Final Contributions
Problems and Methods
of Psycho-Analysis

FINAL CONTRIBUTIONS TO THE PROBLEMS AND METHODS OF PSYCHO-ANALYSIS

BY

SÁNDOR FERENCZI

Edited by
MICHAEL BALINT

Translated by
Eric Mosbacher and others

KARNAC

LONDON　　NEW YORK

Reprinted 1994, with the permission of
Hogarth Press Limited by

H. Karnac (Books) Ltd.
6 Pembroke Buildings
London NW10 6RE

Reprinted 2002

All rights reserved. No part of this publication may be reproduced, stored in a retrieval system, or transmitted, in any form or by any means, electronic, mechanical, photocopying, recording, or otherwise, without the prior written permission of the publisher.

British Library Cataloguing in Publication Data
A C.I.P. for this book is available from the British Library

ISBN: 1 85575 087 2

© Judith Dupont 1955

www.karnacbooks.com

Printed and bound by Antony Rowe Ltd, Eastbourne

Editor's Note

THE appearance of this volume gives English readers the first opportunity of critically appreciating the development of Ferenczi's ideas, as his papers written after 1926, i.e. since the publication of *Further Contributions*, were either scattered in various scientific journals, as often as not in inadequate translations, or had not been translated at all. In the period 1926–33 he produced, it is true, some of his rather problematic writings, but also several of his most stimulating ones. In this respect German readers were in a far better position as the publication of the four volumes of *Bausteine zur Psychoanalyse*, in 1939, made practically all his papers easily accessible. This volume has been compiled with the aim of remedying this state of affairs.

The papers here collected fall into three well-defined groups: (a) papers written after *Further Contributions*, (b) posthumous papers, notes and fragments, and (c) papers which—very likely owing to an oversight—were omitted from *Further Contributions*. The papers in each group are arranged in chronological order.

With the publication of this volume all Ferenczi's important papers are now available for English readers in book form, either (1) in the three uniform volumes: *First Contributions* (title of the American edition: Sex and Psycho-Analysis), *Further Contributions*, and the present one; or (2) in the following independent publications: (a) *Thalassa* (The Psychoanalytic Quarterly, New York, 2nd impr., 1938) (b) (written in collaboration with K. Abraham, E. Simmel, and E. Jones) *Psycho-Analysis of the War Neuroses* (Int. Psycho-Analytical Press, London, 1921) and (c) (written in collaboration with Otto Rank) *The Development of Psycho-Analysis* (Nervous and Mental Diseases Publication Co., New York, 1925).

The work that has been omitted comprises: papers of his preanalytic period, papers of only local (Hungarian) interest, book reviews, polemics, and a few rather popular essays. Apart from these, there remain unpublished for the time being the complete correspondence between Freud and Ferenczi covering a period of twenty-five years, and his scientific diary, written during his last year.

A complete bibliography was published in *Bausteine*, Vol. IV (1939) and subsequently in the second edition of *Further Contributions* (1950). The bibliography in this volume enumerates in chronological order all Ferenczi's papers published in English, giving in each case the volume and page numbers where the paper may be found. It has been compiled by Miss Marie de Lepervanche, the Librarian of the Institute of Psycho-Analysis, London, and I wish to record my grateful appreciation of her conscientious labours.

The index covers the same field as the bibliography, i.e. all books and papers by Ferenczi published in English. It has been prepared by Mrs. Lilla Vészy-Wagner, Ph.D., and I desire to express my thanks for her painstaking and careful work.

Papers Nos. 1, 2, 4, 5, 6, 9, 10, 11 and 12 were first published in various journals, and it has not been possible to trace their translators (some of them needed considerable revision); Nos. 3, 7, 8, 14, 15, 16, 18, 19, 20, 23, 24, 25, 29, 30, 31, 32, 33, 34, 35, 36, 37, 38, 42 and 43 were translated by Mr. Eric Mosbacher, and lastly Nos. 13, 17, 21, 22, 26, 27, 28, 39, 40 and 41 by myself. I am greatly indebted to Dr. Margaret Little for helping me in the translation of 'Notes and Fragments', to Professor L. S. Penrose and Mr. J. O. Wisdom, who kindly read certain parts of this volume, and especially to Mr. A. S. B. Glover, who read the whole book, for most valuable suggestions. The responsibility for the final text, however, is entirely mine.

Finally I desire to acknowledge the courtesy of the proprietors and editors of the following publishing houses and periodicals, in allowing me to reprint articles published by them: *The International Journal of Psycho-Analysis*, *The British Journal of Medical Psychology*, *Archives of Psycho-Analysis*, *Mental Hygiene*, *Nervous and Mental Diseases Publishing Co.*, *Covici-Friede Publ.*

Ferenczi's personality well merits study by any psychoanalyst. Those interested will find revealing material in the obituaries and in the Ferenczi number of the *International Journal of Psycho-Analysis* in volume 30 (1949). A complete list of these is attached to the bibliography at the end of this volume.

MICHAEL BALINT

Contents

Editor's Note   *page* 5

PAPERS WRITTEN AFTER THE PUBLICATION OF 'FURTHER CONTRIBUTIONS TO THE THEORY AND TECHNIQUE OF PSYCHO-ANALYSIS'

1. To Sigmund Freud on his Seventieth Birthday (1926)   11
2. Freud's Importance for the Mental Hygiene Movement (1926)   18
3. Organ Neuroses and their Treatment (1926)   22
4. Present-Day Problems in Psycho-Analysis (1926)   29
5. Gulliver Fantasies (1926)   41
6. The Adaptation of the Family to the Child (1927)   61
7. The Problem of the Termination of the Analysis (1927)   77
8. The Elasticity of Psycho-Analytic Technique (1928)   87
9. The Unwelcome Child and his Death Instinct (1929)   102
10. The Principles of Relaxation and Neocatharsis (1930)   108
11. Child-Analysis in the Analysis of Adults (1931)   126
12. Freud's Influence on Medicine (1933)   143
13. Confusion of Tongues between Adults and the Child (1933)   156

POSTHUMOUS PAPERS

14. More about Homosexuality (*c.* 1909)   168
15. On the Interpretation of Tunes that come into One's Head (*c.* 1909)   175
16. Laughter (*c.* 1913)   177
17. Mathematics (*c.* 1920)   183
18. On Epileptic Fits. Observations and Reflections (*c.* 1921)   197
19. A Contribution to the Understanding of the Psychoneuroses of the Age of Involution (*c.* 1921-2)   205
20. Paranoia (*c.* 1922)   213

21. Notes and Fragments (1920 and 1930-2)	216

I. (1920)

Nocturnal Emission, Masturbation and Coitus	216
'Zuhälter' and 'Femme Entretenante'	217
Anxiety and Free Floating Libido	218
On Affect Hysteria	218

II. (1930)

Oral Erotism in Education	219
Each Adaptation is Preceded by an Inhibited Attempt at Splitting	220
Autoplastic and Alloplastic Adaptation	221
Autosymbolism and Historical Representation	221
On the Analytical Construction of Mental Mechanisms	221
On the Theme of Neocatharsis	223
Thoughts on 'Pleasure in Passivity'	224
Fundamental Traumatic Effect of Maternal Hatred or of the Lack of Affection	227
Fantasies on a Biological Model of Super-Ego Formation	227
Trauma and Striving for Health	230

III. (1931)

Attempt at a Summary	232
On the Patient's Initiative	235
Relaxation and Education	236
On the Revision of the Interpretation of Dreams	238
Aphoristic Remarks on the Theme of being Dead—being a Woman	243
The Birth of the Intellect	244
Fluctuation of Resistance	246
On Masochistic Orgasm	248
Trauma and Anxiety	249

IV. (1932 and undated)

Fakirism	251
The Three Main Principles	252
On Shock (*Erschütterung*)	253
Suggestion=Action Without one's Own Will	254
Repression	255

Scheme of Organizations	256
Accumulatio Libidinis	257
Quantum Theory and Individualism	257
The Technique of Silence	258
Once Again on the Technique of Silence	258
The Therapeutic Argument	260
Psychic Infantilism=Hysteria	260
The Analyst's Attitude to his Patient	261
The Vulnerability of Traumatically Acquired Progressive Faculties (also of Infant Prodigies)	262
The Two Extremes: Credulity and Scepticism	263
Infantility Resulting from Anxiety Concerning Real Tasks	264
The Language of the Unconscious	265
Suppression of the Idea of the 'Grotesque'	267
Repetition in Analysis worse than Original Trauma	268
Pull of the Past (Mother's Womb, Death Instinct) and Flight from the Present	268
Suggestion in (after) Analysis	269
Integration and Splitting	270
Indiscretion of the Analyst in Analysis—helpful	271
Exaggerated Sex Impulse and its Consequences	271
Theoretical Doubt in place of a Personal One	272
Chiromancy	274
On Lamaism and Yoga	274
Abstraction and Memory for Details	275
Abstraction and Perception of Details	275
Yoga-Discipline	276
Psychotrauma	276
Cure Finishing	277
Snake—Hiss	278
Trauma-Analysis and Sympathy	278
Amnesia	278

PAPERS OMITTED FROM PREVIOUS COLLECTIONS

22. Psycho-Analysis and Education (1908)   280

23. The Effect on Women of Premature Ejaculation in Men (1908)   291

24. Stimulation of the Anal Erotogenic Zone as a Precipitating Factor in Paranoia (1911)   295

25. On the Organization of the Psycho-Analytic Movement (1911)   299

26. Exploring the Unconscious (1911)	308
27. Dirigible Dreams (1912)	313
28. On the Definition of Introjection (1912)	316
29. A Case of 'Déjà Vu' (1912)	319
30. Varia: On the Genealogy of the 'Fig Leaf' (1912)	321
31. Varia: Metaphysics=Metapsychology (1912)	322
32. Varia: Paracelsus to the Physicians (1912)	323
33. Varia: Goethe on the Reality Value of the Poet's Fantasy (1912)	324
34. A Forerunner of Freud in the Theory of Sex (1912)	325
35. Philosophy and Psycho-Analysis (1912)	326
36. Interpretation of Unconscious Incestuous Fantasies from a Parapraxis (Brantôme) (1912)	335
37. Taming of a Wild Horse (1913)	336
38. On the Genesis of the Jus Primae Noctis (1913)	341
39. Review of Groddeck's 'Die psychische Bedingtheit und psychoanalytische Behandlung organischer Leiden (1917)	342
40. Review of Groddeck's 'Der Seelensucher' (1921)	344
41. Discussion on Tic (1921)	349
42. Psycho-analysis and the Mental Disorders of General Paralysis (1922)	351
43. Freud's 'Group Psychology and the Analysis of the Ego' (1922)	371
Bibliography	377
Index	387

LATER PAPERS

I

TO SIGMUND FREUD ON HIS SEVENTIETH BIRTHDAY[1]
(1926)

THE duty has fallen to me of conveying to Sigmund Freud on the occasion of his seventieth birthday the greetings and warm congratulations of this Journal. To fulfil this honourable task is no easy matter. Freud is far too outstanding a figure for one who belongs to the circle of his followers and fellow-workers to be able to estimate him in comparison with other great personalities in the evolution of human culture and describe him in relation to his contemporaries. Moreover, his work speaks for itself; it needs no commentary, far less any eulogy. The creator of a science that is austerely honest and wages war on all hypocrisy would certainly dislike the dithyrambs with which it is customary on such occasions to acclaim the leader of a great movement. An objective description of his life-work, however —an enticing theme for an enthusiastic disciple—is superfluous, since the master himself has devoted to this subject more than one essay which for detached and concrete presentation could not be surpassed. He has never withheld from publicity anything that he knows about the origin of his ideas; he has spoken frankly and fully about the vicissitudes his views have undergone and about the attitude of the present generation towards them. So far as his personality is concerned, he has completely taken the wind out of the sails of that modern method of enquiry which attempts to gain fresh insight into the development of a scientist's views by studying the intimate details of his private life. In his *The Interpretation of Dreams* and *Psychopathology of Everyday Life* Freud has undertaken this task himself in a way that was previously unknown, and has not only indicated new

[1] German and English versions appeared simultaneously in 1926 in *Int. Z. f. Psa.* 12, 235 and *Int. J. of PsA.* 7, 297.

lines of research for an enquiry of this kind, but given for all time an example of a candour quite ruthless towards himself. He has also revealed unhesitatingly the 'secrets of the laboratory', and the inevitable vacillations and uncertainties that usually are so carefully kept hidden.

This being so, the most logical course would be for us to forego any kind of demonstration. I am well aware that it would best please the master if we went on quietly with our work without concerning ourselves with arbitrary periods of time and dates that in themselves mean nothing. We, his pupils, have learnt from Freud himself that all modern celebrations are tributes offered in an exalted mood that give expression only to one side of an emotional impulse. It has not always been as now; there was a time when the hostile attitude against the man who had been raised to the throne was not dissembled either. It was Freud who taught us that the most highly honoured figure is regarded even to-day, though it be only unconsciously, with hate as well as love.

In spite of all this, we cannot resist the temptation to bow to convention by way of exception, against our better judgement, and make his birthday the occasion of expressly dedicating to our 'Director' this issue of the *Journal*, and also the issues of the *Zeitschrift* and *Imago* which make their appearance at the same time. Anyone who glances through the annual volumes of these periodicals will at once see, however, that every one of the previous numbers has in reality been dedicated to him; the contents of these volumes, apart from what the master himself has contributed, have been simply a continuation, confirmation, or valuation of his teaching. The present issues therefore, though more ceremonious than usual, do not differ essentially from any of their predecessors; his fellow-workers are merely represented in them in rather more imposing numbers. But instead of inditing a formal introduction to these contributions, I intend to allow myself to set down in an unconnected sequence, as in free association, the feelings and thoughts that naturally arise in me on this occasion. I can take it for granted that these thoughts will be common to many of those who are engaged in the same pursuit.

In a paper in which I once attempted to form an estimate of Freud's *Three Contributions to the Theory of Sexuality*,[1] I stated my conclusion that this work was one of epoch-making importance in the evolution of science; it demolished the boundary wall between mental and natural science. In another paper I described Freud's discovery and exploration of the unconscious as a step forward in human progress, as the first time of functioning of a new sense-organ. One may be disposed to dismiss these assertions forthwith as the exaggerations and uncritical utterances of an enthusiastic disciple; the fact remains that they were not the outcome of any mood of jubilation, but were logical deductions based on a long series of new accessions to knowledge.

Whether and when my prediction will be fulfilled, whether a time will come when the whole world will speak of a pre-Freudian and a post-Freudian epoch, I cannot of course say; it is twenty years now since I followed in his footsteps, and this conviction has not changed in the least. Certain it is that the life of a psycho-neurologist who has had the good fortune to be a contemporary of Freud's, and, better still, to recognize his importance early in his career, is divided into pre-Freudian and post-Freudian periods—two stages that stand in sharpest contrast to one another. In my own case at least, neurological work before Freud, apart from observations on the nerve fibres, which were interesting enough on occasion, was a matter of histrionics, a perpetual profession of friendliness and knowledge to hundreds of neurotic patients whose symptoms were not in the least understood. One was ashamed—at any rate I was—to accept payment for this performance. Even to-day we cannot cure everyone, but we can assuredly help many; and even when we are unsuccessful there remains the mitigating consideration that we have honestly endeavoured to gain knowledge of the neurosis by scientific methods, and can understand why it is impossible to help. We are exempted from the sorry task of promising comfort and aid with an air of professional omniscience; indeed we have finally and completely lost our skill in this art. Psychiatry, which was formerly a museum of abnorm-

[1] Later editions: 'Three Essays on the Theory of Sexuality (1949)'.

alities before which we stood in uncomprehending amazement, has become through Freud's discoveries a fertile field of scientific research, susceptible of coherent comprehension. Is it an exaggeration, then, to assert that Freud has added lustre and honour to our calling? And is it not to be expected that we should be filled with lasting gratitude towards the man whose work has made this possible? It may be a conventional formality to celebrate seventieth or eightieth birthdays, but for Freud's followers such a day is undoubtedly merely an opportunity of giving expression for once to feelings they have long cherished. Would it not be making a concession to the spirit of the age, which is inclined to be so shamefaced in the matter of emotional expression, if we continually suppressed these feelings? We prefer to follow the example of antiquity, and without shame to offer our master for once our open and hearty thanks for all he has bestowed on us.

The day is not far distant when the whole medical profession will recognize that not only psychiatrists and neurologists, but all who are concerned with the cure of disease have ample cause to share in these admittedly lyrical expressions of feeling. The knowledge of the part played in every kind of therapy by the mental relation of the patient to the physician and the possibility of systematically turning this to good account will gradually become the common possession of all medical men. The science of medicine, at present disintegrated by specialization, will once more be restored to unity. The physician will no longer be a dry technician of the laboratory and the dissecting-room; he will be a connoisseur of humanity in both health and sickness, a counsellor to whom everyone will turn with a well-founded hope of understanding and of possible succour.

But signs are multiplying that the physician of the future will be able to count on much greater respect and recognition not only from his patients, but from the whole of society. The ethnologist and the sociologist, the historian and the statesman, the aesthete and the philologist, the pedagogue and the criminologist have even now to turn for confirmation to the physician as the expert in the human soul, if they wish to base their special departments of study, which must ultimately rest in part on psychology, on a more secure foundation than the uncertain ground of arbitrary assumptions. There was once before a time when the physician was respected as a man of science; he it was who was highly versed in knowledge of all plants and animals and the properties of the 'elements', so far as they were then known. I venture to predict the approach of a similar age—an age of 'iatro-philosophy', the foundation stone of which has been laid by the work of Freud. Nor has Freud waited to advance in this direction until all the different schools became conversant with psycho-analysis. Compelled, with the aid of psycho-analysis alone, himself to solve problems connected with allied sciences which he encountered in dealing with nervous patients, he wrote his *Totem and Taboo*, a work that laid down new lines of approach in ethnology; while the sociology of the future will find his *Group Psychology and the Analysis of the Ego* indispensable. His book on *Jokes* is the first attempt to construct a system of aesthetics on a psychological basis, and he has furnished innumerable suggestions relating to possibilities of progressive work in the domain of educational science.

As for the debt that psychology owes to psycho-analysis, the readers of this Journal will hardly require me to waste many words on that. Is it not the fact that before the advent of Freud all scientific psychology was, in essence, merely a refined physiology of sensation, while the complexities of our mental life remained the undisputed territory of *belles lettres*? And was it not Freud who, by creating a theory of the instincts, by inaugurating a psychology of the ego, and by constructing a serviceable scheme of metapsychology, first raised psychology to the level of a science?

This enumeration of achievements, which is by no means complete, is enough to convince the most sceptical that not only his followers and his professional associates, but the whole learned world, have cause to rejoice that the master has reached his seventieth birthday in the full possession of his powers, and to wish that he may long be spared to carry on his great work.

'So we are only to hear panegyrics after all,' many will be thinking; 'what has become of the frankness we were promised about the difficulties and the disputes between the master and his disciples?' It is my duty, therefore, to add a few sentences on this topic, although I do not find it pleasant to come forward, so to speak, as a witness for the Crown, in connexion with incidents which, while they are not without interest, are certainly very painful to all concerned. Let me say then that there is scarcely one of us who has not had to listen occasionally to hints and exhortations from the master which sometimes destroyed magnificent illusions and at the moment of first hearing gave rise to a sense of injury and depreciation. At the same time I must testify that Freud often gives us perfect liberty for a long while, and allows great latitude to individual idiosyncrasies, before he decides to interpose as a moderating influence, or to make decisive use of the means of defence at his command; he resorts to the latter course only when he is convinced that compliance would imperil the cause that to him is more important than anything else. Here he certainly admits of no compromise, and is ready to sacrifice, even though with heavy heart, personal ties and hopes that have become dear to him. In these things he is as severe towards himself as towards another. He watched with sympathetic interest one of his most gifted scholars developing along his own lines, until the latter advanced the claim that he could account for everything with his '*élan vital*'. Once several years ago I myself came forward with the theory that all could be explained by a death-instinct. Freud's verdict was not favourable to the idea, and my faith in him enabled me to bow to his judgement; then one day there appeared *Beyond the Pleasure Principle*, in which his theory of the interplay of death-instincts and life-instincts does far more justice to the manifold facts of psychology and biology than my one-sided conception could do. The idea of organic inferiority interested him as a very promising beginning for the somatic foundation of psycho-analysis. For years he accepted its author's rather peculiar mode of thought as part of the bargain; but when it became clear that the latter was using psycho-analysis simply as a springboard for a teleological philosophy, Freud relinquished all collaboration with him. For a long time he overlooked even the scientific gambols of one of his followers, because he recognized his acute sense for sexual symbolism. The great majority of his adherents, however, have overcome the sensitiveness that is inevitable in this situation, and are convinced that all their legitimate personal efforts will sooner or later be accorded a place in Freudian psycho-analysis.

The exclusiveness of our professional interests should not prevent us on such a day from keeping in mind, also, the feelings of those who stand personally nearest to Freud, of his family above all, among whom Freud lives and works as a human being and not as a mythical figure, who guard with such solicitude a health so precious to us all, and to whom we owe so great a debt of gratitude for their care. The wide circle of sick people who have been treated by this method, and through it have found once more the strength to live, will also join with us in celebrating this memorable day; and not less that still wider circle of sufferers who had kept their health, yet from whom Freud's knowledge has lifted a burden needlessly borne.

Psycho-analysis works ultimately through the deepening and enlargement of knowledge; but, as I have attempted to show in a paper that appears in the following pages, knowledge can be enlarged and deepened only by love. The fact that Freud has succeeded in schooling us to endure more of the truth would alone ensure him the love with which a large and not unworthy section of humanity are thinking of him to-day.

II

FREUD'S IMPORTANCE FOR THE MENTAL HYGIENE MOVEMENT[1]
Written on the Occasion of his Seventieth Birthday
(1926)

It is with great pleasure that I accede to the kind request of Dr. Frankwood Williams to say something about the possible relations between the mental-hygiene movement and the psychological and therapeutical method originated and developed by Freud and called psycho-analysis. For a long time I have been convinced that the importance of those relations has, generally speaking, been too little appreciated. The literature of psycho-analysis has been concerned chiefly with the investigation of neuroses, from which it obtained all its new knowledge. Although this knowledge has at times been applied to the psychoses also, the analysis of the psychoses has remained only applied psycho-analysis, as it were; it has not developed into an independent source of knowledge.

It may nevertheless be asserted that psychiatric science has profited much by the analytic point of view. Before Freud's time psychiatry was not based on psychology. Attempts were made to ascribe the symptoms of mental disease to anatomical changes in the brain. But such attempts were only half successful, and then only in connexion with certain deficiencies in severe organic lesions of the brain (psychotic disturbances in cases of brain tumours, multiple sclerosis, after repeated paralytic strokes, after inflammation of the brain, and in cases of progressive paralysis and senile dementia). All the so-called functional psychoses—mania, melancholia, paranoia, dementia praecox, and hysterical psychosis—remained inexplicable from an anatomical point of view, however much one tried to prove that specific microscopical changes took place in those disorders. The expression 'functional' served merely to veil our ignorance. How could we

[1] English original: *Mental Hygiene* (1926), 10, 673.

be able to give the slightest explanation of the pathological change in the functioning of the psyche when we did not know anything about its normal functioning? Instead of remembering that fact, the authors of psychiatric manuals indulged in fancies about invisible cellular and even molecular changes, which were supposed to be at the bottom of the psychoses. Not one psychiatrist thought of looking for psychological explanations of the psychotic symptoms.

Holding those fixed views, they of course took very little interest in the psychic contents of the acts and expressions of insane persons. These appeared to them to be merely inessential phenomena, attendant on the supposed molecular or functional change in the organ, which, at most, they used as a means for diagnosing the case or giving it the proper label. The psychic performances of the diseased were marked as 'confused', 'disconnected', 'mannered', 'stereotyped', 'fickle', and even as 'incoherent' and as 'verbal salads', and were shown to students and visitors of insane asylums almost as if they were curiosities.

The influence of psycho-analysis has brought about fundamental changes in this field. Freud taught us that the 'psychoses' manifest themselves not simply as the consequences of a psychic 'shock' (which idea was still based, though not admittedly, on the analogy with physical trauma and concussion of the brain), but that their symptoms are the final result of an inner psychic struggle between opposing tendencies. That inner struggle, which in neurotic persons ends in 'repressions' and the formation of neurotic symptoms, is something that so-called normal individuals may also observe directly in themselves by pure introspection. The consequence was that in the first place the neurosis was made accessible to introspective investigation and to therapeutics, and secondly that the partition wall which had been thought of as dividing healthy from neurotic individuals disappeared. Further progress in the investigation showed that the wall separating neurosis and psychosis must also be torn down, and that even the most singular acts and mental processes of the insane are to be reduced to psychic conflicts, analogous to those which exist in 'normal' individuals also. The conduct, too, of insane persons ceased to be senseless and their expressions ceased to be 'verbal salads'; the skilful interpretation of their contents created the possibility of relating even the most scurrilous and confused words of the insane to those frequently tragic conflicts which are understandable by all of us.

The mental activity whose psychic analysis completely removed the chasm between insanity and mental health—which had hitherto been thought unbridgeable—was the activity of the psyche *in dreams*. Even the most normal individual is in a sense psychotic during the night; he has hallucinations; his logical, ethical, and aesthetic personality is completely changed in most cases in the direction of greater primitiveness. Formerly science consistently explained the dream also as an insignificant phenomenon accompanying molecular or other changes of the brain during sleep. But when Freud *interpreted* the first dream—i.e. made it understandable in spite of its senseless make-up—the statement that the sane and the insane could not be compared had to be dropped. The fact that all of us recognized in ourselves the possibility of performing the psychic acts that we call insane was immensely important for the treatment of the unfortunate victims of insanity. The psychiatrists began to pay attention when the insane individual said or did something strange; they began to interpret his conduct and to search for comprehensible associations between the disconnected words of his flow of thoughts; they tried to recognize in the shapes of his visions, in the voices of his auditory hallucinations, the pathogenetically important persons of his life's history. It was by this step that psychiatry freed the insane from their tragic isolation. If the humanitarian spirit of the nineteenth and twentieth centuries did in fact relieve the insane of their chains and drag them forth out of their cells, of what avail was it if they were to remain as before mentally isolated and misunderstood? It was only after their expressions, too, became recognizable as representations of general human tendencies—i.e. after we began *to understand the language of the insane*—that these latter really were accepted as members of human society.

As far as I am informed, one of the main objects of the mental-hygiene movement is to better the lot of the insane, to facilitate their return to ordinary society. The hope exists that psycho-analytical investigation, by penetrating still deeper into the mechanisms of these forms of disease, will in time produce results in the cure of psychoses similar to those which have been produced in our days in the treatment of the psychoneuroses (hysterias and compulsion neuroses). In any case psycho-analysis is at present the only practicable road to the understanding of 'functional' mental diseases, and that understanding could even to-day contribute much to the improvement of the condition of the insane. I therefore think I was right when I asserted at the beginning of this paper that there are bonds of relationship between the aims of psycho-analysis and those of 'mental hygiene'. Ways and means should be found to promote those common aims by co-operative exertions, and that will also be the most dignified manner of celebrating the birthday of the scientist who made such progress possible.

Co-operation might take two forms: some of the most experienced analysts should be given an opportunity to devote themselves for a lengthy period to the study of psychoses in sanatoria, and scholarships should be founded for physicians attached to institutions, to enable them to make use of the facilities available for psycho-analytical training.

III

ORGAN NEUROSES AND THEIR TREATMENT[1]
(1926)

MANY frequently occurring illnesses are mentally determined, though they consist of real disturbances of the normal functioning of one or more physical organs. They are called organ neuroses. The fact that they involve objective as well as subjective disturbances differentiates them from hysteria, though it is not possible to draw sharp dividing lines between them and hysteria on the one hand and a number of organic diseases on the other. This is the result, not only of the defectiveness of the present state of our knowledge, but also of the fact that much organic illness is accompanied by a neurosis of the organ concerned; and in addition hysterical symptoms are often associated with organ-neurotic or organic illnesses, which are then experienced in an hysterically accentuated form.

The most familiar form of organ neurosis is neurasthenia, as it is called, known in German as nervous weakness. It was first described by an American nerve specialist in the first half of the nineteenth century, and was attributed to the allegedly shattering effects on the nervous system of railway travel, which was then new and unfamiliar. The innocuousness of railway travel has long since been demonstrated, but the beautiful Greek word 'neurasthenia' has firmly established itself in medical practice and in the popular mind, and is still used to describe a variety of different conditions—mental depressions, physical sensitivenesses or weaknesses, mental or physical symptoms of anxiety or obsession. It was psycho-analysis which first revealed that in a large proportion of cases of so-called neurasthenia the clinical picture was purely psychological, involving disturbances curable by psychological means. However, after the elimination of

[1] German original in *Das psychoanalytische Volksbuch*, Hippokrates Verlag, Stuttgart, 1926. English translation in *Medical Review of Reviews*, 36, 376. New translation.

all the conditions susceptible of psychological explanation, a group of illnesses remained which we still describe as neurasthenia to-day. Neurasthenics are highly susceptible to mental and physical fatigue, their power of attention is diminished, their sensitivity to external stimuli is accentuated, and they suffer from headaches and digestive disturbances. In the case of men their potency is disturbed; male neurasthenics are often liable to premature ejaculation or involuntary emissions associated with a condition varying in degree between an unpleasant sensation and a violent pain in the back (formerly known as spinal irritation). But no organic illness, or disease of the spinal cord in particular, is present, or is to be feared.

The causes of this neurasthenic condition are sexual malpractices. From the earliest ages the most terrifying beliefs have been current concerning the consequences of self-gratification (masturbation), i.e., the attainment of sexual pleasure by practices on one's body (generally rubbing of the genitals to the accompaniment of pleasurable fantasies). The Bible condemns masturbation as a deadly sin; last century spinal tuberculosis was attributed to masturbation, and in this century it has been held to be responsible for dementia praecox. Even to-day this superstition is not dead. In reality masturbation represents a normal stage in sexual development. Only those who remain at this stage too long and cling to it too strongly, continuing to practise masturbation, often obsessionally, long after reaching the stage of maturity, get neurasthenia from it.

But even in these cases neurasthenia is not the result of the physical act of masturbation, but the psychological result of obsession and guilt-feeling.

It would therefore be as well, before putting oneself down as a neurasthenic or a neuropath, to seek the advice of a physician trained in psycho-analysis, who is often able in such cases to remove most of the symptoms by explanation and by alleviating the burden of guilt. If this is insufficient, proper psychological treatment must be undertaken to remove the obstacles that have stood in the way of normal sexual development. In any case the giving up of the immature method of gratification will result in a cure.

In short, true neurasthenia is nearly always rooted in sexuality and is curable by psychological means or changes in sexual hygiene. What is felt to be severe neurasthenia often vanishes by itself, without medical intervention, when it is realized that masturbation is harmless.

Another illness is so-called anxiety neurosis, in which mental and physical symptoms can also be combined: e.g., baseless or insufficiently based general anxiety, a continual state of apprehensiveness (fear of accidents, pessimistic interpretation of entirely trivial symptoms both in oneself and others, etc.), anxiety attacks accompanied by trembling or sweating, palpitation, nightmares, pressure on the heart, diarrhoea, frequency of micturition, etc. Anxiety symptoms, like neurasthenic symptoms, can also appear as attendant phenomena associated with an unnoticed organic illness, e.g., of the nose, the respiratory organs, or the heart. To distinguish between them a careful physical examination is necessary as well as a psycho-analytic examination. Should these reveal nothing suspicious, attention should be turned to the patient's sex life. When this is done it is frequently found that those who suffer from such symptoms practise sexual intercourse, but in an unhealthy manner. They avoid having children by practising *coitus interruptus*, or deliberately prolong the duration of the act, or engage in fore-pleasure without allowing orgasm to take place.

If the required alteration in the patient's sex life can be brought about, the illness, serious and critical though it may appear, as a rule disappears in a short time (a week or a fortnight). In cases in which this does not occur organic and neurotic illness is involved, both of which require medical treatment.

A not uncommon and most unfortunate combination occurs when a husband who suffers from neurasthenic premature ejaculation is married to a 'frigid' wife with a tendency to anxiety. In such a case the physician will have great difficulty in securing the establishment of that harmony in the sex act which is so important for successful marriage. Economic and social difficulties come into play, and among the social difficulties one of the chief is the excessive difference in the sex life of the sexes before marriage. One of the chief tasks of hygiene should be the abolition or reduction of these differences, though it is not to be denied that other and serious difficulties lie in the way of this.

There are also a whole series of so-called single-symptom neuroses which can be described as organ neuroses. The best-known is so-called nervous asthma. Attacks of difficult breathing occur, generally accompanied by anxiety, with plain indication of morbid contraction of the bronchial muscles. With the end of the spasm sticky mucus is generally coughed up. Of still more frequent occurrence are neurotic disturbances of the digestive organs. In the so-called stomach neuroses either too much or too little acid is secreted. Also of frequent occurrence is 'nervous intestinal disturbance', which, without any organic cause, can take the form of diarrhoea, constipation, secretion of mucus, griping pains, flatulence, or one or more of these symptoms. In the very common so-called heart neuroses the strength and rhythm of the heart-beat is disturbed without any demonstrable organic cause, and the patient has disagreeable sensations which make him think he has heart-disease.

It was only in recent times, that is to say, since Freud showed sex life to be a worth-while object of scientific study, that the idea of organ eroticism became familiar as a scientific possibility. It is now established beyond doubt that not only the sex and the sense organs serve the purpose of obtaining pleasure, but that all our other organs, apart from their activities in the interests of self-preservation, partially serve the purpose of procuring pleasure, thus creating a kind of organ pleasure (Alfred Adler), which can almost be regarded as erotic self-gratification of the organs by their own activity. In infancy a playful pleasure in organ activities of all kinds, of which the child is perfectly conscious, is evident, and it is demonstrable also in all adults, at least in residual form. What is called 'healthy physical enjoyment' is closely connected with the sense of pleasure resulting from healthy functioning of the organs. An example of this pleasure is that of eating, which does not depend only on the satisfaction of hunger and the tastiness of the meal. Most people take more or less pleasure in masticating and swallowing, and most people take pleasure also in the further processes of digestion. In many individuals this organ-pleasure is particularly, often morbidly, accentuated. They cannot suppress the itch to swallow, or to withhold their faeces. The word 'itch'[1] gives a hint of the pleasure associated with this morbid process.

Psycho-analytic investigation has established that in the organ neuroses such infantile play or erotic functioning of an organ is capable of proliferating to such an extent as to hamper its real, useful function. Normally this happens when for psychological reasons normal sexuality has been disturbed. This indicates the path along which a cure may be attained by psychotherapy, and also explains why this kind of illness is so obstinate without ever endangering life.

Let us briefly refer to a few more of the organ neuroses. It is still doubtful whether migraine should be included in this category. There are certainly organ-neurotic kinds of headache. In many cases a tendency to faint, if possible organic causes have been carefully eliminated, is to be regarded as a neurotic disturbance of the innervation of the blood vessels. Particular sensitiveness to the vibration of trains, and the liability to seasickness which is related to it, also have neurotic roots. In conclusion we may also mention that purely organic complaints may leave organ-neurotic disturbances behind after they have healed. A well-known example is the persistence of blinking after catarrh of the eyes, which may continue in the form of a so-called *tic*, or even establish itself as a lasting habit, after the catarrh has disappeared. Similarly children sometimes persist with a nervous cough for years after an attack of whooping-cough. The habitual grimaces and other twitching movements known under the name of *tic* all appear to be organ-neurotic disturbances of function. The local and general nervous phenomena which occasionally appear after operations stand on the border-line between the mental and the organic neuroses; the disturbing effect on the patient of knowing that his life is in danger, and the stimulus given to the organ concerned by the surgical intervention, both contribute to these.

But the course of every organic disease is favourably or unfavourably affected by mental influences. Good news increases

[1] *Reiz*, here translated 'itch', means 'stimulus' and also 'fascination'. (Translator's note.)

the patient's strength and bad news affects it adversely. It is not uncommon for a chronic disease, which had been getting worse and worse, to be brought to an end by a change for the better in the patient's state of mind. In the case of fevers the influence of such events can, so to speak, be read on the temperature chart. The exacerbation of symptoms and of physical pain under the influence of anxiety is also well known, as is its converse, its disappearance upon the arrival of the doctor; a familiar phenomenon is the disappearance of toothache in the dentist's waiting room. That is why entirely unscientific, superstitious practices are sometimes able to cure organic diseases. The effectiveness of such methods depends on the patient's faith in them, his 'suggestibility'.

Freud's psycho-analytic method first made it possible to investigate the unsuspected depths of the instinctual life of man, in which body and mind continually interact. Psycho-analysis attributes suggestibility in the last resort to the ineradicable effects left behind in everyone by his relation with his parents. The omnipotence over the mental and physical life of their patients wielded by many doctors is a repetition of the omnipotent relationship of the parents to the child; in both cases the driving forces leading to exaggerated obedience are love and fear. Psycho-analysis gives the name 'transference' to repetitions of the parent-child relationship; it shows how transferences may be brought about in the patient and then used for curing him.

The chief successes achieved by this transference to the physician have been in the field of the psychogenic neuroses, but successful results have also been obtained in the treatment or psychological influencing of organic disturbances. Analytic therapy of organic diseases has the advantage over all previous attempts of this nature that it is free of all mystery-mongering and remains in close contact with psychology and biology.

Psycho-analysis has already had successes, for example, in dealing with organic diseases of the heart and the lungs. Alleviation of heart action under the influence of transference and after the discovery of repressed mental focuses of disease has actually resulted in the overcoming of a compensatory disturbance of the circulatory system that was threatening to become dangerous.

Incipient tuberculosis of the lungs is so manifestly susceptible to mental influence that every tuberculosis hospital ought to employ an experienced psycho-analyst. If psycho-analysis, by re-establishing harmony in the patient's emotional life, and more particularly in his sex life, is able to cure, not only psychological, but also physical illness, we are forced to the conclusion that it is from the fountain of sexual energy that the regeneration required for a cure derives its strength; as if, when there is a special threat to self-preservation (i.e., illness), it is thrown back on borrowing from preservation of the species.

The development of psycho-analytic treatment of organic disease lies in the future; nothing in it is incompatible with the other kinds of medical treatment that are necessary.

IV

PRESENT-DAY PROBLEMS IN PSYCHO-ANALYSIS[1]

(1926)

PERHAPS one of the chief handicaps which may prevent the American members of our movement from contributing to psycho-analytic knowledge and research through their own original works is due in great measure to the fact that only after considerable time are they able to acquaint themselves with the European literature in translated form. This applies to the translation of German works, and even to certain works of Freud. This may well be the reason why I was invited to give a short résumé of the most important practical and theoretical problems which are now occupying our attention. The time which I have for giving such a résumé is so short compared with the many-sidedness of the subject that I shall limit myself to merely touching upon the problems concerned. What I shall present to you, therefore, will be only a kind of menu, which as you know is not a thing to satisfy hunger. My aim is merely to arouse in you a desire, the satisfaction of which can come only through the study of the original works.

It is a great mistake to gauge a person's age by the number of years he has lived. To remain productive and to be capable of changing one's opinions is to stay young. Both of these attributes are highly characteristic of Professor Freud, as his latest writings attest. One finds in them nothing of stagnation in dogmatic assertions or of exhaustion of the fantasy. Against his own earlier theses he is perhaps often too unsparing, and the breadth of his perspective often exceeds everything which he has created in the past. His style, also, has changed, owing to the greater condensation of his material, and he does not make it so easy for

[1] Delivered before the Midwinter Meeting of the American Psychoanalytic Association, 28 Dec., 1926. First published in *Arch. of PsA.* (1927), 1, 522-30; German version in *Bausteine*, III.

us to follow him as it formerly was. His newest works must be read more often and with greater concentration. I can assert, however, that the gain in intellectual insight will well repay the labour.

Freud's recent contributions are mostly theoretical; his train of thought sheds light in unexpected ways, and gives us an insight into the structure, dynamics, and economy, not only of the various neuroses and psychoses, but also of each individual case which we have to handle and understand. And whosoever is not afraid to take the trouble to follow the sometimes difficult constructions has much more hope of success in his practice, or of understanding the cause of the failures he encounters.

As an example of how an apparently purely speculative view put forward by Freud helps us to understand a particular mental symptom, I would bring to your attention his conception of an instinct which before him had not been taken into consideration either by biologists or by psychologists, namely, the death instinct. Only through this conception are we able to understand masochism, pleasure in pain and the destruction of the self; purely sexual masochism as well as those excesses against one's own ego which afflict one in the form of exaggerated conscience and need for punishment. Freud has called this trait moral masochism, and has been able to trace it as well as all other forms of masochism back to the urge for self-destruction. Pleasure in self-injury has ceased to be a psychological wonder since it has been recognized as the gratification of a particular impulse and therefore the gratification of a wish.

No less important is the practical significance of the developing field of ego-psychology which has been the subject of several of Freud's more recent contributions. I refer to the separation of the apparently united personality into id, ego, and super-ego. The id, as is well known, is the collective conception of all our primitive instinctive impulses: on the one hand the death impulse and on the other the life impulse, which latter is differentiated into erotic and self-preservation instincts. The super-ego is that part of the personality which we have developed and shaped after the pattern or example of the authorities which influenced our bringing up. I mean especially the introjected picture of the father and mother who, in the form of moral force, may then in like manner criticize the intentions of the ego acting from within. Now the ego has not only to withstand the demands of the instinctive id, and to justify itself before the criticisms of the super-ego, but it must in addition take notice of the real possibilities of the outer world; so that the mentally healthy ego must adapt itself in three directions and has to bring the three principles of pleasure, reality, and morals into harmonious relations. These conceptions lead to a new classification in psychopathology and to new notions in pathogenesis. The transference neuroses develop as a result of the exaggerated demands of the instinctive id, which the ego, controlled as it is by morals and reality, cannot recognize and therefore must repress. Freud calls those conditions in which the relation of the ego to the *outer* world is disturbed, psychoses. In Meynert's *amentia*, reality is denied completely, for example, the death of a loved person is simply not recognized. In schizophrenia and paranoia the situation is different. In schizophrenia the interest for the outer world is directed *inward*. In paranoia the outer world is falsified so far as is necessary to make it compatible with the demands of the id and the super-ego. The analysis of the manic depressive cases, which we have up till now classified with the rest of the psychoses, shows that we deal here with a particular form of mental disturbance, a conflict between the ego and the ego-ideals, under whose moral influence we stand. Melancholia is a denial of the depreciation of the ego-ideals connected with withdrawal of libido from the persons with whom one has hitherto identified oneself. Instead of turning against the depreciated authorities, the melancholiac turns—apparently through regression to the instinct of self-destruction (death-wish)—against his own person. Mania, however, is a periodic or temporary attempt to overthrow the tyranny of the super-ego. As a result of their genetically different position, Freud decided to give a particular name to conditions which do not have to do with a conflict with the outer world, but rather with one between the ego and its ideals. He calls these states the narcissistic neuroses. Knowledge about these etiological distinctions brings us nearer to the possibility of a rational therapy for the psychoses.

As another instance, I will mention another apparently purely theoretical explanation which Freud gave us with regard to a hitherto unrecognized element in the formation of paranoid delusion. Freud showed us—a thing which we had already suspected—that the paranoiac is endowed with an over-sharp gift of observation for the *outward* manifestations of the unconscious in his fellow men. Recognizing their sharpened sensitiveness to symbolism, for instance, enabled me some years ago to interpret the dream-symbols in a paranoiac. Now Freud has shown that even in the most abstruse delusional ideas there lies a grain of truth, but of course only truth in the sense of the unconscious. The persecuted insane person, for instance, is not so entirely wrong when he says that people in the street regard him with squinting eyes, and even with murderous intentions. He recognizes and exaggerates all the unconscious reactions and aggressive tendencies which exist in all of us and which we direct against one another as soon as someone stands in our way—for instance, when people hinder our getting into a tube train. Consciously, we feel only a vague anger or irritation. In the unconscious, however, this corresponds to an aggressive and perhaps even a murderous intention. But the sensitive paranoiac reads these unconscious intentions from the play of our features and gestures; he regards them as conscious tendencies and wishes to take revenge on us for the injustice done him. Since this ingenious explanation of Freud has come to my knowledge I have succeeded much better than before in keeping up the transference situation with the paranoiac so that he does not withdraw so soon from the analytic influence. It is not unlikely that on this basis a successful technique for analysing the paranoiac may be built up.

An entirely new sphere of mental conditions was rendered accessible to the influence of the analyst through the progress made in ego-psychology. I refer to the disturbances and peculiarities of the character. Until now in our analyses of the neuroses we have concerned ourselves principally with their symptomatology. In order not to arouse the patient's resistance we have left his character peculiarities untouched; that is to say, we have made a pact with the patient's ego and in reward for this consideration that ego became our ally in the struggle to unmask the symptom originating in the id. But, where neurotic symptoms do not play a great role, the analyst has to treat the character peculiarities of the patient. Abraham was one of the first to study systematically this field of analysis. Of course we have Freud to thank also for the first hint towards an understanding of character formation. He showed us that the development of the early auto-erotic organizations of the libido really proceeds by the transformation of libidinal manifestations of mental energy into typical character traits. The resolving of anal-eroticism, for instance, results in the development of quite distinct anal character traits: cleanliness, avarice, obstinacy, pedantry, ceremoniousness. From the oral-libidinal phase develops, on the one hand, the character trait of greed, perhaps also jealousy, and probably also a need for tenderness, whereas the anal character traits remain connected in their primary amalgamation with hate and sadism. Urethral eroticism is replaced by the traits of shame and ambition, apparently also by the tendency to uncontrolled emotional outbursts. However, only Freud's recent investigations into the more delicate processes of the structure of the ego at the onset of the latency period help us to understand the development of the super-ego, the most important step in character development. Here also we have to do with the transformation of large quantities of energy from the libidinal side to that of the character. The large quantity of libido energy which is used in sublimated form for the building up of the super-ego, develops in man out of a high narcissistic regard for his genitals at the time of the establishment of phallic organization. In this stage there arises out of the earlier undisturbed condition a tragic conflict between the son and his father. Even the slightest suspicion of phallic incestuous tendencies is answered by the father with more or less clear castration threats, and under the pressure of this danger the destruction of the Oedipus complex results. The wish to kill the father and to possess the mother is replaced by a tendency to identify with the parents, especially with the parent of the same sex. The formerly hated father is raised to an ego-ideal, and to attain his power and perfection becomes the paramount aim in life; his formerly hated disciplinary measures now act from with-

B

in as punishments or rewards by the inner father, the conscience. Why castration should be such a terrible punishment and be followed by such permanent effects I have tried to explain in my *Thalassa*.[1] I there came to the conclusion that in the phallic stage the penis becomes the representative of all the individual's libido interest and as such is permitted the pleasure of returning to the woman's body. The castration threat forces the individual to give up a part of his personality and to adapt himself psychically to the father's power.

In the woman the Oedipus conflict does not play the same role as in the man. In connexion with the newest investigations of Freud I can say that only in man is the Oedipus complex the central complex of the neuroses; the greatest difficulties of the woman lie in another direction and set in much earlier. They lie, as Freud has shown us, in the discovery of the anatomical difference between the male and female genitals and in the mental reaction to this discovery. Whereas in the case of the man the fear of losing the penis subdues him into becoming civilized, the woman must become conscious much earlier of the actual inferiority of her genitals as compared to man's. The happy termination of the trauma is the giving up of the wish for phallic (male) satisfaction and the adaptation of the comforting mechanism of vaginal satisfaction and motherhood. Greater willingness to yield, tenderness, an almost organic goodness, understanding, and tact, are the character traits which develop in the woman in the wake of this trauma. In less fortunate cases the penis envy leaves behind an unhealed wound which drives the woman to a permanent protest against the 'superiority' of man and to a battle of competition with him, leading to an accentuating of phallic sexuality, towards vaginal frigidity and towards jealousy and aggressiveness. Naturally we do not find in woman pure character types, but rather a mixture of the two character forms described. The great difference between the sexes, however, is principally this: with the man the castration threat leads to a giving up of nearly all sexual tendencies, whereas with the woman full realization of the unalterable absence of the penis

[1] German original: *Versuch einer Genitaltheorie*, Wien, 1924. In English: *Thalassa. A Theory of Genitality*. New York, 1934.

leads to the development of feminine sexual traits which then enable her to make a sexual approach towards the father. Logically it would follow, and my analytical observations bear this out, that the incest barrier may be originally a purely male device which, however, has been taken over secondarily by woman but without the tragic note which marks the incest problem in man.

I must not fail to mention the new conception which Freud has introduced in the pursuit of this problem. It is the mental process which he calls mastering or resolving (in German: *Überwindung*). Those who are not neurotic appear successfully to evade being overwhelmed for good by the Oedipus complex and render it, so to speak, inactive or non-functioning. We might also put it in this way: with the non-neurotic the emotional content of the Oedipus complex as well as the interest in it is completely given up and is replaced by successful transferences, sublimations, and ego changes. The most important result of this point of view is that we may assume only in the case of neurotics a repressed Oedipus complex which in the unconscious often ties up great quantities of mental energy which quantities under certain conditions may cause severe disturbances in the individual's love-life. It will be one of the problems of the future to study this process more thoroughly. Perhaps such investigations will throw some light on the working methods of the mind, especially on how early primitive methods are superseded during phylogenesis.

Regarding Freud's most recent book, *Hemmung, Symptom und Angst*[1], I would mention two points. One is that the ego does not merely play, as Freud thought previously, a purely passive intermediary role between the id, the super-ego, and the outer world, but occasionally also influences actively in very important ways the end-result of the mental processes. That the ego, despite its comparative weakness, is capable of holding in control great quantities of energy of the id is to be explained by its high organization acquired apparently in its long diplomatic service as intermediary between the various mental powers. The

[1] Appeared in German in 1926. English translation: London, Hogarth, 1936.

ego is weak but clever, the id strong but crude and primitive; it permits itself to be led by higher powers. So the ego becomes the watchman at whose signals the instinctual energy takes this or that direction. One of these signals is anxiety. Freud, reversing an earlier idea with regard to anxiety, regards it not as a case of transformation of libido quantities, but as a signal given by the ego.

We now come to the question which has lately become the subject of much discussion in America also. I refer to the tracing back of every fear to the individual's birth and of every neurosis to the individual's birth trauma. Rank has propounded this theory without, to my mind, supporting it with sufficient evidence. Freud's standpoint, with which I wholly agree, is that anxiety imitates certain characteristics of the birth situation. It was Freud who first called attention to this analogy. That this imitating is more than a symbolic expression for every kind of danger is, however, unsubstantiated. This signal sent out by the ego is most impressive when the most important pleasure representative, the penis, is endangered, and as a matter of fact analysis finds the fear of the castration threat as the principal disturbance behind most of the neuroses. In a lecture[1] which I recently gave before the New York Society for Clinical Psychiatry I attempted to demonstrate by means of some examples that the mother-, womb-, and birth-fantasies and dreams of neurotics are only symbolic substitutes of the—because of the castration danger—most feared coitus situation; in those cases the whole body becomes the symbolic representative of the penis. We are here presented with a really fantastic reversal of the normal development of genitality, at the end of which the penis as deputy for the whole body endeavours to re-create the lost mother-womb situation. However this may be, it is certainly unjustified to base a new technique of psycho-analysis on such a highly disputed theory as the birth trauma which leaves out of account a great part of the valuable data concerning the psychogenesis of the neuroses which Freud and others have collected with so much effort, and to attempt to explain nearly all symptoms on the basis of the experience of the individual birth.

[1] 'Gulliver Phantasies'. In this volume, page 41.

As you will probably have understood from the foregoing, Freud as well as myself rejects this newest theory of Rank's.

Another object of dispute over the psycho-analytic technique is a method which I brought forward some eight or ten years ago under the term of *active therapy*. You will perhaps remember that the central idea of my method consisted in requesting the patient upon occasion, in addition to his free association, to act or behave in a certain way in the hope of gaining thereby, even though at the cost of an increase of unpleasant tensions, mental material that lay buried in the unconscious. These measures were really only a continuation of a line of thought of Freud's concerning our technique, that is the proper relation of the repetition tendency to recollection in analysis. Freud told us that the purpose of analysis and the real triumph of our technique is when we succeed in changing the repetition tendency arising in the analytic situation into recollections. I held that in certain cases it was necessary and advantageous for the analyst first of all not only to permit but to encourage the repetition tendency. The advice I gave really helped the patient's will to fight against certain neurotic habits, that is, to give up the subjective advantage of the primary and secondary gains from his neurosis. Freud accepted my method in so far as he admitted that analyses are best carried out in a state of abstinence. I have always emphasized that this measure can be used only in exceptional cases and then only occasionally. But certain colleagues appear to have misunderstood my method and have identified it with the already well-known educative and habit-forming exercises. Active therapy, however, is only a means to an end. Our purpose remains as before, to bring the unconscious material into consciousness, and to substitute an uncontrollable symptom formation through insight and ways of satisfaction that are compatible with reality.

Exaggeration of active measures leads to a great heightening of resistance in the patient and would endanger the analysis. I was forced to warn against certain exaggerations of this kind which—admittedly—I myself have tried from time to time, and especially against the setting of a time limit for the analysis in order to speed it up. I have returned to the earlier view that the analyst must have more patience than the patient and that under favourable circumstances, even though the material appears to be already exhausted, we should go on quietly with the analytic work until the patient has the feeling that he has overcome the emotional tie to the analyst. The proper time for the termination of treatment and the turning towards reality is decided by the patient himself. This experience does not alter the clinical fact that more courageous interpretation of dreams and symptoms in terms of the analytic situation is followed by good results, as recommended by Rank and by myself. Unfortunately my former colleague, in his most recent work on technique, could not resist the temptation to view the analytic situation too one-sidedly at the expense of the historical material. Looking back on the development of the psycho-analytic technique we must concede that Freud was right, that according to his former view that analysis acts through insight we must endeavour to remove consistently the resistances of the patient. The 'active therapy' is merely a detail of this latter measure. The analyst need not be afraid to arouse the resistance of the patient; that is, one need not always be so careful about the feelings of the former ally in the struggle with the symptom. Exaggerated intellectualization of the analysis is no less wrong than its one-sided emotionalization. The former leads absolutely to the degrading of the analysis into a mere pedagogic measure, that is, to depriving oneself of all the possibilities of the exploration into the unconscious.

The theme of education leads me to the interesting question of child analysis and to the relation of psycho-analysis to pedagogy. My former pupil, Mrs. Melanie Klein of Berlin, has taken the first courageous step in this field. She analysed young children and infants with the same fearlessness as we do the adult. She observed the children during their play, and used my method of forced fantasy or imagination much in the same sense as I advised with adults, and found that neurotic and problem children can be helped by symbolic interpretations and explanations. Another more conservative line of child analysis is being instituted by Miss Anna Freud of Vienna. She is of the opinion that in the case of a child the analyst should not transfer the entire emotional attachment to the analytic situation but should confine himself to creating normal relations to the parents, sisters, brothers, etc. We shall look forward to the publication of her lectures on analytic pedagogy delivered in Vienna. Our analyses so far have merely shown us how we should *not* educate children, but now we hope to receive more positive advice concerning the problem of how parents and teachers should educate children in the light of analytic understanding.

A few more contributions in the field of applied psychoanalysis should be mentioned. In his book, *Geständniszwang und Strafbedürfnis*, Theodor Reik (Vienna) has shown new ways to analytic criminal psychology; August Aichhorn, the director of the Municipal Welfare Department of Vienna, has published an excellent book on analytical techniques in the education of problem children; then there is the important book by Géza Róheim (Budapest) on *Australian Totemism*, and several others. You see how necessary the collaboration of non-medical analysts is to further our knowledge and to extend its application to sociology.

Freud answered the attacks against the lay analysts in a monograph soon to appear in English.[1] Of course, Freud defends only analytic practice by laymen who have been as well trained psycho-analytically as the medical analysts. He also gives advice on how to make possible the co-operation of physician and lay analyst in order to remove any disadvantages so far as the person to be analysed is concerned.

Some time ago Dr. Groddeck (Baden-Baden) attempted with success to extend psycho-analysis to certain cases of purely organic illness. These experiments have been going on, and recently he has been joined by Dr. Felix Deutsch (University of Vienna). This is a field equally important for both biology and therapy.

The scientific activity of European psycho-analysis has received its greatest momentum in recent years from the psychoanalytic institutes, first in Berlin under Dr. Eitingon, later in Vienna, and recently in London, which were all built on the same principle. In Budapest we have already made a successful

[1] *Das Problem der Laienanalyse*, Wien, 1924; English translation, New York, 1927.

beginning in a committee devoted to the post-graduate instruction of analysts.

The next congress of the International Psycho-analytic Association will take place in Stuttgart, and we hope for the active participation of our American colleagues. Exchange of ideas and personal contact between European and American analysts are much to be desired.

V

GULLIVER PHANTASIES[1]
(1926)

Mr. President, Ladies and Gentlemen,
Allow me first of all to thank you for the honour you have done me in asking me to read the opening paper at this Annual Meeting of your learned Society. I take it as an honour done not so much to myself as to psycho-analysis. Seventeen years ago I had the privilege of visiting this country with Professor Freud, and so I am able to compare the position of psycho-analysis in 1909 with its position to-day both in America and in Europe. At that time, apart from the friendly interest shown by two great American scholars, Dr. Stanley Hall and Dr. J. J. Putnam, Freud's method was championed by only one single person in the United States—Dr. A. A. Brill. And in Europe things were certainly not much better. We were only a handful of pioneers scattered about the world—generals without an army; yet we were full of hope and optimism about our work. Our abounding hopefulness in those days reminds me of the old anecdote of the beggar who was dividing his property amongst his sons. To the first he said, 'You may beg in Germany'; to the second: 'You shall have Hungary', while to the third he apportioned Switzerland, and to the fourth, America. Since the time of my visit we have indeed advanced enormously in public recognition, and can boast of a whole host of adherents of psycho-analysis both in your country and in Europe; at any rate, I find a more widespread interest in psycho-analysis in America among people who have not had a proper training in analysis. If I had to account for this fact I should be tempted to say that the spirit of liberty characteristic of the American genius makes it impossible for a young science to be rejected, as has been attempted in certain European universities, for

[1] Read at the Annual Meeting of the New York Society for Clinical Psychiatry, 9 December, 1926.
First published in German: *Int. Z. f. Psa.* (1927), 13, 379. English translation in *Int. J. of PsA.* (1928), 9, 283.

reasons of mere conservatism, without its having first been examined. On the other hand you will, I am sure, allow me to remark that this spirit of liberty is not without its dangers. Once, when I was talking to several eminent Americans, they said that the spirit of liberty in them resented Freud's specially important precept that anyone who wanted to become an analyst must first be analysed himself. I fear that this attitude may rob you of all the advantages which you derive from your love of liberty and may make it impossible for you correctly to evaluate Freud's methods. The larger number and greater importance of scientific contributions to psycho-analysis in Europe are probably accounted for by the fact that there is a larger body of well-trained analysts there, and the possibility of acquiring an analytic training at several psycho-analytic institutes, which in America are non-existent.

In concluding this comparison, I will mention only the following points: In Europe it has become customary for people to appropriate a large part of Freud's life-work, to dish it up in a new form and with a new terminology, and publish it as their own original work. I have come across nothing of this sort in American literature. On the other hand, it seems as though in America (possibly owing to the pressure of public opinion) people are much readier than we are in Europe to accept the watered-down and attenuated views of certain of Freud's former disciples. I have noticed too, over here, something of an exaggerated anxiety about the question of lay-analysis, probably because there are many more dangerous quacks in America than with us. With this danger strongly impressed on your minds, you seem to me to undervalue the advantage we derive from the co-operation of thoroughly well-trained lay-analystis, both in medical practice and in social and educational work. There are not enough members of the medical profession to undertake every case of neurosis and to deal with all 'difficult' children and all adult criminals. Besides, we are obliged to co-operate with non-medical research-workers, analytically trained, in the fields of ethnology, pedagogy, history, and biology. I hope that this difference of opinion between Freud and his American followers will soon be satisfactorily settled.

My original intention in speaking to you to-day was to give a general account of the relation between psychiatry and psycho-analysis. But to have done so would have been merely to add one more to the numerous essays on psycho-analysis which already exist and which you have doubtless read. So I have chosen rather to demonstrate by means of a concrete example how psycho-analysis deals with a special psychiatric problem. I am quite aware of the dangers of this experiment. By leading you to dip into the seething cauldron of psycho-analytic work I shall assuredly rouse the resistance of all those who are not accustomed to contemplate mental symptoms in the light of our analytical understanding of symbols. I hope that the resistance so evoked will be only transitory, and that subsequent experience will convince you that our science is neither as hysterical nor as speculative as it may appear at first glance.

With your permission I will now enter upon the subject of to-day's lecture. In your observation of patients you have all come across psychotics who had hallucinations about giants and dwarfs, such hallucinations being accompanied by feelings of anxiety and fear. Frequently dwarfs and small creatures appear to such persons in terrifying hordes. Microptic and macroptic illusory distortions of the surrounding world are, indeed, rather more rare, but with alcoholics and hysterics they are by no means uncommon. In general, the old text-books of psychiatry made scarcely any attempt to explain this kind of symptom, and, if they did set out to do so, it was upon a purely physiological basis. For example, they explained an entoptic sensation by cramps in the focusing muscles of the eye or by circulatory disturbances in the retina or the optic brain centres.

Probably under the influence of Freud's teaching psychiatrists are now beginning to interest themselves in these symptoms from a more strictly psychological standpoint. Some psychiatrists have given them the name of *Lilliputian* hallucinations.

The deeper psycho-analytical explanation of this symptomatology is, however, still to come. With two decades of psycho-analytical work behind me, I believe that I can throw a little light on this question. Most of my experience in this connexion is derived from the dreams of neurotics, particularly of patients suffering from anxiety neurosis. The dreams in which giants and dwarfs make their appearance are generally, though not invariably, characterized by marked anxiety. Sometimes they have the effect of a nightmare; in other cases, on the contrary, the magnifying or minimizing of a person, an animal, or an inanimate object is accompanied not by anxiety but by a certain pleasurable feeling. In Freud's *The Interpretation of Dreams*, which is the principal source of our knowledge about the nature of dreams, we find an explanation of this type of dream: a visual disproportion is always somehow connected with the earliest period of childhood. My experiences entirely confirm this view. The sudden appearance of giants or magnified objects is always the residue of a childhood recollection dating from a time when, because we ourselves were so small, all other objects seemed gigantic. An unusual reduction in the size of objects and persons, on the other hand, is to be attributed to the compensatory, wish-fulfilling fantasies of the child who wants to reduce the proportions of the terrifying objects in his environment to the smallest possible size. In many dreams the tendency to minimize or magnify is not so plain, because the persons minimized or magnified appear not as living beings but in some symbolical disguise. Dreams of landscapes with mountains and valleys, for instance, which represent male or female bodies, or parts of bodies, might be termed, from the psycho-analytical point of view, Lilliputian dreams, if we compare the size of the dreamer with that of the persons or bodily organs symbolically represented by the landscape. The symbolism of staircases, houses, and deep hollows, representing the mother, and the appearance of the father or his genital organ in the form of a gigantic tower or tree, bear a certain analogy to Gulliver fantasies. One of the most frequently occurring dream-pictures is that of rescuing someone from water—the sea or a deep well, symbolizing the mother's womb. These rescue dreams are interpreted by Freud as symbolic birth-dreams. In other instances, where the dream represents penetrating into a cellar or some other subterranean place, climbing, going up or down in lifts, and so forth, Freud explains it as a distorted coitus-fantasy, generally of coitus with a woman for whom the dreamer has a special respect. In my experiences the fantasies of birth represented by rescue from water or by climbing out of, or sinking down into, holes generally admit of a twofold interpretation. The more superficial one, which the patient readily accepts and sometimes even spontaneously proffers, is the birth-fantasy. The more hidden and not so easily accepted over-determination is the fantasy of sexual intercourse with some woman who is held in special esteem, and whose claims to reverence and whose dangerousness are represented by the large size of the symbol. *The disguise of fantasies of sexual intercourse as a symbolic birth comes about through the dreamer's substituting his whole body for his sexual organs. In my opinion this is the principal motive of Lilliputian dreams.*

You probably know that Freud himself was the first to recognize the significance for the unconscious of fantasies of the mother's womb. Subsequently I worked out the meaning of these fantasies into a genital theory by showing that the sexual act represents symbolically the desire to return to the mother's womb.[1] Next Rank came to regard these fantasies of return to the mother's womb and of being born as the central problem of the whole psychology of the neuroses. He holds that 'the trauma of birth' determines not only the symptomatology of the neurotic but the psychological development of healthy persons. Freud rejects this one-sided and exaggerated view, and I agree with him. We are also unable to adopt the new therapeutic technique which Rank works out on the basis of his theory of the birth-dream.[2] In this he seems to have forgotten many of his own valuable contributions to dream-psychology, especially in connexion with the over-determination of both dream-content and neurotic symptoms. Even when he bears in mind the complicated structure of the dream-fabric he undervalues the true significance of the sexual element and the castration-complex and is too much inclined to take literally every association and every fantasy of the patients which sounds like a reference to the trauma of birth.

[1] *Versuch einer Genitaltheorie*, Wien, 1924. Hungarian translation: Budapest, 1929. In English: *Thalassa*, (2nd imp.). New York, 1938.

[2] Cf. 'Zur Kritik der Rankschen "Technik der Psychoanalyse".' *Internationale Zeitschrift fur Psychoanalyse*, Bd. XIII, 1926. In English, *Int. J. of Ps.A.* (1927) 8.

My experience in the matter of Gulliver fantasies and symbols in neurotics has proved to me beyond any possibility of doubt that fantasies of birth or of return to the mother's womb generally indicate a flight from the sexual trauma to the less terrible idea of being born. For example, one of the most recent of my patients constantly dreamt that she was buried alive in a cave, or else that she was a tiny little person who was obliged to hop rhythmically over the spokes of a wheel which was going round quite fast, so that she was in perpetual danger of being crushed by it. Sometimes, too, she was suddenly tempted to jump out of the window. All these dream-fantasies and impulses are explained by the patient herself as representations of birth, but a more thorough analysis has shown that the whole complex of fantasies of birth and the mother's womb was simply the Lilliputian disguise of sexual temptations. The same patient often dreamt of tiny little black men, and in one of her fantasies during free associations she felt impelled to eat them all up. A quite spontaneous association to these thoughts was that of eating dark-coloured faeces and then of biting and devouring a penis. By eating these up she felt that her whole body was in some way transformed into a male genital; in this guise she could in her unconscious fantasies have sexual intercourse with women. These associations reveal the masculine trend in the patient's disposition as well as the fact that the tiny creatures in her dreams represent not only birth but, in a deeper mental stratum, her sexual tendencies and her penis-envy.

One of my male patients recollects that in the masturbation fantasies of his youth there was a little, imaginary, female figure which he always carried in his pocket and from time to time took out and played with. This patient had had a number of dreams all his life, which recurred also during his analysis, in which he found himself placed in an enormous room. You will already have guessed that this man's sexual potency was very inconsiderable. He came into the category of those men who with women whom they respect and love suffer either from *ejaculatio præcox* or complete inability to achieve erection and are potent only with prostitutes. These are only some of the many instances which have proved to me that Lilliputian fantasies of the uterus are characteristic of persons whose sexual development has not been sufficiently normal for them to make the penis in coitus a completely valid equivalent for the whole body. Freud also came to the conclusion that (as I suggest in my genital theory) persons who cannot attain to this level of sexual reality show a preference for fantasies in which they substitute the whole body for the sexual organ.

A patient who suffers from a severe obsessional neurosis said that in his masturbation fantasies he always imagined himself a big man, surrounded by a whole harem of tiny women, who served, washed, and caressed him, combed his pubic hair, and then played with his genital until ejaculation ensued. In both these last two patients the real anxiety is the fear of castration associated with the idea of sexual intercourse, and both *the Gulliver fantasies and those of the mother's womb are simply substitutes, by a process of displacement, for the painful idea of being castrated on account of incestuous desires.*

Fantasies connected with the birth-trauma may well be compared with examination-dreams which often occur in impotent neurotics during the night before they attempt some sexual activity to which they feel themselves unequal. Generally they dream, with an accompaniment of great anxiety, that they are being examined in some subject in which they are in reality thoroughly versed or even have already successfully passed an examination. Now, the experience of birth is for all of us a test which we have successfully passed, and it can therefore serve as a less terrible substitute for a real, actual sexual task which is dreaded and for the menace of castration with which this is associated. The comparison of Lilliputian and birth fantasies with examination-dreams holds good, I think, in yet another respect, namely the fact that there is no other trauma for which we are so well prepared as for that of birth. Birth itself is, as Freud himself was the first to emphasize, certainly a shock, but the preparation for the difficulties of extra-uterine life and the great care which the maternal instinct lavishes on the child immediately after birth make the trauma as light as possible.

When it comes to the child's sexual development, on the other hand, there appears to be no inherited instinct in either father or mother which can assist it. On the contrary, parents often intimidate their children by threats of castration, and this is the greatest and most important 'trauma' which leads to neurosis. Passing or 'transitory' symptoms[1] which I have observed in my patients during their analyses have sometimes revealed a sudden displacement of genital sensations or sexual excitations to the whole surface of the body. For instance, by a process of hysterical conversion, erection has been represented by a rush of blood to the head. In a whole series of cases of repressed male homosexuality I found that in moments of sexual excitement the whole surface of the skin became burning hot. It is not unlikely that the German slang expression used of homosexuals, 'hot brothers', has its origin in this symptom. In some other cases patients have told me that, instead of an erection, they experience a sudden rigidity of all their muscles. I have found that many cases of neurotic spinal rigidity or passing cramps of the leg-muscles could be similarly explained. Possibly this sort of conversion-symptom forms the physiological substructure upon which is erected the psychic superstructure of the Gulliver fantasies.

As I have already said, it is almost as common to meet with a tendency to magnify or minimize the male body as the female. The material derived from the associations of patients with this kind of fantasy is in the case of male children clearly connected with the boy's dread of a gigantic father—a dread proceeding from the comparison of his own genital organs with those of his father.

The fear of castration and mutilation, or the dread of being eaten up or swallowed, is apparently even greater in the unconscious than the dread of death. So long as we are not mutilated, the unconscious regards being buried, drowned, or swallowed up as a kind of continued existence *in toto*. Apparently it cannot grasp the idea that death betokens a complete cessation of existence, whilst even a slight symbolic suggestion of mutilation, such as cutting the hair or nails, or a threat with a sword, knife, or scissors, or even with the index finger, may produce an intense reaction in the form of an outbreak of castration anxiety.

[1] cf. First Contr., p. 193.

A little boy in his dreams and fantasies prefers to picture himself as a dwarf who is devoured by the terrible father, but whose genital is thereby secure from castration, rather than to imagine that he is natural life-size but that his genitals are exposed to the danger of mutilation. Similarly, a little girl prefers the oral fantasy of being eaten up but preserving her genital organs intact to the idea of being injured in these organs by the penis of the male. (This last would mean accepting without reservation her lack of the penis.)

I must confess that I should not have had the courage to tell you about all these unconscious fantasies, which are only reconstructed from dreams and based on what patients have said, if I were not certain that in your capacity of psychiatrists you must have often had occasion to convince yourselves of the existence of active and passive castration tendencies which frequently manifest themselves quite clearly in psychosis. In my monograph entitled *Versuch einer Genitaltheorie* I tried to account theoretically for this high estimation of the penis by showing that the sexual organs, in particular the penis and the clitoris, are the pleasure-reservoir of the whole individual and are prized by the ego as a kind of second personality which I have termed the libidinal ego. You know how often children and the common people call the genital by pet names as though it were an independent being.

I will now try to enliven the monotony of this dry and somewhat theoretical argument by reading some passages from the two first journeys of our friend and colleague, Gulliver, in the hope that perhaps they will make my constructions seem somewhat more probable.

Let us take the description of Gulliver's awaking in the land of Lilliput: 'When I awaked it was just daylight. I attempted to rise, but was not able to stir: for, as I happened to lie on my back, I found my arms and legs were strongly fastened on each side to the ground; and my hair, which was long and thick, tied down in the same manner. I likewise felt several slender ligatures across my body, from my armpits to my thighs. I could only look upwards; the sun began to grow hot, and the light offended my eyes. I heard a confused noise about me, but in the posture I lay, could see nothing except the sky. In a little time I felt something alive moving on my left leg, which advancing gently forward over my breast came almost up to my chin; when bending my eyes downwards as much as I could, I perceived it to be a human creature, not six inches high, with a bow and arrow in his hands, and a quiver at his back. In the meantime, I felt at least forty more of the same kind (as I conjectured) following the first. I was in the utmost astonishment, and roared so loud, that they all ran back in a fright; and some of them, as I was afterwards told, were hurt with the falls they got by leaping from my sides upon the ground.'

This description has a great similarity to the apparitions seen by our neurotic patients who so often tell us how they are frightened by little animals and manikins sitting on their breasts.

Anyone who wishes to explain everything by the trauma of birth will probably lay stress on another detail, a suspicious number which appears on page 89 of this edition.[1] Here Gulliver states that he lived for nine months and thirteen days in the land of the Lilliputians—a period which exactly corresponds to the duration of pregnancy. On the other hand we may cite the fact that the little Lilliputians were just six inches long and that this number is suspicious from another point of view, especially since Gulliver happens to say that the Lilliputians were 'rather longer than my middle finger' and further, that he could not be mistaken in this estimate 'for I have often held them in my hand'. (He is referring to the Lilliputians!)

A little further on he says: 'Two hundred sempstresses were employed to make me shirts and linen. . . . [They] took my measure as I lay on the ground, one standing at my neck, and another at my mid-leg. . . . Then they measured my right thumb and desired no more; for, by a mathematical computation, that twice round the thumb is once round the wrist, and so on to the neck and waist. . . .' It is significant that it is just the finger, the typical genital symbol, which is taken as the standard measure for the whole body. It will have struck you, as it did me at the time, how similar this fantasy of being served by so many tiny women is to the masturbation-fantasies of one of my patients.

[1] (The author is quoting from the Tauchnitz Edition.—Trans.)

The strong exhibitionistic tendencies of Gulliver and his great desire that the Lilliputians should admire him for the size of his genital are very clearly revealed in the following description of a parade held by the Lilliputian army in his honour: '[The Emperor] desired I would stand like a Colossus, with my legs as far asunder as I conveniently could; he then commanded his general . . . to draw up the troops in close order, and march them under me . . . with drums beating, colours flying and pikes advanced. . . . His Majesty gave orders upon pain of death that every soldier in his march should observe the strictest decency with regard to my person, which, however, could not prevent some of the younger officers from turning up their eyes as they passed under me. And to confess the truth, my breeches were at that time in so ill a condition that they afforded some opportunities for laughter and admiration.'

Does not this sound exactly like the reassurance-fantasy or dream of an impotent man who in waking life suffers from the idea that his penis is too small and in consequence of his sense of inferiority is shy of showing his organ and in dreams basks in the admiration of those whose penises are even smaller than his own?

A still worse offence brings Gulliver into the extreme peril of his life. I refer to the incident of his urinating before the Empress. As you perhaps know, the queen or empress is one of the typical symbols of the mother. A fire breaks out in the Empress's apartments and the Lilliputians are unable to extinguish it.

Fortunately our hero Gulliver is at hand and performs this heroic task as follows: 'I had, the evening before,' he says, 'drank plentifully of a most delicious wine . . . which is very diuretic. By the luckiest chance in the world I had not discharged myself of any part of it. The heat I had contracted by coming very near the flames, and by my labouring to quench them, made the wine begin to operate by urine, which I voided in such a quantity, and applied so well to the proper places, that in three minutes the fire was wholly extinguished. . . .'

Everyone who is acquainted with the mode of expression used by the unconscious will know that the extinguishing of a conflagration in a woman's house, especially when this is done by urinating into it, represents the child's idea of sexual intercourse, the woman being symbolized by the house. The heat mentioned by Gulliver is the symbol of the male's passionate desire (and at the same time fire stands for the dangers to which the genital is exposed). And, in point of fact, with Gulliver the threat of punishment follows hard upon the misdeed and characteristically proceeds from the Emperor, the typical father-substitute: 'I could not tell how His Majesty might resent the manner by which I had performed it. For by the fundamental laws of the realm it is capital in any person of what quality soever to make water within the precincts of the palace. . . .' 'I was privately assured that the Empress, conceiving the greatest abhorrence of what I had done, removed to the most distant side of the Court . . . and . . . could not forbear vowing revenge.' The death penalty is revoked by the mercy of the Emperor, but Gulliver cannot escape punishment in another form. The sentence ran as follows: 'The said Quinbus Flestrin'—(the Man Mountain, the Lilliputians' name for Gulliver)—'in open breach of the said law, under colour of extinguishing the fire kindled in the apartment of His Majesty's most dear imperial consort, did maliciously, traitorously, and devilishly, by discharge of his urine, put out the said fire kindled in the said apartment, lying and being within the precincts of the said royal palace.' But, of his clemency, the Emperor condemned him merely to the loss of his eyes, which would not impair his bodily power and would enable him still to be useful to His Majesty! The punishment, you see, is the same as that which King Oedipus inflicted on himself for his sexual intercourse with his mother. And countless times our analytical experience shows us beyond a shadow of doubt that putting out the eyes may be a symbolic distortion of the punishment of castration.

But even in peril of death and mutilation our hero Gulliver cannot deny himself the satisfaction of suggesting a reason for this sentence, namely, that he was not only able 'to extinguish the fire by discharge of urine in Her Majesty's apartment,' [but he might] 'at another time raise an inundation by the same means to drown the whole palace.'

As you know, Gulliver succeeded in escaping from the Lilliputians, who had by now become so hostile to him, but fate still dogged his footsteps, and on his next journey he fell into the hands of the giants of Brobdingnag. His very first experience with one of the natives of this land is a symbolic representation of the danger of castration. '[The man] appeared as tall as an ordinary spire-steeple,' and had a reaping-hook in his hand 'about the largeness of six scythes'. Gulliver was very nearly cut in two with the reaping-hook, but he 'screamed as loud as fear could make' him, whereupon the huge creature seized him between his forefinger and thumb, regarded him as a curiosity, and then gave him as a plaything to his wife and children. He called his wife and showed him to her; 'but she screamed and ran back as women in England do at the sight of a toad or a spider.'

Women's abhorrence of spiders, toads, and other little creeping things is well known as an hysterical symptom. A disciple of the theory of the trauma of birth would say that this anxiety was simply conditioned by the fact that little reptiles are the symbol for little children who might creep in and out of the genital. My analytical experiences, however, all go to confirm Freud's idea that the deeper meaning of such little creatures, especially of those which move rhythmically, is really that they represent symbolically the genital organ and function, and that the sight or touch of them therefore produces the kind of disgust which is often the woman's primary reaction to her first contact with the genitals. I should not hesitate to interpret a dream in which such creatures appeared as the identification of a whole (here, of an animal's) body with the male sexual organ and to class it with those cases in which women in their dreams or fantasies are made uneasy by little creatures or manikins.

As he became a plaything, Gulliver had the opportunity to observe the most intimate functions of the gigantic women and girls from quite near by, and he is untiring in describing the frightful impressions produced in him by their monstrous dimensions: 'I must confess no object ever disgusted me so much as the sight of her monstrous breast, which I cannot tell what to compare with so as to give the curious reader an idea of its bulk, shape and colour. It stood prominent six foot, and could not be less than sixteen in circumference. The nipple was about half the bigness of my head, and the hue both of that and the dug so varified with spots, pimples, and freckles, that nothing could appear more nauseous: for I had a near sight of her, she sitting down the more conveniently to give suck, and I standing on the table. This made me reflect upon the fair skins of our English ladies, who appear so beautiful to us, only because they are of our own size, and their defects not to be seen but through a magnifying glass; where we find by experiment that the smoothest and whitest skins look rough and coarse and ill-coloured.'

In my opinion it would be far-fetched to explain the dread of the large holes in the women's skin as a recollection of the trauma of birth. It is much more probable that Gulliver is the embodiment of a type of male whose sexual courage vanishes in the presence of a young English lady with her delicate skin and who prefers to complain of the difficulty of the task before him and the lack of charm of the object of his love rather than admit his own inadequacy. An interesting contrast to the extinguishing of the fire is given in a later chapter in a scene where Gulliver is obliged to urinate in the presence of one of the giant women. He signed to her not to look or to follow him, and then he hid himself between two sorrel-leaves and there satisfied the needs of nature. Further he tells us that the young maids of honour often examined him and touched him for the mere pleasure they took in it. 'They would often strip me naked from top to toe, and lay me at full length in their bosoms; wherewith I was much disgusted, because to say the truth a very offensive smell came from their skins, which I do not mention or intend to the disadvantage of these excellent ladies, for whom I have all manner of respect. . . . That which gave me most uneasiness among these maids of honour . . . was to see them use me without any manner of ceremony like a creature who had no sort of consequence. For they would strip themselves to the skin, and put on their smocks in my presence, while I was placed on their toilet directly before their naked bodies; which, I am sure, to me was very far from being a tempting sight, or from giving me any other motions than those of horror and disgust. Their skins appeared so coarse and uneven, so variously coloured when I saw them near, with a mole here and there as broad as a trencher, and hairs hanging from it thicker than pack threads, to say nothing further concerning the rest of their persons. Neither did they at all scruple, while I was by, to discharge what they had drunk, to the quantity of at least two hogshead, in a vessel that held above three tuns. The handsomest among these maids of honour, a pleasant frolicsome girl of sixteen, would sometimes set me astride upon one of her nipples, with many other tricks, wherein the reader will excuse me for not being over particular. But I was so much displeased, that I entreated Glumdalclitch to contrive some excuse for not seeing that young lady any more.'

I am sure that you know that according to the findings of psycho-analysis two dreams dreamt in the same night often throw light on one another. The same could be maintained of the first two sections of *Gulliver's Travels*. The adventure in Lilliput represents the wish-fulfilling part of the dream—it is a description of large size and male potency in his own person. The terrible experiences in Brobdingnag reveal to us the motives of the tendency to self-magnification; his dread lest he should fail in rivalry and in strife with other men and his impotence with women.

Of course, in the story of the second journey there are suggestions of the situations of birth and intra-uterine existence. During the whole period of his sojourn in the land of the giants Gulliver was carried about by a young girl in a travelling box, in which at the four corners of the top a hammock was fixed by silken ropes to break the jolts, and the manner in which he finally escaped from the dangerous land of the giants is still more significant. He woke up and felt his box raised very high in the air and then borne forward with prodigious speed. 'The first jolt had like to have shaken me out of my hammock, but afterwards the motion was easy enough. . . . [I] then began to perceive the woeful condition I was in, that some eagle had got the ring of my box in its beak, with an intent to let it fall on a rock, like a tortoise in a shell, and then pick out my body and devour it. . . .

'I heard several bangs or buffets, as I thought, given to the eagle . . . and then, all on a sudden, felt myself falling perpendicularly down for above a minute, but with such incredible swiftness that I almost lost my breath. My fall was stopped by a terrible squash, that sounded louder to my ears than the cataract of Niagara, after which I was quite in the dark for another minute, and then my box began to rise so high that I could see light from the tops of the windows. I now perceived that I was fallen into the sea. . . . I got with much difficulty out of my hammock . . . to let in air, for want of which I found myself almost stifled. How often did I then wish myself with my dear Glumdalclitch, from whom one single hour had so far divided me!' (Glumdalclitch was the name of the girl who carried him about and whose plaything he was.)

No analyst would take exception to an attempt to interpret this escape as a birth-fantasy—the natural end of pregnancy, which is represented by being carried about in a box. On the other hand, dreams of a similar sort give us no reason to suppose that this scene represents details of the individual birth, as Rank assumes. It is much more probable that Gulliver and other people into whose dreams birth-fantasies enter transform and diminish quite real sexual dangers to which they feel unequal into injuries dating from childhood or even from foetal life. Almost as though the author wished to make clear beyond any doubt that in Gulliver's journey the whole body really represents the male organ and coitus, he adds to the description of the escape that one of the few tokens of remembrance which he had saved from the giant mother was 'a gold ring which one day she made me a present of in a most obliging manner, taking it from her little finger, and throwing it over my head like a collar.' Students of folklore and psycho-analysts agree in the belief that putting on a wedding ring is a symbolic representation of coitus, the ring standing for the female and the finger for the male sexual organ. Thus when the giantess takes her ring from her little finger and throws it round Gulliver's neck she simply expresses by this gesture the idea that only his head would be big enough to fulfil the sexual task for which normally an organ of the size of a finger suffices.

The fact that all creations of genius are characterized by the remarkable number of interpretations which may be put upon them has made it possible for *Gulliver's Travels* to be interpreted in the most varied ways. Despite their superficiality, these interpretations have a certain basis in fact. In his short biography of Jonathan Swift, the author of *Gulliver's Travels*, Walter Scott, tells us how the different classes of society reacted to the book. Readers in higher social circles saw in it a personal and political satire; the common people looked upon it as a story of exciting adventures; romantic persons admired the element of the supernatural which it contained; the young loved its cleverness and wit; thoughtful people read into it moral and political teaching. But neglected old age and disappointed ambition found in it only the maxims of a sad and embittered misanthropy.

These may be called the preconscious interpretations, whereas psycho-analysis would aim at explaining also the unconscious meaning of the *Travels*. Perhaps if we study the life-history of Jonathan Swift it will help us to decide on the value or otherwise of our interpretation. A large number of authors have devoted whole volumes to this extraordinary personality, but, so far as I know, Hans Sachs is the only psycho-analyst who has made Swift the subject of a psycho-analytical study. Even the very fleeting glances which I myself have been able to take at Swift's life-history throw light upon certain data which support my notion about the fantasies of magnifying and minimizing in *Gulliver's Travels*. I will quote briefly some of the most important facts of Swift's life.

Jonathan Swift was born on 30 November 1667. Towards the end of his life he kept his birthday always as a day of fasting and mourning, and never omitted to read the third chapter of the book of Job. Richard Brennan, the servant in whose arms he died, tells us that in the infrequent lucid intervals of Swift's fatal illness he seemed to be conscious of this date, as was seen from the fact that he constantly repeated the words: 'Let the day perish wherein I was born, and the light in which it was said there is a man-child conceived.' Swift was a posthumous child. A remarkable occurrence removed him for a time from the care of his uncle and his mother. The nurse who had charge of the child was so devoted to him that she stole him from his mother and took him across the Channel. His delicate health and the difficulty in those days of finding an opportunity to cross prevented his being sent back for three years.

It is probably not too rash to assume that these abnormal situations and events of his youth made an ineffaceable impression on Swift and exercised a great influence on his subsequent development, possibly also increasing his interest in adventurous travels. It seems to me unnecessary to seek for abnormal physiological difficulties in the child's birth when the pathogenic factors during his childhood are so patent.

Our psycho-analytical experience teaches us that sons who grow up without a father are seldom normal in their sexual life; most of them become neurotic or homosexual. The fixation to the mother is in these cases by no means the result of any birth-trauma, but must be attributed to the lack of a father, with whom a boy has to fight out the Oedipus conflict and whose presence helps to resolve the castration anxiety through the process of identification. Naturally, the excessive spoiling which the boy is likely to receive from mother and nurse makes him less liable to compete with other boys, and this disability is often one of the principal causes of disturbances of sexual potency. Moreover, when there is no father, the mother is the only person in whom resides the power of discipline or—in sexual matters—of castration, and this often leads to an exaggeration of the boy's normal reserve and timidity in his relations with women whom he reveres, or indeed with women altogether. Swift's later behaviour, especially in the sphere of sex, does actually show that he was a neurotic. Thus for example he began a flirtation with a Miss Waring, whom he affectionately called Varina, as his biography tells us: 'The courtship so far as it can be traced is supremely ridiculous. While the lady was coy and cold, nothing could equal the impetuosity of the lover, but when after a long resistance she unexpectedly surrendered at discretion, the lover suddenly disappeared, the warm epistles to "Varina" were changed into a cold formal "Miss Jane Waring" . . . in which it was hinted in unequivocal terms that the impatient suitor would be a reluctant bridegroom. The lady with proper spirit broke off all intercourse and Swift was free to try his arts on a more unfortunate victim.' It is interesting that in contrast to this exaggerated scrupulousness rumour in that part of England has it that Swift committed an indecent assault on the daughter of a farmer and that criminal charges were laid against him on oath before Mr. Dobbs, the mayor of the neighbouring town.

The accounts of his subsequent famous marriage with Mrs. Esther Johnson—better known by her poetic name of Stella—on the other hand show marked dependence and passionateness from the beginning of their acquaintance. Walter Scott, it is true, quotes a remark of Swift's about his love story which seems to contradict this: 'It is a habit which I could easily renounce and which I could leave without regret at the gate of the sanctuary.' And so it actually came about. Swift married Stella only on condition that their marriage should remain secret and that they should continue to live apart. Thus, these details of his private life do really reveal the far-reaching consequences of the disturbances in his development as a child. From the psycho-analytical standpoint one would describe his neurotic behaviour as an inhibition of normal potency, with a lack of courage in relation to women of good character and perhaps with a lasting aggressive tendency towards women of a lower type. This insight into Swift's life surely justifies us who come after him in treating the fantasies in *Gulliver's Travels* exactly as we do the free associations of neurotic patients in analysis, especially when interpreting their dreams. The disadvantage of such an analysis *in absentia* is that the patient cannot confirm our conclusions; the scientific advantage of a posthumous analysis, on the other hand, is that the analyst cannot in this case be accused of having suggested to the patient the statements made by the latter. I think that the biographical argument confirms our supposition that Gulliver fantasies in which persons and objects are magnified or minimized express the sense of genital inadequacy of a person whose sexual activities have been inhibited by intimidation and fixations in early childhood.

My analysis of Swift and his masterpiece has perhaps been too long, but I think it bears out my suggested interpretation of the

Lilliputian and Brobdingnagian fantasies and symptoms met with in psychotic and neurotic patients and in dreams.

I cannot do better than conclude with a slightly altered quotation from Gulliver himself: 'I hope my readers will excuse me for dwelling on these and similar particulars; however insignificant they may appear, yet they may perhaps help a philosopher to enlarge his thoughts and imagination so that he may apply them to the benefit of public as well as of private life.'

I thank you once more for your invitation and for the patience with which you have listened to me.

VI

THE ADAPTATION OF THE FAMILY TO THE CHILD[1]
Being Free Associations on Children's Education
(1928)

THE title which I have given to this paper is rather an unusual one, for we are generally concerned with the adaptation of the child to the family, not that of the family to the child; but our special studies in psycho-analysis have shown that it is we who should make the first adaptation, and that we have in fact made the first step in this direction, which of course is to understand the child. Psycho-analysis is often reproached for being too exclusively concerned with pathological material; this is true, but we learn much from a study of the abnormal that is of value when applied to the normal. In the same way the study of the physiology of the brain would never have advanced so far as it has without a knowledge of the processes of faulty function; by a study of neurotics and psychotics psycho-analysis shows the way in which the different levels or layers, or the different ways of functioning, are hidden behind the surface of normality. In the study of the primitive or the child we find traits which are invisible in more civilized people; indeed we stand in debt to children for the light they have thrown on psychology, and the best and most logical way of repaying that debt (it is in our interest as well as theirs to do so) is to strive to improve our understanding of them through psycho-analytical studies.

I confess that we are not yet in a position to assess precisely the educational value of psycho-analysis, nor to give rules regarding practical details of education, because psycho-analysis, which is ever cautious in giving advice, is primarily concerned with matters which education has either mishandled or left untouched; we can tell you how *not* to educate your child better than we can tell you how to do it; the latter is a much more

[1] Delivered before a joint meeting of the Med. and Ped. sections of the Brit.Ps.Soc. 1927. German original (1928). English translation in *Brit. J.Med.Psych.* (1928), 8, 1.

complicated question, but we are hoping that we shall be able some day to give a satisfactory answer to that too. For this reason in what I have to say I am compelled to be more general in my treatment of the subject than I would like, but I can say that the study of criminals, or normal people, or neurotics, will not be complete until we have made further progress in the analytical understanding of the life of the child.

The adjustment of the family to the child cannot take place until the parents first of all *understand themselves* and thus get some grasp of the mental life of grown-ups. Up to now it has often been taken for granted that parents are endowed with a natural knowledge of how to bring up their children, though there is a famous German saying which states the opposite: 'It is easy to become a father, but difficult to be one.' The first mistake that parents make is to forget their own childhood. Even in most normal people we find an astonishing lack of memories from the first five years of life, and in pathological cases the amnesia is even more extensive. These are years in which the child has in many ways reached the level of adults—and yet they are forgotten! Lack of understanding of their own childhood proves to be the greatest hindrance to parents grasping the essential questions of education.

Before I come to my real topic—the question of education—let me make a few general remarks on *adaptation* and its part in psychic life. I have used the word 'adaptation', and I do so because it is a biological term and draws our attention to biological concepts. It has three different meanings—the Darwinian, the Lamarckian, and a third which can be called the psychological. The first deals with natural selection, and is at bottom a 'statistical explanation' of adaptation in that it concerns itself with general questions of survival. For example, the giraffe, having a longer neck, can reach food that shorter-necked animals cannot; it can therefore satisfy its hunger and live to propagate its kind; this explanation is in fact applicable to all creatures. According to the Lamarckian view, the exercise of a function both helps the individual to become stronger and passes on the increased capacity to posterity; this is a 'physiological explanation' of adaptation. There is a third way in which individuals can adapt themselves to their environment, and that is by psychological means. It is probable that alteration in the distribution of mental or nervous energies may make an organ grow or degenerate. It has become fashionable in America to deny the existence of psychology as a science; every word beginning with 'psych-' is a brand-mark of the unscientific, on the ground that psychology contains a mystic element. Dr. Watson once asked me to say just what psycho-analysis was. I had to confess that it was not so 'scientific' as behaviourism, viewing science, that is to say, solely as a discipline of the measure and scales. Physiology requires that every change should be measured with an instrument, but psycho-analysis is not in a position to deal with emotional forces in this way. Very slight approaches, it is true, have been made to this goal, but they are at present far from satisfying. However, if one explanation fails, it is not forbidden to try others. One such we owe to Freud. He found that by a scientific grouping of the data of introspection one could gain a new insight just as certainly as by grouping the data of external perceptions derived from observations and experiments; these introspective facts, though as yet not measurable, are none the less facts, and as such we have the right to group them and try to find out ways of helping us to something new. By merely regrouping introspective material Freud constructed a psychical system; in this there are of course hypotheses, but these are found no less in the natural sciences. Among them the concept of the unconscious plays a very special part, and with its help we have reached conclusions which were not possible with the hypotheses of physiology and cerebral anatomy. When progress in microscopy and chemistry shows us that Freud's hypotheses are superfluous we shall be ready to resign our claims to science. Dr. Watson is of the opinion that one can understand the child without the help of psychology; he thinks that psychology is unscientific and that conditioned reflexes can explain behaviour fully. I had to answer him that his physiological scheme may lead to an understanding of white mice and rabbits, but not of human beings. But even with his animals he himself is, without admitting it, constantly using psychology—he is an unconscious psycho-analyst! For instance, when he speaks of a fear reflex he uses the psychological term 'fear'. He uses the word correctly because he knows from introspection what fear is; if he had not known it introspectively he would not have realized what running away meant to the mouse. But to return to the question of *adaptation*: psycho-analysis brings forward a new series of facts besides those of the natural sciences—*the working of internal factors which cannot be detected except through introspection.*

I will now try to deal with the practical problems connected with the ways in which parents adapt themselves to their children. Nature is very careless; she does not care for the individual, but we human beings are different; we wish to save the lives of every one of our offspring and spare them unnecessary suffering. Let us therefore turn our special attention to those phases of evolution in which the child has to deal with difficulties. There are a great many of them. The first difficulty is birth itself. It was Freud himself who told us that the symptoms of anxiety were closely connected with the particular physiological changes which take place at the moment of the transition from the mother's womb to the external world. One of his former pupils used this view of Freud's as a springboard from which to leap to a new theory, and, leaving psycho-analytical concepts behind him, tried to explain the neuroses and psychoses from this first great trauma; he called it 'the trauma of Birth'. I myself was very much interested in this question, but the more I observed the more I realized that for none of the developments and changes which life brings was the individual so well prepared as for birth. Physiology and the instincts of the parents go to make this transition as smooth as possible. It would indeed be a trauma if lungs and heart were not so well developed, whereas birth is a sort of triumph for the child and must surely exert as such an influence on its whole life. Consider the details: the menacing suffocation is dealt with, for the lungs are there and begin to expand at the very moment of the cessation of the umbilical circulation, and at the same time the left side of the heart, till then inert, takes up its role with vigour. In addition to these physiological aids, the parents' instincts guide them to make the situation as agreeable as possible, the child is kept warm and protected from the disturbing stimuli of light and sound as far as possible; indeed they make the child forget what has happened, it can make believe that nothing has happened. It is questionable whether an event dealt with so smoothly and speedily should be called a 'trauma'.

Real traumata are more difficult to solve; they are less physiological than birth, they concern the child's entry into the company of his fellow mortals; the intuitions of the parents do not make such good provision in this respect as they did at birth. I refer to the traumata of weaning, training to cleanliness, the breaking of 'bad habits', and, last and most important of all, that breaking off from childhood itself into the adult way of life. These are the biggest traumata of childhood, and for these neither parents in particular nor civilization in general have as yet made adequate preparation.

Weaning is and always has been an important matter in medicine. It is not only the change from a primitive way of feeding to the active act of mastication, that is, it is a change not only of physiological, but also of great psychological, importance. A clumsy method of weaning may influence unfavourably the child's relation to his love objects and his ways of obtaining pleasure from them, and this may darken a large part of his life. We do not, it is true, know much about the psychology of the one-year-old child, but we are beginning to get a faint conception of the deeper impressions which weaning may leave. In the early states of embryonic development a slight wound, the mere prick of a pin, can not only cause severe alterations in, but may completely prevent, the development of whole limbs of the body. Just as, if you have only one candle in a room and put your hand near the candle, half the room may become darkened, so if, near the beginning of life, you do only a little harm to a child, it may cast a shadow over the whole of its life. It is important to realize how sensitive children are; but parents do not believe this, they simply cannot comprehend the high degree of sensitivity of their offspring, and behave in their presence as if the children understood nothing of the emotional scenes going on around them. If intimate parental intercourse is observed by the child in the first or second year of life, when its capacity for excitement is already

c

there but it lacks as yet adequate outlets for its emotion, an infantile neurosis may result which may permanently weaken the child's effective life. Infantile phobias and hysterical anxieties are common in the early developmental years; usually they pass without disturbing later life, but quite often we find that they have left deep impressions on the mind and character of the child. This much for the more or less passive relation of the parents to the young; we must now examine a situation or series of situations in which the parents play an active part in the intimate concerns of the child's emotional life, and it is here especially that we find how necessary it is for the parents to understand their own minds and instinctual reactions before they embark on the task of 'upbringing'.

Toilet training is one of the most difficult phases in the child's development. It is one that can be very dangerous, but it is not always so; there are children who are so healthy and well equipped that they can deal with the silliest parents, but these are exceptions, and even if apparently successful in dealing with their bad upbringing we too often note that they have lost something of the happiness which life can bring. The possibility of loss of happiness through careless or over-vigorous 'training' in cleanliness should make parents and educators pay far more attention than they do to the feelings of the child and appreciate its difficulties. Freud's observations on the emotional changes in the child during the adaptations to the adult code of cleanliness led him to the signal discovery that an important part of the character of the individual is formed during this process. To put it in other words: the way in which the individual adapts his primitive urges to the requirements of civilization in the first five years of life will determine the way in which he deals with all his difficulties in later life. Character is from the point of view of the psycho-analyst a sort of abnormality, a kind of mechanization of a particular way of reaction, rather similar to an obsessional symptom. We expect an individual to be able to adapt himself precisely to the details of the current situation, but consider how far this is compatible with what his character has made out of him! If you know the character of any individual, you can make him perform an action when you wish and as often as you wish, because he behaves like a machine. If you put something into his ear he will shake his head, if you utter a particular name you know he will also shake his head (physical and psychical reflex, i.e. automatic response). He gives this automatic response to your cunningly chosen word because it is 'in his character' to do so. When I was a student too much importance was accorded in medicine to inherited characteristics; physicians believed that we were the product of our constitution. Charcot, one of our best teachers in Paris, gave many important lectures on this topic. I well remember a typical incident which illustrates this. One day a mother came to him at one of his *leçons du mardi* and wished to speak to him about her neurotic child. He began, as always, to ask about its grandfather and what diseases he had and what he died of, and about its grandmother and the other grandfather and grandmother and all its relations: the mother tried to interrupt and tell him of something that had happened to the child a week or a year ago. Charcot became irritated, and did not want to hear about this; he was intent on tracing the inherited characteristics. We psycho-analysts do not deny their importance; on the contrary we believe them to be among the most important factors in the aetiology of neurotic or psychotic disease, but not the only ones. The inherited disposition may be there, but its influence may be modified by post-natal experience or by education. Both heredity and the individual traumata must be taken into account. Cleanliness is not a thing inborn, it is not an inherited quality, so it must be taught. I do not mean that children are not sensitive to this sort of teaching, but I think that, unless taught, children would not acquire this training by themselves.

The natural tendency of the baby is to love himself and to love all those things which he regards as parts of himself; his excreta are really part of himself, a transitional something between him and his environment, i.e. between subject and object. The child has a sort of affection for his excrement; in fact some adult people share this attitude too. I have sometimes analysed so-called normal people, and I have never found very much difference in this respect between them and the neurotics, unless it be that the latter have somewhat more unconscious interest in dirt;

and since hysteria is the negative of a perversion, as Freud has taught us, cleanliness in a normal man is founded on his (repressed) interest in dirt. People generally call it abnormal if a person is interested in the excretory functions, but most of us *are* to a certain extent during the whole of our lives. Do not let us be downhearted about it, for these primitive functions provide us with energy for the great achievements of civilization. If we ignore this and rage cruelly and blindly against the child struggling with difficulties—achieving the repression of these difficulties—we shall only deflect the energies to false paths. The reaction will differ according to the varying constitutions of the individuals; one will possibly become a neurotic, another a psychotic, a third a criminal. If, however, we know our way in these matters and treat the children with understanding, let them work out their impulses in their own way to a certain extent, and by giving way give them a chance to sublimate those impulses, the path will be much smoother and they will learn to turn their primitive urges into the paths of usefulness. Teachers often wish to 'weed out' these primitive urges (which are most important sources of energy) as if they were vices, whereas if led into social channels they can be used for the good of the individual and for the benefit of society.

The real traumas during the adaptation of the family to the child happen in its transitional stages from the earliest primitive childhood to civilization, not only from the point of view of cleanliness, but from the point of view of sexuality. One often hears people saying that Freud bases everything on sexuality, which is quite untrue. He speaks of the *conflict* between egoistic and sexual tendencies, and even holds that the former are the stronger. Psycho-analysts in fact spend most of their time in the analysis of the *repressing* factors in the individual.

Sexuality does not begin with puberty, but with the 'bad habits' of children. These 'bad habits', as they have been erroneously called, are manifestations of auto-eroticism, that is of primitive sexual instincts in the child. Do not be afraid of these manifestations. The word masturbation frightens people immensely. If, in consultation—and how often this happens—the doctor's advice is asked about the auto-erotic activities of children, he should tell the parents not to take it tragically; parents, however, have to be treated tactfully in this matter because of their immense fears and their lack of comprehension. Curiously, what the parents do not comprehend is precisely what the children understand only too well and experience deeply, and what the children cannot fathom is as clear as daylight to the parents. I will explain this riddle later on: it contains the whole secret of the confusion in the relation between parents and child.

I will turn for a moment from this paradox to the salient question of how to deal with the neurotic child. There is only one way of doing this, and that is to find out his motives, which, though hidden in his unconscious mind, are nevertheless active. Several attempts have already been made in this direction; a former pupil of mine and of Dr. Abraham's, Mrs. Melanie Klein, whose paper on 'Criminal Tendencies in Normal Children' appeared in this Journal, Vol. VII, 11, pp. 177-92, has courageously attempted the analysis of children as if they were adults, and has met with great success. Another attempt, on different, more conservative, lines has been made by Miss Anna Freud, Professor Freud's daughter. The two methods are quite different; we shall see some day whether they can be brought together and the difficult problem of a combination of education and analysis solved; at any rate we can say that the beginnings are hopeful.

When in America recently I had an opportunity of studying the methods of a school which is run by psycho-analytically trained and mostly psycho-analysed teachers. This is the Walden school. The teachers try to deal with the children in groups, since separate individual analysis of each child, which would be preferable, is out of the question on account of time. They attempt to educate children in such a way that analysis becomes unnecessary. If they have a really neurotic child they make, of course, a particular study of it, giving it an individual analysis and as much individual attention as it requires. In particular I was greatly interested in the way in which they deal with sex education. The school emphasizes in its conferences with parents the need for answering children's questions on sex in a simple, natural way. Unfortunately they adopt the 'Botanic Method', i.e. they use plant analogies in explaining reproduction in the human species.

I have an objection to make against this. It is too *informative*, that is, not sufficiently *psychological*, in its appraoch. It may be a good beginning, but it does not give full consideration to the internal needs and strivings of the child. For instance, even the most elaborate and physiological explanation of where children come from does not satisfy the child, and the usual way in which children react to this information is by sheer disbelief. They virtually say: 'You tell me this, but I don't believe it.' *What the child really needs is an admission of the erotic (sensual) importance of the genital organs.* The child is not the scientist who wants to know where children come from; it is interested, of course, in this question as it is interested in astronomy, but it is much more desirous of having the admission from parents and educators that the genital organ has a libidinous function, and as long as this is not admitted by the parents no explanation is satisfactory to the child. The child puts to itself such questions as this: how often does sexual intercourse take place? and tries to compare the answer with the number of children in the family. Then he says, perhaps: 'It must be very difficult to produce a child, because it lasts so long.' It guesses that the sexual act occurs repeatedly, not once only, and that it causes pleasure to the parents; sympathetically, as we say, it feels erotic sensations in its own genitals which can be satisfied by certain activities, and it is clever enough to find out and to feel that the genital organ has a libidinous function. It feels guilty because it has libidinous sensations at this stage, and therefore thinks: 'What an inferior person I am to have libidinous sensations in my genitals, whereas my respected parents only use this organ in order to have children.' As long as the erotic or pleasurable function of the genital is not admitted, there will always be a distance between you and your child, and you will become an unattainable ideal in its eyes —or the reverse! This is what I meant by the paradox a few moments ago. The parents cannot believe that the child experiences in its genitals sensations similar to their own; whereas the child, just because of these sensations, feels corrupt and believes that the parents are in this respect pure and immaculate, which the parents find readily acceptable; there is thus a gulf between parent and child on this intimate domestic matter. If a similar gulf developed between a husband and wife—as in fact it not so seldom does—we should not be at all surprised that it led to an 'estrangement': but with the blindness which clouds our vision on nearly all matters connected with the sexual activity of children (due to our infantile amnesia) we expect implicit trust from children while denying them the validity of their own physical and psychical experiences. Often one of the child's greatest difficulties arises later when it realizes that all this high idealization is unfounded, is not true, and it becomes disappointed and mistrusts every authority. One should not deprive the child of its trust in authority, in the truthfulness of its parents and others, but it should not be forced to take everything on trust. Perhaps I can illustrate this best by saying it in another way, that it is a disaster for a child to grow up to disbelieve, to be disappointed too early.

The Walden school does good work, but of course it is only a beginning. Their method of influencing the child's mind through the medium of the parents' understanding is in some cases quite good, and in early cases of neurotic difficulties it might even be successful. We must remember that the first child analysis was done by Professor Freud in this way (Little Hans[1]). He interviewed the father of the neurotic child and all the explanations were given by the father. But the father was analysed by Freud, a fact likewise to be forgotten.

The difficulties of adaptation at the age when the child becomes independent of the family are very much connected with sexual development. This is the stage of the formation of the so-called Oedipus conflict. If you think of the ways in which children sometimes express themselves about this question, then you will probably not find it so tragic. The child sometimes spontaneously tells the father: 'If you die, I shall marry Mother.' Nobody takes it very seriously, because this is said at a time *before* the Oedipus conflict, that is to say at a period when the child is permitted to do and think everything without being

[1] Freud: 'Analysis of a Phobia in a Five-year-old Boy', German original in 1909, *Collected Papers*, Vol. III, pp. 149–289.

punished for it, just because the parents do not comprehend the sexual nature of the child's intentions. Suddenly the child, which until then had fully believed in its complete freedom, finds that at a certain age such things are taken seriously and are punished. In these circumstances the poor child reacts in a very particular way. To help you to understand this, I shall use a simple diagram of the human mind as explained by Freud:

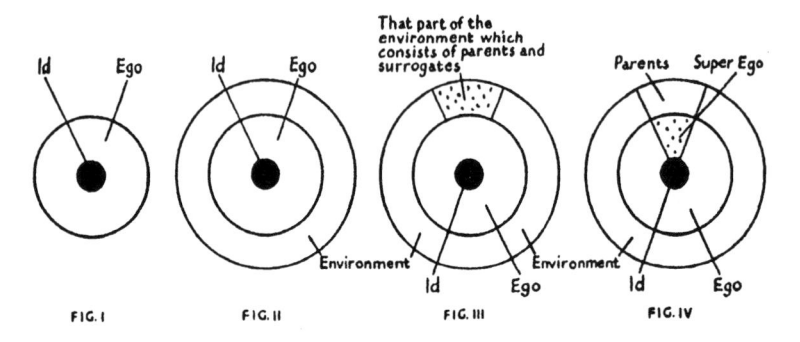

The Id (the instincts) is the central part, the Ego the adaptive peripheral part of the mind, the part which must adjust itself to the environment in any particular relationship. Human beings are a part of the environment, differing greatly in importance from all other objects in the world, particularly in one significant respect: all other objects are always equable, always constant. The only part of the environment which is not reliable is other persons, particularly the parents. If we leave something in any place we can find it again in the same place. Even animals do not vary greatly, they do not lie against their own natures; once known, they can be depended upon. The human being is the only animal which lies. It is this which makes it very difficult for a child to adapt itself to the parental part of its environment; even the most respected parents do not always tell the truth, they lie deliberately, though—as they think—only in the interests of the child. But once a child has experienced this it becomes suspicious. That is one difficulty. The other is the child's dependence on its environment. It is because of the ideas and ideals of its environment that the child is forced to lie. Parents have here set a kind of trap for the child. The child's first judgements are of course its own, that sweets are good, and being trained is bad; it then discovers that another set of standards is firmly implanted in the parents' mind, namely that sweets are bad and being trained is good, and so forth. The former set is derived from its own perceptions of pleasant and unpleasant experience; the latter is thrust upon it by persons who, in spite of these views, are deeply loved. The child, being dependent on the parents both physically and emotionally, has to adapt itself to the new and difficult code. It does this in a particular way, which I will illustrate from a case. I had a patient who remembered his early life very well. He was not what we should call a good child, he was rather bad, and was beaten every week, sometimes in advance. When he was beaten he suddenly began to think consciously: 'How nice it will be when I am a father and can beat my child!', thus showing that in his fantasy he already enjoyed himself in his future role of father. An identification of this kind leads to a change in a part of the mind. The ego has become richer by acquiring from the environment something that was not inherited. This is also the way by which one becomes 'conscientious'. First we are afraid of punishment, then we identify ourselves with the punishing authority. Then father and mother may lose their importance; the child has built up a sort of internal father and mother. This is what Freud calls the super-ego (see diagram).

The super-ego is thus the result of an interaction between the ego and the environment; if you are too strict you can make the life of a child unnecessarily difficult by giving it a too harsh super-ego. I think it will be necessary at some time to write a book not only about the importance and the usefulness of ideals for the child, but also about the harmfulness of exaggerated ideals. In America children are very disappointed when they hear that Washington never told a lie in his life. When one little American heard that Washington never lied, he asked: 'What was the matter with him?' I felt the same dejection when I learned at school that Epaminondas did not lie, even in joke—*Nec joco quidem mentiretur.*

I have only a few points to add. The question of co-education, which I had an opportunity to see working in America, reminds me of the time when I went with my friend Dr. Jones and some other psycho-analysts in America to listen to Freud's first American lectures. We met Dr. Stanley Hall, the great American psychologist, who said to us jokingly: 'You see these boys and girls, they are capable of living together for weeks at a time, and unfortunately it is always without any danger.' This is more than a joke. The repression on which proper behaviour is founded may cause great difficulties in later life. If you think that co-education is necessary you must find a better way of bringing the sexes together, because the present method of herding them together socially and at the same time forcing them to repress their passionate emotions may enhance the development of neuroses. One word only about the ways of meting out punishment at schools: I only want to stress how necessary it is to get rid of the spirit of retaliation, instead of making it just an educational measure.

The idea I had when accepting your invitation was not to say something definitive about the relations between psycho-analysis and education, but just to stimulate you to further interest and further work. Freud called psycho-analysis a kind of *re-education of the individual*, but things seem to develop in such a way that education will have more to learn from psycho-analysis than psycho-analysis from education. Psycho-analysis will teach teachers and parents to treat children in a way which makes this 're-education' superfluous.

[The following took part in the discussion: Dr. Ernest Jones, Mrs. Klein, Dr. Menon, Mrs. Susan Isaacs, Mr. Money-Kyrle, Miss Barbara Low, Dr. David Forsyth.

Dr. Ferenczi then replied as follows:]

In answer to Dr. Jones's objection I regret that I gave the impression of agreeing that measurement is the sole qualification for classing a method as scientific. To begin by sharing the opinion of one's opponents is the best way to overcome them, therefore I accepted it as a *positum sed non concessum*. Although I have a very high opinion of mathematics I really believe that even the best measurement would not make psychology unnecessary. Even if you had a machine that could project the subtlest processes of the brain on a screen, accurately registering every change of thought and emotion, you would still have an internal experience, and would have to connect the two. There is no way out of the difficulty other than to accept both kinds of experience, the physical and the psychical; to try to dispense with this duality is only to approach the unknown.

In reply to Mrs. Klein I can only agree that full freedom in fantasy would be an excellent relief for the whole of life, and if this could be granted to children they would the more easily adapt themselves to the required changes from their autistic activities to a life in a community. Therefore it is very good to allow children to have full freedom of fantasy, but in order to have it the parents must be on an equal level with the children and acknowledge that they themselves have the same sort of fantasies: this, however, does not excuse them from teaching the child the difference between fantasies and irrevocable actions. Where this freedom is granted there is a greater probability that the emotional difficulties of later life will be lessened. You must permit the fullest freedom to fantasy, that is to say you must lead the child to acknowledge in his fantasy that he is allowed to imagine superiority that he actually has not. He will try to take advantage of the situation, and then perhaps comes a point where you have to use your authority. Only unjustified authority is not permitted by psycho-analysis.

I am reminded of an incident with a little nephew of my own, whom I treated as leniently as, in my view, a psycho-analyst should. He took advantage of this and began to tease me, then wanted to beat me, and then to tease and beat me all the time. Psycho-analysis did not teach me to let him beat me *ad infinitum*, so I took him in my arms, holding him so that he was powerless to move, and said: 'Now beat me if you can!' He tried, could not, called me names, said that he hated me; I replied: 'All right, go on, you may feel these things and say these things against me, but you must not beat me.' In the end he realized my advantage in strength and his equality in fantasy, and we became good friends. In fantasy a child should be free, but not in action. That is the great lesson which education has to teach, namely where the limitation of action begins; it is not the same thing as repression, and it is not harmful for the future of the child to learn to control himself. The difficulty arises when the child begins in consequence to think that he does not want to do things.

With regard to the question how to translate symbols to children, we should in general learn symbols from children rather than they from us. Symbols are the language of children; they have not to be taught how to understand them. They have only to feel that the other person has the same understanding of them that they themselves have when acceptance becomes immediate.

I think that is all I can say to-night, and I hope this meeting will act as a stimulus to further work. I will conclude with a little story about Prof. Freud, who, when anyone comes to him with an objection, instead of entering into a discussion of it, replies: 'Excellent, excellent, now write a paper about it and do not dissipate your interest in discussing the subject with me.' Those are my parting words to you; if you make observations and have views on the adaptation of the family to the child—write a paper about them!

VII

THE PROBLEM OF THE TERMINATION OF THE ANALYSIS[1]

(1927)

Address to the Tenth International Psycho-Analytical Congress at Innsbruck, 3 September 1927

Ladies and Gentlemen,
Let me begin by referring to a case which some time ago caused me a great deal of concern. While dealing with a patient who, apart from certain neurotic difficulties, came to analysis chiefly because of certain abnormalities and peculiarities of his character, I suddenly discovered, incidentally after more than eight months, that he had been deceiving me the whole time in connexion with an important circumstance of a financial nature. At first this caused me the greatest embarrassment. The fundamental rule of analysis, on which the whole of our technique is built up, calls for the true and complete communication by the patient of all his ideas and associations. What, then, is one to do if the patient's pathological condition consists precisely in mendacity? Should one declare analysis to be unsuitable for dealing with such cases? I had no intention of admitting such poverty on the part of our scientific technique. Instead I continued with the work, and it was in fact investigation of the patient's mendacity which first enabled me to gain an understanding of some of his symptoms. During the analysis, before the lie was detected, he had on one occasion failed to appear for his appointment, and next day he failed even to mention the fact. When I taxed him with it, he obstinately denied his nonappearance, and, as it was certain that it was not I whose memory was at fault, I pressed him energetically to find out what had really happened. We both soon came to the conclusion that he had completely forgotten, not only his appointment with me, but the events of the whole day in question. He was

[1] German original in *Int. Z. f. Psa.* (1928), 14, 1. First English translation.

able only partially to fill in the gaps in his memory, partly by questioning others. I do not propose to go into the details of this incident, interesting though they are, and shall confine myself to mentioning that he had spent the forgotten day in a state of semi-drunkenness in various places of ill repute in the company of men and women of the lowest sort, all strangers to him.

He turned out to have had such memory disturbances before. When I obtained incontrovertible evidence of his conscious mendacity I was convinced that the split personality, at any rate in his case, was only the neurotic sign of his mendacity, a kind of indirect confession of his character-defect. So in this case the proof of the patient's lying turned out to be an advantageous event for his analysis.[1]

It soon occurred to me that the problem of lying and simulation during analysis had been considered a number of times before. In an earlier paper I offered the suggestion that in infancy all hysterical symptoms were produced as conscious fictional structures. I recalled also that Freud used occasionally to tell us that it was prognostically a favourable sign, a sign of approaching cure, if the patient suddenly expressed the conviction that during the whole of his illness he had really been only shamming: it meant that in the light of his newly-acquired analytic insight into his unconscious drives he was no longer able to put himself back into the state of mind in which he had allowed his symptoms automatically to appear without the slightest intervention of his conscious self. A real abandonment of mendacity therefore appears to be at least a sign of the approaching end of the analysis.

We have in fact met the same set of circumstances before,

---

[1] I have no hesitation in generalizing this single observation, and interpreting all cases of so-called split personality as symptoms of partially conscious insincerity which force those liable to it to manifest in turn only parts of their personality. In terms of metapsychology, one might say that these people have several super-egos which they have failed to fuse. Even scholars who do not *a priori* deny the possibility of 'many truths' about the same thing are probably people whose scientific morality has not developed into a unity.

though under a different name. What in the light of morality and of the reality principle we call a lie, in the case of an infant and in terms of pathology we call a fantasy. Our chief task in the treatment of a hysteria is essentially the seeking out of the automatically and unconsciously produced fantasy structure. During this process a large proportion of the symptoms disappear. We had come to the conclusion that the laying bare of the fantasy, which could be said to possess a special kind of reality of its own (Freud called it a psychical reality), was sufficient for a cure, and that it was a secondary matter from the point of view of the success of the analysis how much of the fantasy content corresponded to reality, i.e. physical reality or the recollections of such reality. My experience had taught me something else. I had become convinced that no case of hysteria could be regarded as cleared up so long as a reconstruction, in the sense of a rigid separation of reality and fantasy, had not been carried out. A person who admits the plausibility of the psychoanalytical interpretations he has been given but is not unquestionably convinced of their secure basis in fact preserves the right to take flight from certain disagreeable events into illness, i.e. into the world of fantasy; his analysis cannot be regarded as being terminated if by termination is meant a cure in the prophylactic sense. One might generalize and say that a neurotic cannot be regarded as cured if he has not given up pleasure in unconscious fantasy, i.e. unconscious mendacity. No bad way of ferreting out such fantasy nests is detecting the patient in one of those distortions of fact, however insignificant, which so often appear in the course of analysis. The patient's pride, his fear of losing the analyst's friendship by disclosing certain facts or feelings, invariably and without any exception whatever betray him into occasional suppression or distortion of facts. Observations of this nature have convinced me that calling on all our patients for full and complete free association from the outset represents an ideal which, so to speak, can be fulfilled only after the analysis has ended. Associations which proceed from such distortions frequently lead back to similar but far more important infantile events, i.e. to times when the now automatic deception was conscious and deliberate.

We can confidently put down every infantile lie as an enforced lie and, as mendacity in later years is connected with infantile lying, perhaps there is something compulsive about every lie. This would be entirely logical. Frankness and honesty are certainly more comfortable than lying, the only inducement to which must be the threat of some greater unpleasure. What we describe by the fine names of ideal, ego-ideal, super-ego, owes its origin to the deliberate suppression of real instinctual urges, which thus have to be denied and repudiated, while the moral precepts and feelings imposed by education are paraded with exaggerated assiduity. Painful though it must be to students of ethics and moral theologians, we cannot avoid the conclusion that lying and morality are somewhat interconnected. To the child everything seems good that tastes good; he has to learn to think and feel that a good many things that taste good are bad, and to discover that the highest happiness and satisfaction lie in fulfilling precepts which involve difficult renunciations. In such circumstances it is not surprising—and our analyses demonstrate it beyond any possibility of doubt—that the two stages, that of original amorality and of subsequently acquired morality, are separated by a more or less long period of transition, in which all instinctual renunciation and all acceptance of unpleasure is distinctly associated with a feeling of untruth, i.e. hypocrisy.

From this point of view, if the analysis is to be a true re-education, the whole process of the patient's character-formation, which was accompanied by the protective mechanism of instinctual repression, must be followed back to its instinctual foundations. The whole thing must, so to speak, become fluid again, so that out of the temporary chaos a new, better-adapted personality may arise under more favourable conditions. In other words, theoretically no symptom analysis can be regarded as ended unless it is a complete character analysis into the bargain. In practice, of course, many symptoms can be cured analytically without such radical changes being effected.

Naïve souls, who do not know how instinctively human beings gravitate towards harmony and stability, will take fright at this, and wonder what happens to a man who loses his character in analysis. Are we able to guarantee delivery of a new character, like a new suit, in place of the old one which we have taken away? Might not the patient, divested of his old character, dash off in characterless nudity before the new clothing was ready? Freud has demonstrated how unjustified is this fear, and how psycho-analysis is automatically followed by synthesis. In reality the dissolution of the crystalline structure of a character is only a transition to a new, more appropriate structure; it is, in other words, a recrystallization. It is impossible to foresee in detail what the new suit will look like; the one thing that it is perhaps possible to say is that it will be a better fit, i.e. that it will be better adapted to its purpose.

Certain characteristics common to those who have been thoroughly analysed can, however, be mentioned. The far sharper severance between the world of fantasy and that of reality which is the result of analysis gives them an almost unlimited inner freedom and simultaneously a much surer grip in acting and making decisions; in other words it gives them more economic and more effective control.

In the few cases in which I have approached this ideal goal I have found myself compelled also to pay attention to certain external features of the patient's appearance or behaviour of a kind which previously we have often left unheeded. In my attempt to gain an understanding of the narcissistic peculiarities and mannerisms of sufferers from *tic* I observed how often relatively cured neurotics remained untouched by the analysis so far as these symptoms were concerned. A thoroughgoing character analysis cannot, of course, stop short at these peculiarities; in the last resort we must, so to speak, hold a mirror up to the patient, to enable him for the first time to become aware of the oddities in his behaviour and even in his personal appearance. Only those who have observed, as I have, how even people who have been cured by analysis continue surreptitiously to be smiled at by everybody because of their facial expressions or bodily posture or awkward mannerisms, etc., though they themselves have not the slightest suspicion that they are peculiar in any way, will shrink from regarding as a fearful but inevitable task imposed by a radical analysis the necessity of making those whom they primarily concern aware of these, so to speak, open secrets.[1] The analyst, who must, of course, always be tactful, must be particularly tactful in his handling of the acquisition by the patient of this particular kind of self-knowledge. I have made it a principle never to tell a patient directly about these things; with the continuation of the analysis he must sooner or later become aware of them himself with our help.

The phrase 'sooner or later' contains a hint of the importance of the time factor if an analysis is to be fully completed. The completion of an analysis is possible only if, so to speak, unlimited time is at one's disposal. I agree with those who think that the more unlimited it is, the greater are the chances of quick success. By this I mean, not so much the physical time at the patient's disposal, as his determination to persist for so long as may be necessary, irrespective of how long this may turn out to be. I do not wish to imply that there are not cases in which patients abundantly misuse this timelessness.

In the course of the time at our disposal, not only must the whole unconscious psychical material be lived through again in the form of memories and repetitions, but the third factor in analytic technique must also be applied. I refer to the factor of analytic working through. Freud has emphasized that this factor is as important as the other two, but its importance has not been properly appreciated. My present aim is to bring this working through, or the effort that we apply to it, into dynamic relation with the repression and the resistance, that is to say with a purely quantitative factor. Finding the pathogenic motivation and the conditions which determined the appearance of the symptom is a kind of qualitative analysis. This can be nearly complete without producing the expected therapeutic change. But further repetition of the same transference and resistance material, which has perhaps been gone through a countless number of times already, sometimes leads unexpectedly to an important advance which we can explain only as the successful effect of the factor of working through. Often

---

[1] This is the point at which psycho-analysis comes for the first time into practical contact with problems of physiognomy and physical constitution (as well as their derivatives, such as mimicry, graphology, etc.).

enough the opposite takes place, i.e. after long working through, access to new memory material is gained which may herald the end of the analysis.

A really difficult but at the same time interesting task, which has in my opinion to be accomplished in every single case, is the gradual breaking-down of the resistances consisting in more or less conscious doubts about the dependability of the analyst. By this we mean his complete dependability in all circumstances, and in particular his unshakable good will towards the patient, to whatever extremes the latter may go in his words and his behaviour. One might actually speak of the patient's unconscious attempt consistently and in the greatest possible variety of ways to test the analyst's patience in this respect, and to test it, not just once, but over and over again. Patients sharply observe the physician's reaction, whether it takes the form of speech, silence, or gesture, and they often analyse it with great perspicuity. They detect the slightest sign of unconscious impulse in the latter, who has to submit to these attempts at analysis with inexhaustible patience; this often makes superhuman demands upon him which, however, are invariably worth while. For if the patient fails to detect the analyst in any untruth or distortion, and comes gradually to realize that it is really possible to maintain objectivity in relation even to the naughtiest child, and if he fails to detect the slightest sign of unfounded superiority in the physician in spite of all his efforts to provoke signs of such a thing, if the patient is forced to admit that the physician willingly confesses the mistakes and inadvertences that he occasionally commits, it is not at all uncommon for the latter to reap as a reward of his labours a more or less rapid alteration in the patient's attitude. It seems to me exceedingly probable that, when patients do these things, they are attempting to reproduce situations in which non-understanding educators or relatives reacted to the child's so-called naughtiness with their own intense affectivity, thus forcing the child into a defiant attitude.

To stand firm against this general assault by the patient the analyst requires to have been fully and completely analysed himself. I mention this because it is often held to be sufficient if a candidate spends, say, a year gaining acquaintance with the principal mechanisms in his so-called training analysis. His further development is left to what he learns in the course of his own experience. I have often stated on previous occasions that in principle I can admit no difference between a therapeutic and a training analysis, and I now wish to supplement this by suggesting that, while every case undertaken for therapeutic purposes need not be carried to the depth we mean when we talk of a complete ending of the analysis, the analyst himself, on whom the fate of so many other people depends, must know and be in control of even the most recondite weaknesses of his own character; and this is impossible without a fully completed analysis.

The analysis of course shows that it was libidinous tendencies and not just the need for self-assertion or the desire for revenge that were the real factors in the patient's character formation and his often grotesquely disguised resistances. After the naughty, defiant child has fired off all the shots in his locker in vain, his concealed demands for love and tenderness come naïvely into the open. No analysis has been completed until most of the fore- and end-pleasure activities of sexuality, both in their normal and abnormal manifestations, have been emotionally lived through in the conscious fantasy. Every male patient must attain a feeling of equality in relation to the physician as a sign that he has overcome his fear of castration; every female patient, if her neurosis is to be regarded as fully disposed of, must have got rid of her masculinity complex and must emotionally accept without a trace of resentment the implications of her female role. This analytic goal more or less corresponds to that resuscitation of primeval innocence which Groddeck demands of his patients. The difference between him and me is that he sets out for this goal straight from the symptoms, while I try to reach it by means of the 'orthodox' analytic technique, though at a slower pace. With the necessary patience the same result falls into our lap without any special pressure on our part.

Renunciation of pressure does not involve renunciation of those technical aids which I once referred to under the name of 'activity'. I still adhere to what I said on the subject at our Homburg congress. Perhaps no analysis can be ended until the patient, in agreement with our advice (which, however, must not contain anything in the nature of a command) decides, in addition to free association, to consider some alterations in his way of life and behaviour, which then help in the discovery and eventual control of certain otherwise inaccessible nuclei of repression. In some cases bringing the analysis abruptly to an end may produce results, but this procedure is in principle to be rejected. While the pressure of an accidental external circumstance sometimes hastens the analysis, pressure imposed by the analyst often unnecessarily prolongs it. The proper ending of an analysis is when neither the physician nor the patient puts an end to it, but when it dies of exhaustion, so to speak, though even when this occurs the physician must be the more suspicious of the two and must think of the possibility that behind the patient's wish to take his departure some neurotic factor may still be concealed. A truly cured patient frees himself from analysis slowly but surely; so long as he wishes to come to analysis, he should continue to do so. To put it another way, one might say that the patient finally becomes convinced that he is continuing analysis only because he is treating it as a new but still a fantasy source of gratification, which in terms of reality yields him nothing. When he has slowly overcome his mourning over this discovery he inevitably looks round for other, more real sources of gratification. As Freud so long ago discovered, the whole neurotic period of his life appears to him in the light of analysis as one of pathological mourning, which he now seeks to displace into the transference situation; and the revelation of its true nature puts an end to the tendency to repeat it in the future. The renunciation of analysis is thus the final winding-up of the infantile situation of frustration which lay at the basis of the symptom-formation.

Another theoretically important experience in really completed analyses is the almost invariable occurrence of symptom transformation before the end. We know from Freud that the symptomatology of neuroses is nearly always the result of a complicated psychical development. The obsessional patient, for instance, only gradually changes his emotions into obsessional behaviour and obsessional thinking. The hysteric may struggle for a long time with painful ideas of some kind before he succeeds in converting his conflicts into physical symptoms. The subsequent schizophrenic or paranoiac starts his pathological career as a victim of anxiety hysteria and succeeds often only after some hard work in finding a kind of pathological self-cure in exaggerated narcissism. We ought therefore not to be surprised if an obsessional begins producing symptoms of hysteria after a sufficient degree of loosening up and undermining of his intellectual obsessional system has taken place, and if the formerly so carefree sufferer from conversion hysteria, after analysis has made his physical symptoms inadequate, begins producing ideas and memories in place of the physical movements lacking in conscious content with which he previously expressed himself. It is thus a favourable sign if an obsessive neurotic begins to manifest hysterical emotion instead of affectless ideas, and if a hysteric temporarily produces obsessional ideas. It is, however, disagreeable if psychotic features make their appearance in the course of symptom transformation, but it would be mistaken to be excessively alarmed by them. I have seen cases in which there was no way to a final cure except through a temporary psychosis.

I have brought all these observations to your notice to-day in support of my conviction that analysis is not an endless process, but one which can be brought to a natural end with sufficient skill and patience on the analyst's part. If I am asked whether I can point to many such completed analyses, my answer must be no. But the sum-total of my experiences forces me to the conclusions that I have stated in this lecture. I am firmly convinced that, when we have learned sufficiently from our errors and mistakes, when we have gradually learned to take into account the weak points in our own personality, the number of fully analysed cases will increase.

VIII

THE ELASTICITY OF PSYCHO-ANALYTIC TECHNIQUE[1]

(1928)

Lecture given to the Hungarian Psycho-Analytical Society, 1927

EFFORTS to make the technique which I use in my psychoanalyses available to others have frequently brought up the subject of psychological understanding. If it were true, as so many believe, that understanding of the mental processes in a third person depends on a special, inexplicable, and therefore untransferable faculty called knowledge of human nature, any effort to teach my technique to others would be hopeless. Fortunately it is otherwise. Since the publication of Freud's 'Recommendations' (1912–15)[2] on psycho-analytic technique, we have been in possession of the first foundations for a methodical investigation of the mind. Anyone who takes the trouble to follow the master's instructions will be enabled, even if he is not a psychological genius, to penetrate to unsuspected depths the mental life of others, whether sick or healthy. Analysis of the parapraxes of everyday life, of dreams, and in particular of free associations, will put him in a position to understand a great deal about his fellows which was previously beyond the range of any but exceptional human beings. The human predilection for the marvellous will cause this transformation into a kind of craft of the art of understanding human nature to be received with disfavour. Artists and writers in particular appear to regard it as a kind of incursion into their domain and, after showing initial interest, summarily reject and turn their backs on it as an unattractive and mechanical technique. This antipathy causes us no surprise. Science is a process of progressive

[1] German original in *Int. Z. f. Psa.* (1928), 14, 197. First English translation.
[2] Reprinted in *Collected Papers*, Vol. II.

disillusionment; it displaces the mystical and the miraculous by universally valid and inevitable laws, the monotony and ineluctability of which provoke boredom and displeasure. However, it may serve as a partial consolation that among the practitioners of this craft, as of all others, artists will from time to time appear to whom we may look for progress and new perspectives.

From the practical point of view, however, it is an undeniable advance that analysis has gradually succeeded in putting tools for the more delicate investigation of the kind into the hands of the physician and student of only average gifts. A similar development occurred in regard to surgery; before the discovery of anaesthesia and asepsis it was the privilege of only a favoured few to exercise that 'healing art'; in the conditions of the time the art of working *cito, tuto, et jucunde* was confined to them alone. True, artists in the technique of surgery still exist to-day, but the progress that has taken place enables all the thousands of physicians of average ability to exercise their useful and often life-saving activity.

A psychological technique had, of course, been developed outside the field of mental analysis; I refer to the methods of measurement used in psychological laboratories. This kind of technique is still in vogue, and for certain simple, practical purposes it may be sufficient. But analysis has much more far-reaching aims: the understanding of the topography, dynamics, and economy of the whole mental apparatus, undertaken without impressive laboratory apparatus, but with ever-increasing claims to scientific certainty and, above all, with incomparably greater results.

Nevertheless, there has been, and still is, a great deal in psycho-analytic technique which has created the impression that it involves a scarcely definable, individual factor. This has been chiefly due to the circumstance that in analysis the 'personal equation' has seemed to occupy a far more important place than we are called on to accept in other sciences. In his first essays on technique Freud himself left open the possibility that there was room in psycho-analysis for methods other than his own. But that expression of opinion dates from before the crystallizing out of the second fundamental rule of psycho-analysis, the rule by which anyone who wishes to undertake analysis must first be analysed himself. Since the establishment of that rule the importance of the personal element introduced by the analyst has more and more been dwindling away. Anyone who has been thoroughly analysed and has gained complete knowledge and control of the inevitable weaknesses and peculiarities of his own character will inevitably come to the same objective conclusions in the observation and treatment of the same psychological raw material, and will consequently adopt the same tactical and technical methods in dealing with it. I have the definite impression that since the introduction of the second fundamental rule differences in analytic technique are tending to disappear.

If one attempts to weigh up the unresolved residue of this personal equation, and if one is in a position to see a large number of pupils and patients who have been analysed by others, and if, like me, one has to wrestle with the consequences of one's own earlier mistakes, one can claim the right to express a comprehensive opinion about the majority of these differences and mistakes. I have come to the conclusion that it is above all a question of psychological tact whether or when one should tell the patient some particular thing, when the material he has produced should be considered sufficient to draw conclusions, in what form these should be presented to the patient, how one should react to an unexpected or bewildering reaction on the patient's part, when one should keep silent and await further associations, and at what point the further maintenance of silence would result only in causing the patient useless suffering, etc. As you see, using the word 'tact' has enabled me only to reduce the uncertainty to a simple and appropriate formula. But what is 'tact'? The answer is not very difficult. It is the capacity for empathy. If, with the aid of the knowledge we have obtained from the dissection of many minds, but above all from the dissection of our own, we have succeeded in forming a picture of possible or probable associations of the patient's of which he is still completely unaware, we, not having the patient's resistances to contend with, are able to conjecture, not only his withheld thoughts, but trends of his of which he is unconscious.

At the same time, as we are continuously aware of the strength of the patient's resistance, we should not find it difficult to decide on the appropriateness or otherwise of telling him some particular thing or the form in which to put it. This empathy will protect us from unnecessarily stimulating the patient's resistance, or doing so at the wrong moment. It is not within the capacity of psycho-analysis entirely to spare the patient pain; indeed, one of the chief gains from psycho-analysis is the capacity to bear pain. But its tactless infliction by the analyst would only give the patient the unconsciously deeply desired opportunity of withdrawing himself from his influence.

All these precautions give the patient the impression of good will on the analyst's part, though the respect that the latter shows for the former's feelings derives solely from rational considerations. In my subsequent observations I shall try in a certain sense to justify the creation of this impression upon the patient. The essence of the matter is that there is no conflict between the tact which we are called upon to exercise and the moral obligation not to do to others what in the same circumstances we should not desire to have done to ourselves.

I hasten to add that the capacity to show this kind of 'good will' represents only one side of psycho-analytic understanding. Before the physician decides to tell the patient something, he must temporarily withdraw his libido from the latter, and weigh the situation coolly; he must in no circumstances allow himself to be guided by his feelings alone.

I now propose to give a few brief examples to illustrate this general point of view.

Analysis should be regarded as a process of fluid development unfolding itself before our eyes rather than as a structure with a design pre-imposed upon it by an architect. The analyst should therefore in no circumstances be betrayed into promising a prospective patient more than that, if he submits to the analytic process, he will end by knowing much more about himself, and that, if he persists to the end, he will be able to adapt himself to the inevitable difficulties of life more successfully and with a better distribution of his energies. He can also be told that we know of no better and certainly of no more radical treatment of psychoneurotic and character difficulties; and we should certainly not conceal from him that there are other methods which hold out quicker and more definite prospects of a cure; and, if patients then reply that they have already submitted for years to treatment by suggestion, occupational therapy, or methods of strengthening the will, we may feel pleased. In other cases we may suggest that they try one of these much-promising methods before coming to us. But we cannot allow to pass the objection usually made by patients that they do not believe in our methods or theories. It must be explained to them at the outset that our technique makes no claim to be entitled to such unmerited confidence in advance, and that they need only believe in us if or when their experience of our methods gives them reason to do so. To another objection, namely that in this way we repudiate in advance any responsibility for a possible failure of the analysis and lay it squarely upon the patient and his impatience, we have no reply, and we have to leave it to the patient himself to decide whether or not to accept the risk of undertaking analysis under these difficult conditions. If these questions are not definitely settled in advance, one is putting into the hands of the patient's resistance a most dangerous weapon, which sooner or later he will not fail to use against us and the objective of the analysis. Even the most alarming question must not divert us from firmly establishing this basis for the analysis in advance. Many prospective patients ask with visible hostility whether the analysis may not last for two, three, five, or even ten years. We have to reply that it is possible. 'But a ten-year analysis would in practice be equivalent to a failure', we have to add. 'As we can never estimate in advance the magnitude of the difficulties to be overcome, we can promise you nothing, and can only say that in many cases the time needed is much shorter. But, as you probably believe that physicians like making favourable prognoses, and as you have probably heard, or will soon hear, many adverse opinions about the theory and technique of psycho-analysis, it will be best, from your point of view, if you will regard analysis as a bold experiment, which will cost you a great deal of toil, time, and money; and you must decide for yourself whether or not the amount of suffering which your difficulties are causing you is sufficient to make the experiment worth while in spite of all that. In any case, think it over carefully before beginning, because without the earnest intention to persist, even in spite of inevitable aggravations of your condition, the only result will be to add one more to the disappointments you have already suffered.'

I believe this preparation, which certainly errs on the side of pessimism, is certainly the better; in any case it is in accordance with the requirements of the 'empathy rule'. For, behind the prospective patient's often all-too-excessive display of faith in us, there is nearly always concealed a strong dose of distrust, which he is trying to shout down by his passionate demands on us for promises of a cure. A characteristic question that is often put to us by a prospective patient, after we have spent perhaps an hour trying to explain to him that we regard his case as suitable for analysis, is: 'But, doctor, do you really think that analysis would help me?' It would be a mistake to reply by simply saying yes. It is better to say that we do not believe in offering further assurances. Even if the prospective patient professes the most glowing opinion of analysis, this does not eliminate his concealed suspicion that the physician is, after all, a business man with something to sell. The patient's concealed incredulity is even more manifest in the question: 'But, doctor, don't you think that your methods might make me worse?' I generally reply to this with a counter-question. 'What is your occupation?' I ask. Suppose the answer is: 'I'm an architect.' 'Well, what would you say,' I reply, 'if you laid the plan for a new building before a client, and he asked you whether it wouldn't collapse?' This generally puts an end to further demands for assurances, because it dawns on the patient that the practitioner of any craft is entitled to a certain amount of confidence on his own speciality, though that does not, of course, exclude disappointments.

Psycho-analysis is often reproached with being remarkably concerned with money matters. My own opinion is that it is far too little concerned with them. Even the most prosperous individual spends money on doctors most unwillingly. Something in us seems to make us regard medical aid, which in fact we all first received from our mothers in infancy, as something to which we are automatically entitled, and at the end of each month, when our patients are presented with their bill, their resistance is stimulated into producing all their concealed or unconscious hatred, mistrust, and suspicion over again. The most characteristic example of the contrast between conscious generosity and concealed resentment was given by the patient who opened the conversation by saying: 'Doctor, if you help me, I'll give you every penny I possess!' 'I shall be satisfied with thirty kronen an hour,' the physician replied. 'But isn't that rather excessive?' the patient unexpectedly remarked.

In the course of the analysis it is as well to keep one eye constantly open for unconscious expressions of rejection or disbelief and to bring them remorselessly into the open. It is only to be expected that the patient's resistance should leave unexploited no single opportunity for expressing these. Every patient without exception notices the smallest peculiarities in the analyst's behaviour, external appearance, or way of speaking, but without previous encouragement not one of them will tell him about them, though failure to do so constitutes a crude infringement of the primary rule of analysis. We therefore have no alternative but to detect ourselves from the patient's associations when we have offended his aesthetic feelings by an excessively loud sneeze or blowing of the nose, when he has taken offence at the shape of our face, or when he feels impelled to compare our appearance with that of others of more impressive physique.

I have on many other occasions tried to describe how the analyst must accept for weeks on end the role of an Aunt Sally on whom the patient tries out all his aggressiveness and resentment. If we do not protect ourselves from this, but, on the contrary, encourage the only-too-hesitant patient at every opportunity that presents itself, sooner or later we shall reap the well-deserved reward of our patience in the form of the arrival of the positive transference. Any trace of irritation or offence on the part of the physician only prolongs the duration of the resistance period; if, however, the physician refrains from defending himself, the patient gradually gets tired of the one-sided battle and, when he has given full vent to his feelings, he cannot avoid confessing, though hesitantly, to the friendly feelings concealed behind his noisy defence; the result being deeper access into latent material, in particular into those infantile situations in which the foundation was laid (generally by non-understanding educators) for certain spiteful character traits.

Nothing is more harmful to the analysis than a schoolmasterish, or even an authoritative, attitude on the physician's part. Anything we say to the patient should be put to him in the form of a tentative suggestion and not of a confidently held opinion, not only to avoid irritating him, but because there is always the possibility that we may be mistaken. It is an old commercial custom to put 'E. & O.E.' ('errors and omissions excepted') at the bottom of every calculation, and every analytic statement should be put forward with the same qualification. Our confidence in our own theories should be only conditional, for in every case we may be presented with a resounding exception to to the rule, or with the necessity of revising a hitherto accepted theory. I recall, for instance, an uneducated, apparently quite simple, patient who brought forward objections to an interpretation of mine, which it was my immediate impulse to reject; but on reflection not I, but the patient, turned out to be right, and the result of his intervention was a much better general understanding of the matter we were dealing with. Thus the analyst's modesty must be no studied pose, but a reflection of the limitations of our knowledge. Incidentally this may suggest the point from which, with the help of the lever of psychoanalysis, an alteration in the attitude of the doctor to the patient may be brought about. Compare our empathy rule with the lofty attitude to the patient generally adopted by the omniscient and omnipotent doctor.

Of course I do not mean that the analyst should be overmodest. He is fully justified in expecting that in the great majority of cases his interpretations, being based on experience, will sooner or later turn out to be correct, and that the patient will end by accepting the accumulation of evidence. But the analyst must wait patiently until the patient makes up his own mind; any impatience on the physician's part costs the patient time and money and the physician a great deal of work which he could very well spare.

A patient of mine once spoke of the 'elasticity of analytic technique', a phrase which I fully accept. The analyst, like an elastic band, must yield to the patient's pull, but without ceasing to pull in his own direction, so long as one position or the other has not been conclusively demonstrated to be untenable.

One must never be ashamed unreservedly to confess one's own mistakes. It must never be forgotten that analysis is no suggestive process, primarily dependent on the physician's reputation and infallibility. All that it calls for is confidence in the physician's frankness and honesty, which does not suffer from the frank confession of mistakes.

Analysis demands of the physician, not only a firm control of his own narcissism, but also a sharp watch on his emotional reactions of every kind. It used to be held that an excessive degree of 'antipathy' was an indication against undertaking an analysis, but deeper insight into the relationship has caused us to regard such a thing as unacceptable in principle, and to expect the analysed analyst's self-knowledge and self-control to be too strong for him to yield to such idiosyncrasies. Such 'antipathetic features' are in most cases only fore-structures, behind which quite different characteristics are concealed; dropping the patient in such cases would be merely leaving him in the lurch, because the unconscious aim of intolerable behaviour is often to be sent away. Knowledge of these things gives us the advantage of being able coolly to regard even the most unpleasant and repulsive person as a patient in need of help, and even enables us not to withhold our sympathy from him. The acquisition of this more than Christian humility is one of the hardest tasks of psycho-analytic practice, and striving to achieve it may incidentally lead us into the most terrible traps. I must once more emphasize that here too only real empathy helps; the patient's sharp wits will easily detect any pose.

One gradually becomes aware how immensely complicated

the mental work demanded from the analyst is. He has to let the patient's free associations play upon him; simultaneously he lets his own fantasy get to work with the association material; from time to time he compares the new connexions that arise with earlier results of the analysis; and not for one moment must he relax the vigilance and criticism made necessary by his own subjective trends.

One might say that his mind swings continuously between empathy, self-observation, and making judgements. The latter emerge spontaneously from time to time as mental signals, which at first, of course, have to be assessed only as such; only after the accumulation of further evidence is one entitled to make an interpretation.

Above all, one must be sparing with interpretations, for one of the most important rules of analysis is to do no unnecessary talking; over-keenness in making interpretations is one of the infantile diseases of the analyst. When the patient's resistance has been analytically resolved, stages in the analysis are reached every now and then in which the patient does the work of interpretation practically unaided, or with only slight prompting from the analyst.

And now let us return for a moment to the subject of my much-praised and much-blamed 'activity'.[1] I believe I am at last in a position to give the details on timing for which I was rightly asked. You know, perhaps, that I was originally inclined to lay down certain rules of behaviour, in addition to free association, so soon as the resistance permitted such a burden. Experience later taught me that one should never order or forbid any changes of behaviour, but at most advise them, and that one should always be ready to withdraw one's advice if it turned out to be obstructive to the analysis or provocative of resistance. My original conviction that it was always the patient and never the physician who must be 'active' finally led me to the conclusion that we must content ourselves with interpreting the patient's concealed tendencies to action and supporting his feeble attempts to overcome the neurotic inhibitions to which he had hitherto been subject, without pressing or even advising

[1] See my papers on technique in *Further Contributions*.

him to take violent measures. If we are patient enough, the patient will himself sooner or later come up with the question whether he should risk making some effort, for example to defy a phobic avoidance. In such a case we shall certainly not withhold our consent and encouragement, and in this way we shall make all the progress expected from activity without upsetting the patient and falling out with him. In other words, it is the patient himself who must decide the timing of activity, or at any rate give unmistakable indications that the time is ripe for it. It remains true, of course, that such attempts by the patient produce changes of tension in his psychical system and thus prove to be a method of analytic technique in addition to the associations.

In another technical paper[1] I have already drawn attention to the importance of working through, but I dealt with it rather onesidedly, as a purely quantitative factor. I believe, however, that there is also a qualitative side to working through, and that the patient reconstruction of the mechanism of the symptom and character formation should be repeated again and again at every forward step in the analysis. Every important new insight gained calls for a revision of all the material previously produced, and may involve the collapse of some essential parts of what may have been thought to be a complete structure. The more subtle connexions between this qualitative working through and the quantitative factor (discharge of affect) must be left to a more detailed study of the dynamics of analytical technique.

A special form of this work of revision appears to occur, however, in every case; I mean the revision of the emotional experiences which happened in the course of the analyses. The analysis itself gradually becomes a piece of the patient's life-history, which he passes in review before bidding us farewell. In the course of this revision it is from a certain distance and with much greater objectivity that he looks at the experiences through which he went at the beginning of his acquaintanceship with us and the subsequent unravelling of the resistance and transference, which at the time seemed so immediate and im-

[1] 'The Problem of the Termination of the Analysis', this vol., p. 77.

portant to him; and he then turns his attention away from analysis to the real tasks of life.

In conclusion I should like to hazard some remarks about the metapsychology of our technique.[1] It has often been said, by myself among others, that the process of recovery consists to a great extent of the patient's putting the analyst (his new father) in the place of the real father who occupies such a predominant place in his super-ego, and his then going on living with the analytic super-ego thus formed. I do not deny that such a process takes place in every case, and I agree that this substitution is capable of producing important therapeutic effects. But I should like to add that it is the business of a real character analysis to do away, at any rate temporarily, with any kind of super-ego, including that of the analyst. The patient should end by ridding himself of any emotional attachment that is independent of his own reason and his own libidinal tendencies. Only a complete dissolution of the super-ego can bring about a radical cure. Successes that consist in the substitution of one super-ego for another must be regarded as transference successes; they fail to attain the final aim of therapy, the dissolution of the transference.

I should like to mention, as a problem that has not been considered, that of the metapsychology of the analyst's mental processes during analysis. His cathexes oscillate between identification (analytic object-love) on the one hand and self-control or intellectual activity on the other. During the long day's work he can never allow himself the pleasure of giving his narcissism and egoism free play in reality, and he can give free play to them in his fantasy only for brief moments. A strain of this kind scarcely occurs otherwise in life, and I do not doubt that sooner or later it will call for the creation of a special hygiene for the analyst.

Unanalysed ('wild') analysts and incompletely cured patients are easily recognizable by the kind of 'compulsive analysing' from which they suffer; in contrast to the unhampered mobility

---

[1] By metapsychology we mean, of course, the sum-total of the ideas about the structure and dynamics of the psychical apparatus which our psycho-analytic experiences have caused us to adopt. See Freud's papers on metapsychology in his *Collected Papers*, Vol. IV.

of the libido which is the result of a complete analysis, which makes it possible to exercise analytic self-knowledge and self-control when necessary, but in no way hampers free enjoyment of life. The ideal result of a completed analysis is precisely that elasticity which analytic technique demands of the mental therapist. This is one more argument for the necessity of the second fundamental rule of psycho-analysis.

Having regard to the great importance of any new technical recommendation, I could not make up my mind to publish this paper before submitting it to a colleague with a request for criticism.

'The title ["Elasticity"] is excellent,' he replied, 'and should be applied more widely, for Freud's technical recommendations were essentially negative. He regarded it as his most important task to emphasize what one should not do, to draw attention to all the temptations and pitfalls that stand in the way of analysis, and he left all the positive things that one should do to what you called "tact". The result was that the excessively docile did not notice the elasticity that is required and subjected themselves to Freud's "don't's" as if they were taboos. This is a situation that requires revision, without, of course, altering Freud's rules.

'True though what you say about tact is, the concessions you make to it seem to me to be questionable in the form in which you have put them. Those who have no tact will find in what you say a justification for arbitrary action, i.e. the intervention of the subjective element (i.e. the influence of their own un-mastered complexes). What in reality we undertake is a weighing up—generally at the preconscious level—of the various reactions that we may expect from our intervention, and the most important aspect in this is quantitative assessment of the dynamic factors in the situation. Rules for making such an assessment can naturally not be given. The decisive factors are the analyst's experience and normality. But tact should be robbed of its mystical character.'

I entirely share my critic's view that these technical precepts of mine, like all previous ones, will inevitably be misused and misunderstood, in spite of the most extreme care taken in drafting them. There is no doubt that many—and not only beginners, but all who have a tendency to exaggeration—will seize on what I have said about the importance of empathy to lay the chief emphasis in their handling of patients on the subjective factor, i.e. on intuition, and will disregard what I stated to be the all-important factor, the conscious assessment of the dynamic situation. Against such misinterpretations repeated warnings are obviously useless. I have even discovered that, in spite of the caution with which I put it forward—and my caution in the matter increases as time goes on—some analysts have used 'activity' as an excuse to indulge their tendency to impose on their patients entirely unanalytic rules, which sometimes border on sadism. I should therefore not be surprised if one day I heard my views on the patience required of an analyst used to justify a masochistic technique. Nevertheless the method which I follow and recommend—the method of elasticity—is not equivalent to non-resistance and surrender. True, we try to follow the patient in all his moods, but we never cease to hold firm to the viewpoint dictated to us by our analytic experience.

My principal aim in writing this paper was precisely to rob 'tact' of its mystical character. I agree, however, that I have only broached the subject and have by no means said the last word about it. I am, perhaps, a little more optimistic than my critic about the possibility of formulating positive advice on the assessment of certain typical dynamic conditions. For the rest, his belief that the analyst should be experienced and normal more or less corresponds to my own belief that the one dependable foundation for a satisfactory analytic technique is a complete analysis of the analyst himself. The processes of empathy and assessment will obviously take place, not in the unconscious, but at the pre-conscious level of the well-analysed analyst's mind.

Obviously under the influence of the above warnings, I feel it necessary to clarify one of the ideas put forward in this paper. I refer to my suggestion that a sufficiently deep character analysis must get rid of any kind of super-ego. An over-logical mind might interpret this as implying that my technique aimed at robbing people of all their ideals. In reality my objective was to destroy only that part of the super-ego which had become unconscious and was therefore beyond the range of influence. I have no sort of objection to the retention of a number of positive and negative models in the pre-conscious of the ordinary individual. In any case he will no longer have to obey his preconscious super-ego so slavishly as he had previously to obey his unconscious parent imago.

IX

THE UNWELCOME CHILD AND HIS DEATH INSTINCT[1]
(1929)

In his short study, 'Cold, Disease and Death',[2] Ernest Jones, linking up his own ideas with some trains of thought in my 'Stages in the Development of the Sense of Reality',[3] and related views of Trotter, Stärcke, Alexander and Rank, traces the tendency of so many people to colds and suchlike illnesses in part to early infantile traumatic impressions, particularly to painful experiences which the child must undergo on removal from the warm maternal environment and which, according to the laws of the 'repetition compulsion', he must later always experience anew. The conclusions drawn by Jones were based chiefly on physiopathological, but partly also on analytic considerations. In the following brief communication I shall put forward a similar train of ideas, ranging, however, over a rather wider field.

Since the epoch-making work of Freud on the irreducible instinctual foundations of everything organic (in *Beyond the Pleasure Principle*) we have become accustomed to look upon all the phenomena of life, including those of mental life, as in the last resort a mixture of the forms of expression of the two fundamental instincts: the life and the death instinct. On one single occasion Freud also mentioned the derivation of a pathological manifestation from the almost complete defusion of these two main instincts; he surmised that the symptoms of epilepsy express the frenzy of a tendency to self-destruction that is almost free from the inhibitions of the wish to live. Psycho-analytic investigations of my own have since in my opinion corroborated

[1] German and English versions appeared simultaneously in Dr. E. Jones's 50th Birthday Numbers of the *Int. Z. f. Psa.* (1929), 15, 149 and of the *Int. J. of PsA.* (1929), 10, 125.
[2] Reprinted in *Papers on Psycho-Analysis*. Originally in *Internationale Zeitschrift für Psycho-analyse*, Bd. IX, 1923.
[3] *First Contributions to Psycho-Analysis*, p. 181.

the plausibility of this interpretation. I know of cases in which epileptic attack followed upon painful experiences which made the patient feel that life was hardly any longer worth living. (Naturally I do not mean this as a pronouncement upon the nature of the attack.)

As physician in charge of a war hospital it was one of my duties to decide upon the fitness of many epileptics for service. After excluding the not infrequent cases of simulation and hysterical attacks, there remained a series of cases with typical epileptic manifestations, in which I was able to examine more closely the expressions of the death instinct. After the tonic rigidity and clonic spasms had run their course, there usually followed (with continuing deep coma and pupillar rigidity) complete relaxation of the musculature and an extremely laboured and inadequate stertorous breathing, evidently caused through relaxation of the muscles of the tongue and larynx. At this stage stopping up the respiratory passages which were still open was very often effective in cutting short the seizure. In other cases this attempt had to be broken off on account of threatening danger of asphyxiation. It was natural to conjecture behind this diversity in the depth of coma a difference in completeness of diffusion of the death-instinct. Unfortunately, however, external circumstances prevented any deep analytic working through of these cases.

I obtained a somewhat deeper insight into the genesis of unconscious self-destructive trends during analysis of nervous circulatory and respiratory disturbances, especially of bronchial asthma, but also of cases of complete loss of appetite and emaciation, not explicable anatomically. All these symptoms fitted on occasion perfectly into the total psychic trend of these patients, who had to struggle a great deal against suicidal tendencies. I also had to interpret the retrospective analysis in two of my cases of infantile glottal spasms as attempts at suicide by self-strangulation. Now in the analysis of these latter cases I came to form the surmise which I wish to communicate here, in the hope that a wider circle of observers (I am thinking particularly of pediatricians) will bring forward further material in its support. Both patients came into the world as *unwelcome guests of the family*, so to speak. One was the tenth child of a mother who was manifestly much overburdened, the other the offspring of a father who was mortally ill and in fact died soon after. All the indications show that these children had observed the conscious and unconscious signs of aversion or impatience on the part of the mother, and that their desire to live had been weakened by these. In later life relatively slight occasions were then sufficient motivation for a desire to die, even if this was resisted by a strong effort of will. Moral and philosophic pessimism, scepticism, and mistrust became conspicuous character traits in these patients. One could also note ill-disguised longing for (passive) tenderness, repugnance for work, incapacity for prolonged effort, and thus a certain degree of emotional infantilism, naturally not without attempts at over-compensation, resulting in a rigid character. A case of alcoholism in a still youthful woman revealed itself as a particularly severe case of aversion to life, existing from infancy. She naturally reacted to difficulties in the analytic situation on several occasions with suicidal impulses, mastered only with effort. She can remember, and members of her family also confirm, that as the third girl in a family without boys she was very ungraciously received. She naturally felt herself innocent, and by precocious brooding she sought to explain the hatred and impatience of her mother. She kept for life a leaning towards cosmological speculation, with a strain of pessimism. Her broodings about the origin of all living things were only, as it were, the continuance of the question which had remained unanswered, why she had been brought into the world at all if those who did so were not willing to receive her with love. As in other cases, so in this, the Oedipus conflict naturally proved an ordeal to which the patient was not equal, any more than she was to the difficulties of adaptation to married life, which happened in her case to be unusually great. She remained 'frigid', just as all the 'unwelcome children' of the male sex observed by me suffer from more or less severe disturbances of potency. The tendency to colds postulated by Jones in similar cases was often present; in one special case there was even a quite peculiar, intense cooling down at night, with subnormal temperatures, difficult to explain organically.

It cannot of course be my task to go at all exhaustively into the symptomatology of this nosogenic type, here presented only in its etiological aspect; for this purpose, as already indicated, the experience of one person would not suffice. I only wish to point to the probability that children who are received in a harsh and unloving way die easily and willingly. Either they use one of the many proffered organic possibilities for a quick exit, or if they escape this fate, they retain a streak of pessimism and aversion to life.

This etiological assumption is based upon a theoretical view differing from the accepted one as to the operation of the life and death instincts at various ages. On account of the dazzling effect of the impressive unfolding of growth at the beginning of life, the view has tended to be that in infants only just brought into the world the life instincts were greatly preponderant. In general, there has been a disposition to represent the life and death instincts as a simple complementary series in which the life maximum was placed at the beginning of life, and the zero point at the most advanced age. This does not appear, however, to be quite accurate. It is true that the organs and other functions develop at the beginning of life within and without the uterus with astonishing profusion and speed—but only under the particularly favourable conditions of germinal and infantile protection provided by the environment. The child has to be induced, by means of an immense expenditure of love, tenderness, and care, to forgive his parents for having brought him into the world without any intention on his part; otherwise the destructive instincts begin to stir immediately. And this is not really surprising, since the infant is still much closer to individual non-being, and not divided from it by so much bitter experience as the adult. Slipping back into this non-being might therefore come much more easily to children. The 'life-force' which rears itself against the difficulties of life has not therefore any great innate strength; and it becomes established only when tactful treatment and upbringing gradually give rise to progressive immunization against physical and psychical injuries. Corresponding to the drop in the curve of mortality and disease in middle age, the life-instinct would only counterbalance the destructive tendencies at the age of maturity.

If we were to assign to cases with this etiology their place among the nosogenic types of neurosis which Freud formulated so early and yet so exhaustively, we must locate them somewhere about the point of transition from the purely endogenous to the exogenous, i.e. among the 'frustration' neuroses. Those who develop so precocious an aversion to life give the impression of a defective capacity for adaptation similar to those who, in Freud's grouping, suffer from an inherited weakness in their capacity for life, but with the difference that in all our cases the innateness of the sickly tendency is deceptive and not genuine, owing to the early incidence of the trauma. There remains of course the task of ascertaining the finer differences in neurotic symptoms between children maltreated from the start and those who are at first received with enthusiasm, indeed with passionate love, but then 'dropped'.

Now there naturally arises the question whether I have anything to say as to a special therapy for this nosogenic group. In accordance with my attempts, published elsewhere, at a certain 'elasticity' of analytic technique,[1] I found myself gradually compelled, in these cases of diminished desire for life, to relax my demands for active efforts on the part of these patients more and more as the treatment went on. Finally a situation became apparent which could only be described as one in which the patient had to be allowed for a time to have his way like a child, not unlike the 'pre-treatment' which Anna Freud considers necessary in the case of real children.

Through this indulgence the patient is permitted, properly speaking for the first time, to enjoy the irresponsibility of childhood, which is equivalent to the introduction of *positive* life-impulses and motives for his subsequent existence. Only later can one proceed cautiously to those demands for privation which characterize our analyses generally. However, such an analysis must, of course, end like every other, with the clearing up of resistances which have inevitably been aroused, and with adaptation to a reality full of frustrations, but supplemented, one hopes, by the ability to enjoy good fortune where it is really granted.

[1] *Internationale Zeitschrift für Psycho-Analyse.* Bd. 14, 1928. English translation in this vol., p. 87.

On an occasion when I spoke of the importance of supplying 'positive life-impulses', that is to say of tenderness in relation to children, a very intelligent woman who had been, however, one-sidedly influenced by 'ego-psychology', immediately retorted: How was this to be reconciled with the significance of sexuality in the etiology of the neuroses, as affirmed by psycho-analysis? The answer gave me no difficulty, since in my *Genital Theory*[1] I had had to advocate the view that the manifestations of life of very young children are almost exclusively libidinal (erotic) but that eroticism was inconspicuous *just because of its ubiquity*. Only after the development of a special organ for eroticism does sexuality become unmistakable and undeniable. This would also be my reply to all those who might attack Freud's libidinal theory of the neuroses on the ground of the present communication. For the remainder, I have already pointed out that often it is only the struggles of the Oedipus conflict and the demands of genitality which reveal the consequences of an aversion to life acquired at an early stage.

[1] *Versuch einer Genitalthorie*, Internationaler Psychoanalytischer Verlag, 1923. English translation: *Thalassa*. New York: *Psycho-Analytic Quarterly*, 1938, 2nd imp.

X

THE PRINCIPLE OF RELAXATION AND NEOCATHARSIS[1]
(1929)

An enlarged version of a paper read at the Eleventh International Psycho-Analytical Congress, Oxford, August 1929, entitled: 'Progresses in Psycho-Analytic Technique'

AT the conclusion of this essay many of you will very likely have the impression that I ought not to have called it 'Progress in Technique', seeing that what I say in it might be more fittingly termed retrogressive or reactionary. But I hope that this impression will soon be dispelled by the reflection that even a retrograde movement, if it be in the direction of an earlier tradition, undeservedly abandoned, may advance the truth, and I honestly think that in such a case it is not too paradoxical to put forward an accentuation of our past knowledge as an advance in science. Freud's psycho-analytical researches cover a vast field: they embrace not only the mental life of the individual, but group psychology and study of human civilization; recently also he has extended them to the ultimate conception of life and death. As he proceeded to develop a modest psychotherapeutic method into a complete system of psychology and philosophy, it was inevitable that the pioneer of psycho-analysis should concentrate now on this and now on that field of investigation, disregarding everything else for the time being. But of course the withdrawal from facts earlier arrived at by no means implied that he was abandoning or contradicting them. We, his disciples, however, are inclined to cling too literally to Freud's latest pronouncements, to proclaim the most recently discovered to be the sole truth and thus at times to fall into error.

My own position in the psycho-analytical movement has made me a kind of cross between a pupil and a teacher, and

[1] German original in *Int. Z. f. Psa.* (1930), **16**, 149. English translation: *Int. J. of PsA.* (1930), **11**, 428.

perhaps this double role gives me the right and the ability to point out where we are tending to be one-sided, and, without foregoing what is good in the new teaching, to plead that justice shall be done to that which has proved its value in days past.

The technical method and the scientific theory of psychoanalysis are so closely and almost inextricably bound up with one another that I cannot in this paper confine myself to the purely technical side; I must review part of the contents of this scientific doctrine as well. In the earliest period of psychoanalysis, a period of which I will give as concise a summary as possible, there was no talk of any such division, and, even in the period immediately succeeding, the separation of technique and theory was purely artificial and was made solely for purposes of teaching.

I

A genial patient and her understanding physician shared in the discovery of the forerunner of psycho-analysis, namely, the cathartic treatment of hysteria. The patient found out for herself that certain of her symptoms disappeared when she succeeded in linking up fragments of what she said and did in an altered state of consciousness with forgotten impressions from her early life. Breuer's remarkable contribution to psychotherapy was this: not only did he pursue the method indicated by the patient, but he had faith in the *reality* of the memories which emerged, and did not, as was customary, dismiss them out of hand as the fantastic inventions of a mentally abnormal patient. We must admit that Breuer's capacity for belief had strict limitations. He could follow his patient only so long as her speech and behaviour did not overstep the bounds marked out by civilized society. Upon the first manifestations of uninhibited instinctual life he left not only the patient but the whole method in the lurch. Moreover, his theoretical deductions, otherwise extremely penetrating, were confined as far as possible to the purely intellectual aspect, or else, passing over everything in the realm of psychic emotion, they linked up directly with the physical.

Psychotherapy had to wait for a man of stronger calibre, who would not recoil from the instinctual and animal elements in the mental organization of civilized man; there is no need for me to name this pioneer. Freud's experience forced him relentlessly to the assumption that in every case of neurosis a *conditio sine qua non* is a sexual trauma. But when in certain cases the patient's statements proved incorrect, he too had to wrestle with the temptation to pronounce all the material they had produced untrustworthy and therefore unworthy of scientific consideration. Fortunately, Freud's intellectual acumen saved psycho-analysis from the imminent danger of being once more lost in oblivion. He perceived that, even though certain of the statements made by patients were untrue and not in accordance with reality, yet the psychic reality of their lying itself remained an incontestable fact. It is difficult to picture how much courage, how much vigorous and logical thinking, and how much self-mastery was necessary for him to be able to free his mind from disturbing affects and pronounce the deceptive unveracity of his patients to be hysterical fantasy, worthy as a psychic reality of further consideration and investigation.

Naturally the technique of psycho-analysis was coloured by these successive advances. The highly emotional relation between physician and patient, which resembled that in hypnotic suggestion, gradually cooled down to a kind of unending association-experiment; the process became mainly intellectual. They joined, as it were, their mental forces in the attempt to reconstruct the repressed causes of the illness from the disconnected fragments of the material acquired through the patient's associations. It was like filling in the spaces in an extremely complicated crossword puzzle. But disappointing therapeutic failures, which would assuredly have discouraged a weaker man, compelled Freud once more to restore in the relation between analyst and patient the affectivity which, as was now plain, had for a time been unduly neglected. However, it no longer took the form of influence by hypnosis and suggestion—an influence very hard to regulate, and one whose nature was not understood. Rather more consideration and respect were accorded to the signs of *transference of affect* and of *affective resistance* which manifested themselves in the analytical relation.

This was, roughly speaking, the position of analytical technique and theory at the time when I first became an enthusiastic adherent of the new teaching. Curiously enough, the first impetus in that direction came to me through Jung's association-experiments. You must permit me in this paper to depict the development of the technique from the subjective standpoint of a single individual. It seems as though the fundamental biogenetic law applies to the intellectual evolution of the individual as of the race; probably there exists no firmly established science which does not, as a separate branch of knowledge, recapitulate the following phases: first, enlightenment, accompanied by exaggerated optimism, then the inevitable disappointment, and, finally, a reconciliation between the two affects. I really do not know whether I envy our younger colleagues the ease with which they enter into possession of that which earlier generations won by bitter struggles. Sometimes I feel that to receive a tradition, however valuable, ready-made, is not so good as achieving something for oneself.

I have a lively recollection of my first attempts at the beginning of my psycho-analytical career. I recall, for instance, the very first case I treated. The patient was a young fellow-physician whom I met in the street. Extremely pale and obviously struggling desperately for breath, he grasped my arm and implored me to help him. He was suffering, as he told me in gasps, from nervous asthma. He had tried every possible remedy, but without success. I took a hasty decision, led him to my consulting-room, got him to give me his reactions to an association-test, and plunged into the analysis of his earlier life, with the help of this rapidly sown and harvested crop of associations. Sure enough, his memory pictures soon grouped themselves round a trauma in his early childhood. The episode was an operation for hydrocele. He saw and felt with objective vividness how he was seized by the hospital attendants, how the chloroform-mask was put over his face, and how he tried with all his might to escape from the anaesthetic. He repeated the straining of the muscles, the sweat of anxiety, and the interrupted breathing which he must have experienced on this traumatic occasion. Then he opened his eyes, as though awaking from a dream, looked about him in wonder, embraced me triumphantly, and said he felt perfectly free from the attack.

I could describe many other 'cathartic' successes similar to this, at about this time. But I soon discovered that, in nearly all the cases where the symptoms were thus cured, the results were but transitory, and I, the physician, felt that I was myself being gradually cured of my exaggerated optimism. I tried by means of a deeper study of Freud's work and with the help of such personal counsel as I might seek from him to master the technique of association, resistance, and transference. I followed as exactly as possible the technical hints that he published during this period. I think I have already told elsewhere how, with the deepening of my psychological knowledge as I followed these technical rules, there was a steady decrease in the striking and rapid results I achieved. The earlier, cathartic therapy was gradually transformed into a kind of analytical re-education of the patient, which demanded more and more time. In my zeal (I was still a young man) I tried to think out means for shortening the period of analysis and producing more visible therapeutic results. By a greater generalization and emphasizing of the principle of frustration (to which Freud himself subscribed at the Congress at Budapest in 1918), and with the aid of artificially produced accentuations of tension ('active therapy'), I tried to induce a freer repetition of early traumatic experiences and to lead up to a better solution of them through analysis. You are doubtless aware that I myself, and others who followed me, sometimes let ourselves be carried away into exaggerations of this active technique. The worst of these was the measure suggested by Rank and, for a time, accepted by myself—the setting of a term to the analysis. I had sufficient insight to utter a timely warning against these exaggerations, and I threw myself into the analysis of the ego and of character-development, upon which in the meantime Freud had so successfully entered. The somewhat one-sided ego-analysis, in which too little attention was paid to the libido (formerly regarded as omnipotent), converted analytical treatment largely into a process designed to afford us the fullest possible insight into the topography, dynamics, and economy of symptom-formation, the distribution of energy between the patient's id, ego, and super-ego being exactly traced out. But when I worked from this standpoint, I could not escape the impression that the relation between physician and patient was becoming far too much like that between teacher and pupil. I also became convinced that my patients were profoundly dissatisfied with me, though they did not dare to rebel openly against this didactic and pedantic attitude of the analyst. Accordingly, in one of my papers on technique I encouraged my colleagues to train their patients to a greater liberty and a freer expression in behaviour of their aggressive feelings towards the physician. At the same time I urged analysts to be more humble-minded in their attitude to their patients and to admit the mistakes they made, and I pleaded for a greater elasticity in technique, even if it meant the sacrifice of some of our theories. These, as I pointed out, were not immutable, though they might be valuable instruments for a time. Finally, I was able to state that not only did my patients' analysis not suffer from the greater freedom accorded them, but, after all their aggressive impulses had exhausted their fury, positive transference and also much more positive results were achieved. So you must not be too surprised if, once more, I have to tell you of fresh steps forward, or, if you will have it so, *backward* in the path that I have followed. I am conscious that what I have to say is not at all likely to be popular with you. And I must admit that I am afraid it may win most unwelcome popularity amongst the true reactionaries. But do not forget what I said at the beginning about progress and retrogression; in my view a return to what was good in the teaching of the past most emphatically does not imply giving up the good and valuable contributions made by the more recent development of our science. Moreover, it would be presumptuous to imagine that any one of us is in a position to say the last word on the potentialities of the technique or theory of analysis. I, for one, have learnt humility through the many vicissitudes which I have just sketched. So I would not represent what I am about to say as in any way final. In fact, I think it very possible that in a greater or lesser degree it will be subject to various limitations as time goes on.

2

In the course of my practical analytical work, which extended over many years, I constantly found myself infringing one or another of Freud's injunctions in his 'Recommendations on Technique'. For instance, my attempt to adhere to the principle that patients must be in a lying position during analysis would at times be thwarted by their uncontrollable impulse to get up and walk about the room or speak to me face to face. Or again, difficulties in the real situation, and often the unconscious machinations of the patient, would leave me with no alternative but either to break off the analysis or to depart from the general rule and carry it on without remuneration. I did not hesitate to adopt the latter alternative—not without success. The principle that the patient should be analysed in his ordinary environment and should carry on his usual occupation, was very often impossible to enforce. In some severe cases I was even obliged to let patients stay in bed for days and weeks and to relieve them of the effort of coming to my house. The sudden breaking-off of the analysis at the end of the hour very often had the effect of a shock, and I would be forced to prolong the treatment until the reaction had spent itself; sometimes I had to devote two or more hours a day to a single patient; often, if I would not or could not do this, my inflexibility produced a resistance which I felt to be excessive and a too literal repetition of traumatic incidents in the patient's childhood; it would then take a long time even partly to overcome the bad effects of this unconscious identification of his. One of the chief principles of analysis is that of frustration, and this certain of my colleagues, and, at times, I myself applied too strictly. Many patients suffering from obsessional neurosis saw through it directly and utilized it as a new and quite inexhaustible source of resistance-situations, until the physician finally decided to knock this weapon out of their hands by *indulgence* (*Nachgiebigkeit*).

I had the greatest conscientious scruples about all these infringements of a fundamental rule (and about many others which I cannot instance in detail here), until my mind was set at rest by the authoritative information that Freud's 'Recommendations' were really intended only as warnings for beginners and were designed to protect them from the most glaring blunders and failures; his precepts contained, however, hardly any positive instructions, and considerable scope was left for the exercise of the analyst's own judgement, provided that he was clear about the metapsychological consequences of his procedure.

Nevertheless, the exceptional cases have become so numerous that I feel impelled to propound another principle, not hitherto formulated, even if tacitly accepted. I mean the *principle of indulgence*, which must often be allowed to operate side by side with that of frustration. Subsequent reflection has convinced me that my explanation of the way in which the active technique worked was really a very forced one: I attributed everything that happened to frustration, i.e. to a 'heightening of tension'. When I told a patient, whose habit it was to cross her legs, that she must not do so, I was actually creating a situation of libidinal frustration, which induced a heightening of tension and the mobilization of psychic material hitherto repressed. But when I suggested to the same patient that she should give up the noticeably stiff posture of all her muscles and allow herself more freedom and mobility, I was really not justified in speaking of a heightening of tension, simply because she found it difficult to relax from her rigid attitude. It is much more honest to confess that here I was making use of a totally different method which, in contrast to the heightening of tension, may safely be called *relaxation*. We must admit, therefore, that psycho-analysis employs two opposite methods: it produces heightening of tension by the frustration it imposes and relaxation by the freedom it allows.

But with this, as with every novelty, we soon find that it contains something very, very old—I had almost said, something commonplace. Are not both these principles inherent in the method of free association? On the one hand, the patient is compelled to confess disagreeable truths, but, on the other, he is permitted a freedom of speech and expression of his feelings such as is hardly possible in any other department of life. And long before psycho-analysis came into existence there were two elements in the training of children and of the masses: tenderness and love were accorded to them, and at the same time they were required to adapt themselves to painful reality by making hard renunciations.

If the International Psycho-Analytical Association were not so highly cultivated and self-disciplined an assembly, I should probably be interrupted at this point in my discourse by a general uproar and clamour. Such a thing has been known to happen even in the British House of Commons, usually so dignified, when a particularly infuriating speech has been made. 'What on earth do you really mean?' some of you would shout. 'We have scarcely reconciled ourselves to some extent to the principle of frustration, which you yourself carried to all lengths in your active technique, when you upset our laboriously placated scientific conscience by confronting us with a new and confusing principle, whose application will be highly embarrassing to us.' 'You talk of the dangers of excessive frustration,' another and no less shrill voice would chime in. 'What about the dangers of coddling patients? And, anyhow, can you give us any definite directions about how and when one or the other principle is to be applied?'

Softly, ladies and gentlemen! We are not yet advanced far enough to enter on these and similar details. My only object for the moment was to prove that, even though we may not admit it, we do actually work with these two principles. But perhaps I ought to consider certain objections which naturally arise in my own mind too. The fact that the analyst may be made uncomfortable by being confronted with new problems surely need not be seriously discussed!

To compose your minds I will say with all due emphasis that the attitude of objective reserve and scientific observation which Freud recommends to the physician remains, as ever, the most trustworthy and, at the beginning of an analysis, the only justifiable one, and that, ultimately, the decision as to which is the appropriate method must never be arrived at under the influence of affective factors but only as the result of intelligent reflection. My modest endeavours have for their object merely a plain definition of what has hitherto been vaguely described as the 'psychological atmosphere'. We cannot deny that it is possible for even the cool objectivity of the physician to take forms which cause unnecessary and avoidable difficulties to the patient, and there must be ways and means of making our attitude of friendly goodwill during the analysis intelligible to him without abandoning the analysis of transference-material or falling into the errors of those who treat neurotics, not analytically, i.e. with complete sincerity, but with a simulation of severity or love.

3

I expect that various questions and objections, some of them I admit, very awkward ones, have arisen in your minds. Before we discuss them, let me state the main argument which, in my view, justifies me in emphasizing the principle of relaxation side by side with that of frustration and of objectivity (which is a matter of course for the analyst). The soundness of any hypothesis or theory is tested by its theoretical and practical usefulness, i.e. by its heuristic value, and it is my experience that the acknowledgement of the relaxation-principle has produced results valuable for both theory and practice. In a number of cases in which the analysis had come to grief over the patient's apparently insoluble resistances, and a new analysis was attempted in which a change was made from the too rigid tactics of frustration hitherto employed, it was attended with much more substantial success. I am not speaking of patients who had failed to get well with other analysts and who gratified me, their new analyst, by taking a turn for the better (partly out of revenge for the old, perhaps). I am speaking of cases in which I myself, with the one-sided technique of frustration, had failed to get any further but, on making a fresh attempt and allowing more relaxation, I had not nearly so long-drawn-out a struggle with interminable personal resistances, and it became possible for physician and patient to join forces in a less disrupted analysis of the repressed material, or, as I might say, to tackle the 'objective resistances'. On analysing the patient's former obstinacy and comparing it with the readiness to give way, which resulted from the method of relaxation, we found that the rigid and cool aloofness on the analyst's part was experienced by the patient as a continuation of his infantile struggle with the grown-ups' authority, and made him repeat the same reactions in character and in symptoms as formed the basis of the real neurosis. Hitherto my idea about terminating the treatment had been that one need not be afraid of these resistances and might even provoke them artificially; I hoped (and to some extent I was justified) that, when the patient's analytical insight had gradually closed to him all avenues of resistance, he would be cornered and obliged to take the only way left open, namely, that which led to health. Now I do not deny that every neurotic must inevitably suffer during analysis; theoretically it is self-evident that the patient must learn to endure the suffering which originally led to repression. The only question is whether sometimes we do not make him suffer more than is absolutely necessary. I decided on the phrase 'economy of suffering' to express what I have realized and am trying to convey—and I hope it is not far-fetched—namely, that the principles of frustration and indulgence should both govern our technique.

As you all know, we analysts do not attach great scientific importance to therapeutic effects in the sense of an increased feeling of well-being on the patient's part. Only if our method results not merely in his improvement but in a deeper insight into the process of his recovery may we speak of real progress in comparison with earlier methods of treatment. The extent to which patients improved when I employed this relaxation-therapy in addition to the older method was in many cases quite astonishing. In hysterics, obsessional neurotics, and even in neurotic characters the familiar attempts to reconstruct the past went forward as usual. But, after we had succeeded in a somewhat deeper manner than before in creating an atmosphere of confidence between physician and patient and in securing a fuller freedom of affect, hysterical physical symptoms would suddenly make their appearance, often for the first time in an analysis extending over years. These symptoms included paraesthesias and spasms, definitely localized, violent emotional movements, like miniature hysterical attacks, sudden alterations of the state of consciousness, slight vertigo and a clouding of consciousness often with subsequent amnesia for what had taken place. Some patients actually begged me to tell them how they had behaved when in these states. It was easy to utilize these symptoms as fresh aids to reconstruction—as physical memory symbols, so to speak. But there was this difference—this time, the reconstructed past had much more of a feeling of *reality and concreteness* about it than heretofore, approximated much more closely to an actual *recollection*, whereas till then the patients had spoken only of possibilities or, at most, of varying degrees of probability and had yearned in vain for memories. In certain cases these hysterical attacks actually assumed the character of *trances*, in which fragments of the past were relived and the physician was the only bridge left between the patients and reality. I was able to question them and received important information about dissociated parts of the personality. Without any such intention on my part and without my making the least attempt to induce a condition of this sort, unusual states of consciousness manifested themselves, which might also be termed autohypnotic. Willy-nilly, one was forced to compare them with the phenomena of the Breuer-Freud *catharsis*. I must confess that at first this was a disagreeable surprise, almost a shock, to me. Was it really worth while to make that enormous detour of analysis of associations and resistances, to unravel the maze of the elements of ego-psychology, and even to traverse the whole metapsychology in order to arrive at the good old 'friendly attitude' to the patient and the method of catharsis, long believed to have been discarded? But a little reflection soon set my mind at rest. There is all the difference in the world between this cathartic termination to a long psycho-analysis and the fragmentary eruptions of emotion and recollection which the primitive catharsis could provoke and which had only a temporary effect. The catharsis of which I am speaking is, like many dreams, only a confirmation from the unconscious, a sign that our toilsome analytical construction, our technique of dealing with resistance and transference, have finally succeeded in drawing near to the aetiological reality. There is little that the palaeocatharsis has in common with this *neocatharsis*. Nevertheless we must admit that here, once more, a circle has been completed. Psycho-analysis began as a cathartic measure against traumatic shocks, the effects of which had never spent themselves, and against pent-up affects; it then devoted itself to a deeper study of neurotic fantasies and the various defence mechanisms against them. Next, it concentrated rather on the personal affective relation between analyst and patient, being in the first twenty years mainly occupied with the manifestations of instinctual tendencies, and, later, with the reactions of the ego. The sudden emergence in modern psycho-analysis of portions of an earlier technique and theory should not dismay us; it merely reminds us that, so far, no single advance has been made in analysis which has had to be entirely discarded as useless, and that we must constantly be prepared to find new veins of gold in temporarily abandoned workings.

4

What I am now about to say is really the logical sequel to what I have said already. The recollections which neocatharsis evoked or corroborated lent an added significance to the original traumatic factor in our aetiological equations. The precautions of the hysteric and the avoidance of the obsessional neurotic may, it is true, have their explanation in purely mental fantasy-formations; nevertheless the first impetus towards abnormal lines of development has always been thought to originate from real psychic traumas and conflicts with the environment—the invariable precursors of the formation of nosogenic mental forces, for instance, of conscience. Accordingly, no analysis can be regarded (at any rate in theory) as complete unless we have succeeded in penetrating to the traumatic material. This statement is based, as I said, on experience acquired in relaxation-therapy; if it be true, it adds considerably (from the theoretical as well as the practical standpoint) to the heuristic value of this modified technique. Having given due consideration to fantasy as a pathogenic factor, I have of late been forced more and more to deal with the pathogenic trauma itself. It became evident that this is far more rarely the result of a constitutional hypersensibility in children (causing them to react neurotically even to a commonplace and unavoidable painful experience) than of really improper, unintelligent, capricious, tactless, or actually cruel treatment. Hysterical fantasies do not lie when they tell us that parents and other adults do indeed go monstrous lengths in the passionate eroticism of their relation with children, while, on the other hand, when the innocent child responds to this half-unconscious play on the part of its elders the latter are inclined to think out severe punishments and threats which are altogether incomprehensible to him and have the shattering effects of a shock. To-day I am returning to the view that, beside the great importance of the Oedipus complex in children, a deep significance must also be attached to the *repressed incestuous affection of adults, which masquerades as tenderness*. On the other hand, I am bound to confess that children themselves manifest a readiness to engage in genital eroticism more vehemently and far earlier than we used to suppose. Many of the perversions children practise probably indicate not simply fixation to a pre-genital level but regression from an *early genital level*. In many cases the trauma of punishment falls upon children in the midst of some erotic activity, and the result may be a permanent disturbance of what Reich calls 'orgastic potency'. But the premature forcing of genital sensations has a no less terrifying effect on children; what they really want, even in their sexual life, is simply play and tenderness, not the violent ebullition of passion.

Observation of cases treated by the neocathartic method gave further food for thought; one realized something of the psychic process in the traumatic primal repression and gained a glimpse into the nature of repression in general. *The first reaction to a shock seems to be always a transitory psychosis*, i.e. a turning away from reality. Sometimes this takes the form of negative hallucination (hysterical loss of consciousness—fainting or vertigo), often of an immediate positive hallucinatory compensation, which makes itself felt as an illusory pleasure. In every case of neurotic amnesia, and possibly also in the ordinary childhood-amnesia, it seems likely that a *psychotic splitting off* of a part of the personality occurs under the influence of shock. The dissociated part, however, lives on hidden, ceaselessly endeavouring to make itself felt, without finding any outlet except in neurotic symptoms.

For this notion I am partly indebted to discoveries made by our colleague, Elisabeth Severn, which she personally communicated to me.

Sometimes, as I said, we achieve direct contact with the repressed part of the personality and persuade it to engage in what I might almost call an infantile conversation. Under the method of relaxation the hysterical physical symptoms have at times led us back to phases of development in which, since the organ of thought was not yet completely developed, physical memories alone were registered.

In conclusion, there is one more point I must mention, namely, that more importance than we hitherto supposed must be attached to the anxiety aroused by menstruation, the impression made by which has only been recently properly emphasized by C. D. Daly; together with the threat of castration it is one of the most important traumatic factors.

Why should I weary you, in a discourse which is surely mainly concerned with technique, with this long and not even complete list of half-worked-out theoretical arguments? Certainly not in order that you may wholeheartedly espouse these views, about which I myself am not as yet quite clear. I am content if I have conveyed to you the impression that a proper evaluation of the long neglected traumatogenesis promises to be fruitful, not only for practical therapy but for the theory of our science.

5

In a conversation with Anna Freud in which we discussed certain points in my technique she made the following pregnant remark: 'You really treat your patients as I treat the children whom I analyse.' I had to admit that she was right, and I would remind you that in my most recent publication, a short paper on the psychology of unwanted children who later become subjects for analysis, I stated that the real analysis of resistances must be prefaced by a kind of comforting preparatory treatment. The relaxation-technique which I am suggesting to you assuredly obliterates even more completely the distinction between the analysis of children and that of adults—a distinction hitherto too sharply drawn. In making the two types of treatment more like one another I was undoubtedly influenced by what I saw of the work of Georg Groddeck, the courageous champion of the psycho-analysis of organic diseases, whom I consulted about an organic illness. I felt that he was right in trying to encourage his patients to a childlike *naïveté*, and I saw the success thus achieved. But, for my own part, I have remained faithful to the well-tried analytical method of frustration as well, and I try to attain my aim by the tactful and understanding application of *both* forms of technique.

Now let me try to give a reassuring answer to the probable objections to these tactics. What motive will patients have to turn away from analysis to the hard reality of life if they can enjoy with the analyst the irresponsible freedom of childhood in a measure which is assuredly denied them in actuality? My answer is that even in analysis by the method of relaxation, as in child-analysis, conditions are such that performance does not outrun discretion. However great the relaxation, the analysis will not gratify the patient's actively aggressive and sexual wishes or many of their other exaggerated demands. There will be abundant opportunity to learn renunciation and adaptation. Our friendly and benevolent attitude may indeed satisfy that childlike part of the personality which hungers for tenderness, but not the part which has succeeded in escaping from the inhibitions in its development and becoming adult. For it is no mere poetic licence to compare the mind of the neurotic to a double malformation, something like the so-called *teratoma* which harbours in a hidden part of its body fragments of a twin-being which has never developed. No reasonable person would refuse to surrender such a *teratoma* to the surgeon's knife, if the existence of the whole individual were threatened.

Another discovery that I made was that repressed hate often operates more strongly in the direction of fixation and arrest than openly confessed tenderness. I think I have never had this point more clearly put than by a patient whose confidence, after nearly two years of hard struggle with resistance, I won by the method of indulgence. 'Now I like you and now I can let you go,' was her first spontaneous remark on the emergence of a positive affective attitude towards me. I believe it was in analysis of the same patient that I was able to prove that relaxation lends itself particularly well to the conversion of the repetition-tendency into recollection. So long as she identified me with her hard-hearted parents, she incessantly repeated the reactions of defiance. But when I deprived her of all occasion for this attitude, she began to discriminate the present from the past and, after some hysterical outbreaks of emotions, to remember the psychic shocks of her childhood. *We see then that, while the similarity of the analytical to the infantile situation impels patients to repetition, the contrast between the two encourages recollection.*

I am of course conscious that this twofold method of frustration and indulgence requires from the analyst himself an even greater control than before of counter-transference and counter-resistance. It is no uncommon thing for even those teachers and parents who take their task seriously to be led by imperfectly mastered instincts into excess in either direction. Nothing is easier than to use the principle of frustration in one's relation with patients and children as a cloak for indulgence in one's own unconfessed sadistic inclinations. On the other hand, exaggerated forms and quantities of tenderness may subserve one's own, possibly unconscious, libidinal tendencies, rather than the ultimate good of the individual in one's care. These new and difficult conditions are an even stronger argument in support of the view I have often and urgently put forward, namely, that it is essential for the analyst himself to go through an analysis reaching to the very deepest depths and putting him into control of his own character-traits.

I can picture cases of neurosis—in fact I have often met with them—in which (possibly as a result of unusually profound traumas in infancy) the greater part of the personality becomes, as it were, a *teratoma*, the task of adaptation to reality being shouldered by the fragment of personality which has been spared. Such persons have actually remained almost entirely at the child-level, and for them the usual methods of analytical therapy are not enough. *What such neurotics need is really to be adopted and to partake for the first time in their lives of the advantages of a normal nursery.* Possibly the analytic in-patient treatment recommended by Simmel might be developed with special reference to these cases.

If even part of the relaxation-technique and the findings of neocatharsis should prove correct, it would mean that we should substantially enlarge our theoretical knowledge and the scope of our practical work. Modern psycho-analysis, by dint of laborious effort, can restore the interrupted harmony and adjust the abnormal distribution of energy amongst the intrapsychic forces, thus increasing the patient's capacity for achievement. But these forces are but the representatives of the *conflict originally waged between the individual and the outside world.* After reconstructing the evolution of the id, the ego, and super-ego many patients repeat in the neocathartic experience the primal battle with reality, and it may be that the transformation of this last repetition into recollection may provide a yet firmer basis for the subject's future existence. His situation may be compared with that of the playwright whom pressure of public opinion forces to convert the tragedy he has planned into a drama with a 'happy ending'. With this expression of optimism I will conclude.

XI

CHILD ANALYSIS IN THE ANALYSIS OF ADULTS[1]
(1931)

I FEEL I ought to say a few words to explain or excuse the fact that I, a stranger, have been chosen to speak at this celebration by a society that includes so many who are worthy—more worthy than myself—to fulfil this honourable task. It cannot be merely the precedence accorded to those twenty-five years during which I have had the privilege of being in close contact with Professor Freud and under his leadership—for there are amongst you some of our colleagues who have been his faithful disciples even longer than I. Let me therefore look for some other reason. Perhaps you wanted to take this opportunity of giving the lie to a certain statement which is widely current and much favoured by the uninitiated and the opponents of psycho-analysis. Over and over again one hears irresponsible remarks about the intolerance, the 'orthodoxy' of our master. It is said that he will not suffer his associates to criticize any of his theories, and that he drives all independent talent out of his circle in order tyrannically to impose his own will in matters scientific. People talk of his 'Old Testament' severity, and even account for it on racial grounds. Now it is a sad truth that in the course of time certain men of conspicuous talent and many lesser lights have turned their backs on Freud after following him for a longer or shorter period. Were they in leaving him really actuated by purely scientific motives? It seems to me that their sterility in scientific work since then does not testify in their favour.

I should like to throw into the scales your kind invitation to me as an argument against this notion of the 'orthodoxy' of the International Association and its spiritual leader, Professor Freud. I have no wish to measure my own standing against that of the colleagues to whom I have alluded; but it is a fact that I

[1] German original: *Int. Z. f. Psa.* (1931), **17**, 161. English translation: *Int. J. of PsA.* (1931), **12**, 468.

am fairly generally regarded as a restless spirit, or, as someone recently said to me at Oxford, the *enfant terrible* of psychoanalysis.

A considerable majority of you have criticized as fantastic, as altogether too original, the technical and theoretical suggestions which I have submitted for your judgement. Nor can I say that Freud himself agrees with all that I publish. He did not mince matters when I asked his opinion. But he hastened to add that the future might show me to have been right in many respects, and neither he nor I dream of suspending our collaboration because of these differences in method and in theory; for on the most important principles of psycho-analysis we are in perfect agreement.

In one respect Freud is certainly orthodox. He is the creator of works which have now for several decades stood unchanged, intact—crystallized, as it were. His *Interpretation of Dreams*, for example, is so highly polished a gem, so closely knit in content and in form, that it withstands all the changes of time and of the libido, so that criticism scarcely ventures to approach it. Let us thank the fates that we have the good fortune to be fellow-workers with this great spirit—this *liberal* spirit, as we can proclaim him to be. Let us hope that his seventy-fifth year may restore to Professor Freud bodily health to match the unfailing vigour of his spirit.

Now let us turn to the theme of my address to-day. During the last few years it has happened that certain facts of analytic experience have grouped themselves in my mind round ideas which urge me to temper materially the antithesis, hitherto so sharp, between the analysis of children and that of adults.

The first beginnings of child-analysis came from among your group. Leaving aside one isolated attempt of Freud's (which certainly pointed the way), we may say that the Viennese analyst, Frau von Hug-Hellmuth, was the first to work methodically at the analysis of children. We have to thank her for the idea that such analysis should, as it were, start in the form of play. She and, later, Melanie Klein found that, if they wanted to analyse children, they would have to make considerable alterations in the technique used in adult analysis, mostly in the direction of mitigating its usual technical strictness. The systematic works on this subject of one of your members, Anna Freud, are universally known and esteemed, as is the masterly skill of Aichhorn's devices for making even the most difficult children tractable in analysis. I for my part have had very little to do with children analytically, and I have myself been surprised to come upon the self-same problems in quite a different quarter. How has this happened? I can answer this question in a few words, but before I do so, it will, I think, not be irrelevant to tell you something of an idiosyncrasy in the direction my own work has taken. I have had a kind of fanatical belief in the efficacy of depth-psychology, and this has led me to attribute occasional failures not so much to the patient's 'incurability' as to our own lack of skill, a supposition which necessarily led me to try altering the usual technique in severe cases with which it proved unable to cope successfully.

It is thus only with the utmost reluctance that I ever bring myself to give up even the most obstinate case, and I have come to be a specialist in peculiarly difficult cases, with which I go on for very many years. I have refused to accept such verdicts as that a patient's resistance was unconquerable, or that his narcissism prevented our penetrating any further, or the sheer fatalistic acquiescence in the so-called 'drying up' of a case. I have told myself that, as long as a patient continues to come at all, the last thread of hope has not snapped. Thus the question constantly forced itself upon me: Is it always the patient's resistance that is the cause of the failure? Is it not rather our own convenience, which disdains to adapt itself, even in technique, to the idiosyncrasies of the individual? In the cases which appeared to have 'dried up', and in which for long periods of time analysis brought neither fresh insight nor therapeutic progress, I had the feeling that what we call free association was still too much of the nature of a conscious selection of thoughts, and so I urged the patient to deeper relaxation and more complete surrender to the impressions, tendencies, and emotions which quite spontaneously arose in him. Now the freer the process of association actually became, the more naïve (one might say, the more childish) did the patient become in his speech and his other modes of expressing himself. More and more frequently there were mingled with his thoughts and visual ideas little expressive movements, and sometimes 'transitory symptoms', which, like everything else, were subsequently analysed. Now in certain cases it transpired that the analyst's cool, expectant silence, and his failure to manifest any reaction had the effect of disturbing the freedom of association. The patient has barely reached the point of really forgetting himself and yielding up everything that is going on in his mind, when he suddenly rouses himself with a start from his absorbed state, and complains that he really cannot take the current of his emotions seriously when he sees that I am sitting tranquilly behind him, smoking my cigarette and at most responding coolly and indifferently with the stereotyped question: 'Now what comes into your mind about that?' I said to myself then that there must be some way or means of eliminating this disturbance of the association and affording the patient an opportunity of unfolding more freely the repetition-tendency as it strove to break through.

But it was a very long time before the first suggestions of how to do this came to me, and, once more, they came from the patients themselves. For example, a patient in the prime of life resolved, after overcoming strong resistances, and especially his profound mistrust, to revive in his mind incidents from his earliest childhood. Thanks to the light analysis had already thrown on his early life, I was aware that in the scene revived by him, he was identifying me with his grandfather. Suddenly, in the midst of what he was saying, he threw his arms round my neck and whispered in my ear: 'I say, Grandpapa, I am afraid I am going to have a baby!' Thereupon I had what seems to me a happy inspiration: I said nothing to him for the moment about transference, etc., but retorted, in a similar whisper: 'Well, but what makes you think so?'[1]

As you see, I was entering into a game, which we might call a game of questions and answers. This was perfectly analogous to the processes described to us by those who analyse children,

[1] Translator's note.—In this dialogue both patient and analyst use the intimate pronoun 'du'.

and for some time this little device was quite successful. But you must not suppose that I am able in this kind of game to ask every sort of question. If the question is not simple enough, not really adapted to a *child's* comprehension, the dialogue is soon broken off, some patients even reproaching me straight out with having been clumsy and having, so to speak, spoilt the game. Often this has happened because I introduced into my questions and answers things of which the child, at that time, could not possibly have known. I met with even more decided rebuffs when I attempted to give learned, scientific interpretations. I need hardly tell you that my first reaction to such incidents was a feeling of outraged authority. For a moment I felt injured at the suggestion that my patient or pupil could know better than I did. Fortunately, however, there immediately occurred to me the further thought that he really must at bottom know more about himself than I could do with my guesses. I therefore admitted that possibly I had made a mistake, and the result was not that I lost my authority, but that his confidence in me was increased. I may mention in passing that a few patients were indignant because I called this method a game. They said that that was a sign that I did not take the matter seriously. There was a certain amount of truth in this too: I was soon forced to admit to myself and to the patient that many of the serious realities of childhood were concealed beneath this play. I had a proof of this when certain patients began to sink out of this half-playful behaviour into a kind of hallucinatory abstraction, in which they enacted before me traumatic occurrences, the unconscious memory of which lay, in fact, behind the dialogue of the game. Curiously enough, I made a similar observation at the outset of my analytical career. Once, when a patient was talking to me, he suddenly fell into a kind of hysterical 'twilight state' and began to enact a scene. On that occasion I shook the man vigorously and shouted to him that he was to finish what he had just been saying to me. Thus encouraged, he succeeded, though only to a limited extent, in making contact, through me, with the world again and was able to communicate something of his hidden conflicts to me in intelligible sentences instead of in the gesture-language of his hysteria.

You see that in my procedure I have linked up the technical device of 'play-analysis' with a certain preconception, which, however, was based on a number of observations; I assumed that one has no right to be satisfied with any analysis until it has led to the actual reproduction of the traumatic occurrences associated with the primal repression, upon which character and symptom-formation are ultimately based. When you consider that, according to our experience hitherto and to the premises with which we start, most pathogenic shocks take place in childhood, you will not be surprised that the patient, in the attempt to uncover the origin of his illness, suddenly lapses into a childish or childlike attitude. Here, however, several important questions arise, which I had in fact to put to myself. Is there any advantage in letting the patient sink into the primitive state of the child and act freely in this condition? Does that really accomplish any part of the analytic task? Are we not simply providing confirmation of the charge often brought against us that analysis fosters the sway of uncontrolled instincts, or that it simply provokes hysterical attacks, which might quite well suddenly occur for external reasons, without analytic help, and which only provide temporary relief? And, in any case, how far is it legitimate to carry such analytic play? Are there any criteria by which we may determine the limit up to which this childlike relaxation is permissible and beyond which educative frustration must begin?

Of course the task of analysis is not fulfilled when we have reactivated the infantile level and caused the traumas to be re-enacted. The material re-enacted in play or repeated in any other way has to be thoroughly worked through analytically. Of course, too, Freud is right when he teaches us that it is a triumph for analysis when it succeeds in substituting recollection for acting out. But I think it is also valuable to secure important material in the shape of action which can then be transformed into recollection. I too am in principle opposed to uncontrolled outbreaks, but I think it is expedient to uncover the hidden tendencies to acting out as fully as possible, before setting about intellectual work on them and the training in self-control which goes with this. You must catch your hare before you can cook him. So do not think that the analyses which sometimes bring down to the level of a game are fundamentally so very different from analysis as hitherto practised. The sessions begin, as always, with thoughts originating from the surface level of the mind, and much time is spent—just as usual—on the events of the previous day. Then perhaps there comes a 'normal' dream-analysis, which, however, tends readily to go off into an infantile situation or into acting out. But I never let an analytic hour pass without thoroughly analysing the material provided by the acting out, of course making full use of all that we know (and have to bring to the patient's consciousness) about transference and resistance and the metapsychology of symptom-formation.

The second question—up to what point is active expression in play to be permitted?—may be answered as follows. Adult patients, too, should be free to behave in analysis like naughty (i.e. uncontrolled) children, but if the adult himself falls into the mistake with which he sometimes charges us, that is to say, if he drops his role in the game and sets himself to act out infantile reality in terms of adult behaviour, it must be shown to him it is he who is spoiling the game. And we must manage, though it is often hard work, to make him confine the kind and extent of his behaviour within the limits of that of a child. In this connexion I would put forward the conjecture that the friendly affective attitudes of children—especially where they are also libidinal—are originally derived from the tender relation between mother and child, and that their naughtiness, fits of passion, and uncontrolled perversions are generally a later result of tactless treatment by those around them.

It is important for the analysis that the analyst should be able to meet the patient as far as possible with almost inexhaustible patience, understanding, goodwill, and kindliness. By so doing he lays up a reserve by means of which he can fight out the conflicts which are inevitable sooner or later, with a prospect of reconciliation. The patient will then feel the contrast between our behaviour and that which he experienced in his real family and, knowing himself safe from the repetition of such situations, he has the courage to let himself sink down into a reproduction of the painful past. Here what happens reminds us vividly of the occurrences described by the analysts of children. Thus, for instance, a patient, when he confesses to a fault, suddenly seizes my hand, imploring me not to hit him. Very often patients try to provoke an expression of the ill-will which they imagine us to be concealing, by their bad behaviour, by sarcastic or cynical remarks, by all sorts of rudeness, and even by making faces. It is not satisfactory to go on playing even in these circumstances the part of the grown-up who is always indulgent and kind; it is better to admit honestly that we find the patient's behaviour unpleasant, but that we feel it our duty to control ourselves, since we know that he is not going to the trouble of being naughty for no reason. In this way we discover a good deal about the insincerity and hypocrisy which he often could not fail to observe in the display or assertions of love made by those around him in his childhood, though he hid his criticism from everyone, and, later, even from himself.

Not infrequently patients, often in the middle of their free associations, produce little stories which they have made up, or even poems and rhymes, and sometimes they ask for a pencil so as to make us a present of a drawing, generally of a very naive sort. Naturally I let them indulge in this and make the little gifts a starting-point for further fantasy-formations, which I afterwards analyse. Does not this by itself sound as if it came from the analysis of children?

I should like at this point to confess to you an error in tactics, the remedying of which taught me a great deal on an important matter of principle. I refer to the problem of how far my method with my patients may be called hypnosis or suggestion. Our colleague, Elizabeth Severn, who is doing a training-analysis with me, once pointed out to me, when we were discussing this amongst a number of other subjects, that I sometimes disturbed the spontaneity of the fantasy-production with my questions and answers. She thought that I ought to confine my assistance to stimulating the patient's mind to further efforts when it faltered, to overcoming inhibitions due to anxiety, and so on. It would be even better, she considered, if my stimulation took the form of very simple questions instead of statements, which should compel the patient to continue the work by his own exertions.

The theoretical formulation which follows from this, and which I have acted on with much gain of insight, is that the suggestion, which is legitimate even in analysis, should be of the nature of general encouragement rather than special direction. This, I think, is materially different from the suggestion customarily practised by psychotherapists; it is really only a reinforcement of what in analysis we cannot help asking the patient to do: 'Now lie down and let your thoughts run freely and tell me everything that comes into your mind.' The fantasy itself is only a similar, though certainly a strengthened encouragement.

The question about hypnosis may be answered in the same way. In all free association there is necessarily an element of self-forgetful abstraction. It is true that, when the patient is called upon to go further and deeper in this direction, it sometimes happens—with me, let me frankly confess, very frequently—that a more profound abstraction develops. Where this takes a quasi-hallucinatory form, people can call it auto-hypnosis if they like; my patients often call it a trance-state. What is important is that one should not abuse this phase, in which the subject is unquestionably much more helpless than usual, by urging upon his unresisting mind one's own theories and fantasies. On the contrary, we ought to use our undeniably great influence here to deepen the patient's capacity for producing his own material. Putting it in a somewhat inelegant way, we might say that in analysis it is not legitimate to suggest or hypnotize things *into* the patient, but it is not only right but advisable to suggest them *out*. Here we get light, of some significance for education, on the course which we ought also to follow in the rational upbringing of children. Their suggestibility and their tendency, when they feel themselves helpless, to lean, without any resistance, on a 'grown-up' (that is to say an element of hypnotism in the relation between children and adults) is an undeniable fact, with which we have to reckon. But instead of doing what is commonly done, that is to say, going on using the great power which grown-ups have over children to stamp upon their plastic minds our own rigid rules as something externally imprinted, we might fashion that power into a means of educating them to greater independence and courage.

If, in the analytic situation, the patient feels hurt, disappointed, or left in the lurch, he sometimes begins to play by himself like a lonely child. One definitely gets the impression that to be left deserted results in a split of personality. Part of the person adopts the role of father or mother in relation to the rest, thereby undoing, as it were, the fact of being left deserted. In this play various parts of the body—hands, fingers, feet, genitals, head, nose, or eye—become representatives of the whole person, in relation to which all the vicissitudes of the subject's own tragedy are enacted and then worked out to a reconciliatory conclusion. It is noteworthy, however, that over and above this we get glimpses into the processes of what I have called the 'narcissistic split of the self' in the mental sphere itself. One is astonished at the large amount of auto-symbolic self-observation or unconscious psychology revealed in the fantasy productions of both patients and, obviously, of children. I have been told little tales like the one about the wicked animal which tries to destroy a jelly-fish by means of its teeth and claws, but cannot get at it because the jelly-fish with its subtleness eludes each jab and bite and then returns to its round shape. This story may be interpreted in two ways: on the one hand it expresses the passive resistance with which the patient meets the attacks of his environment, and on the other it represents the splitting of the self into a suffering, brutally destroyed part and a part which, as it were, knows everything but feels nothing. This primal process of repression is expressed even more clearly in fantasies and dreams, in which the head, i.e. the organ of thought, is cut off from the body and goes about on feet of its own, or is connected with the body only by a single thread. All this calls for interpretation not only in terms of the patient's history, but also of auto-symbolism.

I do not at present want to consider more closely the metapsychological significance of all these processes of splitting and reunion. It will be enough if I can convey to you my own surmise that in reality we have still a great deal to learn from our patients, our pupils, and obviously also from children.

Many years ago I made a short communication on the relatively common occurrence of a typical dream: I called it the dream of the wise baby.[1] I was referring to those dreams in which a new-born or very young infant in the cradle suddenly begins to talk and to give wise advice to its parents or other grown-ups. Now in one of my cases the split-off intelligence of the unhappy child in the analytic fantasy behaved like a separate person whose duty it was to bring help with all speed to a child almost mortally wounded. 'Quick, quick! what shall I do? They have wounded my child! There is no one to help! He is bleeding to death! He is scarcely breathing! I must bind up his wound myself. Now, child, take a deep breath or you will die. Now his heart has stopped beating! He is dying! He is dying!...' The associations which followed from the analysis of a dream now ceased, and the patient was seized with an opisthotonus and made movements as though to protect his abdomen. He was almost comatose, but I succeeded in establishing contact again and inducing him, with the help of the kind of encouragement and questions that I have described, to tell me about a sexual trauma of his early childhood. What I want to emphasize now is the light that this observation, and others like it, throw on the genesis of the narcissistic split of the self. It really seems as though, under the stress of imminent danger, part of the self splits off and becomes a psychic instance self-observing and desiring to help the self, and that possibly this happens in early —even the very earliest—childhood. We all know that children who have suffered much morally or physically take on the appearance and mien of age and sagacity. They are prone to 'mother' others also; obviously they thus extend to others the knowledge painfully acquired in coping with their own sufferings, and they become kind and helpful. It is, of course, not every such child who gets so far in mastering his own pain: many remain arrested in self-observation and hypochondria.

There is no doubt that the united forces of analysis and of observation of children have a colossal task still before them in solving problems to which the common features in the analyses of children and of adults have led us.

It might justly be said of my method with my patients that it is like 'spoiling' a child. In following it, one gives up all con-

[1] 'The Dream of the Wise Baby'. *Further Contributions*, p. 349.

sideration of one's own convenience, and indulges the patient's wishes and impulses as far as is in any way possible. The analytic session is prolonged till the emotions roused by the material are composed. The patient is not left to himself until the inevitable conflicts in the analytic situation have been solved in a reconciliatory way by removing misunderstandings and by tracing the conflicts back to infantile experiences. The analyst's behaviour is thus rather like that of an affectionate mother, who will not go to bed at night until she has talked over with the child all his current troubles, large and small, fears, bad intentions, and scruples of conscience, and has set them at rest. By this means we can induce the patient to abandon himself to all the early phases of passive object-love, in which—just like a real child on the point of sleep—he will murmur things which give us insight into his dream-world. But even in analysis, this tender relation cannot go on for ever. *L'appetit vient en mangeant.* The patient, who has become a child, goes further and further with his claims and thus tends to put off more and more the advent of the situation of reconciliation, in order to avoid being left alone, i.e. to escape the feeling of not being loved. Or else he tries, by making more and more alarming threats, to impel us to some act of punishment. The deeper and the more satisfying the transference-situation, the greater, of course, will be the traumatic effect of the moment when we are finally compelled to put an end to this unrestrained licence. The patient finds himself in the situation of frustration which we know so well. This reproduces from the past the helpless rage and ensuing paralysed state, and we have to take great pains and show much tactful understanding in order to bring back reconciliation even in these circumstances, in contrast to the lasting alienation of the same situation in childhood.

This process gives us an opportunity of observing something of the mechanism of the genesis of a trauma. First, there is the entire paralysis of all spontaneity, including all thinking activity and, on the physical side, this may even be accompanied by a condition resembling shock or coma. Then there comes the formation of a new—displaced—situation of equilibrium. If we succeed in making contact with the patient even in these phases, we shall find that, when a child feels himself abandoned, he loses, as it were, all desire for life or, as we should have to say with Freud, he turns his aggressive impulses against himself. Sometimes this process goes so far that the patient begins to have the sensations of sinking and dying. He will turn deadly pale, or fall into a condition like fainting, or there may be a general increase in muscular tension, which may be carried to the point of opisthotonus. What we here see taking place is the reproduction of the mental and physical agony which follows upon incomprehensible and intolerable woe. I will just remark in passing that these 'dying' patients also sometimes tell me interesting things about the next world and the nature of existence after death: to attempt to evaluate such statements psychologically would take us too far from our subject.

All these manifestations, often very alarming, suggested to Dr. Rickman of London, with whom I discussed them, the question whether I kept remedies at hand in order to intervene if necessary to save the patient's life. I was able to reply that I did, but that, so far, I had never had to use them. Tactful and calming words, reinforced perhaps by an encouraging pressure of the hand, or, if that is not enough, a friendly stroking of the patient's head, helped to mitigate the reaction to a point at which he again becomes accessible. In contrast to our own procedure, we then learn of the ill-advised and inappropriate actions and reactions of adults in the patient's childhood in the presence of the effects of traumatic shocks. Probably the worst way of dealing with such situations is to deny their existence, to assert that nothing has happened and that nothing is hurting the child. Sometimes he is actually beaten or scolded when he manifests traumatic paralysis of thought and movement. These are the kinds of treatment which make the trauma pathogenic. One gets the impression that children get over even severe shocks without amnesia or neurotic consequences, if the mother is at hand with understanding and tenderness and (what is most rare) with complete sincerity.

I am prepared here for the doubt whether it is really necessary first to lull the patient by over-indulgence into a delusion of unfounded security, in order to subject him later to a trauma which must be all the more painful. My excuse is that I did not bring about this process intentionally: it developed as the result of what I considered a legitimate attempt to enhance the freedom of association. I have a certain respect for such spontaneous reactions; I therefore let them appear without hindrance, and I surmise that they manifest tendencies to reproduction which should not, in my opinion, be inhibited, but should be brought to full development before we try to master them. I must leave it to educationists to decide how far similar experiences are also to be met with in the ordinary upbringing of children.

The patient's behaviour when he awakes from this infantile-traumatic abstraction is very remarkable, and, I can confidently say, highly significant. We get genuine insight here into the way in which particular parts of the body are selected for the symptoms which set in after subsequent shocks. For instance, I had a patient who had a tremendous rush of blood to the head during the traumatic convulsion, so that she turned blue in the face. She woke as though from a dream, knowing nothing of what had happened or of the causes, but merely feeling that the headache, which was one of her usual symptoms, was unusually severe. Are we not here on the track of the physiological processes which bring about hysterical displacement of a purely psychic emotional disturbance on to a bodily organ? I could easily cite half a dozen such examples. One or two may suffice. One patient, who as a child had been forsaken by father and mother and one might almost say by God and man, had been exposed to the most painful bodily and mental suffering. He awoke from a traumatic coma with one hand insensible and pallid like a corpse's; otherwise, except for the amnesia, he was fairly composed and almost at a stroke became fit for work. It was not difficult to catch in the very act, as it were, the displacement of all his suffering and even of death on to a particular part of the body: the corpse-like hand represented the whole agonized person and the outcome of his struggle in insensibility and death. Another patient began to limp, after the reproduction of the trauma. The middle toe of one foot became flaccid and obliged him to pay conscious attention to every step. Apart from the sexual symbolism of the middle toe, its behaviour expressed the warning which the patient had given himself: 'Take care before you make a step, so that the same thing does not happen again.' His native language being English, he followed up my interpretation with the remark: 'You mean that I am simply acting out the English expression: "Watch your step".'

Now if I suddenly stop here and imagine the words which are on the tips of my listeners' tongues, I seem to hear on all sides the astonished question: 'Can you really still apply the term "psycho-analysis" to what goes on in these "child-analyses" of grown-up people? You speak almost exclusively of emotional outbursts, of reproductions of traumatic scenes, so vivid as to amount to hallucination, and of spasms and paraesthesias which may safely be called hysterical attacks. What has become of the fine dissection, economic, topographical and dynamic, of the reconstruction of the symptom-formation; what of the tracing of the changing energy-cathexes of the ego and the super-ego—and all the characteristic procedure of modern analysis?' It is true that in this lecture I have confined myself almost entirely to the evaluation of the traumatic factor, but in my analyses this is not in the remotest degree what happens. For months and often years at a time, my analyses, too, proceed on the level of the conflicts between the intra-psychic forces. With obsessional neurotics, for instance, it sometimes takes a year or even longer before the emotional element secures expression at all. During these periods all that the patient and I can do, on the basis of the material which he produces, is to seek to track down intellectually the original causes of his protective measures, the ambivalence in his affective attitude and behaviour, the motives of his masochistic self-torment, and so forth. So far as my experience goes, however, there comes sooner or later (often, I admit, very late) a collapse of the intellectual superstructure and a breaking through of the fundamental situation, which after all is always primitive and strongly affective in character. Only at this point does the patient begin to repeat, and find a fresh solution for, the original conflict between the ego and its environment, as it must have taken place in his early childhood. We must not forget that a little child's reactions to pain are in the first instance always physical: only later does he learn to control his bodily expressions, those prototypes of all hysterical symptoms. It seems, indeed, that nerve specialists are right in saying that in our day it is becoming much more rare for people to produce obvious hysterias such as, only a few decades ago, were described as comparatively widespread. It seems as if, with the advance of civilization, even the neuroses have become more civilized and adult. But I believe that, if we are sufficiently patient and persevering, even firmly consolidated, purely intrapsychic mechanisms can be demolished and reduced to the level of the infantile trauma.

Another difficult question which will be immediately put to me is that of the therapeutic results. You will understand only too well that as yet I can make no definite pronouncement on this point. But I must confess two things: that my hope of considerably *shortening* the analysis by the help of relaxation and catharsis has, so far, not been fulfilled, and that this method has made the analyst's work considerably more laborious. But what it has done—and I trust will do still more—is to deepen our insight into the workings of the human mind in health and in disease and to entitle us to hope that any therapeutic success achieved, being based on these deeper foundations, will have a better prospect of permanence.

And now let me conclude with a question of practical importance. Is it necessary and possible in *training*-analyses, likewise, to penetrate to this deep infantile stratum? If so, the indefinite length of my analyses leads to tremendous practical difficulties. And yet I believe that anyone who has the ambition to wish to understand and help others should not shrink from this great sacrifice. Even those who undergo analysis for purely professional reasons must thus submit to becoming slightly hysterical, i.e. slightly ill, during its course, and it becomes evident then that even character-formation is to be regarded as a remote consequence of very strong infantile traumas. But I think that the cathartic result of being submerged for a time in neurosis and childhood has ultimately an invigorating effect, and that, if the work is carried right through, it does no sort of harm. In any case the procedure is much less dangerous than the self-sacrificing experiments of many medical men, who have studied the effects of various infections and poisons upon their own persons.

If the line of thought which I have endeavoured to present to you to-day comes at any time to receive recognition, the credit will in fairness have to be shared between me and my patients and colleagues. And of course, also with those analysts of children whom I have already named. I shall think myself happy if I have succeeded in making at least a beginning towards more intimate co-operation with them.

I should not be surprised if this paper, like some others which I have published of late years, gave you the impression of a certain *naïveté* in my outlook. It may strike you as odd that anyone, after working at analysis for twenty-five years, should suddenly begin to regard with wonder the fact of psychic traumas. It is like an engine-driver I knew, who when pensioned off after fifty years' service, used to go down to the station every afternoon and gaze in wonder at a train just going out, often exclaiming: 'Isn't a locomotive a marvellous invention!' Perhaps this tendency or ability to contemplate naïvely what has long been familiar is also something I have learnt from our teacher, who, during one of our unforgettable summer holidays together, surprised me one morning by announcing: 'You know, Ferenczi, dreams really are wish-fulfilments!' He went on to tell me his latest dream, which certainly was a striking confirmation of his inspired theory of dreams.

I hope you will not forthwith reject what I have told you, but will defer your judgement until you have procured some experience under the same conditions. In any case I thank you for the courteous patience with which you have listened to my remarks.

XII

FREUD'S INFLUENCE ON MEDICINE[1]
(1933)

IF WE wish to assess in a constructive manner the significance of one man to science or to a branch of science, it is of importance to describe first the state of the development of science before the man in question appeared, and also the changes brought about by his influence. But even such a description would hardly satisfy the deeper desire for causality. We would have to assess in detail whether existent material had merely been synthesized by a constructive mind or whether an intellectual light had, like a meteor, struck an unsuspecting and unprepared world. Finally, we cannot evade asking to what degree chance and to what extent rare personal qualities are to be considered the decisive factors in the discovery of a new science and its formulation into theory. When the investigation has been carried up to this point, there still remains the task of supplementing the contributions with a kind of personality study.

To portray Freud's influence on medicine, I must limit myself to remarks on these problems, but above all, I must expound the accidental factors. Without doubt it was an accident that the Viennese physician, Dr. Josef Breuer, had an intelligent female patient under hypnotic treatment, who observed in herself the favourable effect of talking about the contents of her fantasies and called her physician's attention to her observation. In a strict sense, *she* is the discoverer of the original cathartic method. It was another accident which later brought Sigmund Freud into personal contact with Breuer. But it was certainly no accident that Breuer, despite his profound insight into the importance of the discovery from the psychological as well as from the pathological angle, soon lost interest in these problems and no longer associated himself with Freud or his further studies. It is

[1] Published in full in *PsA Bewegung*, 1933. A somewhat abridged translation appeared in *Psycho-Analysis to-day*, ed. S. Lorand. Covici-Friede, New York, 1933. George Allen & Unwin Ltd., London, 1948.

no longer a secret to what qualities in him Freud owes his perseverance and his results in the scientific development of psycho-analysis. Of these qualities I would select for mention his objectivity, which remained unaffected even in the face of the problems of sex. Strange as it sounds, it is nevertheless true that, before Freud, even those who considered themselves enlightened were not free of moral scruples in sex matters; they left untouched the psychological side of love-life.

Only two courageous men had dared, at least descriptively, to make the most repulsive peculiarities of sexual life the subject of extensive study. These were the Viennese Krafft-Ebing and the Englishman Havelock Ellis. Their example was soon followed by some German and Swiss scholars. The first attempts of Freud at finding an explanation for Breuer's discovery soon led him to the investigation of sexual problems. His friends and colleagues, who recognized his genius only as long as he concerned himself with such moral and harmless questions as aphasia and cerebral infantile paralysis, took to their heels and deserted him. Soon even Breuer joined the ranks of those who did not wish to collaborate with Freud in his study of these unaesthetic, hence unedifying things, and from then on Freud stood alone. There began what deserves to be called the heroic period in his life, that in which he produced *The Interpretation of Dreams*, the permanent foundation of all of his later creation. To-day, more than thirty years after its first publication, we still see the rejecting attitude of the rest of the world, which certainly points to the fact that psycho-analysis did not come up to the expectations of scientific and medical circles.

Another characteristic which predestined Freud to become the discoverer of psycho-analysis was his unrelenting criticism of the shortcomings of the therapeutic ability and theoretical knowledge of that day, which showed itself in inadequacy and perplexity when dealing with neuroses. He became convinced of the futility of electro-therapy for dealing with the neuroses at a time when, almost as to-day, the faradic and galvanic apparatus was the physician's chief weapon for dealing with the so-called functional diseases. The transient and unreliable occasional results obtained by hypnotic and suggestive influence prompted Freud to give up these methods as well. It would have been easy, particularly in the medical atmosphere in which he grew up, to accept the smug idea of medical nihilism, and to enjoy without further worry his rapidly growing neurological practice. But through a particular trait in Freud, his zealous drive for truth, which did not permit him to halt at mere criticism of the prevailing order of things, and his inquisitive mind gave him no rest until the questions which he had once raised had been solved, and that wholly without external aid. The work involved seemed impossible to cope with, for it was a matter of solving a problem with many unknowns. As Breuer and Freud had already recognized, the causes of neurotic symptoms were supposed to lie in the unconscious psychic life, which is inaccessible to direct examination. As we have just mentioned, Freud deliberately dropped the methods of hypnosis and suggestion which permitted partial access to this unconscious system. He believed that, measured by the standard of psychological knowledge of that time, the efficacy of these methods must appear inexplicable or even mystical. All knowledge gathered by their use would bear the marks of the mystical and would not meet the scientific requirements of clarity. Yet Freud had success with the improbable; the apparently unfathomable was exposed by his *method of free association.*

It is not easy to define the conception of genius, but it seems to me that the term can appropriately be used of one who finds a solution to a hopeless situation of the kind outlined above. I do not hesitate to say that with this idea of Freud the future of psychology and all its applications have been settled. It is no exaggeration to attribute to this idea, which arose in Freud's mind, all later developments in these sciences. At the moment Freud's main idea was conceived modern psychology was born.

It then became necessary to sift the enormous amount of material which the new method had collected and to classify it scientifically. Whether for good or for evil, Freud soon had to formulate a skeletal framework for his theory, a construction which, though it has been many times altered, modified, and remodelled, remains sound in its main structure up to the present day. This construction is what is called metapsychology.

Briefly, I shall try to explain what we understand by this. Freud could not explain the origin of neurotic symptoms without imagining mental functions in some spatial system where forces of a certain intensity and quality were interacting. The first topical division in mental functions was the separation of the conscious and unconscious systems, and the first idea of their dynamics was that there was a conflict between the forces operating in each system. The outcome of this conflict depended on the economic relation between the two mental forces, yet the sum total of the two could be considered as practically constant. We need not be startled by the fact that the uninitiated regard this construction as fantastic; if we wish, we may call it a scientific fantasy. But every scientific theory is fantasy, and it is serviceable as such just as long as it meets practical requirements and agrees with the facts of experience. Freud's metapsychological system does this fully. It places us in a position to understand the disturbances in the mental life of a patient as a result of such and similar conflicts, and even enables us to influence favourably the faulty distribution of the two forces. Freud's later work caused this very simple system to be superseded by a much more complicated one. He was able to trace the motor forces behind the mental life to their biological sources and to confirm their analogy with physical driving forces. Unperturbed by practical considerations, he did not permit himself either to be led astray into denying the multiformity which manifested itself here, nor did the illusion of a premature system of unification cause him to abandon his ideas, which, though they showed gaps and were not fully satisfactory, were yet in accord with reality.

I do not hesitate to say that this construction of Freud's is in itself of the highest scientific importance. It means nothing less than the first attempt to solve something pertaining to the physics and physiology of mental phenomena. The only means to this end was penetrating psycho-analytic research into the mental life of the sick and the normal person. Up to this time anatomy and physiology had contributed absolutely no information about the finer mental processes. Medical science stared rigidly, as if hypnotized, into the microscope, and anticipated, from a knowledge of the development and the course of nerve fibres in the brain, the 'how' of mental functioning. But these developments showed no more than the crudest facts about motor and sensory functions. Since no neurosis or functional psychosis revealed any changes in the brain, medical science was at a loss what to do about these pathologic conditions. The mistake lay in the fact that physicians before Freud's time were trained one-sidedly and materialistically. The striking mental facts which play such an important part in our personal lives, as well as in the lives of the patients, were considered as a kind of reality of minor importance to which no serious-minded scientist could apply himself. Psychology *per se* was abandoned and left to dilettanti and littérateurs. Dislike of unfounded generalization guarded Freud from the error of uniting prematurely the mental and physical into materialistic monism, as was customary in other quarters. His honesty of spirit brought him to recognize the fact that mental life was accessible only through introspective methods, that is, from the subjective side; further, that facts that become accessible through subjective methods must be fully accepted as psychic reality. Thus Freud became a dualist, a term which most physical scientists have regarded, and still regard, as almost opprobrious. I do not believe that Freud objected essentially to the monistic conception of knowledge. His dualism says only that unification is not possible at present, nor in the near future, and perhaps cannot be ever achieved completely. On no account should we confuse Freud's dualism with the naïve separation of a living organism into a body and a mind. He is always mindful of the anatomic-physiological facts concerning the nervous system. He pursues his psychological investigations up to the point of human impulses, which he looks upon as a dividing line between the mental and the physical, a line which he does not believe psychological interpretation should cross, because as yet it seems incompetent to do so. On the other hand, just as his metapsychological system, which is constructed on the pattern of the reflex arc, shows, he must rely on analogies to natural science even in his purely psychological investigations. To describe this form of dualism I must coin a new word, *utraquism*, and I believe that this method of research in natural as well as mental science well merits wide applications.

One of the most remarkable achievements of Freud's psychology is that it not only gives the content, i.e. a dictionary of the unconscious, but also formulates the rules of the peculiar grammar and primitive logic which reign there, so that the strange productions of the dream, the slips of everyday life, and neurotic and psychotic symptoms become meaningful and intelligible. One must admit that a physician who understands the language of the psychotic and neurotic patient and who can use it, so to speak, etiologically and etymologically, faces these sicknesses with a very different understanding from that of the natural scientist who is little concerned about the origins of any individual phenomenon and who, in the treatment of this condition, is guided exclusively by his artist-like intuition. No one will wish to deny that even before Freud there were distinguished psycho-therapists who in the treatment of psychosis and neurosis were surprisingly efficient and successful. But their art could not be learned; the fortunate ones who possessed such talents could not, even with the best intentions, teach the manner of their approach. The relation between patient and physician would be called by the psycho-analyst a dialogue between two unconscious minds. The unconscious of the physician understood the unconscious of the patient and then permitted the appropriate answer or the idea of a proper remedy to arise in the physician's conscious mind. The progress which psycho-analysis has brought to medical practice lies chiefly in that it has changed this therapeutic art into a science which can be learned by every intelligent physician with as much ease or difficulty as he learns surgery or internal medicine. Naturally there will always be artists in psycho-analysis, as there are in the other branches of healing. But presupposing the proper preparation and adherence to the theories laid down by Freud in his works, there will be no obstacle in the way towards such training, even to the degree demanded of the specialist.

Those of practical disposition may have become impatient by now, not having had enough information about the practical results of psycho-analysis. Are we able through its application to obtain more thorough and more frequent results and in shorter time when all other psycho-therapeutic measures fail? Is it the one form of psycho-therapy which leads to happiness, and are there no cases where other methods are preferable? In order to answer these questions freely I will disillusion those who believe that the motto of the surgeon, *Cito, tuto et jucunde*, is applicable to analysis. Analysis is no quick method of cure, but rather a very prolonged one. Usually an analysis lasts for months, in severe cases years. This can hardly be called a matter of convenience. It promises no absolute painlessness; in fact tolerance of mental pain which cannot be avoided and which has a real basis is one of the ends it hopes to bring about in the patient. One can also permit oneself no more than a surmise about the certainty of the final result. In no event does psycho-analysis belong to that group of enviable methods such as hypnotism which can simply blow symptoms away. It places no faith in the permanence of such methods; it is certain that the dust raised by such a process must settle somewhere. It rather seeks radically to clean up the psychopathic foci. If the proverb, *Si duo faciunt idem non est idem*, applies anywhere, it is here. Psycho-analysis acknowledges that it is not suitable in all cases of neurosis; other forms of psycho-therapy also have their field of application. At present it is not adapted to mass treatment. What it does anticipate for the future, however, is that the other methods will become permeated by its spirit. As a hypnotist, a psycho-therapist, or a director of an asylum, the trained analyst will have much better results and will show much better judgement than he who makes no effort to discover the probable etiology of the psychogenic symptoms from the data at hand. In this sense we can confidently prophesy that no form of psycho-therapy will be able permanently to avoid being influenced by Freud's ideas. This is actually true to-day to a large extent, even though the process is masked under various devices.

The great changes which have taken place in psychiatry since Freud's concepts penetrated the walls of asylums are well-known facts. No one is satisfied any longer with the traditional descriptive method of labelling cases according to their symptomatic grouping. There is a need for intelligible relationships and connexions which certainly were not conspicuous in pre-Freudian literature. We can predict that the mental hospital will be transformed into a psycho-therapeutic institution in which psycho-analytically trained physicians will occupy themselves with each case every day, and, if possible, for an hour a day. No matter how difficult it is to attain this ideal, it will hardly be possible to shun it. What the old master of French psychiatry, Pinel, following the goodness of his heart, accomplished externally—releasing the psychotic from the unnecessary chains—Freud has repeated, starting from the inside. Owing to his discovery, the symptoms of the insane have ceased to be a collection of abnormalities which by the unthinking were declared to be crazy, ridiculous, and meaningless. The psychotic also speaks a language which is intelligible to the properly trained expert. Thus the deep chasm which exists between the mentally normal and the mentally deranged person has been bridged for the first time.

The great transformation in the study of the neuroses and psychoses which Freud not only inaugurated but brought to a kind of completion in more than thirty years of indefatigable work, may be compared to the transformation in internal medicine through the clinical methods of percussion, auscultation, measurement of temperature, X-rays, bacteriology and chemistry. Before these discoveries there were sensitive, successful physicians too. But to-day no physician of normal mentality would depend exclusively on his keen senses, and intentionally fail to convince himself objectively of the correctness or incorrectness of his provisional diagnosis. Psycho-analysis has raised knowledge about the neuroses and psychoses to a new scientific level, and this work can never now be undone. Of course there are many ways in which medicine can make use of the Freudian ideas. One would be for psycho-analysis, as a distinct science, to be further suppressed and repressed so that its fruitful ideas had to seep along all possible underground routes into all branches of science. In this way it would be ploughed under like a fertilizer, so that the moral and aesthetic sense of gentlemanly scholars would not be injured by its unappetizing aspects. Thus they would be permitted to enjoy in composure the beautiful blossoms nourished by it. But to consider that this is a serious possibility is unbelievable. It was the good fortune of the discoverer of psycho-analysis to live long enough to establish his work on a firm basis and to protect it from these numerous attempts at dissolution.

Freud was also able to bring sufficiently near to completion the neglected research into the hidden powers behind instinctual life so that finally he could turn to the more obvious and acceptable function of consciousness. I refer to his beginning in scientific ego psychology, which finally contained, in substantial form, explanations of the higher psychic functions—intelligence, conscience, morality, idealism, etc. Such explanations were sorely needed by his contemporaries. Freud certainly did not occupy himself with the aberrations of sexual life and with the animal aggressive instincts because of a personal preference, but because there was no other Hercules to bring order into this Augean stable. He was a simple investigator of reality; social views and prejudices concerned him little. Yet from the very beginning he recognized that besides instinctual life the power of repressing forces, social adjustment, and sublimation of the instincts were factors of equal if not greater importance in his studies. The consistent overlooking of this point can be attributed only to the blind hate or blind fear of his contemporaries. The result, however, was that some said he delved into the dirty instincts; others branded his teachings as 'pansexuality' and 'a dangerous psychic epidemic'.

But the day of these reactions of fury seems to be coming to its close. Even though they speak timidly, more and more voices, distinguished ones among them, at least partially confirm Freud's teachings. It is striking that such confirmations come not only from psychiatrists, but from circles of clinicians, gynaecologists, pediatricians, dermatologists, and so on. They state that many a problematic case in their own fields of speciality has become intelligible and accessible to therapy only because of a psycho-analytic explanation. Consideration of unconscious psychic factors in the pathogenesis of disease seems to spread almost like an epidemic. Many distinguished physicians occupy themselves intensively with analytic therapy in organic disease. To be sure, these are only promising beginnings, but their future significance cannot be denied. To medical science which has been segmented into numerous specialities, psycho-analysis has been a benefactor, for it reminds one, in every form of disease, to treat the patient as well as the condition. This need has always been recognized in principle, but rarely in practice, because of the want of real psychological knowledge. To use a gross exaggeration, we might say that heretofore medicine has acted as though a patient were anencephalous and as though the highest comprehending powers, those which we call mental, had nothing to say in the matter of the struggle of the organs against the disease. It is certainly time that we should take seriously the expression 'the individual treatment of the patient'.

The separatist movements which manifest themselves in all great ideas did not leave psycho-analysts untouched. But it is out of place to go into them in detail here. Suffice it to say that the importance of the individual schismatics is small compared with Freud's. It is unfair to mention their names along with his, as so many scientific publications often do. The whole matter reminds one of the satirical words of that thoughtful and original Viennese professor of pathology, Samuel Stricker, who supplemented the communications of his own discoveries with the remark: 'But now it is Mr. Modifier's turn.' This does not imply that such efforts contain nothing of value or interest.

All institutes solely devoted to psycho-analysis owe their establishment to private initiative. Occasionally they have had to combat the indifference, even the hostility, of official groups. Everywhere the universities have been the most conservative in their attitude. Nothing illustrates this better than the fact that the creator of psycho-analysis was never approached to give an official course of study, though he was awarded the honorary title of professor for his accomplishments.

It was a divine inspiration which prompted Freud to preface his *Interpretation of Dreams* with the prophetic phrase, *Flectere si nequeo superos, Acheronta movebo*. By this he meant to characterize the scientific fact that the most important problems of the human mind are attacked only from the depths of the unconscious. But the motto may be interpreted in another sense. The fortresses of science still resist the intrusion of psycho-analysis into the medical curriculum. It will be some time before the knocking of the medical world at large at the gates of the universities becomes louder, because to-day it does not amount to more than a low rumble from the depths. Only then will psycho-analysis be able to take its rightful place in the medical curriculum.

Perhaps this day will come sooner than many think. One need be no talented prophet to foretell that one day numerous courses will compensate psycho-analysis for previous contempt. The successors of the present professors of medicine will then do justice to the real importance of Freud. I can state that before Freud, medicine had been taught as a purely natural science. One attended a technical high school for physical health, from which one graduated with much theoretical and practical knowledge, yet ignorant of the human psyche. But out in the world of medical practice the psychological factor in therapy is as important as the objective finding in the organs. I can imagine how much effort and pain might have been spared had I as a student been taught the art of dealing with transference and resistance. I envy the medical student of the near future who will be taught this. The humanization of the medical curriculum will become an absolute necessity, and in the end it will come about.

A particular difficulty in learning psycho-analysis lies in the fact that its method, as we have said, is dualistic or utraquistic. Accurate observation of the objective attitude of the patient including what he says, that is his so-called 'behaviour', is not enough. Psycho-analysis demands of the physician untiring sensitivity to all of the patient's ideational associations, his emotions, and his unconscious processes. For this it is necessary that the physician himself have a flexible, plastic mind. He can attain this only by being analysed himself. How the future medical student will acquire this profound self-knowledge is a difficult question to answer. The training of a psycho-analytic specialist requires, apart from theoretical study, a didactic analysis of at least a year's duration. One cannot demand so much of the practitioner of the future, yet this sometimes painful process cannot be dispensed with altogether. It is an old, well-known fact that diabetic physicians are most sensitive while treating diabetic patients, and the same is true of the tuberculous physician. The Viennese professor Oser who lectured on gastric pathology told us that he was interested in the subject because of his own weak stomach. Naturally we cannot expect the future physician to expose himself to and to contract all manner of infectious diseases in order better to understand and treat patients with such diseases. Yet psycho-analysis demands something of this kind when it requires a high mental sensitivity on the part of the physician to the abnormalities of the patient. The difference between this situation and the one just mentioned lies, however, in the fact that each of us has, according to the discoveries of psycho-analysis, a virtual potentiality for sympathetic sensitivity in his own unconscious. We need only remove the acquired resistance to this unconscious power to make it conscious, so that it becomes serviceable in the understanding of the patient. I am convinced that efforts in such directions are more than worth while. Scientifically founded knowledge of mankind will help to bring back to the general practitioner the authority which he has lost as adviser to the individual, to his family, and to society, when he finds himself in difficult situations. I trust that he will then remember the man whose life work was dedicated to restoring his status and dignity.

A few more words about the geographical extension of psycho-analysis, or as Hoche called it, the psycho-analysis plague. Completely misunderstanding the essentials of the discovery, some particularly vicious antagonists of Freud asserted that psycho-analysis, or, as they termed it, sexual psycho-analysis, could have been produced only in the frivolous, gay atmosphere of Vienna. One comment from an Anglo-Saxon country was: 'Perhaps one dreams such things in Austria's capital city, but our dreams are more respectable.' Psycho-analysis claims that repression of libidinal tendencies is the cause of neuroses. Hence, if Freud's opponents were right, such a teaching ought to have arisen in a land where prudery and repression find themselves at home. But in reality countries not particularly characterized by prudery were most resistant to the recognition of psycho-analysis. France, Austria, and Italy are such countries where psycho-analysis met with the greatest opposition, while England and America, countries with a particularly rigid sex morality, showed themselves much more receptive.

Some did not miss the opportunity to judge Freud's work from a racial angle and to attribute it to his Semitic blood. It is said that Lord Balfour, in dedicating the new University of Jerusalem, called Freud one of the representatives of intellectual Judaism. But many others referred to his Semitic origins with much less goodwill. I do not believe that our knowledge of racial psychology has developed to a point where we can say anything definite as to the soundness of these remarks. At any rate, such comments are rather an honour to the Jewish race than a denigration of Freud.

In conclusion, I wish to point out that Freud tore down the rigid wall of demarcation between natural and mental science. Psycho-analysis has not only promoted mutual understanding between physician and patient, but it has also made natural and mental science comprehensible to each other where before they were strange and foreign. To attain such an end Freud had to renounce that feeling of self-complacency which characterized the physician of the past. He began by accepting the saying of Schweniger, that 'every human being must be a physician and every physician must be a human being'.

Freud's influence on medicine signifies a formal change, a radical stimulus to the development of this science. Potentiality for such development might have existed for a long time, yet for its translation into act it had to await the coming of a personality like Freud.

XIII

CONFUSION OF TONGUES BETWEEN ADULTS AND THE CHILD[1]
(1933)

The Language of Tenderness and of Passion[2]

It was a mistake to try to confine the all too wide theme of the exogenous origin of character formations and neuroses within a Congress paper. I shall, therefore, content myself with a short extract from what I would have had to say on that subject. Perhaps it will be best if I start by telling you how I have come to the problem expressed in the title of this paper. In the address given to the Viennese Psycho-Analytic Society on the occasion of Professor Freud's seventy-fifth birthday, I reported on a regression in technique (and partly also in the theory) of the neuroses to which I was forced by certain bad or incomplete results with my patients. By that I mean the recent, more emphatic stress on the traumatic factors in the pathogenesis of the neuroses which had been unjustly neglected in recent years. Insufficiently deep exploration of the exogenous factor leads to the danger of resorting prematurely to explanations—often too facile explanations—in terms of 'disposition' and 'constitution'.

The—I should like to say imposing—phenomena, the almost hallucinatory repetitions of traumatic experiences which began to accumulate in my daily practice, seemed to justify the hope that by this abreaction large quantities of repressed affects might obtain acceptance by the conscious mind and that the formation of new symptoms, especially when the superstructure

[1] German original in *Int. Z. f. Psa.* (1933), **19**, 5. English translation in *Int. J. of PsA.* (1949), **30**, 225.
Paper read at the Twelfth International Psycho-Analytical Congress, Wiesbaden, September, 1932.

[2] The original title of the paper as announced was 'The Passions of Adults and their Influence on the Sexual and Character Development of Children'. Published in *Int. Z. f. Psa.* (1933), **19**, 5–15 and subsequently in *Bausteine zur Psychoanalyse*, Vol. III. Berne, 1939.

of the affects had been sufficiently loosened by the analytic work, might be ended. This hope, unfortunately, was only very imperfectly fulfilled and some of my patients caused me a great deal of worry and embarrassment. The repetition, encouraged by the analysis, turned out to be too good. It is true that there was a marked improvement in some of the symptoms; on the other hand, however, these patients began to suffer from nocturnal attacks of anxiety, even from severe nightmares, and the analytic session degenerated time and again into an attack of anxiety hysteria. Although we were able to analyse conscientiously the threatening symptoms of such an attack, which seemed to convince and reassure the patient, the expected permanent success failed to materialize and the next morning brought the same complaints about the dreadful night, while in the analytic session, repetition of the trauma occurred. In this embarrassing position I tried to console myself in the usual way —that the patient had a much too forceful resistance or that he suffered from such severe repressions that abreaction and emergence into consciousness could only occur piecemeal. However, as the state of the patient, even after a considerable time, did not change in essentials, I had to give free rein to self-criticism. I started to listen to my patients when, in their attacks, they called me insensitive, cold, even hard and cruel, when they reproached me with being selfish, heartless, conceited, when they shouted at me: 'Help! Quick! Don't let me perish helplessly!' Then I began to test my conscience in order to discover whether, despite all my conscious good intentions, there might after all be some truth in these accusations. I wish to add that such periods of anger and hatred occurred only exceptionally; very often the sessions ended with a striking, almost helpless compliance and willingness to accept my interpretations. This, however, was so transitory that I came to realize that even these apparently willing patients felt hatred and rage, and I began to encourage them not to spare me in any way. This encouragement, too, failed to achieve much, for most of my patients energetically refused to accept such an interpretative demand although it was well supported by analytic material.

Gradually, then, I came to the conclusion that the patients

have an exceedingly refined sensitivity for the wishes, tendencies, whims, sympathies and antipathies of their analyst, even if the analyst is completely unaware of this sensitivity. Instead of contradicting the analyst or accusing him of errors and blindness, the patients *identify themselves with him*; only in rare moments of an hysteroid excitement, i.e. in an almost unconscious state, can they pluck up enough courage to make a protest; normally they do not allow themselves to criticize us, such a criticism does not even become conscious in them unless we give them special permission or even encouragement to be so bold. That means that we must discern not only the painful events of their past from their associations, but also—and much more often than hitherto supposed—their repressed or suppressed criticism of us.

Here, however, we meet with considerable resistances, this time resistances in ourselves as well as in our patients. Above all, we ourselves must have been really well analysed, right down to 'rock bottom'. We must have learnt to recognize all our unpleasant external and internal character traits in order that we may be really prepared to face all those forms of hidden hatred and contempt that can be so cunningly disguised in our patients' associations.

This leads to the side issue—the analysis of the analyst—which is becoming more and more important. Do not let us forget that the deep-reaching analysis of a neurosis needs many years, while the average training analysis lasts only a few months, or at most, one to one and a half years.[1] This may lead to an impossible situation, namely, that our patients gradually become better analysed than we ourselves are, which means that although they may show signs of such superiority, they are unable to express it in words; indeed, they deteriorate into an extreme submissiveness obviously because of this inability or because of a fear of occasioning displeasure in us by their criticism.

A great part of the repressed criticism felt by our patients is directed towards what might be called *professional hypocrisy*. We greet the patient with politeness when he enters our room, ask him to start with his associations and promise him faithfully that we will listen attentively to him, give our undivided inter-

[1] Written 1932.

est to his well-being and to the work needed for it. In reality, however, it may happen that we can only with difficulty tolerate certain external or internal features of the patient, or perhaps we feel unpleasantly disturbed in some professional or personal affair by the analytic session. Here, too, I cannot see any other way out than to make the source of the disturbance in us fully conscious and to discuss it with the patient, admitting it perhaps not only as a possibility but as a fact.

It is remarkable that such renunciation of the 'professional hypocrisy'—a hypocrisy hitherto regarded as unavoidable—instead of hurting the patient, led to a marked easing off in his condition. The traumatic-hysterical attack, even if it recurred, became considerably milder, tragic events of the past could be reproduced *in thoughts* without creating again a loss of mental balance; in fact the level of the patient's personality seemed to have been considerably raised.

Now what brought about this state of affairs? Something had been left unsaid in the relation between physician and patient, something insincere, and its frank discussion freed, so to speak, the tongue-tied patient; the admission of the analyst's error produced confidence in his patient. It would almost seem to be of advantage occasionally to commit blunders in order to admit afterwards the fault to the patient. This advice is, however, quite superfluous; we commit blunders often enough, and one highly intelligent patient became justifiably indignant, saying: 'It would have been much better if you could have avoided blunders altogether. Your vanity, doctor, would like to make profit even out of your errors.'

The discovery and the solution of this purely technical problem revealed some previously hidden or scarcely noticed material. The analytical situation—i.e. the restrained coolness, the professional hypocrisy and—hidden behind it but never revealed—a dislike of the patient which, nevertheless, he felt in all his being—such a situation was not essentially different from that which in his childhood had led to the illness. When, in addition to the strain caused by this analytical situation, we imposed on the patient the further burden of reproducing the original trauma, we created a situation that was indeed unbearable. Small wonder that our effort produced no better results than the original trauma. The setting free of his critical feelings, the willingness on our part to admit our mistakes and the honest endeavour to avoid them in future, all these go to create in the patient a confidence in the analyst. *It is this confidence that establishes the contrast between the present and the unbearable traumatogenic past*, the contrast which is absolutely necessary for the patient in order to enable him to re-experience the past no longer as hallucinatory reproduction but as an objective memory. Suppressed criticisms felt by my patients, e.g. the discovery with uncanny clairvoyance, of the aggressive features of my 'active therapy', of the professional hypocrisy in the forcing of relaxation, taught me to recognize and to control the exaggerations in both directions. I am no less grateful to those of my patients who taught me that we are more than willing to adhere rigidly to certain theoretical constructions and to leave unnoticed facts on one side that would injure our complacency and authority. In any case, I learnt the cause of my inability to influence the hysterical explosions and this discovery eventually made success possible. It happened to me as it did to that wise woman whose friend could not be wakened from her narcoleptic sleep by any amount of shaking and shouting, to whom there came, suddenly, the idea of shouting 'Rock-a-bye baby'. After that the patient started to do everything she was asked to do. We talk a good deal in analysis of regressions into the infantile, but we do not really believe to what great extent we are right; we talk a lot about the splitting of the personality, but do not seem sufficiently to appreciate the depth of these splits. If we keep up our cool, educational attitude even *vis-à-vis* an opisthotonic patient, we tear to shreds the last thread that connects him to us. The patient gone off into his trance is *a child indeed* who no longer reacts to intellectual explanations, only perhaps to maternal friendliness; without it he feels lonely and abandoned in his greatest need, i.e. in the same unbearable situation which at one time led to a splitting of his mind and eventually to his illness; thus it is no wonder that the patient cannot but repeat now the symptom-formation exactly as he did at the time when his illness started.

I may remind you that patients do not react to theatrical phrases, but only to real sincere sympathy. Whether they recognize the truth by the intonation or colour of our voice or by the words we use or in some other way, I cannot tell. In any case, they show a remarkable, almost clairvoyant knowledge about the thoughts and emotions that go on in their analyst's mind. To deceive a patient in this respect seems to be hardly possible and if one tries to do so, it leads only to bad consequences.

Now allow me to report on some new ideas which this more intimate relation to my patients helped me to reach.

I obtained above all new corroborative evidence for my supposition that the trauma, especially the sexual trauma, as the pathogenic factor cannot be valued highly enough. Even children of very respectable, sincerely puritanical families, fall victim to real violence or rape much more often than one had dared to suppose. Either it is the parents who try to find a substitute gratification in this pathological way for their frustration, or it is people thought to be trustworthy such as relatives (uncles, aunts, grandparents), governesses or servants, who misuse the ignorance and the innocence of the child. The immediate explanation—that these are only sexual fantasies of the child, a kind of hysterical lying—is unfortunately made invalid by the number of such confessions, e.g. of assaults upon children, committed by patients actually in analysis. That is why I was not surprised when recently a philanthropically-minded teacher told me, despairingly, that in a short time he had discovered that in five upper class families the governesses were living a regular sexual life with boys of nine to eleven years old.

A typical way in which incestuous seductions may occur is this: an adult and a child love each other, the child nursing the playful fantasy of taking the role of mother to the adult. This play may assume erotic forms but remains, nevertheless, on the level of tenderness. It is not so, however, with pathological adults, especially if they have been disturbed in their balance and self-control by some misfortune or by the use of intoxicating drugs. They mistake the play of children for the desires of a sexually mature person or even allow themselves—irrespective of any consequences—to be carried away. The real rape of girls who have hardly grown out of the age of infants, similar sexual acts of mature women with boys, and also enforced homosexual acts, are more frequent occurrences than has hitherto been assumed.

It is difficult to imagine the behaviour and the emotions of children after such violence. One would expect the first impulse to be that of reaction, hatred, disgust and energetic refusal. 'No, no, I do not want it, it is much too violent for me, it hurts, leave me alone,' this or something similar would be the immediate reaction if it had not been paralysed by enormous anxiety. These children feel physically and morally helpless, their personalities are not sufficiently consolidated in order to be able to protest, even if only in thought, for the overpowering force and authority of the adult makes them dumb and can rob them of their senses. *The same anxiety, however, if it reaches a certain maximum, compels them to subordinate themselves like automata to the will of the aggressor, to divine each one of his desires and to gratify these; completely oblivious of themselves they identify themselves with the aggressor.* Through the identification, or let us say, introjection of the aggressor, he disappears as part of the external reality, and becomes intra- instead of extra-psychic; the intra-psychic is then subjected, in a dream-like state as is the traumatic trance, to the primary process, i.e. according to the pleasure principle it can be modified or changed by the use of positive or negative hallucinations. In any case the attack as a rigid external reality ceases to exist and in the traumatic trance the child succeeds in maintaining the previous situation of tenderness.

The most important change, produced in the mind of the child by the anxiety-fear-ridden identification with the adult partner, is *the introjection of the guilt feelings of the adult* which makes hitherto harmless play appear as a punishable offence.

When the child recovers from such an attack, he feels enormously confused, in fact, split—innocent and culpable at the same time—and his confidence in the testimony of his own senses is broken. Moreover, the harsh behaviour of the adult partner tormented and made angry by his remorse renders the child still more conscious of his own guilt and still more ashamed. Almost always the perpetrator behaves as though nothing had happened, and consoles himself with the thought: 'Oh, it is only a child, he does not know anything, he will forget it all.' Not infrequently after such events, the seducer becomes over-moralistic or religious and endeavours to save the soul of the child by severity.

Usually the relation to a second adult—in the case quoted above, the mother—is not intimate enough for the child to find help there; timid attempts towards this end are refused by her as nonsensical. The misused child changes into a mechanical, obedient automaton or becomes defiant, but is unable to account for the reasons of his defiance. His sexual life remains undeveloped or assumes perverted forms. There is no need for me to enter into the details of neuroses and psychoses which may follow such events. For our theory this assumption, however, is highly important—namely, that *the weak and undeveloped personality reacts to sudden unpleasure not by defence, but by anxiety-ridden identification and by introjection of the menacing person or aggressor.* Only with the help of this hypothesis can I understand why my patients refused so obstinately to follow my advice to react to unjust or unkind treatment with pain or with hatred and defence. One part of their personalities, possibly the nucleus, got stuck in its development at a level where it was unable to use the *alloplastic* way of reaction but could only react in an *autoplastic* way by a kind of mimicry. Thus we arrive at the assumption of a mind which consists only of the id and super-ego, and which therefore lacks the ability to maintain itself with stability in face of unpleasure—in the same way as the immature find it unbearable to be left alone, without maternal care and without a considerable amount of tenderness. Here we have to revert to some of the ideas developed by Freud a long time ago according to which the capacity for object-love must be preceded by a stage of identification.

I should like to call this the stage of passive object-love or of tenderness. Vestiges of object-love are already apparent here but only in a playful way in fantasies. Thus almost without exception we find the hidden play of taking the place of the parent of the same sex in order to be married to the other parent, but it must be stressed that this is merely fantasy; in reality the child—

ren would not want to, in fact they cannot do without tenderness, especially that which comes from the mother. If *more love or love of a different kind from that which they need*, is forced upon the children in the stage of tenderness, it may lead to pathological consequences in the same way as the *frustration or withdrawal of love* quoted elsewhere in this connexion. It would lead us too far from our immediate subject to go into details of the neuroses and the character mal-developments which may follow the precocious super-imposition of love, passionate and guilt-laden on an immature guiltless child. The consequence must needs be that of confusion of tongues, which is emphasized in the title of this address.

Parents and adults, in the same way as we analysts, ought to learn to be constantly aware that behind the submissiveness or even the adoration, just as behind the transference of love, of our children, patients and pupils, there lies hidden an ardent desire to get rid of this oppressive love. If we can help the child, the patient or the pupil to give up the reaction of identification, and to ward off the over-burdening transference, then we may be said to have reached the goal of raising the personality to a higher level.

I should like to point briefly to a further extension of our knowledge made possible by these observations. We have long held that not only superimposed love but also unbearable punishments lead to fixations. The solution of this apparent paradox may perhaps now be possible. The playful trespasses of the child are raised to serious reality only by the passionate, often infuriated, punitive sanctions and lead to depressive states in the child who, until then, felt blissfully guiltless.

Detailed examination of the phenomena during an analytic trance teaches us that there is neither shock nor fright without some trace of splitting of personality. It will not surprise any analyst that part of the person regresses into the state of happiness that existed prior to the trauma—a trauma which it endeavours to annul. It is more remarkable that in the identification the working of a second mechanism can be observed, a mechanism of the existence of which I, for one, have had but little knowledge. I mean the sudden, surprising rise of new faculties after a trauma, like a miracle that occurs upon the wave of a magic wand, or like that of the fakirs who are said to raise from a tiny seed, before our very eyes, a plant, leaves and flowers. Great need, and more especially mortal anxiety, seem to possess the power to waken up suddenly and to put into operation latent dispositions which, un-cathected, waited in deepest quietude for their development.

When subjected to a sexual attack, under the pressure of such traumatic urgency, the child can develop instantaneously all the emotions of mature adult and all the potential qualities dormant in him that normally belong to marriage, maternity and fatherhood. One is justified—in contradistinction to the familiar regression—to speak of a *traumatic progression*, of a *precocious maturity*. It is natural to compare this with the precocious maturity of the fruit that was injured by a bird or insect. Not only emotionally, but also *intellectually*, can the trauma bring to maturity a part of the person. I wish to remind you of the typical 'dream of the wise baby' described by me several years ago in which a newly-born child or an infant begins to talk, in fact teaches wisdom to the entire family. The fear of the uninhibited, almost mad adult changes the child, so to speak, into a psychiatrist and, in order to become one and to defend himself against dangers coming from people without self-control, he must know how to identify himself completely with them. Indeed it is unbelievable how much we can still learn from our wise children, the neurotics.

If the shocks increase in number during the development of the child, the number and the various kinds of splits in the personality increase too, and soon it becomes extremely difficult to maintain contact without confusion with all the fragments, each of which behaves as a separate personality yet does not know of even the existence of the others. Eventually it may arrive at a state which—continuing the picture of *fragmentation*—one would be justified in calling *atomization*. One must possess a good deal of optimism not to lose courage when facing such a state, though I hope even here to be able to find threads that can link up the various parts.

In addition to passionate love and passionate punishment there is a third method of helplessly binding a child to an adult.

This is the *terrorism of suffering*. Children have the compulsion to put to rights all disorder in the family, to burden, so to speak, their own tender shoulders with the load of all the others; of course this is not only out of pure altruism, but is in order to be able to enjoy again the lost rest and the care and attention accompanying it. A mother complaining of her constant miseries can create a nurse for life out of her child, i.e. a real mother substitute, neglecting the true interests of the child.

I am certain—if all this proves true—that we shall have to revise certain chapters of the theory of sexuality and genitality. The perversions, for instance, are perhaps only infantile as far as they remain on the level of tenderness; if they become passionate and laden with guilt, they are perhaps already the result of exogenous stimulation, of secondary, neurotic exaggeration. Also my theory of genitality neglected this difference between the phases of tenderness and of passion. How much of the sado-masochism in the sexuality of our time is due to civilization (i.e. originates only from introjected feelings of guilt) and how much develops autochthonously and spontaneously as a proper phase of organization, must be left for further research.

I shall be pleased if you would take the trouble to examine in thought and in your practice what I said to-day and especially if you would follow my advice to pay attention more than hitherto to the much veiled, yet very critical way of thinking and speaking to your children, patients and pupils and to loosen, as it were, their tongues. I am sure you will gain a good deal of instructive material.

Appendix

This train of thought points only descriptively to the tenderness of the infantile eroticism and to the passionate in the sexuality of the adult. It leaves open the problem of the real nature of this difference. Psycho-analysis willingly agrees with the Cartesian idea that passions are brought about by suffering, but perhaps will have to find an answer to the question of what it is that introduces the element of suffering, and with it sado-masochism, into the playful gratifications at the level of tenderness. The argument described above suggests that among others it is the *guilt feelings* that make the love-object of both loving *and* hating, i.e. of *ambivalent* emotions, while the infantile tenderness lacks as yet this schism. It is hatred that traumatically surprises and frightens the child while being loved by an adult, that changes him from a spontaneously and innocently playing being into a guilty love-automaton imitating the adult anxiously, self-effacingly. Their own guilt feelings and the hatred felt towards the seductive child partner fashion the love relation of the adults into a frightening struggle (primal scene) for the child. For the adult, this ends in the moment of orgasm, while infantile sexuality—in the absence of the 'struggle of the sexes'—remains at the level of forepleasure and knows only gratifications in the sense of 'saturation' and not the feelings of annihilation of orgasm. The 'Theory of Genitality'[1] that tries to found the 'struggle of the sexes' on phylogenesis will have to make clear this difference between the infantile-erotic gratifications and the hate-impregnated love of adult mating.

[1] *Thalassa*, 1938, New York. *The Psycho-Analytic Quarterly Inc.* (German original published in 1924.)

POSTHUMOUS PAPERS

XIV

MORE ABOUT HOMOSEXUALITY[1]
(1909)

THE following notes apply to both the homosexuals whom I am now treating (C. is a homosexual with inhibitions, who has made heterosexual attempts; T. is entirely uninhibited, but has some religious scruples (fear of hell)):

Homosexuals love women too strongly (terrible intensity, mostly a sadistic colouring of love, perverse fantasies). They shrink back from it in terror. Repression. Return of the repressed in the form of homosexuality, which for the unconscious still represents the old, intolerably strong fantasies (attached to mother or sister). They idealize women (for them women who have coitus are whores), and this is accompanied by the following unconscious fantasy:

I. I (the homosexual) am mother (whore), who requires a a different man each time (both cases identical in this); the man with whom I have relations is myself. (For this reason the homosexual is never completely satisfied, because his young male partner can never be sufficiently like himself.) Both patients seek out only quite young men. The uninhibited one longs quite consciously for a young man in a sailor suit, such as he once wore himself. Other homosexuals (the more passive ones) prefer older, bearded men. In this case the fantasy is: 'I am mother, he father.'

One patient (the uninhibited T.) likes to remain in the dark about the young man's genitals. He never does anything with the young man's genitals, likes him to wear short swimming trunks, which conceal them, and he rubs his member against his thighs. He generally satisfies himself with kissing.

T.'s recklessness and unconcern (his father occupies one of

[1] Posthumous paper. Published in German: *Bausteine*, IV (1939). First English translation.

the highest positions in the state police, and he himself is a lieutenant of *gendarmerie*) means:
  (i) he wants to deprive his father of his position (unconsciously he means his position in the family);
  (ii) to be 'brought down' himself.
    (*a*) to be 'brought to bed', to give birth (*megesni* in Hungarian means literally 'to fall', colloquially 'to be made pregnant'.
    (*b*) to become a rogue, murderer, robber (to kill his father).

He longs, for instance, for a young, handsome *apache* (*apa* in Hungarian=father), i.e. he would like to be one himself (a parricide).

II. The inhibited patient (C.) is making real progress. In addition to the fantasy already described (in the unconscious he is himself or his father; the man with whom he has relations is his mother (back=chest, shoulder-blades=breasts, anus= vagina), the following unconscious fantasies were reconstructed (certain!):

1. He is mother (whore), the young man is himself (exactly as in the case of T.).

2. The left half of his body is similar to that of his mother, while the right half is male, himself. The two halves copulate. His father is dead, murdered. (In his unconscious now he himself and now his mother figures as the murderer.) In his passion to spare his father from death, he sometimes turns himself (the right half of his body) into his father, so that his father and mother copulate; he is 'between' them, and he kisses his mother and father in turn (he always kisses his mother first, and then kisses his father to console him). He carries all these things over into the transference:
  (*a*) he puts me in his father's place and murders me a hundred times a day;
  (*b*) he puts himself in my place and makes me copulate with my mother, or:
  (*c*) he identifies me with himself and himself with his mother and lets himself copulate through me.

While telling me such things one of his legs stiffens instead of an erection (his penis remains limp). At the same time he often has cramps or a stiff neck.

The meaning of the two halves of the body always betrays itself by *passagère* sensations which generally last until he (or mostly I) find the right solution.

I regard as the fundamental characteristic of homosexuality the reversal (inversion) of roles which in neurosis as in dream means mockery and contempt and at the same time concealed revolt against the lie.

I find the origin of this method of representation in the infantile. If a child wishes to express its ridicule (of a statement made about its parents, for instance) in a form unintelligible to adults it does so:

1. By exaggerating the opposite (e.g. exaggerated acceptance of a paternal statement that he finds incredible).
2. By inversion (reversal):
    (*a*) of words (word said backwards);
    (*b*) of a relationship (e.g. 'the lamb gobbles up the wolf').

I owe this remark (about the lamb) to my small nephew, aged five, with whom I occupy myself a great deal. He and his parents moved into Budapest not long ago from a provincial town. He is very intelligent, but his stupid nurse has filled him with superstitious and frightening ideas, from which I am gradually freeing him. She has frightened him, for instance, with stories about wild animals, and these have recently been plaguing him in his dreams (tendency to anxiety, as with little Hans, determined by fear of the father). To reassure him, I told him that lions were frightened of men; they were dangerous only when they were attacked. 'And aren't wolves frightened of lambs, Uncle Sandor?' he said. 'Because a lamb could gobble a wolf up, couldn't it?' Such statements are generally attributed to children's stupidity, but I saw through his little trick, and said he didn't want to believe me when I told him that lions were afraid of men. He blushed, kissed me, and said: 'You won't be angry with me, will you, Uncle Sandor?'

This kind of secret language of children, in which they may perhaps be intelligible to one another, but which is perhaps really made up for their own use, to relieve their own inner tension (urge for truth), ought to be intensively studied. It might result in the explanation of many characteristics of the neuroses.

My patient C. brings up things exactly like this. Inverted words, dates, spring to his mind, and, senseless, inverted situations and pictures. They always mean mockery, contempt, and disbelief (about his parents, myself, analysis, etc.). I could quote a hundred examples.

By this way of reacting of his (taken in conjunction with the above-mentioned experience with children) he produces another of the 'fundamental reasons' of homosexuality.

Homosexuality is a wholesale inversion (inversion *en masse*). Recognition of the sexual lie in themselves and in adults cannot be repressed by children without a substitute formation, and a number choose for the representation (which gradually becomes unconscious) of their feelings the formula which children use otherwise also for the representation of an untruth: inversion. But the inversion of the libido generally takes place only in puberty, when sexual desires are biologically strengthened and are therefore inhibited and transposed to the infantile level. There must, of course, be a 'primary homosexuality'; what I mean is that such an inversion must really have already taken place in infancy if the subsequent repression is to lead to homosexuality (a form of psychoneurosis).

Translated into terms of reason, homosexual inversion means roughly the following:

'*It is as true that my parents are decent and chaste as that I am my mother and that my mother is myself.*'

(The idea that 'I am you and you are me' often came into the head of my patient C. (who when he identified himself with his mother spoke German); compare the childish jingle:

> *Ich und du,*
> *Müllers Kuh,*
> *Müllers Esel,*
> *Das bist du!*[1]

---

[1] 'I and you, miller's cow, miller's donkey, that is you!'

He learned this jingle from his mother, who used to point to him and to herself alternately as she recited it. The game was to repeat the jingle in such a way that you were pointing at the other person when you finished up on the last syllable, *du*.)

Or another idea that struck him was: 'All right, it's not true that I should like to sleep with my mother instead of my father and do such things with her, and that I should like to do away with my father—but in that case I'm mother and my mother is her son' (i.e. it isn't true!).

In the subsequent sexual revolution (puberty) this infantile structure proves itself invaluable in the repression drive. The boy on the threshold of manhood is filled with fear of his own sexual impulses (which are still directed at his parents) and represses them. As a substitute (if the necessary preconditions dating from his infancy are present) he becomes homosexual. Homosexuality contains the whole truth in completely inverted form:

Conscious	*Unconscious*
Men, father, over-estimated	Father murdered
Women, mother, hated	Mother loved
Women idealized	All women, including mother, are whores
I love young men	Young man=myself myself=mother I copulate with my mother
I copulate with a man from behind	I copulate with a woman from in front
etc., etc.	

The credit of establishing that the chief role in homosexuality is played by the mother belongs to Sadger. He thus cleared the way for the discovery that homosexuality was a psychoneurosis, and that its foundation was therefore the nuclear complex of all neuroses. This does not explain the essence of homosexuality, however, because the nuclear complex is common to every neurotic (and every normal person). Only the elucidation of its more detailed structure can help to show us the way in which one neurosis or another is built up out of the nuclear complex. That will leave open only the problem of the choice of neurosis, but in solving this final question the structure can give us some help.

Homosexuality is a neurosis closely related to impotence; the flight from women is common to both. An impotent man suppresses the genital reflex. (He is perhaps helped by some physical factor, the 'somatic compliance'.)

Impotence is noticeably often a family phenomenon; three or four men in the same family (brothers). The homosexual is less able to repress; his conscious sexuality is displaced towards men, but he remains loyal to the other sex in his unconscious.

Impotence, like homosexuality, can only be cured if it causes the patient suffering.

I do not believe in innate homosexuality. At most I am prepared to admit that degree of inherent inclination (sexual constitution) that must also be assumed in the explanation, e.g. of hysteria. A person with a given sexual constitution can then be made a hysteric or a homosexual by events ('the vicissitudes of the libido'). The sexual constitution is something potential; the neurosis on sexual grounds must be present for it to be able to exercise its power of influencing the direction taken. It is by no means the only factor; exogenous factors can also exercise an influence on the direction taken (the choice of neurosis). Thus an individual with a hysterical or homosexual constitution need not necessarily become a hysteric or a homosexual.

The 'third sex' theory was invented by homosexuals as a scientific form of resistance.

Homosexuality in the sense of pederasty (the third sex) does not exist in the animal world (I am not speaking of hermaphroditism). The attraction of opposites draws the young male to the young female more than to another young male. Male dogs play with each other (male monkeys do so too). Thus a certain amount of libido among animals of the same sex is certainly present. But such play is not to be compared with the earnestness of the heterosexual love impulse.

I am convinced that the same applies to human beings, and that, wherever excessive homosexuality appears, it is to be attributed to the repression of heterosexuality; probably to the repression of excessively powerful heterosexuality (intolerable to the ego), which persists undiminished in the unconscious and lives on under the mask of homosexuality.

XV

ON THE INTERPRETATION OF TUNES THAT COME INTO ONE'S HEAD[1]
(about 1909)

I WAS walking in the street, wondering whether the tunes that occur to one were determined by associations other than their verbal content, and I said to myself that hitherto I had always been able to find a verbal association to explain why a tune had occurred to me.

A few moments later I caught myself humming a tune with which I could find no association. What was it? Oh, of course, one of Mendelssohn's *Songs without Words*. The association was simply a continuation of what I had been thinking about—my preconscious had supplied a contradiction and called on me to explain it. For, of course, there are songs without words (i.e. tunes with no verbal accompaniment, which often occur to me, symphonies, sonatas, etc.). But I said to myself at once that, just as in this instance the occurrence to my mind of the 'Song without Words' had turned out to have a meaning, so there would turn out to be a demonstrable meaning in other similar cases, or because of some other temporal, spatial, or causal association with the wordless tune.

But I am not prepared to deny that there may also be purely musical associations. If I start humming a tune, very soon another, based on pure similarity, occurs to me. I am very musical, but unfortunately no musician. The laws of musical association will have to be established by a psycho-analytically trained musician. Probably a rhythm corresponding to one's mood is often sufficient to cause a wordless tune to 'occur' to one. Sometimes a spirited waltz (in my case) means: 'I am so happy that I should like to dance.' (Unfortunately this does not happen very often.) The rhythm of the tunes that occur to me generally

---

[1] Posthumous paper. Published in German: *Bausteine IV*. (1939). First English translation.

175

corresponds exactly with the degree of my cheerfulness or gloom.

In my pre-analytic period I formed a theory about the striking tone-painting in Wagner's operas. I said to myself that every idea, every word, every situation (on the stage, for instance) awakens a certain feeling in people, to which there must correspond a neuro-physical process (oscillation) of definite quantitative proportions (wave lengths, building waves into complicated systems, rhythms, etc.); and that music, by the combination of sounds and sound-sequences, must be able to create acoustic structures having the same quantitative relations as those of the nervous oscillations. That was why on the one hand music associated itself with ideas and moods, and on the other why ideas and moods associated themselves with music. Music was really only the product of emotion; man went on varying the notes until they corresponded to his moods; a natural musical instrument (the organ of Corti) and its connexions with the central nervous system were the regulating factors in musical production.

Since analysis and reading the work of Kleinpaul I have dropped the whole of this fantasy. I now believe it to be probable that music (like speech) is only a direct or indirect representation or imitation of (organic or inorganic) natural sounds or noises, and as such is in a position to awaken moods and ideas just as any natural sound is.

For a musical tune to occur to one two things are generally necessary:

(i) a purely musical association of mood;
(ii) from among the tunes suitable for association by reason of their mood (rhythm, pitch, structure) those are selected which also offer points of contact by reason of their content.

XVI

LAUGHTER[1]
(1913)

The pleasure and unpleasure mechanism of laughter: a repetition of the pleasure and unpleasure in being born.

* * *

Bergson (p. 26):[2] Bergson recognizes, not laughing, but only laughing at.
Bergson: The laughter laughs at what is dead (the mechanical).
Bergson: Because he is disgusted by it.
Ferenczi: Because he longs for it (*cliché*).

* * *

Bergson (p. 27): Why is the mechanical funny? The idea of doing something automatically without any effort of thought is pleasurable (flatters one's laziness). For example: directing a crowd with a button. The magic of omnipotence. Omnipotence of behaviour or words. The army.

* * *

Predetermination. Automatism just as valid for the tragic as for the comic.

* * *

On Bergson (p. 32): Main argument against Bergson.
Bergson: 'Rigidity, which is out of harmony with the immanent plasticity of life, provokes laughter', 'the mechanical that goes behind life provokes laughter'. (To frighten us away from the rigid, the dead, etc.). He never speaks of the reason for laughter, but only about its purpose.

[1] Posthumous paper. First published in German: *Bausteine* IV (1939). First English translation.
[2] Editor's Note.—The page numbers refer to the Hungarian edition of Bergson's *Le Rire*, Budapest, 1913.

If the aim of the affect were the maintenance of order, what sense would there be in the feeling of pleasure which accompanies the affect? The sight of disorder should cause us to weep, mourn, be angry.

* * *

Bergson's social theory applies only to laughing at, not to laughing.

* * *

There are two things to be considered: (i) laughing in itself; (ii) laughing at. The essence of laughing: How much I should like to be as imperfect as that! The essence of laughing at: How satisfactory it is that I am so well behaved, not so imperfect as that!

* * *

Making a virtue of necessity:
  (i) How difficult it is to be perfect, says the child who is being brought up to be orderly.
  (ii) How pleasing it is to be perfect, says the child who has been brought up to be orderly.

Thus in the first place the child can only laugh (be glad) at orderliness.

The conscious attitude of the adult at the sight of disorder is: I am glad that I am not so. Unconsciously he enjoys the fantasy: How satisfactory it is to be so disorderly. Behind every laughing at there is concealed unconscious laughing.

* * *

On p. 8) Laughter and feeling of guilt.
  (i) The feeling of the comic is always a break-through of pleasure at an a-social (sinful) impulse, upon a temporary break-through of the sense of sin by which mankind is continually burdened. (Connexion with the totem sin.)
  (ii) Sin only enjoyable in groups. Mutual forgiveness.
  (iii) Where security is lacking (the presence of strangers) there is embarrassment, and it is impossible to join in the laughter. The communion of the guilty is lacking.

Anxiety.
(i) He who forgives a sin really commits it too.
(ii) He who loves someone shares all the latter's sins and forgives them. (The communion of accomplices.)

* * *

Happiness. Smiling (the child after being quieted; absence of all needs).

Laughter = defence against excessive pleasure.

* * *

What takes place in laughter:
(i) Break-through of feeling of pleasure.
(ii) Defensive measures against this feeling of pleasure (attempt at regression).
(iii) What gives rise to the defence is the same (original) sense of guilt, the conscience.

* * *

An individual who does not join in the laughter (a stranger) does not permit the feeling of pleasure to arise and therefore does not need the defence.

* * *

Laughter is an automatic intoxication with CO_2 (tissue suffocation).

Weeping is an automatic inhalation of O_2.

* * *

Laughter and the comic are yet another result of the censorship.

Laughter is a general physiological defence against discomfort-causing pleasure. A completely bad man prevents the release of pleasure and remains *serious*. If a *consciously moral* person releases unconscious pleasure, his ego defends itself by means of laughter against the advancing pleasure (a counter-poison).

* * *

Laughter is a failure of repression. A defence symptom against unconscious pleasure.

* * *

Remaining serious is successful repression.

* * *

A simply bad man gives rein to his pleasure at the comic (the unseemly, the incongruous) in others without defence (therefore does not laugh, forms no counter-poison to his pleasure).

An individual whose badness is incompletely repressed always starts laughing when incongruousness in others awakens pleasure in him.

A completely moral person laughs no more than a completely immoral one. The release of pleasure is lacking.

Thus a bad person does not laugh, because he simply enjoys his badness (pleasure) without defence (without pleasure).

The good man does not laugh because his pleasure is well repressed—it does not come out, and therefore laughter is superfluous.

The ambivalent individual whose badness is incompletely repressed can laugh. Conflict between the conscience (morality) and pleasure in the bad; the badness makes the pleasure, conscience the laughter.

* * *

Freud: In laughing we feel ourselves into the physical condition of the comic and get rid of the superfluous provision of affect by means of laughter.

I suggest that laughter consists of:
 (i) discharge of physical energy in Freud's sense;
 (ii) compensation for this discharge by the respiratory muscles' becoming the site of the discharge. (And the face muscles (?).)

Laughter is apparently a derivative of general muscle clonuses (and tonuses) which have become available for special purposes (aims). Just as expressive gestures arose from general reactions (cramps).

The respiratory muscular system is thus appropriate to the expression of emotion because it permits (i) abreaction, as well as (ii) different shades of feeling and delicate gradations of inhibition.

The face muscles are similarly adapted to the discharge of more delicate quantities of affect and at the same time to the regulation of breathing by the expansion and constriction of the openings of the nose and mouth (expansion=more pleasure breathed out. In weeping, snivelling movements).

Probably *all* expressive movements consist of an active and a reactive component (compensation)?

(i) More inhibition than explosion.
(ii) More explosion than inhibition.
(iii) Equilibrium, with a slight predominance of one or the other.

* * *

Analogy between laughter and vomiting. Laughter is the vomiting of breath (oxygen) from the lungs. Weeping is the drinking in of air. Breathing is accentuated in maniacs, inhibited in melancholics.

Gross's mechanism of mania. Analogy between alcoholic and oxygen consumption.

* * *

Why does the cheerful man need to drink wine (or oxygen)? Is it needed only when one is sad?

* * *

One can laugh only at oneself. (One can only love oneself!) (Pleasure=love; conscious (irony) or unconscious (comic, jokes).

* * *

Mother, can you order me to do anything? Of course! No, you can order me to do only what I order myself (Freud).

* * *

The comic and laughter.

We are always delighted by the naïve (the childish) element in the comic and it rouses the unconscious child in us (the pleasure factor in laughter). At the same time our conscious ideal is stimulated and sees to it that the pleasure does not become excessive (defence, expiration).

* * *

(Modification of Freud's definition.)

The effect of the comic consists of: (i) laughter; (ii) laughing at (secondary, cultural product, Bergson).

Why must I emphasize that I am *not* like that? Because I *am* like that!

* * *

Forms of laughter deduced theoretically:
 (i) The more laughing at, the more expiration;
 (ii) The more laughing, the less expiration (and the more muscle abreaction).

* * *

After much laughter, dejection (*post coitum triste*).

Laughter and coitus break through guilt feeling.

Difference between man and woman: man *triste*, woman not *triste*. (Cf. religion!) Woman would be easy to enlighten (enlightened). Religiousness not deep.

XVII

MATHEMATICS[1]
(*c.* 1920)

1. Pcs and cs: Organs for ucs psychic qualities.
   Ucs: Organ for physiological qualities (perception-recollection).
   Sense organs: Organs for physical qualities.
   (*Qualities are distinguishable quantities.*)

* * *

2. (i) Psychic reality is arithmetically
   (ii) Physiological reality is algebraically
   (iii) Ucs reality is symbolically (paralogically) (Primary process)
   (iv) Pcs reality is } logically (Secondary
   (v) Cs (?) reality is } process)
   } Individuation
   measured. Counting machine 'Comparison with the study of quantities' (Mathematics).

* * *

3. *Contrast* between the purely introspective mathematician and the purely extraspective primitive *Naturmensch*, man of action.
   Mathematician—knocked down.
   No idea of mathematics—skilful.
   Skill demands an immensely precise calculation.[2]
   Even a dog can do that.
   Thinking animals. Introspection into their own Physis.

* * *

4. *Pure* mathematics is autosymbolism (Silberer).

[1] Posthumous paper. Published in German: *Bausteine IV*, 1939. First English translation.
[2] In the notes there followed here sketches representing achievements demanding high skill, such as catching something moving, etc. (Editor's note).

5. *A priori* knowledge about the processes of the brain (mind).

* * *

6. Mathematics is *instinct*.

* * *

7. Mathematician not necessarily clever. (Idiots): peculiar combination (introspection).

* * *

8. *Genius*: combination of strongly-developed introspection with strong instincts.
   (i) Manifestations of instinctual beings are elaborated by a (syst.) cs capable of combination.
   (ii) Genius elaborates his own inst. 'ideas'.[1]

* * *

9. *The problem of mathematical talent*. The psycho-analysis of Breuer and Freud hardly occupied itself in the beginning with the problems of 'talent'. It turned its interest almost exclusively to the changes which the human mind has to undergo after its birth under the influence of the environment. For quite a long while it held itself to be incompetent for research into the constitutional factors, into the innate predispositions and faculties. It was in its beginnings a science centred on therapy and practice, and it was naturally concerned above all with the pathological changes of mental life which, acquired during life, were to be reversed by the analyst's efforts, while it was not able to do much therapeutically with congenital constitution. This first 'traumatic-cathartic' period in psycho-analysis was a wholesome reaction against the pre-analytic psychiatry and psychology, which completely withdrew from the investigation of the qualities acquired during life, and tended to explain everything mental by the formula of 'innate disposition', and everything psychiatric by that of 'degeneration'.

[1] In German 'Einfälle' (Editor).

10. The second great epoch in psycho-analysis is connected solely with the name of Freud and deserves to be called a 'theory of libido'. For the first time, the following-up of the *developmental phases* from birth to involution of one instinct, that of sexuality, was accomplished, and it became possible to describe all its possible issues and to trace them to their causes. Psycho-analysis could no longer confine itself in this phase to pathology. In order to understand pathology better it had to pay attention to the phenomena of the normal psyche, or those which lay in the borderland between normal and pathological (dreams, jokes, slips, criminality), to the products of the group-mind (myths, folklore, religion, languages), to art, philosophy, science, etc., and had to examine the conditions under which such expressions of the mind arise. But only after the scanty bridging by analytical knowledge of the great gaps in post-natal mental development was it possible for psycho-analysis to extend the connecting links so as to include among the factors also the congenital constitution, this time with good prospect of scientific results. Its material limited it, however—it is true at first somewhat one-sidedly—merely to the discovery of the sexual constitutions and their development; from here, however, some ray of light was thrown on to the sources of other, not sexual, abilities and talents.

11. The third, the present-day, phase of Freud's psycho-analysis is characterized by *metapsychology*, this unique construction which, without even the slightest help from anatomy, histology, chemistry, or physics of the nerve substance—tries to divine and build up, purely on the basis of mental analysis, the topical, dynamic, and economic laws (connexions) which govern both the whole mental life and all its normal or abnormal mental acts. In addition, the one-sidedness of the psycho-analytic material was later balanced by the creation of an *ego-psychology*, based on the study of specific ego-illnesses, and through it the biogenetic parallel was extended to the mind.

It is to be expected that this trend of development in

psycho-analysis, which takes into account, in addition to the congenital factor, also the formal and quantitative moments, will further the investigation of the various 'talents' which until now have been regarded only as rather more or less of one essentially uncertain (anatomical) 'disposition'. Such researches, however, are not yet in existence. I have prefaced my article with this cursory survey of the place of mental talent in psycho-analytical theory in order to demonstrate the narrow foundation on which research into one particular talent has to be built, and the various, often completely heterogeneous, strong-points which would have to be used in such building. The furthering and inhibiting post-natal influences, constitutional factors of the ego, and of sexuality, metapsychological considerations, must all help in motivating a special talent.

12. The foundations on which such a construction could be built up were too narrow and the whole building was too labile and insecure to justify any attempt at systematic investigation. Thus we must content ourselves with trying, armed with the tools of psycho-analytical knowledge, to bring nearer to our understanding one special talent, that of mathematics.

13.
(i) Arithmetic = Physics
(ii) Algebra = Physiology (sensory qualities) (symbol!)
(iii) Higher mathematics (differential—integral calculus) = Symbolism
(iv) = Logic

Arithmetic = Physics
Algebra = Physiology
Symbolism = Ucs Psychic
Logic = Pcs cs

1920 MATHEMATICS

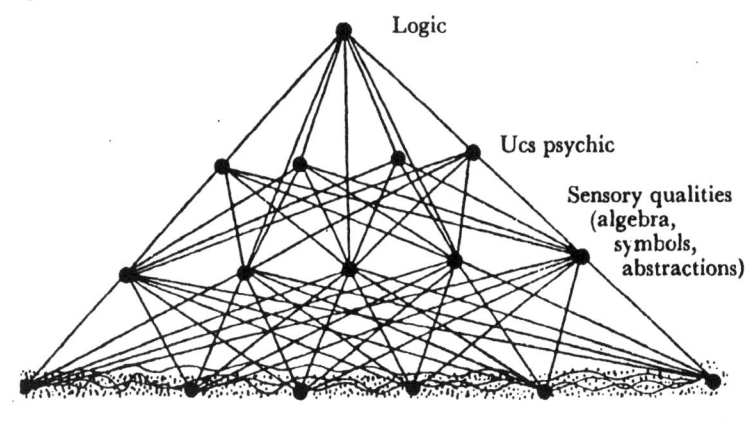

Diagram: a pyramid of interconnected nodes labeled:
- Logic (apex)
- Ucs psychic
- Sensory qualities (algebra, symbols, abstractions)
- Arithmetic. Chaotic (base)

Progressive abstraction (screening) with the help of phylogenetically acquired functions.

* * *

14. *Proof for the reality of the external world.*
    The *introspectively* acquired (*a priori*) mathematical laws prove to be valid also in the 'external world'.

* * *

15. *Man* is the *sum total* of physical, physiological, ucs mental, pcs mental, and cs *energy forms*.
    Inter-relation of physical, physiological and psychological forces during the whole life, perhaps also *regressively*.

   The brain as a counting machine.
   Censure a filter. Rheostat.
   Sense organs are screens (mathematical).
   Mathematical genius is self-observation.
   Not objective.
   Symbolism is self-observation of the latent ontogenetic disposition.
   Logic.

   (i) Auto-arithmetics: perception of the individual sense impressions.

(ii) *Symbolism*: summation of sense impressions (amphimixis-condensation).

(iii) *Logic*: regression to arithmetics at a higher level.
Reckoning with *higher units* (which as such are condensations).
Reckoning with symbols (notions) is *measuring* of the symbols (notions).

* * *

16. The summation of *kindred* or *similar* elements is one of the preconditions of the reckoning (counting) function, but is at the same time the preparatory work for association between two ideas, association according to certain definite categories (similarity, simultaneity, equal affective importance, objective or subjective valuation, etc.).
The *tendency to associate* would be a special expression of the *tendency to economize*. Thinking is after all only a means of preventing *squandering through action*. (Trial action with small quantities). When, instead of counting each time with the fingers, one puts a figure as a symbol in the place of a row of figures, much mental effort is saved.
The closer connexion of action based on cautious thinking with the *tendency to economize* (anal character), and its origin in anal-eroticism, is thus understandable.

17. The fusion of numerous single impressions of the external world into a *unit* and the combination of this with a *symbol* is one of the most fundamental phenomena of mental life. In the ucs the fusions (elementary process) happen according to the principle of *similarity* (especially similarity of the pleasure tones), in the pcs according to the principle of *identity* or of equivalence (reality principle).

18. *Association* is an *incomplete* fusion of two sensory impressions which therefore means that only part of their contents coincide.

* * *

19. (i) *Mathematician: self-observation* for the metapsychological process of thought and action.

(ii) *Thinker*: trial admission to action 'under displacement of minimal qualities'.

(iii) *Active man, man of action*: automatic transformation (performance) of the results of the counting machine into action.

20. (Thinker=transitional type between mathematician and man of action.
'Sicklied o'er with the pale cast of thought').

* * *

21. *Mathematician* can sense only the *formal* in the process of intra-psychic excitation.
Thinker: sense for the *content* of the process of excitation.
Man of action: no interest for it.
(Description of the two types.)

* * *

22. *Mathematical talent.*
Scientific works to date on mathematical talent dealt with:
   (i) *Phrenological* problems on the place of the mathematical sense (Gall, Möbius): third left frontal gyrus which has already to look after so many functions (speech, intelligence, etc.). In contrast to it observations such as those about the great mathematician, Gauss, whose skull was allegedly microcephalous and whose brain-weight was extremely small.
   (ii) Connexion between musical and mathematical talent —an obviously secondary question.
   (iii) Much more important are psychiatric observations on the coincidence of great mathematical ability with otherwise strong backwardness of the other kinds of intellectual and moral development, often amounting to imbecility, or even idiocy.

* * *

23. *Mathematics*=*self-observation of one's own cs function.*

24. (i) *Perceptions* work on the pattern of a screening apparatus,

unifying the impression of the *homogeneous influences* of the external world into an *algebraic unit*.

A *total impression* in which the individual impressions have been united (?). The individual excitement species are sorted out in this way from the chaos of movements of the external world (already an abstraction).

(ii) These simple perceptions are summed up into a higher *algebraic unit: symbol*—everything similar connected by some superior common factor.

(iii) The elimination (a further screening) of the differences, another *abstraction*, allows of the formation of *conceptions* which can stand up to reality testing.

(iv) The relating of these conceptions to each other and the trial admission of action based on them (conception of the consequence) = thinking.

25. The psychologist is in the last instance a self-observer (?) + object, "oscillating" between introspection and observation of objects.

* * *

26. Inhibition as a *principle of action* already valid with the play of the *counting machine*. (Protective mechanisms against stimuli.)

27. *Utraquism.*
A 'Weltanschauung', as far as possible faultless, demands a utraquistic attitude (oscillating between introspection and object observation) out of which a reliable reality can be constructed.

* * *

28. The pure logician is the mathematician among the psychologists. He has interest only for the formal in the pcs and projects it into the external world. The psychologist must, in addition to logic, also take into account the *sub-intellectual*, the ucs ideas and their (fantastic) interplay, also the *instincts* which are the basis of everything psychic—for it is only the aims of the instincts and their derivatives which form the *content* of the mind. The psyche is ruled by the

tendency to care that the instincts receive satisfaction, and are steered eventually into certain harmless channels which prevent unpleasure, that disturbing external stimuli be removed either by adaptation or by changing the external world, or be diminished as far as possible.

The psychologist must not be the mathematician of the mind, for he must take into account the contents of the mind (which are basically illogical and determined by the instincts).

* * *

29. Logic=mathematics of the pcs
Pleasure principle=mathematics of the ucs

* * *

30. *Sense organs* are better mathematicians than the ucs (less personal). The pcs tries to repair the errors in calculation committed by the ucs, which is ruled by the pleasure principle.
Insensitive bodies are the most real calculating organs (photography, expressionism).

* * *

31. *Screening*.
Where this mechanism is present the processes of excitation occasioned by the physiological and psychological stimuli must each time go through a new screening, i.e. being sorted and classified according to quantities. (Light filters in colour photography: (1) separation, (2) synthesis.)

Cs *memory systems*—pcs
Sorting into the *memory systems of the ucs* | Progressive
Sorting according to sensory qualities | screening
(perc. system)
Excitation of the senses

* * *

32. *Conceiving* would mean then a function which strives to condense all these impressions separated into their elements into a unit (conception).

Ucs conception thinks in *fantasies*, that is to say it integrates the psychic rudiments scattered in the memories according to the *rules of association of the ucs*, such as high-speed process in time (*no absolute timelessness*), no subtle contrasts. *Principle of similarity*.

The principal systems of the ucs: *pleasure and unpleasure* memory system: overruling; decisive for the eventual fate of the conception. (An attempt to restore the world of objects out of its elements.)

Sense organs separate the world into elements, the mind restores it.

This *condensation* is a *magnificent mathematical achievement*. Pcs: independent of pleasure principle, is able to reconstruct *reality* out of conceptions and to base on it an action suited to the purpose (*zweckmässig*).

* * *

33. *Mathematics of the ucs:*
Very primitive, approximative mathematics of similarities, but mathematics nevertheless. Mathematics of the *pcs* strict.

34. The mathematician must therefore gain insight into the processes of his pcs mental systems, if his results are to correspond with external reality.
(Children's mathematics?) ⎱ No!
(Idiot's mathematics?) ⎰
Arithmetic: addition, subtraction—function of the sense organs.
Algebra: combination of higher order; permutation, geometrical calculations, reckoning with time—function of the ucs. (This is to be supposed also in animals: the dive of the eagle on his prey, the spring of the tiger—demand calculation. Differential and integral calculus, geometrical functions, even though no *knowledge* of geometry.)

* * *

35. *Mathematics* is a *psychic* organ projection in the same way that mechanics appears to be a *physiological* organ projec-

tion. *Music* is likewise a projection outwards of the *metapsychological* processes which accompany the affective and emotional processes; the congeniality of the musician and the mathematician is based on the same ability for fine self-observation.

36. *Sense organs* are *screening mechanisms* for the sorting of a variety of impressions out of the chaotic external world. The first sorting takes place according to certain gross differences in the sense organs which, with the help of their specific *protective barriers against stimuli*, screen off all the stimuli with the exception of those to which they are sensitive (sight, smell, hearing).
A second screening seems to take place within each *sensory field* according to certain quantitative relations (particular light qualities according to intensity and colour). *Similarly* the organ of hearing screens the first fairly chaotic acoustic sense impressions and differentiates between the various noises, and leads to the abstraction of certain acoustic impressions which are pleasurably toned because of their uniformity, as musical *tones*.

* * *

37. Condensation is the process corresponding to association in the ucs. The *condensation* into an algebraic unit, the summation, through something common, of numerous separate impressions, which is then the *sum total* of these separate impressions, can be demonstrated also in the manifest dream elements and in the neurotic symptoms, which are all 'over-determined'.

* * *

38. The work of an acting man is a magnificent *condensation performance*; the condensed result of a vast quantity of separate calculations and considerations—which may be unnoticed, ucs—gives a result which is the sum total of all these calculations, and this residual sum (result) becomes then capable of being discharged 'in the residual direction'.

39. The mathematician is a man who has a fine capacity for self-observation of this condensation process, i.e. of the formal, of the 'functional' phenomena in *Silberer's* sense; with this, however, he seems to have spent himself so much that he has $\begin{Bmatrix} \text{no} \\ \text{hardly any} \end{Bmatrix}$ mental energy for *performing* of actions. Contrariwise the obviously more objectively orientated man of action.

* * *

40. First function of the psychic: *separation* of the sense impressions into their elements, *sorting* according to qualities, and according to differences in quantities respectively. Sense impressions are deposited in the memory systems in this form. *Keeping control* over this vast material demands condensations (tendency to economy and simplification).

41. Such '*condensations*' (formation of conceptions, of memory images, also speculative processes) are always formed afresh from the split-up material of the ucs, according to the actual aims (fantasies).
    The ucs *fantasies* are thought-forms of the ucs. They conform much more to the pleasure principle, but are, however, already bound in a way by the laws of similarity, of succession, etc.
    The ucs is therefore not really *timeless*, only much less dependent on chronological order than the pcs (*ceteris paribus* simultaneous memories have also here a better chance of being linked associatively, that is to say, of being condensed). In the same way the ucs is not illogical, only paralogical. After finishing the operation of active thinking (condensation) the connexions created for the moment, so to speak *ad usum Delphini*, again disintegrate into their categories.

* * *

42. The mathematician appears to have a fine self-observation for the metapsychic (also probably physical) processes and finds formulas for the operation in the mind of the conden-

sation and separation functions, *projects them*, however, *into the external* world, and believes that he has learnt through *external experience*.

A very strong argument against this is the eminently *intuitive* nature of mathematical talent, its connexion with detachment from reality, even with imbecility.

43. Surprisingly these formulas prove valid as 'applied' mathematics also in the physical world (technique). Indeed, an argument for the 'monism' of the universe, at least for the identity in essence of the metapsychic with the physical.

* * *

44. Query: is mathematics *abstraction from external experience?* or: *a priori knowledge?*

Solution of this problem perhaps: self-observation is in itself an inner 'experience', out of which mathematics is abstracted. That is, on both sides of the P-system mathematical abstractions do occur. In other words: is mathematics *internal* or *external* perception? (Up to the present mathematical knowledge *has been considered as* abstraction (induction?) from external experience.) Here the tracing back of mathematical knowledge and abstraction to *internal* (self-) observation is attempted.

* * *

45. It is not improbable that we must think of the screening work of the sense organs as a prototype of what happens in the higher mental field, in the ucs. The sorting according to certain categories characterizes the whole memory system, which constitutes the ucs, according to *Freud*.

The memory systems of the ucs are still sorted—with regard to (achronic) time, to space, etc.—according to the principle of similarity.

What *Freud* calls a further over-cathexis by the pcs would only be a renewed screening based on the *principle of equivalence or identity* (reality principle). Separation of the

heterogeneous from that which *according to the pleasure tone* (or otherwise) is similar: *logic*.
With the help of *'verbal residues'*.
Cs is after all no system, but a special mental act (?).

XVIII

ON EPILEPTIC FITS
OBSERVATIONS AND REFLECTIONS[1]
(about 1921)

As registrar in a hospital for incurables, the Budapest Salpêtrière, I had in my time to observe hundreds of epileptic fits. This turned out to have been a useful experience during the war years, when I became medical superintendent of a department of a military hospital, where one of my duties was the 'verification' of such fits. I do not propose here to go into the difficult and sometimes insoluble problems presented by individual cases in which we were called on to decide whether we were confronted with malingering, hysteria, or true, 'genuine' epilepsy, but shall confine myself to a few observations and reflections on those cases in which the typical picture of true epilepsy was presented without any doubt—that is to say, dilated, reactionless pupils, tonic-clonic spasms, complete extinction of sensibility, including corneal sensibility, biting of the tongue, noisy, laborious breathing, foaming at the mouth, ejection of the contents of the bowels, and post-epileptic coma.

The impression made on the psycho-analyst by these fits is of a regression to an extremely primitive level of organization in which all inner excitations are discharged by the shortest motor path and all susceptibility to external stimuli is lost. In observing such cases I was continually reminded of the first attempt[2] made by me long ago to classify epilepsy among the psycho-neuroses. I then suggested that an epileptic fit signified a regression to an extremely primitive level of infantile ego-organization in which wishes were still expressed by unco-

---

[1] Posthumous paper. First published in German: *Bausteine III* (1939). First English translation.

[2] In 'Stages in the Development of the Sense of Reality'. First published in 1913. Reprinted in *First Contributions to Psycho-Analysis*, Hogarth Press, London, 1952.

ordinated movements. It will be remembered that this suggestion was subsequently taken up by the American psycho-analyst McCurdy, who modified it by showing that the epileptic's regression went back even further, to the intra-uterine situation, that of the unborn child in the womb. A similar opinion was expressed by my colleague Hollós, who in a paper read to the Hungarian branch of the International Psycho-Analytical Association compared the mental state of an epileptic during a fit to the unconsciousness of an unborn child.

Observation of innumerable epileptic fits during the war years caused me to move nearer to the views of these two authors. One of the chief symptoms of such a fit is obviously the breaking off of all contact with the outer world, of the *vie de relation*, as the great Liébeault would put it. This, however, is something which an epileptic fit has in common with the ordinary state of sleep, which psycho-analysis regards as a regression to the antenatal state.[1] In sleep all interest is withdrawn from the outside world and sensibility to external stimuli is noticeably diminished. Epilepsy, however, must be regarded as a state of exceptionally deep sleep, from which the sleeper is not to be awakened even by the strongest external stimulus.

The conflict between my original view ('epileptic fit=regression to infantile omnipotence by means of uncoordinated movements') and its modification ('epileptic fit=regression to intra-uterine situation') was resolved, however, when I took the whole course of the fit into consideration. The seizure generally begins with the patient's collapse (with or without a loud scream or cry), and this is followed by general tonic contractions and clonic spasms. The duration of the period of tonic-clonic convulsions varies, but is interrupted by shorter or longer periods of rest, during which, however, unconsciousness, dilation of the pupils, stertorous breathing accompanied by signs of threatening oedema of the lungs (foaming at the mouth), and strong palpitations persist. During these pauses the epileptic's attitude certainly resembles that of the foetus in the womb, which we must think of as completely motionless and unconscious (as well

[1] Cf. my paper quoted above, 'Stages in the Development of the Sense of Reality', on the first sleep of the newly born.

as apnoeic, of course). The first period of collapse and convulsions is, however, in my opinion much more reminiscent of the uncoordinated expressions of unpleasure of a newly-born child that is dissatisfied or has been irritated in some way. It is thus possible that both the original and the modified view of the level of regression involved may be correct, in the sense that during the seizure the epileptic goes through a whole gamut of regression, from the infantile to the intra-uterine-omnipotent situation. In cases in which periods of rest and convulsions alternate, we must think of the excitation as going up and down through the whole gamut. The 'post-epileptic' stage, and the transition stage which normally intervenes before the patient comes round, is much more like ordinary sleep. The patient makes defence movements, his pupils react again, and only an inclination to 'ambulatory automatism', a kind of sleep-walking, provides evidence of a remaining pathological, generally violent, hypermotility.

An experiment that I undertook, needless to say with the greatest precautions, enabled me in numerous cases to disturb the stage of 'epileptic rest' as described above and to provoke a repetition of the convulsions, or even the sudden awakening of the patient. During the stage of rest the patient's teeth are firmly clenched and his tongue and palate are sunk backwards, as is shown by his loud snoring; respiratory movements of the thorax take place, but no breathing is possible through the mouth, and the encumbered respiration leads to a congestion of the pulmonary circulatory system and the expectoration of large quantities of serous sputum. If the patient were unable to breathe through the nose, persistence of the seizure would cause him to suffocate (as does happen in certain cases). If during the stage of rest I held the patient's nostrils, so that he could not breathe at all, tonic-clonic spasms (i.e. a less deep state of non-reaction) generally set in again immediately, and if I went on holding his nostrils he generally awoke and his pupillary reaction and his sensibility returned. This experiment is, of course, not without its dangers; if the patient's breathing were stopped too long, he might really suffocate. There were instances in which the patient's condition did not alter after 20–30 seconds;

of course, in such cases I did not force the experiment. During it I always carefully observed the patient's pulse.

I learned from it, however, that an epileptic in a fit is far more sensitive to interference with his remaining breathing capacity than he is to other external stimuli, however painful these may be (application of heat or cold, blows, touching the cornea, etc.). If we regard the rest stage of the seizure as a regression to the intra-uterine, this is intelligible. In an epileptic seizure, as in ordinary sleep, the illusion of the womb can be maintained only if a minimum supply of oxygen is steadily maintained from outside. If the patient's restricted breathing is stopped by holding his nostrils, he is compelled to wake up and breathe through his mouth, just as a new-born child is compelled to breathe and to awaken from its intra-uterine unconsciousness by the cutting off of the blood-supply through the umbilical cord.

In the paper mentioned above I indicated that the epileptic should be regarded as a special human type, characterized by the piling up of unpleasure and by the infantile manner of its periodic motor discharge. To this it should be added that these people are able to interrupt their consciousness, their contact with the outer world, and take refuge in a completely self-contained and self-sufficient way of life as it was lived in the womb, that is to say, before the painful cleavage between the self and the outer world took place.

Individual differences in the various forms of attack may originate from the fact that in some cases it is the motor discharge which is emphasized, while in others it is the apnoeic regression. Even in the same patient, one fit may show the former and the next the latter characteristic of the epileptic process.

The fact that there are traumatic, toxic, and also 'reflex' epilepsies apart from constitutional ones need not, since the acceptance of the Freudian complemental series in the aetiology of the neuroses, cause us any difficulty. Obviously no one is completely immune to epileptic regression, but in one case a severe head injury, or chronic alcoholic poisoning, or a very painful irritation of the peripheral nerves is required to cause an epileptic fit, while in another, where there is a disposition to it, it may take place without such contributory factors.[1]

In the absence of a methodical psycho-analytic investigation, nothing definite can be said about the nature of the affects discharged in epileptic fits. It is, however, to be expected that sado-masochistic instinctual components will turn out to play at any rate a large part in them.

I also suspect that epilepsy—like *tic* in my opinion[2]—will turn out to occupy a border-line position between the transference and narcissistic neuroses.

When the fit is at its height we may assume a state of narcissistic regression far exceeding that of ordinary sleep and resembling cataleptic rigidity and the wax-like flexibility of catatonia. On the other hand, in the motor discharge and in post-epileptic delirium the patient rages at the outer world or turns his aggression inwards against himself; he thus clings fast to his 'object-relationship'.

The regression theory of epilepsy throws some light both on the close connexion between epileptic fits and the state of sleep (that is to say, a milder state of the same regression) and on the combination of epileptic dispositions with other disturbances of organic development and atavisms.

Let me return for a moment to those cases in which the epileptic really suffocates instead of being awakened by having his breathing stopped. Cases have, of course, been described in medical literature in which the patient has collapsed head forwards into a shallow pool and drowned in a situation in which the slightest movement would have saved his life; I have been told about a patient, whose seizures always occurred at night in bed, but who invariably lay on his stomach as if he were deliberately seeking out the position in which he would be most likely to suffocate because of the pillow. (He subsequently died during one of his seizures, but no one was present, so that the exact circumstances of his death could not be established.) It

---

[1] Jacksonian epilepsy, which arises from a purely mechanical irritation of the motor centres of the brain, is not to be included with the psychogenic epilepsies dealt with above.

[2] See 'Psycho-Analytical Observation on Tic'. *Further Contributions*, p. 172.

could be said that the name of epileptic is truly deserved only in those cases in which the unconsciousness is so complete that there is no reaction to an interruption, or attempted interruption, of the breathing. Another view which deserves attention is that there are various degrees of epileptic unconsciousness, and that the extreme case is when the patient really suffocates, for then he has regressed through the pre-natal and the intrauterine stages to the stage of not living at all.[1]

Instances are known in nature in which animals save themselves from intolerable pain by self-dismemberment or mutilation (autotomy). That might well be the phylogenetic pattern of the 'turning against oneself' to be observed in many neuroses (hysteria, melancholia, epilepsy). The metapsychological assumption behind this would be the withdrawal of libidinal cathexis from one's own organism, which is then treated as something alien, i.e. hostile, to the self. Great suffering or great physical pain can so accentuate the longing for absolute rest, i.e. the rest of death, that anything that stands in its way provokes defensive hostility. I was able to observe this not long ago in the sad case of a woman dying in unspeakable agony who reacted to all attempts of the physician to awaken her from her increasing lethargy with angry and often desperate defensive movements. From this point of view epileptic fits can be regarded as more or less serious attempts at suicide by suffocation; in mild cases the suicide is indicated only symbolically, but in extreme cases it is carried out in reality.

It is possible that the respiratory erotogenous zone which D. Forsyth (London) found to be the chief factor in certain respiratory disturbances in children may be the dominant zone in epileptics.

For those who are aware of the immense real importance of symbolism in life, and of the regularity with which the symbolism of death and that of the maternal body are associated with each other in dreams and neuroses,[2] it will be no surprise if epileptic fits turn out to have that double meaning.

[1] See Freud's remarks on the death instinct in *Beyond the Pleasure Principle*.

[2] See my recent papers on symbolism: 'The Symbolism of the Bridge' (1921) and 'Bridge Symbolism and the Don Juan Legend' (1921), both reprinted in *Further Contributions*, Hogarth Press, 1926.

According to this interpretation, the epileptic would appear to be a person of strong instincts and violent affects who succeeds for long periods in protecting himself from outbursts of his passions by extremely powerful repression of his urges, or sometimes by exaggerated humility and religiosity; but at appropriate intervals his instinctual drives break loose and rage, sometimes with bestial ruthlessness, not only against his whole environment, but against his own person, which has become alien and hostile to him. This discharge of affect then brings about, often only for a few very brief moments, a sleep-like state of rest, the pattern of which is that of the unborn child in the womb, or alternatively death.

In certain cases, particularly in the aura, the state of epileptic fugues and 'equivalents', aggression against the environment predominates, and may express itself in impulses to mass murder and a blind, destructive fury. In other cases the violence is chiefly turned inwards and does not rest until the unconscious aim of suicide has been achieved. In so-called *petit mal*—attacks of temporary unconsciousness unaccompanied by convulsions, the temporary happiness of the same embryonic state of rest is achieved without the dramatic discharge of affect, simply by withdrawal of libido and interest from the outer world, the apparatus of perception merely ceasing to function.

The importance of the place occupied by sexuality among the instincts to which an epileptic fit gives rein is shown by the exceptional frequency of so-called sex criminals among epileptics, and the numerous sexual perversions, often in quite remarkable combinations, to be found among them, as described, for instance, by Maeder.[1] In a number of cases the fit appears to be actually a 'coitus equivalent', as in the case of a patient observed by me who was able to avoid fits only by having coitus daily, and sometimes several times daily. That epileptic fits (and, according to Freud, hysterical fits also) recall the sex act in many respects (convulsions, alterations in breathing, disturbance of consciousness) was correctly recognized by the older doctors. I hope to be able to give a theoretical clue to the

---

[1] In Sexualität und Epilepsie: *Jahrbuch für psychoanalytische und psychopathologische Forschungen* (1909), 1, 19.

explanation of the numerous analogies between sleep, fits, and orgasm on another occasion, when I shall have something to say about the meaning of that remarkable combination of aggressive actions and alterations in the psycho-physical state which we call the sex act and which recurs in such a remarkably similar manner in so many different kinds of animals.[1]

For the time being I shall confine myself to remarking that in the state of orgasm the whole personality (the ego) identifies itself, in my opinion, with the genitals, and (as in sleep and in certain stages of epileptic fits) demands a hallucinatory return to the mother's body; and that the male organ advancing towards the womb attains this aim partially, or more correctly 'symbolically', and that only the genital secretion, the semen, attains this destiny in reality.

---

[1] See S. Ferenczi, *Thalassa* (1922). English translation, 2nd imp., 1938.

XIX

A CONTRIBUTION TO THE UNDERSTANDING OF THE PSYCHONEUROSES OF THE AGE OF INVOLUTION[1]

(about 1921-2)

THE cases in which I have had the opportunity of studying analytically the conditions in which the psychoneuroses of the age of involution arise can be summed up as follows: they were all persons who failed to make the change in the distribution of their libido which accompanies the involutionary processes, or were unable to adapt themselves to the new distribution of libidinal interests.

Since Professor Freud drew my attention to the fact, I know (and can only confirm) that with age the 'emanations of the libido'[2] tend to be withdrawn from the individual's love-objects and his no doubt quantitatively diminished libidinous interests tend to be devoted to his own ego. The old become narcissistic again—like children; much of their interest in family and social matters fades away, and they lose a great deal of their former capacity for sublimation, particularly in the sphere of shame and disgust. They become cynical, malicious, and mean; that is to say, their libido regresses to the 'pre-genital stages of development', and sometimes expresses itself in undisguised anal and urethral eroticism, voyeurism, exhibitionism, and a tendency to masturbation.[3]

The process is thus apparently the same as that which Freud describes as underlying paraphrenia; in both cases there is the

---

[1] Posthumous paper. First published in German: *Bausteine* III (1939). First English translation.

[2] See Freud, 'On Narcissism', 1914. Reprinted in *Collected Papers*, Vol. IV.

[3] Voyeurism in old age is illustrated in the story of Susanna and the Elders, in which Susanna is lewdly observed by the Elders while bathing; exhibitionism is a common symptom of so-called senile dementia. Freud's paper, 'The Predisposition to Obsessional Neurosis', 1913 (reprinted in *Collected Papers*, Vol. III, p. 122) draws attention to regression in ageing women to pre-genital forms of eroticism (sadism and anal eroticism).

same abandonment of object-cathexis and the same regression to narcissism. But in paraphrenia we must think of the libido as being quantitatively unaltered but entirely directed towards the ego, while at the change of life the ebbing of libido production leads to a diminution of its total quantity, which first makes itself perceptible in the loosest and most external libidinal cathexes, the 'emanations' on the object. The symptoms of paraphrenia are like islands that rise suddenly out of the depths in an earthquake; the symptoms of the change of life are like rocks left exposed by the receding waters of an inlet fed by no river and abandoned by the sea.

Noticeably little of all these mental signs of ageing are shown by those whom the climacteric affects neurotically. On the contrary, they show exaggerated family and social helpfulness, unselfishness and modesty, are generally liable to depressions, and are plagued by ideas of guilt and impoverishment which induce melancholy, from which they tend to seek refuge by falling into the arms of religion. But these depressions may be interrupted by their violent falling in love, which the sufferer tries vainly to fight against because of its incompatibility with the decorum required by his or her age. It is this type which has given the climacteric its popular name of the 'dangerous age'.

Nevertheless I believe that these noisy love affairs are comparable with the roll of drums used at executions to drown the shrieks of the victim, which in this case is object-libido. The patient's libido has in reality been withdrawn from its object, and it is only the ego which forces the individual to cling to his love ideals, and to conceal by his loud proclamation of love the regression which has in fact taken place. Thus the disastrous failure of ego and libido development to march hand-in-hand follows mankind into old age and forces him to repress that which runs counter to his ideals.

The exaggerated dissipation of sexual interests of many people at the climacteric is a symptom of over-compensation, of the healing tendency, while the real state of the distribution of the libido is represented by the ideas of impoverishment and guilt which accompany the patient's depression. These are the functional expression of the impoverishment of the libidinal object-cathexes and betray the regression to a-social (hence 'guilty') narcissism and auto-eroticism. The depression itself is the expression of the unpleasure and repugnance of a highly civilized consciousness at such incompatible appetites.

As a characteristic instance of this let me describe a case I recently observed. The patient, who had enjoyed a lifelong reputation as a woman-hunter and had had innumerable gallant adventures in which he had cheerfully risked his by no means inconsiderable social position and family interests, succumbed at the age of fifty-five to attacks of depression, with a notable tendency to ideas of impoverishment and guilt for which there was in reality no justification. These fits of depression were interrupted from time to time by periods of (extra-marital) coitus compulsion, during which, however, he turned out to be more or less impotent. Analysis showed that the precipitating cause of the neurosis was the threat, actually by no means a dangerous one, uttered by a husband who had noticed the patient's gallant intentions towards his wife. The threat was in fact far less dangerous than a hundred others to which he had cheerfully exposed himself in the past, but the slight shock that he had on this occasion was sufficient to release the illness. Further analysis showed that in the course of the years his personal security, his reputation as husband and father, and his money, had grown far more valuable to him than he realized; while amorous adventures had simultaneously lost a great deal of their attraction for him, though he had effectively concealed this from himself by exaggerating the interest he took in women and actually pushing this to the extreme of coitus compulsion. His impotence turned out to be the result of his narcissistic castration-anxiety. Although this had originally been very strong, he had been able to ward it off easily for many years, but, with the regression of libido due to his age, it had gained ground to such an extent that whenever there was the slightest threat of his personal security, his money, or his honour being 'cut off' it came immediately into play. In the course of analysis he rapidly adapted his attitude and his way of life to the real distribution of his libidinal interests and dropped his woman-hunting and his superfluous extravagances, whereupon his attacks of depression ceased and his potency returned; but only in relation to his previously neglected wife, and then only when before coitus she touched his genitals, thereby symbolically demonstrating her good will and the danger-free nature of the undertaking. The patient was satisfied with this result, and on financial grounds abandoned further analysis, which would certainly have profited him still further. Thus he succeeded by way of analysis in exchanging the ways of a dashing young man about town for the more modest ways of an elderly Philistine; a process that so many others succeed in accomplishing without medical aid. However, cases such as this show that in the process of growing old man has nearly as many awkward reefs to navigate if he is to avoid falling ill as he had in the transition from childhood to sexual maturity.

Psycho-analytic insight into cases in which libido-impoverishment and its defence reactions appear as the result of alterations induced by age throw light also on circumstances in which this impoverishment is due to other causes. I am thinking in the first place of the consequences of excessive masturbation. Masturbation—and the natural popular feeling in the matter is not to be altered by any 'masturbation-advocate'—is unquestionably a waste of libido which can be indulged in only at the cost of other interests of the organism. The endless complaints of masturbators about 'neurasthenic' disturbances have the same kind of basis in reality as—according to Freud—the hypochondriacal sensation in the organs has in real alterations of the distribution of the libido. But in hypochondria the libido is dammed up, while in neurasthenia it is wasted. The states of depression that accompany masturbation, the ideas of guilt and impoverishment, are perhaps similar to those of the involutionary neuroses—the psychical expression of the libido-impoverishment that has taken place and the damage done to the beloved ego by the waste of libido, the 'sin against oneself'.

Temporary depression following normal sexual intercourse, the well-known *omne animal post coitum triste est*, might also perhaps be regarded as an ego reaction to the perhaps excessive self-forgetfulness of sexual transports, i.e. as an expression of concern for one's own well-being and of narcissistic regret at the loss of precious bodily secretions. The path from the sensation of semen-loss to the idea of impoverishment goes by way of anal eroticism, while the tendency to extravagant masturbation or ejaculation in general seems to be a derivative of urethral eroticism. Post-coital and post-masturbatory organic and mental depression would then be the unpleasure-reaction of all the eroticisms constituting narcissism to the excessive claims on the libido made by a single zone—it is true, the dominant, uro-genital zone. While I thus am trying to trace back the involutionary neuroses to a conflict between object-libido and narcissism, I believe that in post-coital and masturbatory depressions in addition to these a conflict of auto-eroticisms within the individual's narcissism also plays a part.[1]

The fact that in the saying quoted above woman is said to be an exception to the rule of post-coital depression (which apparently is true) could have two causes. In the first place woman does not 'forget herself' so completely in sexual intercourse as man does; her narcissism prevents an excessive 'emanation' of the libido upon the object, and she is therefore partially spared post-coital disappointment. In the second place she 'loses' nothing in coitus; on the contrary, she is enriched by the hope of a child. When once one has been convinced by experience of the tremendous importance of bodily narcissism, which is always essentially and entirely primitive, one is in a better position to understand man's ineradicable fear of 'loss of bodily fluid'.

The fashion in which many neurotics of the climacteric seek to compensate for their dwindling interest in the external world by frantic libido-production is reminiscent of O. Gross's view of the state of manic exaltation. The manic phase, according to Gross, is the result of a kind of endogenous pleasure-production, the object of which is to conceal feelings of unpleasure. This manic pleasure-production occasionally reminds me of alcoholism;[2] but the alcoholic attains forgetfulness by taking in his drink from outside, while the manic is able to produce his

---

[1] I propose shortly to give pathological examples based on analytic investigation in support of these probably only provisional suggestions for an understanding of the 'hierarchy of the eroticisms'. (Cf. *Thalassa* (1933) Ed.)

[2] Cf. *Alkohol und Neurosen*, 1911. Reprinted in *Bausteine*, Vol. I, 145.

stimulant endogenously. The manic's real and fundamental mood—melancholic depression—makes its appearance only when the manic intoxication is over and the endogenous pleasure-production has faded away. After the above experiences of neurotic states in the elderly—which are often reminiscent of melancholia—the question arises whether it is not possible that melancholic depression in the non-elderly (together with the characteristic delusions of guilt and impoverishment) may not be only a reaction of narcissism to damage by libido-impoverishment.

In the few cases of melancholic depression which I have had the opportunity of studying analytically, the ideas of impoverishment have always concealed fear of the consequences of masturbation, and the delusion of guilt has always been the expression of a capacity for object-love that was constitutionally defective, or had become defective.[1] Also I invariably found in the pre-history of my patients a clinical picture that could be described only as neurasthenia. Moreover, the physical disturbances accompanying the melancholia were also reminiscent of the physical symptoms accompanying neurasthenia, in particular insomnia, weariness, temperatures below normal, headaches, and obstinate constipation.

Thus the actual neurosis underlying the melancholic depression is possibly nothing but neurasthenia, caused originally by a squandering of the libido in masturbation, which might be the organic root of manic-depressive psychosis, just as anxiety neurosis lies at the root of the paraphrenic states.

Consideration of the libido distribution in extreme old age may perhaps contribute something to the understanding of the picture, confusing as it is, of senile dementia. Hitherto the consequences of senile cerebral atrophy have alone been taken into consideration; but, apart from these, it should be possible to explain some of the symptoms as signs of senile libido alterations, others as compensatory attempts to cope with them, and

---

[1] Cf. Abraham, who in his paper 'Notes on the Psycho-Analytical Investigations and Treatment of Manic-Depressive Conditions and Allied Conditions' (1911) (reprinted in *Selected Papers*, p. 137. Hogarth Press, 1927) emphasized the defective capacity for object-love of manic-depressives.

others again as 'residuary phenomena' (cf. Freud's grouping of paraphrenic symptoms in his paper 'On Narcissism'). It strikes me as being very likely that the noticeable loss of receptivity for new sensory impressions in the aged, side by side with their retention of old memories, may be the result, not of histopathological alterations in the brain, but of impoverishment of the available object-libido; old memories spring to the mind so readily because of the lively feeling-tone—a residue of still undiminished object-libido—which still remains associated with them, though the present interest in the outside world is no longer sufficient for the acquisition of new lasting memories.

In any case, in senile dementia, as a consequence of sheer anatomical and psychical alterations, there disappears a large part of that difference between the level of ego-interests and of the libido which in the case of involuntary neurosis leads to repression and the symptom-formation associated with it. In dementia the level of intelligence also regresses to that lower level to which only the libido regresses in the case of senile neurotics. There takes place in them that undisguised breakthrough of the normally repressed which Gulliver observed among the Struldbrugs. The Struldbrugs, Swift says, cannot die and are condemned to eternal life: 'By degrees they grew melancholy and dejected, increasing in both till they came to fourscore.' After reaching this age the depression disappears, but instead they become 'not only opinionative, peevish, covetous, morose, vain, talkative, but uncapable of friendship, and dead to all natural affection. . . . Envy and impotent desires are their prevailing passions. . . . They have no remembrance of anything, but what they learned and observed in their youth and middle age. . . . The least miserable among them appear to be those who turn to dotage and entirely lose their memories; these . . . want many bad qualities which abound in others.'

This is an admirable description of the effects of mental conflict in old age, as well as of their final outcome.

XX

PARANOIA[1]
(about 1922)

Interpretation of the paranoid alcoholic's increased capacity for projection after alcoholic indulgence: one might suppose that censorship in the sense of repression (driving into the unconscious) did not exist in the paranoiac, as everything unconscious comes through to the conscious (if only in the form of projection); that alcoholic indulgence leads only to an accentuation of the libido, an activation of the unconscious, resulting in an increase in the work of projection.

The most noticeable feature of alcoholic paranoia is the break-through of homosexuality, masked by hypocritical jealousy of the other sex. In normal men also homosexual sublimation is relaxed after alcoholic indulgence (kissing, embracing, etc.).

The Paranoiac's Struggle against the Evidence of his Senses and his Memories

What one loves becomes absorbed into one's ego (introjection), for in the last resort one can love only oneself. When the transition to object-love takes place one introjects (subjectivizes) objective perception. What one does *not* love (the bad, the vicious, the recalcitrant) is rejected from the conscious by one of the paths available (repression or projection). In paranoia the sense organs for a time correct the originally indefinite, objectless ideas of reference. But soon both sense perceptions and memories submit to the wish to bring the reference feelings into connexion with appropriate objects (illusions, hallucinations, tricks of memory). The paranoiac projects 'on the basis of the slightest aetiological excuse'.

The paranoiac obviously associates his passions and his un-

[1] Posthumous paper. First published in German: *Bausteine* IV (1939). First English translation.

pleasurable ideas of reference with the fact that his sharpened vision correctly perceives that slight degree of continuous sexual interest, which one might call the tonus of the neuroses, which all men, though they are unconscious of it, display in relation to all living beings; but he exaggerates it quantitatively in his own way.

But paranoiac complaints not only contain an element of truth (Freud) in so far as they are a description of an endopsychic reality; they also possibly contain a trace of objective reality, but distorted into a delusional form.

The paranoiac's hallucinatory falsifications are a dream-like-wish-fulfilling confirmation of his delusional idea; they represent the victory of the projection wish over the evidence of his senses. The sensation of being watched when wearing new clothes is projected exhibitionism. (A subject for inquiry is whether this sensation is the same in relation to both sexes.)

Analogies between Dreams and Paranoia

A dream is a paranoid projection, the transformation into the objective (representation) of a subjective state, of something of which the dreamer is deprived, with a changed symbol[1] (wish-fulfilment).

The thing of which the dreamer is deprived is ejected from the ego (to assure the sleeper his rest) and is materialized in the outer world with a changed symbol.[2]

In dreams we are like erotomaniacs: every woman is in love with us (i) because we are in reality unsatisfied; (ii) because we hate them.

Paranoid Self-Observation

A patient reported to me a peculiar feeling of being looked at that he experienced on several occasions immediately after full sexual satisfaction. Walking in the street, he had the feeling that the women he passed looked at him with much more in-

[1] I.e. mathematical symbol, e.g. + changed to —. (Translator's note.)
[2] Mathematical symbol as above. (Translator's note.)

terest than he was usually aware of. My first thought was that a feeling of shame must be concealed behind this impression, but this was contradicted by (i) his impression that the women looked at him, not inquisitively or inquiringly, but actually erotically and at the same time provocatively (as he had perfectly correct ideas about his quite inconspicuous physique, he found this perplexing); (ii) the fact that he had this feeling only in relation to the opposite sex spoke against its being projected anxiety; and finally (iii) this tentative explanation did not prevent his having the same sensation on subsequent occasions when the same circumstances were repeated.

I attached greater importance to the matter only when the patient's wife described the same experience in almost the same words (she had the feeling that men looked at her more than usual).

I then said to myself that projection must be at work, a kind of *passagère* erotomania. We are capable of attaining sexual satisfaction only at intervals; hence there is a great difference in the level of heterosexual feelings before and after it. The man had projected his sudden lack of interest in the other sex into a feeling of being erotically looked at by women; similarly his wife had projected her feelings into the men who for the time being interested her so little.

Perhaps they also made use of the sexual tonus of passers-by, which they disregarded when they were themselves sexually 'hypertonic'. The tonus betrays itself in attitude, look and expression.

The feeling of lack of interest for the other sex seems to be so hard to bear that one involuntarily ejects it from the ego and over-compensates for it. Motives: (i) vanity; (ii) a kind of logic, which refuses to admit the existence of such fluctuations in emotional life. (Analogy in paranoia: delusional jealousy on cooling off of interest. Motive: desire to maintain marital loyalty.)

A confirmation from everyday life: so long as one is passionately in love, one is never sure that the feeling is reciprocated; no manner how many signs of her favour are shown by the beloved, doubt persists, and one goes on asking: Do you love me?

However, so soon as one is in 'peaceful possession', as the saying is, of one's partner's love, so soon as one knows for certain that one is loved, one already has a trace of erotomania; a projection of indifference or turning-away-from with a changed symbol.[1]

This analysis may have been responsible for the fact that for some time my patient has no longer had this feeling. That would make him my first practically cured case of paranoia.

On the Technique of Analysing Paranoiacs

(i) Paranoiacs must not be argued with.
(ii) Their delusional ideas must be accepted, i.e. treated as possibilities, though with certain precautions.
(iii) A trace of transference can be secured by a little flattery (in particular remarks recognizing their intelligence. All paranoiacs are megalomaniacs).
(iv) Paranoiacs interpret their dreams best themselves. They know how to interpret dreams (lack of censorship).
(v) It is difficult to get them to talk about more than they themselves produce. But a paranoiac (when he is in a good mood) readily condescends to indulge in useless play with ideas (that is his conception of analysis). This enables one, however, to discover the most important things; but it is not easy to make the paranoiac keep to them. If, therefore, one observes that trying to make him do so only makes him worse, one should let him go back again to associating in his own way.
(vi) The paranoiac is offended if one takes the liberty of showing him his 'unconscious'; for nothing is 'unconscious' to him, he knows himself completely. In fact he knows himself much better than I do non-paranoiacs; what he does not project is readily available to him.

---

[1] Mathematical symbol as above. (Translator's note.)

XXI

NOTES AND FRAGMENTS[1]
(1920 and 1930-32)

Editor's Note

ON Ferenczi's death a number of notes were found among his papers. These were jottings of ideas that were to be worked up later, if occasion arose, into more permanent form. They were for his private use, in the four languages which served as the medium of his thought, and were scribbled on odd bits of paper, using abbreviations for phrases and ideas which needed some effort to discover and correctly to transcribe.

Ferenczi's literary executors translated the bulk of these notes into German (where that language was not originally used) and published them in the *Bausteine*, Vol. IV.

The originals were burnt when Ferenczi's charming house in Buda was destroyed in the siege of 1944-5.

I (1920)

26.9.1920

Nocturnal Emission, Masturbation, and Coitus

1. Nocturnal emission is *always* unconscious masturbation (often brought about by means of unconscious fantasies).

2. It always follows as a substitute on the giving up of masturbation. In some cases masturbation in sleep slips in as a transitory stage.

3. Complementary series. Onanism=masturbation+fantasy. The more the masturbation, the smaller the role played by fantasy, and *vice versa*. Fantasy is more exhausting, both physically and morally.

4. Therapy: nocturnal emission can be changed into onanism, and it is only the onanism that can be converted into coitus.

5. *Precocious ejaculation* reduces the friction to a minimum and

---

[1] Posthumous. First published in German: *Bausteine* IV (1939). First English translation. (Various parts printed previously in *Int. Z. f. Psa.* (1934), 20, 5; *Indian J. of Psych.* (1934), 9, 29, and *Int. J. of PsA.* (1949), 30, 231.

increases to the extreme the mental aspects of the emotion (and of fantasy). It corresponds to a diurnal emission.

6. Forepleasure gratifications are as far as possible to be forbidden to patients suffering from precocious ejaculation.

7. *The tendency to onanism* is probably connected with increase of urethralism. (Tendency to ejaculation outweighs tendency to retention.) Such urethralism would be characteristic of the *neurasthenic constitution*, while the *tendency to retention* (anal-erotic) could go together with the *constitution for anxiety neurosis*. (Tendency to coitus reservatus, interruptus, incompletus.)

In the same way:

I/1. Urethral-erotic constitution=tendency to enuresis—tendency to onanism (to nocturnal emission).

2. Inordinately great discharge—*manifestation* of *neurotic symptoms*=impoverishment of the organ (or organs) in libido.

II/1. Anal-erotic constitution—tendency to retention.

2. Retention—anxiety neurosis (manifest).

What could the hypochondriac constitution be? Tendency to accumulate organ libido (organ eroticism). (Fixation to this eroticism).

Perhaps: already an accumulation of protonarcissistic (genital —anal and urethral—) libido in the organs.

26.9.20
'Zuhälter' and 'Femme Entretenante'

Being kept by a prostitute is not simply 'moral insanity', but also fixation (regression) to the desire of being kept by the mother. Many impotents are unconsciously *Zuhälter* who cannot surrender in love to a woman if they have to give anything in return or sacrifice something. Amongst other things, ejaculation is such a sacrifice.

(Parallel: woman who keeps a man—mother type, one who provides, a cook.)

30.9.20
Anxiety and Free Floating Libido

The association of a patient brought a striking confirmation of the correctness of Freud's ideas, according to which anxiety is to be explained by the libido becoming free and remaining unsatisfied: 'My wife used to have fears when she had to fetch something from a dark room; her method of protection against this was to take her baby into the room with her; if she pressed the child to herself she did not feel any anxiety at all.'

The efficacy of this remedy proves to us *ex iuvantibus* that anxiety in this case was brought about by a relative frustration of libido satisfaction. This corresponds to a similar case described by Freud of a child who was not afraid in the dark if he could hear his mother speak. Hearing her voice, the darkness for him became '*lighter*'.

30.9.20
On Affect Hysteria

Exaggerated disgust is directed against everything that is in any way connected with genitality. (*Fat* women, *over-full* breasts, pregnancy, confinement, newly born babies.) *Idiosyncrasies* against certain kinds of food and drink.

'Squandering of affect' in the work of introjection.
Genital excitement is discharged in non-genital affects.
Conversion is (Breuer, Freud) also *discharge of affect*.
Conversion: an affect acquired ontogenetically.
Affect: conversion acquired phylogenetically.

Stigmas are trivial (inherited) conversion symptoms.
Stigmas and excessive affects are *petite hystérie*.

II (1930)

Oral Eroticism in Education

10.8.1930

1. It is not impossible that the question of how much oral eroticism (sucking the breast, the thumb, the dummy—kissing) should be allowed or even offered to the suckling, and later in the period of weaning, is of paramount importance for the development of character.

2. Tactless, un-understanding education provokes outbursts of rage and thus conditions the child to discharge tensions through aggressivity and destruction.

3. Simultaneously with these outbursts attempts at compensation develop: gratification by means of permitted parts of the body. (Screen memory: in the flat—the first remembered—sitting on the pot and rhythmically pushing a little toy (a tiny bell) up inside the nose. It remains stuck in the cavity of the nose, a doctor is called, attempts at escape. This screen memory emerged under the pressure of feelings of confusion and anxiety. The patient (woman) is essentially aggressive and negativistic. The relative friendliness of the analyst deprives her of the possibility of a fight; behind the aggressive tendencies anxiety becomes manifest, which then leads to the screen memory quoted above.) Obviously the love life of the newly born begins as complete passivity. Withdrawal of love leads to undeniable feelings of being deserted. The consequence is the splitting of the personality into two halves, one of which plays the role of the mother (thumb sucking: thumb is equalled with the mother's breast). Prior to the splitting there is probably a tendency to self-destruction caused by the trauma, which tendency, however, can still be inhibited—so to speak—on its way: out of the chaos a kind of new order is created which is then adapted to the precarious external circumstances.

10.8.1930
Each Adaptation is preceded by an Inhibited Attempt at Splitting

1. Probably each living being reacts to stimuli of unpleasure with fragmentation and commencing dissolution (death-instinct?). Instead of 'death-*instinct*' it would be better to choose a word that would express the absolute passivity of this process. Possibly complicated mechanisms (living beings) can only be preserved as units by the pressure of their environment. At an unfavourable change in the environment the mechanism falls to pieces and disintegrates as far (probably along lines of antecedent historic development), as the greater simplicity and consequent plasticity of the elements makes a new adaptation possible. Consequently autoplastic adaptation is always preceded by autotomy. The tendency to autotomy in the first instance tends to be complete. Yet an opposite movement (instinct of self-preservation, life-instinct) inhibits the disintegration and drives towards a new consolidation, as soon as this has been made possible by the plasticity developed in the course of fragmentation. It is very difficult to form a conception of the true essence of this instinctual factor and its function. It is as if it could command sources of knowledge and possibilities which go infinitely far beyond everything that we know as faculties of our conscious intelligence. It assesses the gravity of the damage, the amounts of energy of the environment and of the surrounding people, it seems to have some knowledge of events distant in space and to know exactly at what point to stop the self-destruction and to start the reconstruction. In the extreme case when all the reserve forces have been mobilized but have proved impotent in the face of the overpowering attack, it comes to an extreme fragmentation which could be called dematerialization. Observation of patients, who fly from their own sufferings and have become hypersensitive to all kinds of extraneous suffering, also coming from a great distance, still leave the question open whether even these extreme, quasi-pulverized, elements which have been reduced to mere psychic energies do not also contain tendencies for reconstruction of the ego.

10.8.1930
Autoplastic and Alloplastic Adaptation

Contrasted with the form of adaptation described above is alloplastic adaptation, i.e. the alteration of the environment in such a way as to make self-destruction and self-reconstruction unnecessary, and to enable the ego to maintain its existing equilibrium, i.e. its organization, unchanged. A necessary condition for this is a highly developed sense of reality.

10.8.1930

Autosymbolism and Historical Representation should be taken into consideration in equal measure when interpreting dreams or symptoms; the former hitherto much neglected. In hysterical symptoms a subjective moment of the trauma is essentially always repeated. First: the immediate sensory impressions; second: the emotions and the physical sensations associated with them; third: the accompanying mental states, which are represented also as such. (For instance: representation of unconsciousness by the feeling of the head being cut off or lost. Representation of confusion as vertigo, of distressing surprise as being caught in a whirlwind, and of the impotence of dying as being projected into a lifeless thing or animal. The splitting of the personality is mostly represented as being torn to pieces, the fragmentation as an explosion of the head.) Hysterical symptoms seem to be mere autosymbolisms, that is, reproductions of the ego memory-system, but without any connexion with the causative moments. One of the main methods of making something unconscious seems to be the accentuation of the purely subjective elements at the cost of knowledge about external causation.

10.8.1930
On the Analytical Construction of Mental Mechanisms

The topic-dynamic-economic construction of the mental apparatus is based exclusively on the elaboration of subjective data. We relate the sudden disappearance of one part of the content of the conscious, occurring simultaneously, seemingly without any motive, with the appearance of another idea, to a displacement of mental energy from one mental locality to another. A particular case of this displacement process is repression.

Certain observations urge us not to exclude out of hand the possibility of other processes in the mental apparatus. With the same right with which one speaks of the process of repression one may accept as valid statements by patients, that is to say, one may allow the topical point of view in cases in which the personality is described as torn into two or more parts and after this disintegration the fragments assume, as it were, the form and function of a whole person. (Analogy with zoological observation, according to which certain primitive animals can disintegrate and then the individual fragments can reconstitute themselves as whole individuals.) Another process requiring topical representation is characterized in the phrase 'to get beside oneself'.[1] The ego leaves the body, partly or wholly, usually through the head, and observes from outside, usually from above, the subsequent fate of the body, especially its suffering. (Images somewhat like this: bursting out through the head and observing the dead, impotently frustrated body, from the ceiling of the room; less frequently: carrying one's own head under one's arm with a connecting thread like the umbilical cord between the expelled ego components and the body.) Typical examples:

1. The ego suddenly acquires a widely extended vision and can move with ease in these endless plains. (Turning away from pain and turning towards external events.)

2. At a further increase of the painful tension: climbing the Eiffel Tower, running up a steep wall.

3. The traumatic force catches up and, as it were, shakes the ego down from the high tree or the tower. This is described as a frightening whirlwind, ending in the complete dissolution of connexions and a terrific vertigo, until finally

4. the ability, or even the attempt, to resist the force is given

[1] German original: 'ausser sich geraten.' (Editor)

up as hopeless, and the function of self-preservation declares itself bankrupt. This final result may be described or represented as being partially dead.

In one case such 'being dead' was represented in dreams and associations as maximal pulverization, leading finally to complete de-materialization.

The de-materialized dead component has the tendency to drag the not yet dead parts to itself into non-existence, especially in dreams (particularly in nightmares).

It is not impossible that, by further accumulation of experience, the topical point of view will be able to describe, in addition to displacement and repression, also the fragmentation and pulverization of complex mental structures.

17.8.1930
On the Theme of Neo-catharsis

It appears that we must make an exact differentiation between that part of catharsis which appears spontaneously when approaching the pathogenic mental content and that which, as it were, can only be elicited by overcoming strong resistance. The single cathartic outbreak is not essentially different from the spontaneous hysterical outbreak with which patients ease their tensions from time to time. In neo-catharsis such an outbreak indicates merely the place where further detailed exploration has to begin, that is to say, one must not content oneself with what is given spontaneously, which is somehow adulterated, partially displaced, and quite often attenuated; one must press on (of course as far as possible without suggesting contents) to obtain from the patient more about his experiences, the accompanying circumstances, and so on. After the 'waking up' from this trance state, the patient feels more stable for a time; that state is soon dissipated, however, and gives way to feelings of insecurity and doubt, which often deteriorate into hopelessness. 'Well, all this sounds all right', they say frequently —'but is it also true? I shall never, never find security based on true recollections.' The next time the cathartic work sets in at quite a different place, and leads, not without energetic pressure from ourselves, to the repetition of other traumatic scenes. This hard task must be repeated innumerable times until the patient feels, as it were, surrounded, and cannot but repeat before our eyes the trauma which originally had led to mental disintegration. (It is as if one had, by strenuous mining operations, to open a cave filled with gas under high pressure. The earlier, smaller outbreaks were like cracks from which some of the material could escape, but which soon closed up spontaneously.) In the case of Tf. the cathartic work lasted longer than a year, after a preceding analysis of four years, it is true with some interruptions. It must be admitted, however, that my lack of knowledge of the neocathartic possibilities may be responsible for the long duration of the analysis.

24.8.1930
Thoughts on 'Pleasure in Passivity'

The problem of bearing, accepting, even enjoying unpleasure seems to be insoluble without far-reaching speculations. The assertion and defence of egoistic interests is certainly a well-tried form of securing an unendangered tranquillity. At the moment when all defensive forces have been exhausted (but also, when the suddenness of aggression overpowers the defensive cathexes), the libido apparently turns against the self with the same vehemence with which it has defended it till then. Indeed, one could speak of identification with the stronger victorious opponent (on the other hand the role of the opponent can be taken also by some unspecified, impersonal elemental forces). The fact is that such self-destruction can be associated with feelings of pleasure and it *is* necessarily so associated in cases of masochistic surrender. Whence this pleasure? Is it only (as I ventured to interpret it earlier) the identification in fantasy with the destroyer—or have we rather to suppose that the enjoyment of the egoistic tranquillity—after the recognition that it cannot be preserved any longer and that a new form of equilibrium has become necessary—veers suddenly round to a pleasure in self-sacrifice, which could confidently be called 'altruistic pleasure'? The example of the bird, fascinated by the sight of a serpent or by the claws of the eagle, which, after a short period of resistance, throws itself to its own ruin, can be quoted here. In the moment when one must cease to use the environment as material for one's own security and well-being (i.e. when the environment does not consent any longer to accept the role of being incorporated in this way), one accepts the role of sacrifice, so to speak, with sensual pleasure, i.e. the role of material for other, stronger, more self-asserting, more egotistic, forces. Egotistic and altruistic tranquillity were, accordingly, only the two extremes of a higher general principle of tranquillity, including both. The instinct of tranquillity is accordingly the principal instinct, to which the life (egotistic) and death (altruistic) instincts are subjected.

The change of direction of the libido does not always happen in this sudden way nor is it always complete. One could say that the pleasure in self-destruction often (but not always) goes no further than it is driven by the irresistible forces. As soon as the rage of the elements (or of the human environment, most frequently of the parents and adults) has exhausted itself, the part of the ego which remained intact immediately starts to build up a new personality from the preserved fragments, a personality which, however, bears the traces of the endured struggle fraught with defeat. This new personality is called one that is 'adjusted to the conditions'. Each adaptation is accordingly a process of destruction interrupted in its course. In some cases of fragmentation and atomization after a shock the pleasure in one's own defeat was expressed in:

1. Admiration for the greatness and power of the opponent or of the operative elemental force; a rather objective appreciation which could be called aesthetic pleasure.
2. Enjoyment of one's own wisdom and intellectual superiority which is compared with the ruthless brutal, i.e. completely unintelligent opponent to one's own favour. Brutal force always makes the impression of something absurd, mad, and consequently comical. (When veering round to self-destruction the concomitant mood expresses itself occasionally as interminable *laughter*. This laughter means

at the same time the recognition of the senselessness of the struggle which could have been avoided.)
3. The acknowledgment and appreciation of the naïve brutality of another ego (or force) has definitely something superior and maternal in it. Indeed here we can get the first idea of the nature of the superior femininity and motherliness. Child and man show ruthless egoism. If the infant is not fed he is doomed to die. Femininity and motherliness bear witness to the intuitive insight into the true state of affairs and the distribution of forces, and are also able to draw the correct conclusions from this appreciation.

I have the feeling that with these points the motivation of the pleasure of self-destruction is far from being exhausted and would like to add that partial destruction (immediately after a trauma or shock)—as represented in fantasies and dreams—shows the previously unified personality in a secondarily narcissistic splitting, the 'dead', 'murdered' part of the person—like a child—nursed, wrapped up in, by the parts which remained intact. In one of my cases it came, in later years, to a repeated trauma which, for the most part, destroyed also this nursing outer shell (atomization). Out of this as it were pulverized mass there developed a superficial, visible, even partly conscious, personality, behind which the analysis was able to reveal not only the existence of all previous layers, but was also able to revive these layers. In this way it was possible to dissolve quite ossified character traits, products of adaptation, forms of reaction, and to reawaken stages apparently long superseded.

Behind this 'pleasure of adaptation' or 'altruistic pleasure' it was possible to reveal the defeated egotistic pleasure. To be sure, this pleasure had first to be strengthened by the force of analytic encouragement. With our help the analysand is able to face, to bear, even to react to, situations which formerly were too much for him in his state of isolation and helplessness to which he had had to surrender unconditionally, even surrender with pleasure. Far-going homosexual bondages can occasionally be traced back to their traumatic sources and the adaptive reaction be retransformed into a reactive one.

Expressed in biological terms this means: Re-activation of the traumatic conflicts and dealing with them in an alloplastic way instead of the previous autoplastic one.

31.8.1930
Fundamental Traumatic Effect of Maternal Hatred or of the Lack of Affection

T.Z. speaks incessantly of hate waves which she has always felt as coming from her mother, according to her fantasy even when still in mother's womb. Later she felt unloved because she was born a girl and not a boy. Identical conditions in Dm. and B.

Dm. has always had the compulsion to seduce men and to be thrown into disaster by them. In fact she has done so only to escape from the loneliness which was brought upon her by her mother's coldness. Even in the overpassionate ruthless expressions of love by her mother, she felt her mother's hatred as a disturbing element (difficult birth, although no actual contraction of the pelvis).

S. had to be brought up by the father because of his mother's aggressiveness. The father died when the child was eighteen months old and then he was delivered over to the cruelty of the mother and the grandfather. These traumata have led to disturbance of all object relations. Secondary narcissism.

The relation between the strong heterosexual trauma (father) and the defective mother fixation must remain problematic for the time being. Further experience needed.

7.9.1930
Fantasies on a Biological Model of Super-ego Formation

H.'s spontaneous statement on her fatness: 'all this fat is my mother'. If she felt freer inside from the disastrous (introjected) mother-model, then she noticed a decrease in the fat padding, and at the same time she lost weight.

During the week, in which, for the first time, he faced up

defensively to his cruel mother: S. felt he had lost weight. At the same time, however, he had the idea that this fat was that of his equally cruel grandfather.

These observations lead to the idea that formation of the super-ego occurs as the final outcome of a fight, in reality lost, with an overwhelming (personal or material) force, roughly in the following way:

A precondition is the existence of an 'intelligence' or a 'tendency to deal with things economically', with an exact knowledge of all the qualitative and quantitative energy charges and possibilities of the body, also of the ability of the mind to accomplish, to bear, and to tolerate; in the same way this 'intelligence' can estimate with mathematical exactitude the distribution of power in the external world. The first normal reaction of a living being to external unpleasure is an automatic warding off, that is to say a tendency to self-preservation. If beaten down by an overwhelming force, the energy (perhaps in fact the external power of the trauma) turns against the self. In this moment the 'intelligence', which is concerned above all with the preservation of the united personality, seems to resort to the subterfuge of turning round the idea of being devoured in this way: with a colossal effort the 'intelligence' swallows the whole hostile power or person and imagines[1] that it itself has devoured somebody else and, in addition, its own person. In this way man can have pleasure in his own dismemberment. Now, however, his personality consists of a devoured, over-great (fat) aggressor and a much smaller, weaker person, oppressed and dominated by the aggressor, that is, his pretraumatic personality. Many neurotics symbolize their illness in dreams and symptoms as a bundle that they have to carry on their backs; in others this bundle becomes part of the body and turns into a hump or growth; also favoured is the comparison with an enveloping great person which, as it were, enwraps maternally the former personality.

The psychological 'devouring' seems to be associated with greedy voracity and increased hunger for assimilation: putting on fat as a hyserictal symptom. If, by the analytic revision of the

[1] In German: 'bildet sich ein' is used. (Editor)

traumatic struggle, the person has been freed from the overwhelming power, then the obesity, the physiological parallel phenomenon, may disappear.

Physiological and chemical aspects: the muscle and nerve tissues consist, in essence, of protoplasm, that is to say mainly of proteins. Protein is specific for each species, perhaps even for each individual. Foreign protein acts as poison; it is therefore broken down and the specific protein synthesized anew out of the harmless constituents. Not so with unspecific fat. Pork fat, for instance, is stored in the cells as such, and can quite well stand as the organic symbol, or the organic tendency to manifestation, which runs parallel with the devouring of the external powers.

Here a still quite vague idea emerges. Is it possible that the formation of the super-ego and the devouring of the superior force in defeat may explain the two following processes:

(1) 'Eating up the ancestors', and (2) adaptation in general.

1. Plants grow and develop through the incorporation of minerals. Thereby the possibility of existence within the organism is offered to minerals (inorganic substances) which, however, is equivalent to being devoured by the organism. How far the inorganic matter as such is destroyed or dissolved, however, remains problematic. Quantitative analysis rediscovers the consumed inorganic substances to the last grain. When the plant is devoured by a herbivorous animal, the plant organism is destroyed, that is to say reduced to organic or even partly inorganic components. It remains problematic whether or not, despite this, part of the plant substance survives and conserves its individuality, even in the body of the herbivorous animal. In this way the animal body is a superstructure of organic and inorganic elements. Expressed psycho-analytically (although at first glance highly paradoxical) this means: the animal organism has devoured one part of the (menacing?) external world and thus provided for the continuation of its own existence.

The same thing happens at the devouring of animal organisms. It is possible that we harbour in our organism inorganic, vegetative, herbivorous, and carnivorous tendencies like chemical valencies. The likewise highly paradoxical aphorism here is as follows: 'Being devoured is, after all, also a form of existence.'

The idea then emerges that one ought to consider in this process the possibility of a mutual devouring, that is to say a mutual super-ego formation.

2. Adaptation in general appears to be a mutual devouring and being devoured, whereby each party believes that he has remained the victor.

21.9.1930
Trauma and Striving for Health

The immediate effect of a trauma which cannot be dealt with at once is fragmentation. Query: is this fragmentation merely a mechanical consequence of the shock? or is it as such already one form of defence, i.e. adaptation? Analogy with the falling to pieces of lower animals when subjected to excessive stimulation and continuation of existence in fragments. (To be looked up in biological text books.) Fragmentation may be advantageous (*a*) by creating a more extended surface towards the external world, i.e. by the possibility of an increased discharge of affects; (*b*) from the physiological angle: the giving up of concentration, of unified perception, at least puts an end to the simultaneous suffering of multiple pain. The single fragments suffer for themselves; the unbearable unification of all pain qualities and quantities does not take place; (*c*) the absence of higher integration, the cessation of the interrelation of pain fragments allows the single fragments a much greater adaptability. Example: at a loss of consciousness, changes in the shape of the body (being stretched, strained, bent, compressed to the limit of physical elasticity) appear to be possible, whereas a simultaneous defence reaction would increase the danger of irreparable fractures or tears, cf. examples of terrible injuries in childhood, for instance violation, with ensuing shock and rapid recovery.

By the shock, energies which have hitherto been quiescent or used up in object relations are suddenly awakened in the form of narcissistic care, concern, and helpfulness. The certainly quite unconscious internal force, as yet unrecognized in its essence, which estimates with mathematical accuracy both the severity of the trauma and the available ability for defence, produces with automatic certainty and according to the pattern of a complicated calculating machine the only practical and correct psychological and physical behaviour in a given situation. The absence of emotions and speculations which might disturb the senses and distort reality permits the exact functioning of the calculating machine, as if in sleep-walking.

As soon as the shock has, in a way, been dealt with by means of the above processes, the psyche hastens to concentrate in a unit the individual fragments which have now once more become manageable. Consciousness returns, but is completely unaware of the processes since the trauma.

It is much more difficult to explain the symptom of retroactive amnesia. Probably it is a defensive mechanism against the memory of the trauma itself.

Further examples of the regenerative tendency to be worked out in detail.

III (1931)

Attempt at a Summary

9.3.1931

1. *Technical.* Further development of neocatharsis: contrary to the conception previously current, according to which pathogenic material must be probed only associatively so that it may discharge and emotionally empty itself spontaneously and, because of its strong tension, with great vehemence (and at the same time creating and leaving behind it the feeling of the reality of having experienced a trauma), there occurs, to one's astonishment, soon and occasionally immediately after each such discharge a revival of the doubts about the reality of all that has been experienced in the trance state. In some cases the feeling of well-being lasts the whole day, yet nightly sleep and dreaming, especially the awakening from them, bring a complete reappearance of the symptoms, complete loss of the confidence of the previous day, even once more the feeling of complete hopelessness. There may then follow days, even weeks, of complete resistance; until the next successful absorption in the deepest layers of the spheres of experience reaches the same moment of experience, complements it with new convincing details, and brings a renewed strengthening of the reality feeling with somewhat more permanent effect.

Absorption in the real sphere of emotional experience inevitably demands as complete as possible an abandonment of present reality. In principle so-called free association is in itself such a diversion of attention from actual reality, yet this diversion is rather superficial and is maintained at a rather conscious, at the most pre-conscious, level both by the intellectual activity of the patient and by our attempts to explain and interpret following one on the other in more or less rapid succession. It indeed requires of the patients a colossal trust to allow such absorption in the presence of another person. They must first have the feeling that, even in our presence (*a*) they can allow themselves everything in words, gestures, emotional outbreaks, without fear of punishment or of being pulled up by us in any way; and more than that [they can expect]¹ complete sympathy and full understanding of everything, come what may. It is in addition a precondition that they should safely feel that we mean well and are willing to help, and that they must also have the hope that we are indeed able to help. (*b*) No less important is the feeling of reassurance that we are sufficiently powerful to protect the patient against all excesses which might be harmful to him, to us, to other persons and things, and especially that we are both willing and able to bring him back from this 'mad unreality'. Some secure our goodwill in a truly childish fashion by clutching our hand or holding it fast during the whole period of the absorption in the trance. What one calls trance is, therefore, a kind of state of sleep in which communication is yet kept up with a reliable person. Slight changes in the force of the grip here become the means of expressing emotions. Responding or not responding to the changing pressure of the grip may then be taken as the measure and direction of the analyst's reaction. (In an emergency, for instance in the case of too great anxiety, a firm pressure can prevent a frightened awakening; the limpness of our hand is occasionally felt and evaluated as a mute contradiction or as a partial dissatisfaction with the material.)

ESCAPE OF THE PATIENT FROM CONTACT WITH THE ANALYST

After this communication with the patient has lasted for a more or less longish time, just like a conversation in half-sleep, which has to be guided with extraordinary tact and the greatest possible economy and adaptation, it may happen that the patient is suddenly overpowered by an extremely strong hysterical pain or spasm, not infrequently by a true hallucinatory nightmare, in which he acts out in word and gesture some inner or external experience. There is always present the tendency to awake immediately afterwards, to look round for some seconds as if dazed, and then to reject all that has happened as a stupid and senseless fantasy. With some skill we can succeed, however, in restoring contact with the patient who is still in the fit. This

¹ (Inserted by the Editor.)

must be done rather forcefully. Without actually giving him direct hints, the patient can be brought to tell us about the causes of his pain, the meaning of his defensive struggle, still apparent in his muscles. We may thus succeed in getting from him details of his emotional and sensory processes and of the exogenic causes of those traumas and sensations, and the defences against them. Often the responses at first appear very indistinct and vague. After some urging, however, an enveloping cloud, a weight pressing heavily on the chest, may gradually assume definite outlines; there may then be added to it the taut features of a man which, according to the patient's feelings, express hatred or aggressiveness; the indistinct sensations of pain and congestion in the head may reveal themselves as remote consequences of a sexual (genital) trauma; when we then put all these formulations to the patient and urge him to combine them into a whole, we may experience the re-emergence of a traumatic scene with distinct indications of the time and place at which it occurred. Not infrequently we then succeed in differentiating the autosymbolic representation of the mental processes after the trauma (e.g. fragmentation as falling to bits, atomization as explosion) from the real external traumatic events, and in this way reconstruct the total picture of both the subjective and objective history. There often follows, then, a state of calm relaxation, with a feeling of relief. It is as if the patient had with our help succeeded in climbing a hitherto unscaleable wall which awakes in him a feeling of increased internal power, with the help of which he has now succeeded in conquering certain dark forces whose victim he had been until now. However, as already mentioned, we should not place too much hope on the permanence of this success; the next day we may find the patient in full rebellion and desolation again, and often it is only after some days' effort that we may succeed in getting near once more to the painful point, or in getting out of the depths new painful points which are interwoven with the previous ones as it were in a traumatic web.

Budapest, 13.3.1931
On the Patient's Initiative

To continue the previous paper on the humility of the analyst: this could be extended also to the way of keeping the work going. In general it is advantageous: to consider for a time *every one*, even the most improbable, of the communications as in some way possible, even to accept an apparently obvious delusion. Two reasons for this: thus, by leaving on one side the 'reality' question, one can feel one's way more completely into the patient's mental life. (Here something should be said about the disadvantages of contrasting 'reality' and 'unreality'. The latter must in any case be taken equally seriously as a *psychic* reality; hence above all one must become fully absorbed in all that the patient says and feels. Connexions here with metaphysical possibilities.) As a professional man the physician feels uneasy, of course, when the patient not only expresses his own opinion of the interpretations, which opinion is in complete contradiction to the current (analytic) convictions, but also criticizes the methods and techniques used by the physician, ridicules them for their inefficiency, and puts forward his own technical propositions. There are two motives which might lead one to change the usual technique in some way, even in the sense of the patient's propositions: (1) if one has not made progress with work lasting weeks, months, or even years, and the analyst is faced with the possibility of dropping the case as incurable. It is indeed more logical, before giving it up completely to try out on the case some of the patient's propositions. Of course therapeutically this has always been so, only the physician had to know that what he then did was no longer analysis, but something different. I would like to add, however, that the occasional accepting of 'something different' may enrich even the analysis itself. Analytical technique has never been, nor is it now, something finally settled; for about a decade it was mixed with hypnosis and suggestion . . . [Continuation not found. Editor.]

Relaxation and Education

22.3.1931

It appears that patients arrive at a point—even if granted the greatest toleration and freedom for relaxing—where the freedom must be somewhat restricted out of practical considerations: e.g. the desire to have the analyst constantly present, the desire to change the transference situation into a real lasting relation, must remain unfulfilled. The consequent, often extraordinarily strong emotional reaction repeats the shock which led originally to symptom formation. The analyst's great compliance and acquiescence bring for a while—as if by contrast—many bad, hitherto unconscious, experiences of the infantile period into consciousness or make reconstruction feasible. Finally it becomes possible to reduce—so to speak—the whole pathological fabric to the traumatic core and then almost all dream analyses become centred around a few staggering infantile experiences. Occasionally during such analyses the patients are carried away by their emotions; states of severe pain both mental and physical, deliria with more or less deep loss of consciousness, and coma mix themselves into the work of pure intellectual associations and constructions. One urges the patient in this state to give information about the causes of the various emotional and perceptual disturbances. The insight achieved in this way brings about a kind of gratification which simultaneously is emotional and intellectual and is worthy to be called a conviction. But this gratification does not last long, often for some hours only; the next night brings the distorted repetition of the trauma perhaps in the form of a nightmare, without the slightest feeling of understanding; the whole conviction has completely gone. The transitory, intellectual and emotional conviction is torn to bits again and again and the patient oscillates, now as before, between the symptom in which he feels all the unpleasure and does not understand anything, and the conscious reconstruction in which he understands everything yet feels little or nothing. A deep change of this often tiresome and automatic oscillation is brought about by the need mentioned above to restrict the relaxation. It is the high degree of our compliance that makes even the slightest refusal by us uncommonly painful; the patient feels as if he were struck off his balance, produces the most intense degrees of shock and resistance, he feels deceived but inhibited in his aggressiveness, and ends in a kind of paralysed state which he experiences as dying or being dead. If we then succeed in directing this state away from us and back to the infantile traumatic events, it may happen that the patient seizes the moment in which, at that time, knowing and feeling led, under the same symptoms of helpless rage, to self-destruction, to splitting of the mind in unconscious feeling and unfelt knowing,[1] i.e. to the same process that Freud assumes to be the basis of repression. Our analyses will and apparently can go back also to these preliminary stages of the process of repression. It is true that to achieve this one must give up completely all relation to the present and sink completely into the traumatic past. The only bridge between the real world and the patient in this state of trance is the person of the analyst, who, instead of the simple gesticulatory and emotional repetition, urges the patient struggling with his affects to intellectual work, encouraging him incessantly with questions.

A surprising but apparently generally valid ct fain this process of self-splitting is the sudden change of the object-relation that has become intolerable, into narcissism. The man abandoned by all gods escapes completely from reality and creates for himself another world in which he, unimpeded by earthly gravity, can achieve everything that he wants. Has he been unloved, even tormented, he now splits off from himself a part which in the form of a helpful, loving, often motherly, minder commiserates with the tormented remainder of the self, nurses him and decides for him; and all this is done with deepest wisdom and most penetrating intelligence. He is intelligence and kindness itself, so to speak a guardian angel. This angel sees the suffering or murdered child from the outside (consequently he must have, as it were, escaped out of the person in the process of 'bursting'), he wanders through the whole Universe seeking help, invents fantasies for the child that cannot be saved in any other way, etc. But in the moment of a very strong, repeated

[1] In German: 'unbewusstes Fühlen und ungefühltes Wissen.'

trauma even this guardian angel must confess his own helplessness and well meaning deceptive swindles to the tortured child and then nothing else remains but suicide, unless at the last moment some favourable change in the reality occurs. This favourable event to which we can point against the suicidal impulse is the fact that in this new traumatic struggle the patient is no longer alone. Although we cannot offer him everything which he as a child should have had, the mere fact that we can or may be helpful to him gives the necessary impetus towards a new life in which the pages of the irretrievable are closed and where the first step will be made towards acquiescence in what life yet can offer instead of throwing away what may still be put to good use.

26.3.1931

On the Revision of the Interpretation of Dreams

In Freud's *Interpretation of Dreams* the wish-fulfilling transformation of the disturbing unpleasurable residues of the day is represented as the sole function of the dream. The importance of these day's and life's residues is elucidated with almost unsurpassable accuracy and clarity; I think, however, that the recurrence of the day's residues in itself is one of the functions of the dream. While following up the connexions, it strikes us more and more that the so-called day's (and as we may add, life's) residues are indeed repetition symptoms of traumata. As is known the repetition tendency fulfils in itself a useful function in the traumatic neuroses; it endeavours to bring about a better (and if possible a final) solution than was possible at the time of the original shock. This tendency is to be assumed even where no solution results, i.e. where the repetition does not lead to a better result than in the original trauma. Thus instead of 'the dream is a wish-fulfilment' a more complete definition of the dream function would be: every dream, even an unpleasurable one, is an attempt at a better mastery and settling of traumatic experiences, so to speak, in the sense of an *esprit d'escalier* which is made easier in most dreams because of the diminution of the critical faculty and the predominance of the pleasure principle.

I would like the return of the day's and life's residues in the dream not to be considered as mechanical products of the repetition instinct but to presume that behind it is the functioning of a tendency (which should be called psychological) towards a new and better settlement, and the wish-fulfilment is the means which enables the dream to achieve this aim more or less successfully. Anxiety dreams and nightmares are neither wholly successful nor even almost entirely unsuccessful wish-fulfilments, but the beginnings of this are recognizable in the partially achieved displacement. Day's and life's residues are accordingly mental impressions, liable to be repeated, undischarged and unmastered; they are unconscious and perhaps have never been conscious; these impressions push forward more easily in the state of sleep and dreaming than in a waking state, and make use of the wish-fulfilling faculty of the dream.

In a case, observed for many years, each night brought two and often several dreams. The first dream, experienced in the hours of the deepest sleep, had no psychic content; the patient awoke from it with a feeling of great excitement with vague recollections of pain, of having experienced both physical and mental sufferings and with some indications of sensations in various organs of the body. After a period of remaining awake she fell asleep with new, very vivid dream images which turned out to be distortions and attenuations of the events experienced in the first dream (but even there almost unconsciously). Gradually it became clear that the patient could and must repeat the traumatic events of her life, purely emotionally and without any ideational contents, only in a deep unconscious, almost comatose sleep; in the subsequent less deep sleep, however, she could bear only wish-fulfilling attenuations. Theoretically important in these and similar other observations is the relation between the depth of the unconsciousness and the trauma, and this justifies the experiments of searching for the experiences of shock in an intentionally induced absorption in trance. An unexpected, unprepared for, overwhelming shock acts like, as if it were, an anaesthetic. How can this be? Apparently by inhibiting every kind of mental activity and thereby provoking a state of complete passivity devoid of any resistance.

The absolute paralysis of motility includes also the inhibition of perception and (with it) of thinking. The shutting off of perception results in the complete defencelessness of the ego. An impression which is not perceived cannot be warded off. The results of this complete paralysis are: (1) The course of sensory paralysis becomes and remains permanently interrupted; (2) while the sensory paralysis lasts every mechanical and mental impression is taken up without any resistance; (3) no memory traces of such impressions remain, even in the unconscious, and thus the causes of the trauma cannot be recalled from memory traces. If, in spite of it, one wants to reach them, which logically appears to be almost impossible, then one must repeat the trauma itself and under more favourable conditions one must bring it *for the first time* to perception and to motor discharge.

Returning to the trauma: the state of unconsciousness, the state of sleep, favours not only the dominance of the pleasure principle (wish-fulfilling function of the dream), but also the return of unmastered traumatic sensory impressions which struggle for solution (traumatolytic function of the dream). In other words: the repetition tendency of the trauma is greater in sleep than in waking life; consequently in deep sleep it is more likely that deeply hidden, very urgent sensory impressions will return which in the first instance caused deep unconsciousness and thus remained permanently unsolved. If we succeed in combining this complete passivity with the feeling of ability to re-live the trauma (i.e. to encourage the patient to repeat and to live it out to the end—which often only succeeds after innumerable unsuccessful attempts and at first usually only piecemeal) then it may come to a new, more favourable and possibly lasting mastery of the trauma. The sleep itself is unable to achieve this—at most it can lead only to a new repetition with the same paralysing end result. Or it may happen that the sleeper wakes with the feeling of having experienced various mental and physical unpleasurable sensations, then falls asleep again and in his dream the distorted mental contents appear. The first dream is purely repetition; the second an attempt at settling it somehow by oneself, i.e. with the help of attenuations and distortions, consequently in a counterfeited form. Under the condition of an optimistic counterfeit the trauma may be admitted to consciousness.

The main condition of such a counterfeit seems to be the so-called 'narcissistic split', i.e. the creation of a censuring instance (Freud) out of a split off part of the ego which, as it were, as pure intellect and omniscience, with a Janus head estimates both the extent of the damage and that part of it which the ego can bear, and admits to perception only as much of the form and content of the trauma as is bearable, and if necessary, even palliates it by a wish-fulfilment.

An example of this type of dream: Patient to whom the father made advances on several occasions in childhood and also when she reached adult age, for many months brings material that indicates a sexual trauma in her fifth year; yet despite innumerable repetitions in fantasy and in half-dream, this trauma could not be recollected, nor could it be raised to the level of conviction. Many times she wakes up from the first deep sleep 'as if crushed' with violent pains in her abdomen, feeling of congestion in her head, and all 'muscle-wrenched as if after a violent struggle', with paralysing exhaustion, etc. In the second dream she sees herself pursued by wild animals, being thrown to the ground, attacked by robbers, etc. Minor details of the persecutor point to the father, his enormous size to childhood. I regard the 'primary dream' as the traumatic-neurotic repetition, the 'secondary dream' as the partial settlement of it without external help by means of narcissistic splitting. Such a secondary dream had roughly this content: a small cart is pulled uphill by a long row of horses along a ridge so to speak playfully. To right and left are precipices; the horses are driven in a certain kind of rhythm. The strength of the horses is not in proportion to the easiness of the task. Strong feelings of pleasure. Sudden change of the scene: a young girl (child?) lies at the bottom of a boat white and almost dead. Above her a huge man oppressing her with his face. Behind them in the boat a second man is standing, somebody well known to her, and the girl is ashamed that this man witnesses the event. The boat is surrounded by enormously high, steep mountains so that nobody can see them from any direction except perhaps from an aeroplane at an enormous distance.

The first part of the secondary dream corresponds to a scene partly well known to us, partly reconstructed from other dream material, in which the patient as a child slides upwards astride the body of her father and with childish curiosity makes all sorts of discovery trips in search of hidden parts of his body, during which both of them enjoy themselves immensely. The scene on the deep lake reproduces the sight of the man unable to control himself, and the thought of what people would say if they knew; finally the feeling of utter helplessness and of being dead. Simultaneously in an autosymbolic way: the depth of unconsciousness, which makes the events inaccessible from all directions, at the most perhaps God in heaven could see the happenings, or an airman flying very very far away, i.e. emotionally uninterested. Moreover, the mechanism of projection as the result of the narcissistic split is also represented in the displacement of the events from herself on to 'a girl'.

The therapeutic aim of the dream analysis is the restoration of direct accessibility to the sensory impressions with the help of a deep trance which regresses, as it were, behind the secondary dream, and brings about the re-living of the events of the trauma in the analysis. Consequently after the normal dream analysis in a waking state there followed a second analysis in trance. In this trance one endeavours to remain in touch with the patient which demands much tact. If the expectations of the patients are not satisfied completely they awake cross or explain to us what we ought to have said or done. The analyst must swallow a good deal and he must learn to renounce his authority as an omniscient being. This second analysis frequently makes use of some images of the dream in order to proceed through them, as it were, into the dimension of depth, i.e. into reality.

After the trance and before the waking up it is advisable to sum up what has been lived through into one total experience and then present it to the patient. After this then follows the process of waking up which demands special precautions, e.g. it is useful after the waking up to talk over again what has happened in the session. (Here one could possibly insert the train of thought about the difference between 'suggestion of content' in the earlier hypnoses and the pure suggestion of courage in the neo-catharsis: the encouragement to feel and to think the traumatically interrupted mental experiences to their very end.)

2.4.1931
Aphoristic Remarks on the Theme of being Dead—being a Woman

Continuing the train of thought about adaptation—each adaptation is a partial death, a surrender of one part of the personality; condition: traumatically disorganized mental substance from which then an external power may take away some pieces or into which it may add foreign elements—we must arrive at the question whether the problem of the theory of genitality—the genesis of the differences of sexes—should not be regarded also as a phenomenon of adaptation, i.e. of partial death? If this is so, it is perhaps not impossible that the higher intellectual faculties which I assumed to exist in woman might be explained by her having experienced a trauma. In fact a paraphrase of the old adage: the wiser one gives in. Or more correctly: he (she) who gives in becomes wiser. Or better still: the person struck by a trauma comes into contact with death, i.e. with the state in which egotistic tendencies and defensive measures are shut off, above all resistance by friction, which in the egotistic form of existence brings about the isolation of objects and the self in time and space. In the moment of the trauma some sort of omniscience about the world associated with a correct estimation of the proportions of the own and foreign powers and a shutting out of any falsification by emotivity (i.e. pure objectivity, pure intelligence), makes the person in question—even after consequent consolidation—more or less clairvoyant. This could be the source of feminine intuition. A further condition is naturally the supposition that the instant of dying—if perhaps after a hard struggle the inevitability of death has been recognized and accepted—is associated with that timeless and spaceless omniscience.

But now here is again the confounded problem of masochism! Whence the faculty, to become not only objective and, as far as is necessary, to renounce or even to die, but also to obtain pleasure out of this destruction? (i.e. not only acceptance of unpleasure but also addiction to unpleasure).

1. The voluntary searching for, or even hastening of, the unpleasure has subjective advantages *vis-à-vis* what may be a prolonged expectation of unpleasure and death. Above all it is I alone who prescribe for myself the tempo of living and dying; the motive of anxiety about something unknown is shut out. Compared with the expectation of death coming from outside, suicide is relative pleasure.

2. The voluntary hastening in itself (the flight of the little bird towards the claws of the bird of prey, in order to die more quickly) must mean some sort of gratifying experience.

3. There is a good deal in favour of associating such kind of voluntary surrender with compensatory hallucinations (deliria of rapture; displacement of unpleasure on to others, mostly on to the aggressor himself; fantastic identification with the aggressor; objective admiration of the power of the forces attacking the self; and lastly the finding of ways and means of real hope of possible vengeance and superiority of another kind even after defeat).

9.4.1931

The Birth of the Intellect

Aphoristically expressed: intellect is born exclusively of suffering. (Commonplace: one is made wise by bad experiences; reference to the development of memory from the mental scar-tissue created by bad experiences. *Freud.*)

Paradoxical contrast; intellect is born not simply of common, but only of traumatic, suffering. It develops as a consequence of, or as an attempt at, compensation for complete mental paralysis (complete cessation of every conscious motor innervation, of every thought process, amounting even to an interruption of the perception processes, associated with an accumulation of sensory excitations without possibility of discharge). What is thereby created deserves the name of unconscious feeling. The cessation or destruction of conscious mental and physical perceptions, of defensive and protective processes, i.e. a partial dying, seems to be the moment at which, from apparently unknown sources and without any collaboration from consciousness, there emerge almost perfect intellectual achievements; such as most exact assessment of all given external factors, and grasping of the only correct or only remaining possibilities, fullest consideration of one's own and others' psychological possibilities, both in their qualitative and quantitative aspects. Brief examples:

1. Sexual aggression of intolerable intensity against small children: unconsciousness; awakening from the traumatic shock without memory but with changed character: in boys, effeminization, in girls, the same or the exact opposite, 'masculine protest'. It is to be called intelligent when the individual, while still unconscious or comatose, assessing correctly the proportion of powers, chooses the only way of saving life, that is, giving in completely; it is true at the price of more or less mechanized, permanent change and the partial loss of mental elasticity.

2. Succeeding in achieving an almost impossible acrobatic performance, such as jumping down from the fourth floor, and, during the fall, jumping into the corridor of the third.

3. Sudden awakening from a traumatic-hypnotic sleep lasting more than ten years, immediate comprehension of the hitherto almost or completely unconscious past, immediate assessment of the deadly aggression to be expected with absolute certainty, decision of suicide, and all that in one and the same moment.

Here we are faced with intellectual super-performances, which are inconceivable psychologically and which demand metaphysical explanation. At the moment of transition from the state of life into that of death there arrives an assessment of the present forces of life and the hostile powers, which assessment ends in partial or total defeat, in resignation, that is to say, in giving oneself up. This may be the moment in which one is 'half dead', i.e. one part of the personality possesses insensitive energy, bereft of any egoism, that is, an unperturbed intelligence which is not restricted by any chronological or spatial resistances in its relation to the environment; the other part, however, still strives to maintain and defend the ego-boundary. This is what has been called in other instances narcissistic self-splitting. In the absence of any external help one part of this split-off, dead, energy, which possesses all the advantages of the insensibility of lifeless matter, is put at the service of preservation of life. (Analogy with the development of new living beings after mechanical disturbance or destruction which turns into productivity, as, for instance, Loeb's experiments in fertilization; see the relevant chapter in my *Theory of Genitality*.[1] The only 'real' is emotion=unscrupulous acting or reacting, i.e. what one otherwise calls mad.)

Pure intelligence is thus a product of dying, or at least of becoming mentally insensitive, and is therefore *in principle madness, the symptoms of which can be made use of for practical purposes.*

30.7.1931
Fluctuation of Resistance

(Patient B)

Sudden interruption of a fairly long period of productive and reproductive fertile work (scenes, almost physically experienced in the sessions, of seduction and overpowering by the father at the age of 4(?) years), then the sudden emergence of a practically insurmountable resistance. In any case the preceding sessions and also the intervening period were filled with almost unbearable feelings and sensations: as if the back were being broken in two; an enormous weight obstructing breathing which, after a transitory aphonia and nearly suffocating congestion in the head, was suddenly replaced by breathlessness, deadly pallor, general paralytic weakness and loss of consciousness. The crisis of these symptoms of repetition was represented by: (1) a dream of hallucinatory reality in which a thin, long rubber tube penetrates the vagina, is pushed up to the mouth and is then withdrawn, thus producing at each repeated penetration rhythmic feelings of suffocation; (2) a marked swelling of the abdomen: imagined pregnancy becoming more and more

[1] *Thalassa; a Theory of Genitality* (New York, 2nd ed., 1938).

enormous, painful, and menacing. One morning the patient appeared suddenly without pains, unproductive in every respect but without symptoms; my good-humoured question whether her pregnancy had been terminated by abortion was followed by obstinacy and a feeling of being offended, which lasted for weeks. Everything achieved up till then lost its value. Patient full of doubts, hopeless, impatient. I show her consistently the tendency to escape. All in vain; with strong logical consistency she marshals her motives for being justifiably in despair over both her analysis and her whole future; often she sharply criticizes the behaviour of analysts and patients whom she knows and who are partly tied up with me. But, as she is unable to admit of any other solution than psycho-analysis, her whole endeavour and pondering comes to nothing except a general pessimism with hints of suicide.

To-day, after I had shown her that her accusations and despair were really only a disguise for her idea of interrupting the analysis, she spoke, among other things, of her inability to stop thinking and instead of it to uncover her unconscious with the help of really free association. I urged her somewhat energetically to produce free fantasies, and she immediately became absorbed in the unpleasurable sensation of the pain in her back (as if broken). After further urging, she located these sensations again in her birthplace; further she associated them with lying in grass, then the feeling: something horrible had happened to her (by whom?). 'I don't know, perhaps my father.'

In any case, my energetic urging to free associations, and simultaneous making her aware of my sincere sympathy, succeeded in breaking through the resistance.

Similar fluctuations, with the same suddenness, happened previously. What do they mean? Are they (1) simply attempts to escape from pain which is becoming too great? (2) Does the patient wish to indicate in this way the suddenness of the change in her life through the shock? (In fact, she became an obstinate child, difficult to manage.) Or (3) was this really provoked by my hurting her unexpectedly (admittedly sensitized by her previous history)?

General conclusion: the rhythm, the suddenness or slowness

in the change of resistance and transference may also represent autosymbolically parts of the previous history.

Another confirmation of the importance of literally free associations.

Occasional need to come out of passivity and, without threatening, to urge energetically towards greater depth.

4.8.1931

On Masochistic Orgasm

B.'s dream: She walks on her knees; under her knees the torn-off right and left leg of an animal, whose head faces backwards between the legs of the dreamer. The head is triangular, like a fox's. She passes a butcher's shop and there sees how a huge man with one skilful stroke cuts in two a similar small animal. In this moment the dreamer feels pain in her genitals, looks between her legs, sees there the animal dragged along and similarly cut in two, and suddenly notices that she herself has a long slit between her legs on the painful spot.

The whole scene is an attempt to displace the past or just happening violation to another male being, in particular to his penis. A huge man slits not her but an animal in the butcher's shop, then an animal between the dreamer's legs, and only the pain on awakening shows that the operation has been performed on herself. The moment of the orgasm is indicated first by the fact that after this scene a 'masculine ejaculation' with strong flow has taken place, and second by another dream fragment in which three girl friends handle something very clumsily. She thereby expresses her admiration of the cruel but confident man in contrast to the woman, however masculine.

Normal orgasm seems to be the meeting of the two tendencies to activity. The love relation apparently comes about—neither in Subject A nor in Subject B—but between the two. Love therefore is neither egoism nor altruism, but mutualism, an exchange of feelings. The sadist is a complete egoist. When overpowered by a sadist, at the moment of his ejaculation into a vagina which is mentally completely unprepared and unable to respond: the woman's first reaction is shock, i.e. fear of death and dissolution; the second a plastic empathy into the sadist's emotions, a hallucinatory masculine identification. The therapy consists in the unmasking of the weakness behind the masculinity, the tolerance of the fear of death, even the admiration. Chiefly, however, the desire for reciprocated love as a counterbalance.

31.12.1931
Trauma and Anxiety

Anxiety is the direct sequel of each trauma. It consists in the feeling of *inability* to adapt oneself to the unpleasure situation by (1) withdrawing oneself from the stimulus (flight), (2) by removing the stimulus (annihilation of the external force). Rescue fails to appear. Hope of rescue appears out of the question. Unpleasure increases and demands 'outlet'.[1] *Self-destruction* as *releasing some anxiety* is preferred to silent toleration. Easiest to destroy in ourselves is the cs—the integration of mental images into a unit (physical unit is not such an easy prey to the impulses of self-destruction): Disorientation
helps 1. directly, as a process of self-destruction (outlet);[2]
    2. further perception of the unpleasure (especially of the higher 'moral' kind) ceases. *I* do not suffer any more, only one physical part of me.
    3. *wish-fulfilling new formation* out of the *fragments*, on the level of the pleasure principle.

Dm.: not she outraged,[3] she is the father.

U.: he is strong, has colossal success in business (this fantasy is feared as mad).

Anxiety is fear of madness, but transformed. In the paranoiac the tendency *to protect oneself* (to ward off dangers) outweighs the wholly helpless anxiety.

---

[1] This English word was used in the German MS. (Editor)
[2] See previous footnote. (Editor)
[3] See previous footnote. (Editor)

In most cases 1. delusion of persecution
2. delusion of grandeur   } is unconscious
3. omnipotence to destroy everything

Analysis must penetrate all these layers.

Dm.: must see that she intends to kill by *roundabout ways* and can only live with this fantasy. In the analysis she sees that the analyst *understands her*—that she is not bad, that she *must* kill—and knows that she has been, and is, inexpressibly good and would still like to be so in the future. Under these conditions she admits her weakness and badness (and confesses that she wanted to steal my ideas, etc.).

I. and S. I allowed to go away in anger instead of protesting against their desire to cut me to pieces.

IV
(1932 and undated)

Fakirism

10.6.1932

Production of organs for the purpose of 'outlet'.[1] By this, organism frees itself from ruinous tension (sensibility). The *reactions* are displaced somewhere else . . . into the future, into future possibilities which are more satisfactory. One enjoys the better future in order to forget the bad present.

That is repression.

Counter-cathexis of unpleasure with pleasure images.

Query: is such a makeshift organ capable of creating something real?

Can it influence the photographic plate? Allegedly yes. After all, it is also matter, only of a much more mobile nature (of finer structure).

One must not be so selfish, if one would like to reach and use the outer sphere. Out there, there is no (or much less) *friction*—only mutual yielding. Is this the principle of *kindness*, of mutual *regard*?

The fact that things can be influenced (are capable of tolerating unpleasure) is in itself proof of the existence of the II (kindness) principle.[2]

Death instinct? Only death (damage)[3] of the individual.

Is it possible (?) *to make friends* with the ucs? (free-flowing, extra organic expression).

COURAGE FOR MADNESS

WITHOUT ANXIETY.

Has one then still the desire to find the way back to everyday life? And: is one then still capable of passions at all?

---

[1] The English word was used in the German MS. (Editor)
[2] Cf. 'The Three Main Principles', p. 259 of this volume. (Editor)
[3] The English word was used in the German MS. (Editor)

Biarritz, 14.9.1932
The Three Main Principles

The integration of knowledge about the Universe can be compared to the finding of the centre of gravity of a multitude of interconnected elements. Up to now I have thought of only two principles which can be grasped by man's understanding: the principle of *egoism* or of *autarchy* according to which an isolated part of the world-total (organism) possesses in itself—as far as possible—independent of its environment, all the conditions for its own existence or development and tries to preserve them. The corresponding scientific attitude is extreme materialism and mechanism (Freud) and denial of the real existence of 'groups' (family, nation, horde, mankind, etc., Róheim). The minimum (?) or the complete absence (!) of 'considerations', or of altruistic tendencies, that go beyond the limits of egotistic needs or of the favourable returns for the welfare of the individual, are the logical sequel of this train of thought.

Another principle is that of *universality*; only groups, only world-total, only associations exist; *individuals* are 'unreal', as far as they believe themselves to exist outside these associations and neglect the *relations* between individuals (hatred, love) while leading a kind of narcissistic dream-life. Egoism is 'unreal' and *altruism*, i.e. mutual consideration, identification are justified—peace, harmony, voluntary renunciation are desirable because they alone are in conformity with reality.

A third point of view could attempt to do justice to those two opposites and, as it were, to try to find a point of view (centre of gravity) which comprehends both extremes. This would regard universalism as an attempt on the part of nature, uninfluenced by pre-existing autarchy-tendencies, at restoring mutual identification and with it peace and harmony (death instinct). On the other hand, egoism as another, more successful attempt by nature to create in decentralized forms organizations to preserve quiescence. (Protection against stimuli): (Life-instinct): Man is a very well-developed microcosmic integration; one could even think of the possibility that man might succeed in centring the whole external world around himself.

The furthest going unification would recognize the existence of both tendencies and regard, for instance, the feeling of guilt as an automatic signal that the boundaries created by reality had been crossed either in the direction of egoism or of altruism. Consequently there are two kinds of guilt feelings: first, if more has been given to the environment (groups, etc.) than is tolerable for the ego, then the ego has been sinned against; sequel: *ego-indebtedness, culpability* because of offending or neglecting the ego. And secondly, external-world- (group-) indebtedness: neglecting and offending altruistic obligations, i.e. what is commonly called social guilt. (Until now only this form and this motive of guilt have been recognized.)

Yet all this is only speculation, so long as cases fail to prove to my satisfaction that the *A.B.C.-Principles* and the *A.- and B.-guilt* do really exist. *Neurasthenia* was described by me a long time ago as having sinned against one's own ego, as ego-indebtedness (masturbation, forced stripping the ego of libido, melancholia *subjectiva*, or egoistica) ... *Anxiety neurosis:* retention of the libido beyond the measure demanded by narcissism ... guilt towards others, towards the external world; *hoarding* of *libido* ('thesauring'); repression of the tendency *to give* to others (out of the surplus). ... In the case of the identification reaction of a child subjected to early traumatic attack, neurasthenia and subjective-egoistic melancholia might be the consequences (suppressed is the feeling of weakness/inferiority/, pressed to the fore are vigour and efficiency, which, however, easily come to grief). (Forced libido-sequels.) With *libido-frustration:* anxiety.

Is in both cases rage because of enforced or frustrated love the first reaction? and is this rage identical in both cases?

Biarritz, 19.11.1932

On Shock (Erschütterung)

Shock=annihilation of self-regard—of the ability to put up a resistance, and to act and think in defence of one's own self; perhaps even the *organs* which secure self-preservation give up their function or reduce it to a minimum. (The word *Erschütterung* is derived from *schütten*, i.e. to become 'unfest, unsolid', to lose one's own form and to adopt easily and without resistance, an imposed form—'like a sack of flour'). Shock always comes upon one *unprepared*. It must needs be preceded by a feeling of *security*, in which, because of the subsequent events, one feels *deceived*; one trusted in the *external world too much* before; after, too little or not at all. One had to have overestimated one's own powers and to have lived under the delusion that *such things* could not happen, not *to me*.

Shock can be purely physical, purely moral, or both physical and moral. Physical shock is always moral also; moral shock may create a trauma without any physical accompaniment.

The problem is: Is there, in the case of shock, *no reaction* (defence), or does the momentary, transitory attempt at defence prove to be so weak that it is immediately abandoned? Our self-regard is inclined to give preference to the latter proposition; an unresisting surrender is unacceptable even as an idea. Moreover, we notice that in nature even the weakest puts up a certain resistance. (Even the worm will turn.) In any case flexibilitas cerea and death are examples of lack of resistance and of phenomena of disintegration. This may lead to atom-death, and finally to the cessation of all material existence whatsoever. Perhaps to temporary or permanent 'universalism'—the creation of a distance, viewed from which the shock appears minimal or self-evident.

Biarritz, 19.9.1932

Suggestion=Action without one's own Will (with the will of another person. Case: Inability to walk. Fatigue with pains, exhaustion. Someone takes us by the arm (without helping physically)—we lean (depend) on this person who directs each of our steps. We think of everything possible and watch only the direction indicated by this person, which we follow. *Suddenly* walking becomes laborious, each action seems to demand a double expenditure of effort: the *decision* and the *performance*. Incapacity to decide (weakness) may make the simplest movement difficult and exhausting. Surrendering the will (decision) to someone else makes the *same* action easy.

Muscular activity itself here is undisturbed, smooth. Only the will to action is paralysed. This must be contributed by someone else. In hysterical paralysis this will is lacking and must be transmitted by way of 'suggestion' by someone else. How and by what ways and means?: (1) Voice, (2) Percussion sound (music, drum), (3) Transmitting the idea 'you can do it', 'I am going to help you!'

Hysteria is regression to the state of complete *lack of will* and to acceptance of another's will as in childhood (child on mother's arm): (1) Mother takes care of the whole of locomotion, (2) *Child can walk if supported and directed* (not without this help). The safe feeling, that the power supporting us will not let us fall.

Question: is suggestion (healing) necessary after (or even during) the analysis? When relaxation is very deep, a depth may be reached in which only well-intentioned and kindly directed help must replace the absent or lacking act of will. Perhaps as reparation for a former suggestion which *demanded only obedience*; this time a suggestion which awakens (or bestows) a power of individuality must be given. Consequently: (1) Regression to weakness, (2) Suggestion of power, increase of self-esteem in place of the previous suggestion of obedience (relapse into the state of absence of will, and the counter-suggestion against the frightening earlier suggestion of obedience).

Luchon, 26.11.1932

Repression cs-(ego-) functions are pushed out (displaced) from the cerebrospinal into the endocrine system. The body begins to think, to speak, to will, to 'act out' instead of only carrying out (cerebrospinal) ego-functions.

The facility for it appears to be present already in a rudimentary form in the embryo. But what is possible for the embryo is harmful for the adult. It is harmful when the head, instead of thinking, acts as the genital (emission=cerebral haemorrhage); it is likewise harmful when the genital starts to think instead of carrying out its function (genitalization of the head and cerebralization of the genital).

Tripartitum:
1. Cerebro-spinal system corresponds to the conscious superstructure. Organ of reality sense. With possibilities for intra-psychic displacement (superstructure).
2. Sympathetic system: organ neurosis.
3. Endocrine system: organic illness.

Organic illness: when the chemistry of the body expresses ucs thoughts and emotions instead of caring for its own integrity. Perhaps still stronger, more destructive emotions and impulses (murderous intentions) which change into self-destruction. Paralysis in place of aggression (revenge). Bursting, shaken to bits. What causes the change of direction? (1. quantitatively unbearable aggression [gun] 2. premodelled as trauma.)

26.9.1932
Scheme of Organizations

1. The purely *physical* organization is universal.
2. The *chemical* is individualizing.
   The individual compounds endeavour to maintain their own particular existence against the influence—dividing or agglutinating influence—of the external world.
3. The *physiological* organization (*plexus sympathicus*) protection of the individual by means of a nervous reflex system.
4. The *psycho-physiological*: cerebro-spinal organization.

The developments of the organizations are processes of progressive abstraction.

Symbolic (algebraic) superstructure: (mathematical, condensed) symbolization of the purely physical, simpler (atomistic?) vibrations. *Condensation* is physiologically a kind of *association*. The idea is already 'associated' to a high degree, the association of ideas to a still higher degree. The idea of the 'world' combines everything (similarly with gravitation; it is not only I who am attracted by the earth, but I too attract the earth—and the whole universe). The tendency to draw the world together is an *ideal power*, even if its success is for the time being hardly perceptible. Should this power (under particular conditions) become stronger, the idea may work *magically* (telekinesis, telepathy).

Each long-distance action is telekinetic= mental (tendency to co-(sub-)ordinate something from outside the ego into the will of the ego).

Mutual co-(sub-)ordination: two disparate world elements *want the same*, such as:

1. One wants to dominate, the other to be dominated.
2. One wants to dominate more than to be dominated. The other, the other way round. (Bisexuality and preponderance of one sex.)
3. (After orgasm.) Both want to rest and have no fear (self-consciousness) of each other in surrendering to relaxation. Neither wants to dominate. Mutual mother-child relation (no ego tendencies, or reciprocal fully satisfied ego tendencies).

2.10.1932
Accumulatio Libidinis

A life, in which one can continuously exchange less libido than one would like, may become intolerable.

But what is that peculiar process of exchanging libido? Is it the accepting of the sovereignty of the 'second principle' (compromise, harmony)? that is a kind of physical process between two people (things) with different tensions?

Is it a simultaneous giving and taking? It seems that it is only 'satisfactory' in the latter case.

Oct., 1932
Quantum Theory and Individualism

The changes of the *external world*, as well as those of *one's own personality*, do not occur as continua, but in jerks. The maintenance of the form and of the way of acting until the external influences reach a certain point shows *the attempt of the individual* to resist change. After passing the boundary *the individual changes*; it succumbs to the external superior power, it *identifies* itself under duress with the will of the external world. 'Inertia' is resistance against external influences.

Oct., 1932
The Technique of Silence

The disadvantages of 'going on talking'. Obstacles to 'relaxation'. Communication makes things 'clear conscious' and speculative. Associations remain on the surface (or go round in circles; *piétiner sur place*). Relation to analyst remains conscious.

Longish 'keeping quiet': deeper relaxation, dreams, images, somewhat more 'dreamlike'—far from the conscious thought material.

But when afterwards *must* it come to speaking?

Should the analyst interrupt (surprise) the silence? (Not so bad).

When should such 'silent sessions' begin?

(B. demanded them herself!)

Fresh technical problems.

My self-analysis: silence until production of quite dreamlike images or scenes, 'hypnagoga'. These replace the dreams of the night which are completely lacking.

24.10.1932
Once Again on the Technique of Silence

'Free association' is also a *passagère* 'relaxation', in fact a silence (and switching off of conscious thinking) until the next association; then the silence (and the will not to think) is interrupted either spontaneously or at the analyst's question (What is in your mind?). In reality the patient is usually silent somewhat longer, has more—deep and superficial—associations, often forgets in the meantime the presence of a 'third' person, and communicates to us a *series* of associations which occasionally lead far, and often in unexpected directions, from the first still conscious idea, and may have come nearer to the material of the unconscious (repressed). There is therefore no difference in principle between my (occasionally used) technique of silence and that of free association. It is only a difference of degree. *A priori* probable that a somewhat longer silence (i.e. a not conscious thinking) will lead rather further, perhaps also deeper.

Instances: 1. The patient felt disturbed and irritated by the often repeated 'signs of understanding' ('Hm'—'yes'—'of course', etc.) on the part of the analyst; had the feeling that something was being interrupted by them. Interpretations prematurely given were particularly disturbing. Perhaps he would have arrived at the same interpretation (explanation) on his own if only it had not been 'communicated' to him. *Now* he did not know how much of the interpretation was spontaneous, that is, acceptable, and how much 'suggestion'. The greatest possible economy of interpretation is an important rule.

2. Analysis of B.: she literally shouted at me: 'Do not talk so much, do not interrupt me; now everything has been spoiled again.' Frequently interrupted free associations tend to remain more on the surface.

Any communication or talk brings the patient back into the present situation (analysis) and may hinder him from sinking deeper.

The other extreme is abstraction (trance) with total or partial loss of the reality of time and place and with very vivid, often hallucinatory, reproduction of experienced or imagined scenes. On 'waking up' the feeling of conviction with regard to the (probably really experienced) events mostly *disappears*. This argues *against* the suggestive nature of the hallucination. Repeated reproduction leads then later to (*a*) exactly the same scene, or (*b*) *modifications* of it.

Here is the problem: how much of the reproduction is fantasy and how much reality; how much *subsequent* displacement to *persons and scenes which have only later become significant*? How much 'historical dressing up' of a real-life situation? (the analytical amongst others).

Here quotation of Freud.[1]

[1] English words in the German original. (Editor)

Signs of resistance against reality argue *rather* (not always) *for* reality.

24.10.1932
The Therapeutic Argument

After several reproductions with unending suffering and without cs recollection, an accidental interruption is followed by striking improvement and feeling of independence; a hitherto *hidden* tendency to pluck up courage to venture out of the analysis and into *life*. Is this a sign

1. Of the correctness of the interpretation?
2. Of the end of the period of reproduction?
3. Of the beginning of the period of *forgetting* (at least of the emotional actuality)?
4. Of the period of 'healing' of the analytic wounds and of pointing to possibilities which remain (Jung)?

Re 2 (above): In the following period to *encourage* and to *allay* is probably not superfluous (Tf. *necessary*). Revision of the point of view according to which strengthening comes about quite spontaneously without any special help and need not be influenced by suggestion. After all, each instruction is a suggestion (cf. the double meaning of this word in English); especially for the child and, when the encouragement is *well founded in reality*, i.e. when one suggests the truth, one only accelerates a process which could be acquired by experience though much more slowly. (Similarly, with the teaching of things which have been discovered by others; not every child has to find out everything for himself, e.g. history: impossible). At any rate the *Socratic art* of suggestion is of advantage.

26.10.1932
Psychic Infantilism = Hysteria

1. *Adult* man has two systems of memory:
   Subjective = emotions = bodily sensations.
   Objective = projected sensations (sensations referred to the environment, 'external events').

2. Infant has in the beginning only subjective sensations and bodily reactions (movements of expression).

3. Children in the (? 3-4) first years of life have not many cs memories of events, but only of sensations (pleasurable and unpleasurable tones) and consequent bodily reactions. *The 'memory' remains fixed in the body* and *only there* can it be awakened.

4. In the moment of trauma the world of objects disappears partially or completely: everything becomes *objectless sensation*. Conversion is indeed only a regression to the purely bodily, subjective way of reacting (the theory of James-Lange is valid for children, but not for adults).

5. It is unjustifiable to demand in analysis that something should be *recollected consciously* which has never been conscious. Only *repetition* is possible with subsequent objectivation for the first time *in the analysis*. Repetition of the trauma and *interpretation* (understanding)—in contrast to the purely subjective *'repression'*—are therefore the double task of analysis. The hysterical attack can be only a partial repetition, analytical attack must bring it to a complete development.

6. Repeated reiterations of the re-experiencing with interpretations becoming more and more accurate may or indeed must satisfy the patient. Instead of forced and unceasing search for cs memories (an impossible task in which the patient gets exhausted without being able to become independent), one must pay attention to and encourage the patient in his efforts to separate himself from the analyst—from the analysis. Now it is the time for 'encouragement' to the 'tasks of life'—future happiness, instead of pondering and digging in the past.

29.10.1932
The Analyst's Attitude to his Patient

Accused by G. and Tf. (*a*) for lack of energy (therefore no support), (*b*) lack of sympathy.[1]

(G) 'Confession and absolution is no solution; rather a motive for repeated repression.' (No possibility offered of getting rid of *hatred*, to liberate it.)

[1] English sentence in the original German MS. (Editor)

(Dilemma: *strictness* provokes repression and fear
         kindness ,,   ,,   ,, consideration
G.: OBJECTIVITY (neither strict nor kind) is the best attitude. In any case: a sympathetic, friendly objectivity.

Is this not Freud's technique? In some respects it is, but *forcing one's own theory* is not objective—a kind of tyranny. Also the whole attitude is somewhat *unfriendly*.

Tf.: It is my (the analyst's) fault that the transference has become so passionate—as a result of my *coldness*. A much too literal repetition of the father-daughter dependence: *promises* (forepleasure gratifications, leading to expectations) and then nothing given. Effect: flight from one's own person (body) (splitting of the personality).

30.10.1932
The Vulnerability of Traumatically Acquired Progressive Faculties (also of Infant Prodigies)

Ability to achieve is no proof of real will to achieve and of real pleasure in achievement. Traumatically acquired ability to excessive achievements is (because of the always strong ucs tendency to regression) mostly *passagère* (in the mental sphere aphoristic), and has not the character of permanence and of resistance against emerging obstacles. It is also vulnerable: a new trauma (attack) leads easily to a 'collapse' (to regression to a total inability to deal with life, to mental paralysis), i.e. to regression to the childish and infantile with longing for protection and support; dream and fantasy world are playful-infantile (especially: longing to be without *responsibility*). Analysis leads to precocious overburdening with as yet unwanted responsibility, knowledge, seriousness of life, secrecy (compulsion to discretion). Sexual: masturbation (fantasy), *no* coitus, *no* marriage ('I am a bad liar.' Every secret that has to be kept is a burden.) Rules, duties, ordinances are unbearable. Desire for *finding out for oneself*, in contrast to suggestion and protection. *Oral* passions (eating) bind a great part of the total interest. Longing for *idyllic* life, simplicity, life on the land (democracy).

Colossal effort when learning, yet ambition to be first (Adler's type). Cramming for examinations and *forgetting* of dates (intelligence like that of a child perceiving only what is actual, present, but surprisingly deep on *this* level).

Childhood was not *lived out*.

In the normal way the child must be saturated with play and only a surplus of the interest will be turned towards reality.

Patient U.: Infantile, primitive niveau, up to the age of thirteen.

Patient Dm.: Fixation to mother, forcedly dissolved *much too early*. Compulsion and *overflow*.

(Ucs: Drive back to mother.)

Break through of the (feminine) homosexuality.

Break through of the (masculine) childishness. 'Superego' not assimilated.

Even normal development is enforced more or less.

Yet: at the right time (i.e. readiness already present) and *gradually*, so to speak by *small traumata* easy to overcome.

(Patients Dm., G.): compulsion to solve even the *most difficult* problems.

(Several cases) in reality: desire, but without the least burden imposed.

Ability for finding solutions is present, yet 'flashlike'.

30.10.1932
The Two Extremes: Credulity and Scepticism

'Psychognostic', '*Gnosis*' = the view that it is possible to reach by correspondingly deep relaxation to the direct experience in the past, which then may be accepted as true without any further interpretation.

Scepticism: The idea that all thoughts and ideas must be examined first very critically and that they represent: (1) Absolutely nothing of the real happening, or (2) A very distorted version of it ('Telescoping', Frink).

In fact *there is* in the end something that cannot, need not, and must not, be interpreted—or else analysis becomes an endless substitution of emotions and ideas mostly by their opposites.

On the other hand: the 'mental' events of the past (childhood) may have left their memory traces in a language of gestures, un-understandable to our cs (i.e. in the body) as organic-physical 'mnems'; a pcs perhaps did not exist at all then, only feeling (pleasure-unpleasure) reactions in the body (subjective memory traces)—so that only *fragments* of the external (traumatic) events can be reproduced. (Perhaps only the first moments of the trauma which could not yet be 'repressed' (displaced into the organic) because of the element of surprise (lack, or delay, of counter-cathexis).) If this is so, then some memories of childhood cannot be ever raised as such into the cs, and even in physical symptoms and hallucinations are always mixed with dreamlike (wish-fulfilling) distortions of defence and of turning into the opposite, e.g. as regressions (hallucinations of the moments preceding the trauma).

Could (or can) one take right into the body the present *quality of pre-consciousness* (which may accept the unpleasure)?

2.11.1932
Infantility Resulting from Anxiety Concerning Real Tasks

Jung is right in propounding and describing this kind of anxiety; also in that as a physician one has the task of overcoming this anxiety. Only with regard to the *art* of this therapy is he not quite right. *Encouragement, alone* or after only a cursory retrospection into the causation of this anxiety, cannot have a *permanent* effect. (In the same way as pre-analytical suggestions fail with only few exceptions.) First full realization of the existence of that infantility must be reached—and this can truly be achieved only (*a*) through complete return to the causative past by means of reproduction (recollection and/or acting out) or (*b*) through experience and interpretation of the repetition tendencies in the course of analysis.

(Patient Dm.: Sudden crying when preparing a dinner for U. Has never given up *playing*. She wanted only to play at cooking but was compelled to bear real burdens which were much too difficult. (Sex!)—Effort to *identification*.) *Suggestion without analysis=superimposing the hypnotist's superego.* (Over exertion.)—Correct therapy: (*a*) return to childhood—permission to give full vent, (*b*) waiting for the *spontaneous* tendency of 'growth',—here then encouragement certainly has its right place. Courage must be suggested.

Spontaneous *tendency to grow* emerges when play can no longer satisfy the present quantum of energy. (Physical and mental organs develop and demand to be used.)

Embryology: 'Organanlagen' exist in the individual before functions; when they have developed to real *organs* they demand activity (functions). The embryo *plays* with the phylogenetic possibilities (stages of fish, of frog, etc.), and in the same way the child plays as long as provision is made in reality for all his needs. 'Reality' begins when desires are not satisfied completely —needs are not assured and purposeful activity has become unavoidable. One starts to work for food and love, even to fight for them, i.e. to *bear unpleasure* in the meantime. This latter happens probably with the help of splitting off a part (of the suffering part) of the personality, i.e. of *objectivation*—and of its *reunion* with the ego, i.e. *subjectivation*, after the goal has been achieved, the pain, the suffering, has ceased to be. *Repression* is a much too successful *permanent 'alienation'*. Here is the difference between *suppression* and *repression*. With suppression one does not feel the pain, only the *effort* which is necessary to 'alienate over' the pain. With repression one does not even feel this any longer. Even the defence situation may appear *pleasurable* (pleasure creeping in behind the pain).

2 Nov.

The Language of the Unconscious

If the intellectual cs urge to communicate is completely eliminated and the speech organs are given free rein (as the hand of a medium with automatic writing and drawing) there comes—after senseless vowels and consonants (as in the play of *infants* with lips and tongue) *imitations* of things, animals, and people.

The *imitation magic* is here:

1. the only way to *abreact* emotional impressions of the external world by one or several repetitions.

2. to *impart* to another person what has happened, as a complaint or to find sympathy and help=dilution through imparting (=parting!, shared suffering, shared emotions).[1]

3. This 'imparting' has two parts: (1) imitating something *alien* (primitive form of objectivation of the processes in the external world); (2) a *self-imitatory* repetition of the emotional reaction experienced at the event (pleasure, unpleasure, pain, anxiety).

(In certain respects it is also the 'ego' that is objectivized.)

Somewhat more objective (yet still not so much as the preconscious) are the means of representation of the *dream*. Also in dreams there are elements in which *the ego imitates the environment*. (Dog=*I bark*, bites=*it hurts me*.) Caution in assessing the subjective elements, how far they represent something objective—and the objective elements, how far they represent something subjective. Admittedly something objective may also represent objective, something subjective, subjective. To be guessed (divined, conjectured) with the help of the meaning of the whole.

The dream may therefore be interpreted historically (partly distorted in the direction of *wish-fulfilment*).

In a masturbation fantasy often three people are 'experienced', all of them subjectively (primal scene: man, woman and the child itself).

In masturbatory orgasm the objective images disappear—everything unites in a purely subjective feeling. The 'after pains' (bitter after-taste) represent not only remorse but also (after disappearance of the excitement): (1) the insight that reality was lacking; (2) the consequence of the effort (exhaustion) which was necessary to represent the unreal as real (hard *work*). [The onanist feels (*a*) alternatively the emotions of two

---

[1] In the German original: *Mitzuteilen* (=*teilen!*, *geteiltes Leid*, *geteilte Emotion*) = *Verdünnung durch Mitteilen*. Unfortunately it has been found impossible to give an exact English equivalent. (Editor)

people, (*b*) finally of both at the same time. Coitus: reality is there *without effort* and remains in existence (as an affectionate union) after the ending (peace and satisfaction). Where there is lack of satisfaction after coitus it is really masturbation in vaginam.]

From these processes ways lead to the understanding of the *permanent imitation* (identification, super-ego formation), i.e. a kind of *mimicry*, which may be responsible also for organic physical resemblances.

2 Nov.

Suppression of the Idea of the 'Grotesque'

A neglected motive for 'identification' is imitation as a contemptuous grimace.

1. Oft-recurring reproduction and its self-punishing perseveration of an old woman (mother, wife) pot-bellied, with rolls of fat, as a grotesque figure, as in a woodcut.

2. The same kind of picture of a man with a huge nose (with warts on it), pot-bellied (like Falstaff), breaking wind. Comic gestures in praying. Reaction formation: respect, urging the attitude of not caring about 'public opinion'[1] (to let oneself be seen with him in the street) (public opinion=projection of one's own displeasure).

3. Seemingly independent of it (Tf.'s grotesque!): stories about the power of attraction of the young daughter (sister imago); as if I would say 'she is much more beautiful'; this idea is then repressed and the mother now treated ambivalently, ucs mockery, cs devotion. Grimace 'stays so' (is the wording of the punitive sanction). Similar grimace: one *accepts the grotesque for oneself* instead of seeing it on respected persons. (Compulsion to draw grotesque heads, to find them in ornaments, in spots scattered formlessly, in wallpapers, shadows, imitations of father's handwriting.)

Up to the present always interpreted only as *wish-fulfilling identification*—now contemptuous imitation with reaction formation.

[1] English words in the German original. (Editor)

Oedipus situation: penis—a comical appendage, coitus—ridiculous, *in childhood* no real feeling yet for its attractiveness.

4.11.1932
Repetition in Analysis worse than Original Trauma[1]

It has to be born *consciously*.
Habitual forms of reactions have to be left (resistance).
Much *encouragement* needed.

Knowledge as a means of doubt (resistance).
Trauma having been *told* and not *found out*.

Traumatogenesis being *known*; the doubt, whether reality or fantasy, remains or can return (even though everything points at reality). Fantasy theory=an escape of *realization* (amongst resisting analysts too). They rather accept their (and human beings') mind (memory) as unreliable than believe that such things with *those* kinds of persons can *really* have happened. (Self-sacrifice of one's own mind's *integrity* in order to save the parents!)

Cure for knowledge-incredulity. 'You must not *believe*, you just tell things as they come. Do not force feelings of any kind, least of all the feeling of conviction. You have time to judge things from the reality point of view afterwards. (In fact, the series of pure images sooner or later turns into highly emotional representations.) 'You have to admit that (exceptionally) even things can have happened of which somebody told you something.'

5 Nov.
Pull of the Past (Mother's Womb, Death Instinct) and Flight from the Present

The latter much too neglected. A bomb explosion, if intensive enough, makes anybody 'mad'—unconscious.[2] Fever: if high

---
[1] The whole note was originally in English. (Editor)
[2] In German two words: *unbewusst, bewusstlos* are used. (Editor)

enough, makes everybody delirious. It is going too far to speak also in such cases of infantile disposition as an essential cause (although the latter *partly determines* the content and the form of the psychosis). *A potiori fit denominatio.* In order to understand the symptom fully, and perhaps also in order to cure it, one can and should also identify in the pathogenesis the primal instincts aroused by the trauma. There is no development without infantile traumas, to which—if they had not brought about too strong and persistent a fixation—one would never have regressed without a strong external blow from the present. One must always estimate individually the *tendency to flee* from the present and the *power of attraction* of the past. Psycho-analysis has underestimated the first of these 'releasing causes'. Only at the end of an analysis which, unprejudiced, has considered *both* (disposition and trauma) can one assess the contribution of the one and of the other. However: in general . . .

(Continuation lost. Editor.)

10.11.1932

Suggestion in (after) Analysis

1. Only what is true may be suggested (to children and patients).

2. But truth cannot be discovered quite spontaneously, it *must* be 'insinuated', 'suggested'. Children are unable without this help to acquire convictions. Really this is not even their 'job'. Children want to 'get' truth in the same way (without work) as they get food, i.e. without effort on their part. Neurotics, however, *are* children, at least a very great proportion of them *are*. There is *no* completely adult man; everyone is happy if he may play when work is done. To acquire knowledge by play is indeed the desire of all of us. To be a good teacher means: to spare the learner exertion by means of examples, parables, metaphors—so to speak, to make him 'experience' everything—just like a fairy tale, only then does one get the meaning of the whole ('aha'-experience).

3. The apparently superfluous statements of a third person, which in fact one has thought of for oneself consciously, have

quite a different effect and call forth emotions. (Example: expressions of gratitude by two patients: the analyst too is in need of appreciation and this must be said in so many words.)

4. 'Healing' is the reassuring effect of encouragement and of tenderness (possibly also of kindly stroking of the painful part of the body.) (Wart, anal fissure.)

5. Analysis is preparation for suggestion. The intrapsychic adjustment of the cathexes of id-ego-superego is not sufficient. 'Synthesis'? Friendly encouragement (possibly also some 'electromagic') from another person makes the removal of the self-splitting possible and with it the 'surrender' as a reintegrated person. An 'adult' is never 'unsplit'—only a child and one who has again become a child. An adult must 'take care of himself'. A child is taken care of. *Trust* must be acquired analytically, by the passing of all sorts of tests set by the patient. One must have stood all the tests. Then he brings his confidence spontaneously. Neurotics have been disappointed heavily in their trust. Great disappointment of neurotics in medical science in general. None of them will believe: (1) that one really can help, (2) that one really wants to help. (Kindness.)

(Lack of ability and lack of will may be made up by admitting them.)

11.11.1932
Integration and Splitting

Each 'adult', who 'takes care of himself' is split (is no single psychic unit). Apparent contradiction: Sense of reality is possible only on the basis of a 'fantasy' (=unreality) in which a part of the person is *sequestrated* and is regarded 'objectively' (externalized, projected); this, however, is only possible with the help of a partial suppression of emotions (repression?)—Analyses which are carried through on the level of reality never reach the depth of the processes of splitting. Yet each succeeding development depends on the way it occurs (on its vehemence), on the time factor, and on the conditions, of the original splitting (primal repression). Only in earliest childhood, or before the original splitting, was anyone 'one with himself'. Deep analysis must go back under the level of reality into pre-traumatic times and traumatic moments, but one cannot expect a proper resolution unless this time the resolution is different from the original one. Here intervention is necessary (regression and new beginning). Cf. the kindly understanding, the 'permission to give vent' and the encouraging calming reassurance ('Suggestions').

20.11.1932
Indiscretion of the Analyst in Analysis—helpful[1]

Even a father-confessor is occasionally compelled, for the sake of 'higher' truthfulness, to deviate from a literal obedience to his duty of discretion (for instance, to save a life). 'One should not tempt providence'—has its limitations. By and large this is right, but exceptions are inevitable. For instance, with psychotics (complete lack of, or faulty, sense of reality).

Nov. 24
Exaggerated Sex Impulse[2] *and its Consequences*

—as the consequence of infantile 'compulsion for super-achievements'—are the model for the 'wise baby' *in general*. The 'wise baby' is an abnormality, behind which is hidden repressed infantile passivity, as well as rage over the forcible interruption of that passivity; *peril of life* presses towards prematurity. All *child prodigies* may have developed and broken down[3] in this way. Example: intercourse with unorgiastic ending: damage to self and partner. Exaggerated tasks with break down[4] or with much too rapid, unmethodical success (aphoristic writings[5])—remaining on this level always means progress on the fantasy level.

[1] English title in the original. (Editor)
[2] English words in the original. (Editor)
[3] In English in the original. (Editor)
[4] In English in the original. (Editor)
[5] In English in the original. (Editor)

Therapy: admitting, making up for lost infantility (being idle)—new formation of the personality. Breakdown=feeling of inferiority, i.e. flight from tasks and responsibility. Regression from intercourse to (passive) masturbation. At least this latter should be 'allowed': (1) permitted by partner and approved of; (2) tolerated without inner guilt.

Retrograde Effect on the Analysis: Hatred of work of any kind—setting of exaggerated tasks for himself—breakdown (with repressed unpleasure).

— illness. *Advantages* for the patient.

— deeper reaching *disadvantages:* being hated.

That is, it is good for the *deepening*—difficulty of *influencing* because of negative counter-transference.

Protection (Prevention): dealing with it in one's own analysis.

Therapy: terminating one's own analysis with the patient's help.

(Example: hitting nose against partner's teeth in the moment of orgasm.—The orgasm *of another person* is too great a task. Still unable to love—desire merely to be loved. Premature marriage).

Play becomes *reality*, tolerated with great difficulty.

False potency, even over-potency. *Ejaculation up to the ceiling.* Fantasies of grandeur *facilitate* super-performance. This ability, however, is not of any duration. *Impotence* behind super-performance.

26.11.1932
Theoretical Doubt in place of a Personal One[1]

(U.) The day before: Questions: (1) *Can* I help him (financially)? Answer: *No*. (2) *Would* I help him if I had the possibility? Answer: *Yes*. Reaction (immediate): 'I cannot imagine that you have not got the money.' Reaction the following day: discussion of, and attack on, the validity of the psycho-analytical propositions which I developed in the 'developmental stages'. One does *not* pine for the mother's womb. Instead of asking what his doubt means (disbelief in my answers) and admitting

[1] English title in the original. (Editor)

that even if I had the money it is inadvisable from the analytical point of view to lend it to him, and that he should try to make himself financially independent of both me and his girl friend, and, further, admitting my unwillingness to risk the money, I simply *said yes and no*, that is to say I kept certain things from him; instead of admitting the possibility that I did not *care* to lend him the money— i.e. although I could go so far in my role of father and would be able, with a certain effort, to get together the 5,000 dollars, still I did not want to lend it to him. *The love of the analyst does not go so far.*—Most probably I will have to remedy this and admit the truth.—

(He also doubts the existence of the ucs.)

From this incident one should certainly find connexions with disbelief in reality and in the limitations of parental help and love (i.e. parental egoism). He must fend for himself alone.

On the same day I learn from another patient that U. (and another female patient) cracked jokes about my leaving my correspondence lying about on my desk so that it could be read at certain moments by either of them. (Scepticism and enquiries about *real* personal feelings and in general about my personality. U., for instance, finds that I treat one particular patient *too hard* in my letters, i.e. in fact I am harder than I wish to appear.) This also must be clarified: (1) Admitting the fact and the 'professional hypocrisy' on my part; (2) connecting this with similar events in the patient's past (parents are not as good as they wish to appear. One cannot count on them completely).

S. adds that *indiscretion in analysis is necessary*, especially when the patient knows that through the analysis of a second person I am getting indirect news (messages)[1] from him. One must, therefore, bring to discussion the things which a patient tells to another patient and not behave as if one knew nothing about them. The analysis of two people who are in some way closely connected with each other (siblings, lovers, married couples) may proceed in this way without one of them harming the other. Condition: not to bring to discussion anything of which either the first or second patient has no knowledge.

[1] In English in the original. (Editor)

Chiromancy

31.11.1932

The folds of the palm may give information about habitual muscle innervations—(actions and impulses, emotions; expressive movements of the hands).

Graphology gives us for the time being information about the cs or ucs character of the intentions and experiences. *Chiromancy* may enable us to make this discrimination: the right palm may possibly show the cs actions and emotions, and the left the ucs (and unknown) character traits.

On Lamaism and Yoga

31.11.1932

I came completely unawares (1) to the discovery that breathing can be stopped for much longer when one *drinks* cool water; this may lead to the explanation of why drowned people usually have their stomachs filled with water. (Before they drown they inhale water—they first drink themselves full). A protecting device. Maybe one of the ucs. realizations (progressions) in extreme need (I may have experienced this in my *dreams*). Feelings and delusions of *intoxication* may perhaps only be symbols of the repression of reality at the achievement of adjustment in the trauma.

2. Another lamaistic discovery: one can endure suffocation longer when one *thinks*, *sings*, or *counts* during it than without this. (Buddhistic murmuring of phrases in Yoga practice.)

3. The idea of the *wise baby* could be discovered only by a *wise baby*.

4. Chiromancy: right hand shows an unbroken, strong 'lifeline', the left: one weak and interrupted in several places; *cs holding off of death* (by means of intelligence, directing away of the painful emotions by *cs* thinking, chanting, counting, willing, smoking, tics, manic delusions, denial of unpleasure).

31.11.1932
Abstraction and Memory for Details

These two abilities are usually mutually exclusive. *Is abstraction the primordial one? The more primary one?* (An argument for this idea is that memory for details is the first to break down in the case of degeneration.) Can one consider feelings of pleasure and unpleasure (with no closer precision or localization) as the *most general* and *most primitive* contents of the cs, in which all the *particular and singular conceptions* are rooted? Each perception is at first a feeling of change. ('Something has become different'
$\begin{cases} 1.\ \text{better} \\ 2.\ \text{worse} \end{cases}$ (Indifference cannot be felt, only the establishment of an *error:* the *new* is neither better nor worse.) Perhaps originally everything new is a *disturbance*. (The warding off of any change at all.) Or, if the *present* emotional situation is painful, one *expects* a change for the better. (In such a case any insufficient change is *disappointing*.) If one feels relatively well any change is at first a disturbance.

1.12.1932
Abstraction and Perception of Details

Idiots and imbeciles must be the best and most reliable 'Abstractionists' because they have no organ for the perception of detail (cf. association of mental deficiency with mathematical talent). Animals with very little idea of detail reckon *instinctively* (e.g. reckoning of distance when jumping) or after very little experience.—Their perception of pleasure and unpleasure (fear of everything new) is far *safer* than the intelligent calculation of a danger.

22.12.1932
Yoga-Discipline

1. First body is to be treated.
   [Body—Mind—Universum
   [Mind—Body—Vicious or benign circle
2. Afterwards, and then simultaneously, the mind as well.
3. Breaking from } { bad   } habits { mind
   Training to   } { good }   { body
4. Bodily unpleasure } { tolerated { expiration } position
   Bodily pleasure   } { deepened { inspiration }
5. Urethr. sphincter strengthening.
Breaking from self-indulgent muscle actions which neglect self-regulation. (Sphincter contraction of urethrality—Sphincter relaxation of anality. Motility of the bowels.)
6. As result: enhanced ability for actions against the pleasure principle (toleration of thirst, hunger, pain; toleration of thoughts, desires, actions and emotions repressed because of unpleasure) undoing the repression.

Depth of Analysis.

Aggravating { of the narcissistic reactions
Easing   {
Extraversion.

26.12.1932
Psychotrauma

I. *Great unpleasure, which, because of its sudden appearance, cannot be dealt with. What is the meaning of 'dealing with'?*
1. True warding off of the harming factor (altering the external world in the sense of removing the *cause* of the disturbance—alloplastic reaction).

2. Production of *ideas* about future altering of reality in a favourable sense; *holding on* to these ideas which therefore are pleasurably toned '*in spe*' enables us to 'tolerate' the unpleasure, that is, to feel it much less or not at all as such. These ideas act as antidotes against unpleasure (like an anaesthetic) and enable

us to behave sensibly for the duration of the unpleasure or the painful influences. (Extraction of teeth—it will soon be over, 'only a moment'—then everything will be good again.) Simultaneously mostly also *'substitute reactions'* (e.g. muscle contractions) which should be called already illusory because they lead to actions of defence and removal of innocent (but analogous) objects and persons: (1) mostly inanimate things instead of living; (2) but also often on oneself; for instance, tearing one's hair. This second way of dealing with unpleasure is alloplastic *'in spe'*; partly, however, it is mixed up with primary processes in which similarity stands for identity.

Composite formations of allo- and autoplastic reactions, i.e. of reality *'in spe'* and *fantasy*. In any case, the fantastic nature of the substitute actions remains cs or can easily be brought to consciousness.

But what happens in cases of helplessness or general hopelessness?

Cure Finishing[1]

(*a*) To *recognize* all repressed fantasies and hopes, infantile plays, desires.
(*b*) To *acquiesce* in the still attainable and renounce the impossible or even highly improbable.
(*c*) To *reflect* on age, space, time and fitness.
(Correct estimation of the conditions.)

Another formulation: (1) a clear separation of fantasy (=childish play) from real intention and action.
This intends, but ought not, to be: an *over-acquiescence*—that is, giving up also what is possible. Not even the giving up of fan-

[1] English title in the original. (Editor)

tasying, i.e. of play with possibilities. Yet before *action*, before definitive *forming of an opinion*, achievement of the above-mentioned clear separation.

Snake—Hiss

Asthma=rage. Rage=contraction of the bronchial muscles with pressure from below (abdominal muscles) (colic of the bronchi).

Why is it that repressed rage causes just these external movements? Bodily symbol of the mental (psychic) state or process. Perhaps all expressive movements are bodily symbols=tics= hysterical representations or adjustments of mental processes.

Trauma-Analysis and Sympathy

1. Deep (traumatogennic) analysis is not possible if no more favourable conditions (in contrast to the situation at the original trauma) can be offered:

(*a*) by life and by the external world

(*b*) —mainly—by the analyst.

(*a*) is partly contained in the contra-indications of analysis by Freud (misfortune, age, hopelessness) (*b*) may partly replace (*a*), but here emerges the danger of a lifelong fixation to the analyst (adoption—yes, yet how to 'disadopt'?).

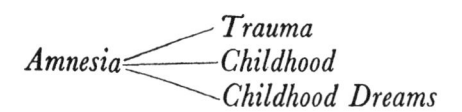

$$Amnesia \begin{cases} Trauma \\ Childhood \\ Childhood\ Dreams \end{cases}$$

Cannot be *remembered* because it has *never* been cs. It can only be *re-experienced* and *recognized* as the past.

Child cannot be analysed, analysis with a child takes place at the still ucs stage—no *proper experiences*, mostly only *suggestions* that make up mental life. The *child* lives in the present. 'Unhappy child of the moment.'

The unpleasurable memories remain reverberating *somewhere* in the body (and emotions).

Child analysis. Education is super-ego *intropression* (by adults).

PAPERS OMITTED FROM PREVIOUS COLLECTIONS

XXII

PSYCHO-ANALYSIS AND EDUCATION[1]
(1908)

[A Hungarian version of this paper was printed first in *Gyógyászat* (a Hungarian medical weekly journal) in 1908, and subsequently included in *Lélekelemzés* (a collection of Ferenczi's early psycho-analytical papers, printed in book form) in 1909. This version differs considerably from the German version found in manuscript among Ferenczi's papers after his death: (*a*) The social consequences of repression are described more in detail, (*b*) The second half of the paper is a completely new version. The most likely explanation is that the manuscript version is the original paper as read at the Congress; when translating it into Hungarian Ferenczi included in it some 'second thoughts'. These two differing parts are printed here as Appendices. In the text of the original it is indicated where they should be inserted.—*Editor*]

A CLOSE study of Freud's work together with psycho-analyses conducted by ourselves, teaches us that faulty education is not only the source of faulty character development, but is also the source of serious illnesses; moreover, we find that present-day education is literally a forcing house for various neuroses.

While analysing our patients and therefore—willy-nilly—subjecting ourselves and our own development to revision, we become convinced that even an education inspired by the noblest intentions and carried out under the most favourable conditions has, through being based on faulty but generally accepted principles now prevalent, a harmful influence in many

[1] Paper read at the First Psycho-Analytical Congress in Salzburg, 1908. First published in Hungarian in *Gyógyászat* (1908); then in German: *Bausteine* III (1939). English translation in *Int. Jour. of PsA* (1949) **30**, 220.

respects upon the development of the child. If we have succeeded in remaining healthy despite these adverse factors, then it is due to our robust, resistant mental make-up. Further, we learn that even he who by good luck has not become ill has, nevertheless, endured much unnecessary mental pain and suffering because of inappropriate pedagogical methods and theories, and we discover that most people are almost wholly unable to find unselfconscious pleasure in the natural joys of life.

What then are the practical advantages education can derive from these experiences? This is not a purely scientific question; it is to psychology (the subject of main interest to us) as horticulture is to botany. Freud, starting from a practical discipline —the pathology of the neuroses—has subsequently been able to gain surprising psychological insight. We must not, therefore, fight shy of penetrating into the nursery. I would hasten to add that this question cannot be solved by one single worker. The co-operation of all of us here will be necessary for the solution, and it is for this reason that I bring up the subject as a problem and invite my colleagues, and above all Professor Freud, to take part in the discussion.

First of all, I should like to mention some general points of view that have come to my mind.

The tendency to maintain existence without pain or tension, the unpleasure principle, must be considered, as Freud considers it, to be the original and natural regulator of the mental apparatus as it appears in the new-born infant. Despite the later superimposing of more complicated mechanisms, a somewhat sublimated unpleasure principle remains paramount in the mind of the civilized adult which takes the form of a natural tendency to experience the greatest possible gratification at the price of the least possible strain. Every education ought to reckon with this tendency. Present-day education does not. Instead, it burdens the mind with still more compulsions than even the already sufficiently pressing external circumstances demand, and does so by strengthening the repression which was originally an adequate and purposeful defensive measure, but if in excess, leads to illness. (Appendix I.)

The primary aim of the educational reform to which we

should aspire should be an attempt to spare the child's mind the burden of unnecessary repression. After that—an even more important task—should be a reform of our social institutions so that freedom of action is given to those wish-impulses which cannot be sublimated. We can afford to ignore the reproach that such views are inimical to civilization. For us civilization is not an end in itself, rather is it an appropriate means whereby a compromise between one's own interests and those of one's fellow men may be attained. If this can be achieved by less complicated means, we need not be afraid of the epithet 'reactionary'. Respect for the reasonable and natural demands of others must always be the limiting factor in deciding the extent to which liberty may run. Ignorance of the true psychology of man and disregard for it in the course of education to-day create in social life numerous pathological phenomena, and expressions of the illogical working of repression become apparent. Were we acting only in consideration of the few people specially predisposed to neuroses, there would be no need to alter the existing state of affairs. But I think—and here I am supported in my belief by Freud's as yet unpublished communications—that the excessive anxiety of most civilized people, their fear of death, their hypochondriasis—all these must be derived from the libido being repressed during the process of education. Similarly, clinging to meaningless religious superstitions, to traditional cult of authorities, to obsolete social institutions, are pathological phenomena of the folk-mind—so to speak, obsessive acts and ideas of the collective mind—their motivating forces being the repressed wish-impulses which have been made rampant by erroneous education. (Appendix II.)

In his excellent lectures on the pedagogical duties of the physician, Professor Czerny, the pediatrician, reproaches parents for being unable to educate their children either because they (the parents) are unable to remember their own childhood at all or else, if they do remember it, they do so unreliably and indeed self-deceptively. We cannot but agree with him, and in fact we could tell him—using the knowledge gained from Freud—what a remarkable mental mechanism it is that causes this infantile amnesia. This in itself is sufficient explanation why education has not made any noticeable progress since time immemorial. It is a vicious circle. The unconscious compels the parents to bring up their children in the wrong way, while wrong education, in its turn, piles up unconscious complexes in the children. Somehow, this vicious circle must be broken. To start with radical reforms in education would be a hopeless beginning. Correction of the infantile amnesia, the enlightenment of grown-ups, holds greater promise. The first and most important step towards a better future lies—in my opinion—in the propagation of the knowledge of the true psychology of the child as discovered by Freud. This wholesale enlightenment would mean a cure for mankind suffering from unnecessary repressions, a sort of inner revolution which each one of us must have experienced whilst incorporating Freud's teachings. Liberation from unnecessary inner compulsion would be the first revolution to bring real relief to mankind, for political revolutions have achieved only that the external powers, i.e. the means of coercion, have changed hands, or that the number of the oppressed has risen or fallen. Only people liberated in this real sense will be able to bring about a radical change in education and prevent permanently the return of similar undesirable circumstances.

In addition to this work of preparation for the future, we must look to the next generation and discover, with this increased insight, what could be changed without delay in the bringing up of children.

First, however, we must discuss the arguments of the nativists who maintain that education has no effect whatsoever, and that the entire mental development is predetermined organically. Freud has shown that the same sexual constitution will produce various outcomes according to the further elaborations of the affective influences, and that infantile experiences have an important part in determining the subsequent course of development. All this pleads for the effectiveness of pedagogical measures. Conversely, not only untoward events, but also purposeful and benign influences—i.e. true education—can make use of the child's tenacity and capacity for fixation.

For the reform of education, I think it is highly desirable to obtain the co-operation of the pediatricians, who have such a great influence upon the public. Moreover, through direct observation of infantile mental life, they could obtain further proofs of the conclusions arrived at—following Freud—from the dreams of the healthy and from the symptoms of the neurotic in relation to the method of working and to the development of the child's mind. It may be assumed that such observations will yield fruitful results in the field of the psychology of the neuroses.

For the time being, however, these new ideas seem to have failed to arouse the understanding and interest of pediatricians. This is all the more remarkable since there are numerous points of contact between Freud's psychology and the pediatric observations uninfluenced by Freud.

If we take Czerny's book, which I have already quoted, as an example, we observe with pleasure that he ascribes to correct handling of the baby during the first year of life a far-reaching effect. Using Freud's terminology, we shall put the problem thus: is the baby to be educated at all and, if so, how is this to be done during the period of almost exclusive paramountcy of the unconscious mental system?

According to what we know of the later role of the unconscious instinctual impulses, there must be the least possible inhibition of the motor discharges of the infant. That is why I consider the present-day custom of swaddling—i.e, tying up of the child—to be objectionable. The child should have ample freedom of movement. The only thing that at this age might be deemed 'education' is to limit the amount of external stimuli reaching the infant. Czerny is absolutely right when he condemns the all-too-early pinning down of the infant's attention by strong visual or auditory stimuli.

As a means of reassurance, Czerny mentions feeding at healthily proper intervals. Further he maintains that rocking, rolling, and thumb-sucking, condemned by so many physicians, are absolutely harmless. Nevertheless, had he known of the possible consequences of excessive stimulation of the erotic senses, of the accompanying sexual effects of rhythmic swaying, he would have advocated some precaution. It is certain that children need these and similar sensations for their full sexual development, but only in limited quantities, and a sensible education must, therefore, regulate the amount of these stimuli which might be harmful if permitted in excessive quantities.

It is interesting to note that Czerny favours breast-feeding as a means whereby those emotional contacts between mother and child develop the relations 'which are so highly valued if they exist between parents and children'. This is a true observation but at the same time a very cautious periphrasis of the decidedly sexual nature of those relations.

The sexual theme is treated cursorily in this book—just as in all similar ones; a few notes about infantile masturbation is all that is offered to the readers. If the pediatricians did but know even a little of Freud's discoveries, then they would not condemn kissing the child on the mouth merely because of the possibility of its being a means of infection, or Escherich would not consider the problem of sucking as finally dealt with by his invention of the boric acid dummy.

The only source of knowledge in this field—for the time being—is Freud's *Three Contributions to the Theory of Sexuality*. The experiences described there should be appraised from the point of view of education, and an attempt should be made to work out whether, and how, the predominance of certain erotogenic zones, component instincts or tendencies to perversions could be prevented, and excessive reaction formation be checked. Education, however, must always bear in mind that it should not aim at strangling these components which are indispensable to the building up of a normal sexuality, but should aim at preventing them from reaching beyond the bounds of expediency into a luxurious indulgence. A wise education will know how to achieve the condition wherein transformation of sexual emotions, repressions, etc., need have no more pathogenic effect. The present-day custom of leaving children alone during the most violent crises of their sexual development, without support or instruction, explanation or assurance, is cruel. Instead, the child should be given successive explanations that will correspond with the current stage of his intelligence.

Only when the hypocritical mysteriousness in sexual matters has ceased to exist, when everyone will know of the processes of his own body and mind—i.e. only with conscious cathexis—will sexual emotions be truly mastered and sublimated. As long as the emotions repressed into the unconscious are free from our control they will, like a 'foreign body', disturb the peace of our mental life. The double meaning of the word '*selbstbewusst*'[1] shows that language had some idea of the connexions between knowledge of oneself and character.

How the possible breakdown of the sexual latency period, the fixation of auto-erotic mechanisms and of incestuous phantasies, the unfortunately frequent seduction by adults, are to be prevented, I am afraid I cannot—for the time being—even imagine.

The methods of correction, praise, command and reprimand, corporal punishment—all these need a thorough revision. Because there is much wrong committed in this field, it often happens that the seeds of subsequent neuroses are sown. On the other hand, the spoiling and pampering of children, i.e. overburdening them with expressions of love by adults—can also have harmful delayed effects, as is well known by any one who has conducted analyses. But once parents are clear in their own minds as to the importance of these implications, their love of the child will prevent any such excesses.

Now, as before, great attention must be paid to the development of the symbols of speech and of the higher mental systems. These have been the almost exclusive aim of present-day pedagogy. The knowledge that thinking in words means a new cathexis of the instinctual life can show teachers why the child's self-control grows parallel with his increasing knowledge. The lack of control in deaf-mute children may possibly be traced back to the lack of this over-cathexis by words. In any case, it should be seen that teaching is made more interesting and that the teacher does not handle the children as a severe tyrant but as a father—whose representative, in fact, he really is.

Whether we shall ever succeed in moulding and forming the character of man by purposeful influences during early childhood is the task of future experimental pedagogy. After what we have quite recently learnt from Freud—I mean the paper

[1] Only in German and in Hungarian. This word also means 'self-esteem', 'self-respect'. In English 'self-conscious' has the opposite meaning.

'Character and Anal Eroticism'—such a possibility is not wholly unthinkable. But we must work to learn much before we can seriously contemplate trying out this idea in practice.

Yet even without this new science, the victory of Freud's ideas will bring much that is good to education. A rational education based upon those ideas may discard a great part of the pressing burdens. And even if the people—because they need no longer surmount such colossal obstacles—may not have such intensive gratifications, their share will be a quiet, cheerful existence, no longer tormented by day by unnecessary anxieties, nor by night by nightmares.

Appendix I

What is repression? Perhaps it could be best described as a denial of facts. But, while the liar tries to cheat others in concealing the truth from them, or by inventing things that do not exist, present-day education has set out to achieve that man should cheat himself in disowning thoughts and feelings stirring within him.

Psycho-analysis teaches that thoughts and impulses thus repressed from consciousness are by no means annihilated, but remain stored in the unconscious, and organize themselves into a dangerous complex of instincts, anti-social and dangerous to the self—a kind of parasitic 'second personality', the tendencies of which are diametrically opposite to those capable of becoming conscious.

It could be contended that this state of affairs is expedient as it makes socially purposeful thinking so to speak automatic, and prevents any harmful effects arising from the anti-social or asocial tendencies by relegating them to the unconscious. Psycho-analysis has proved, however, that this kind of neutralizing of the asocial tendencies is uneconomic and ineffective. The tendencies hidden in the unconscious can be kept suppressed and hidden only by the automatic action of powerful safety measures, a process which consumes much too much mental energy. The prohibiting and deterring commands of moralizing education based on repression are comparable with the post-hypnotic suggestion of a negative hallucination; for just as with a sufficiently strong command one can render a hypnotized man, when awake, unable to perceive or recognize certain visual auditory or tactile stimuli, so nowadays is mankind educated to *introspective blindness*. The man thus educated, like the one who is hypnotized, draws much mental energy from the conscious part of his ego and so impairs considerably his own ability for action, first because he breeds in his unconscious another—a parasitic—person, whose natural egotism and tendency for unscrupulous wish-fulfilment represents the dark phantom, the negative of all the good and beautiful on which the higher consciousness prides itself; and secondly, because the conscious is forced to expend its greatest power in creating a defence against being forced to recognize and appreciate the asocial impulses hidden behind the charity and kindness, by surrounding them with ramparts of moralistic, religious and social dogmas. Such ramparts are, for example, sense of duty, honesty, respect for authority and legal institutions, etc. In a word, all those moral qualities which compel us to respect the rights of others and to suppress our own egotism.

Appendix II

The anaesthesia of hysterical women and the impotence of neurotic men correspond to the strange and unnatural tendency of society towards asceticism. In the same way as behind the exaggerated reaction-formation of the unconsciously perverse, as behind the pathological over-cleanliness and over-honesty of the neurotic, smutty thoughts and repressed libidinous impulses are lying in wait, so do we find that behind the respect-exacting mask of the over-strict moralist there exist unconsciously all the thoughts and wish-impulses which he so strongly condemns in others. The over-strictness saves the moralist from seeing himself and at the same time enables him to live out one of his repressed unconscious urges, namely his aggressiveness.

None of that is meant as an accusation: the best members of our society are men of this kind. I want only to show by what means moralizing education based on repression calls forth a modicum of neurosis, even in the healthy. Only in this way are such social circumstances possible in which behind the catchword 'patriotism' obviously egotistic tendencies can hide themselves, where under the name of 'social reform' tyrannical suppression of the individual freedom is propagated, where religion receives homage partly as a drug against fear of death (i.e. a drug serving egotistical purposes) and partly as a permissible means of mutual intolerance, where in the sexual sphere nobody wants to notice what everyone does continuously. Neurosis and hypocritical egotism are the ultimate effects of education that is based on dogmas and fails to pay attention to the true psychology of man; in the later effect it is not the egotism that must be condemned—without it no living being on this earth can be imagined—but the hypocrisy, the most characteristic symptom of the present-day civilized man's neurosis.

There are some who admit the truth of this, but they are frightened by the prospect of what may possibly happen to human culture when appeal can no longer be made to dogmatic principles nor their discussion tolerated, and when these will no longer guide education and the everyday life of man. Will the egotistic instincts, now freed from their fetters, not destroy all the creations of the millennial human civilization? will it be possible to substitute anything for the categorical imperative of morals?

Psychology has taught us that a substitute is possible. When, after a psycho-analytic cure, a hitherto seriously neurotic patient becomes aware of the unconscious wish-impulses of his mind, impulses condemned by the ruling morals or by his own conscious moral notions, his symptoms disappear. And this happens also when the wish which manifested itself in symbolic form in the neurotic symptom must remain ungratified because of insurmountable obstacles in its way. Psycho-analysis does not lead to an unrestrained rule of egoistic instincts that are or may be inexpedient for the individual, but instead to a liberation from prejudices hindering self-knowledge, to discernment of the hitherto unconscious motives and to control over the now conscious impulses.

Repression is replaced by conscious condemnation, says
K

Freud. The external circumstances, the way of life, need hardly change.

A man with true self-knowledge becomes modest—apart from the exalting feeling created by this knowledge. He is lenient towards the faults of others, willing to forgive; moreover, from the principle '*tout comprendre, c'est tout pardonner*' he aspires only to understand—he does not feel justified to pardon. He analyses the motives of his own emotions and thereby prevents their increase into passions. He watches with cheerful humour the human groups scrambling under various banners; in his actions he is not led by loudly proclaimed morals, but by sober efficiency, and this urges him to keep a watch over and to control those of his wishes whose gratification might offend the rights of other men (which might thus in their later repercussions, become dangerous to him also), but without, nevertheless, denying their existence.

When I stated above that to-day the whole of society is neurotic, it was not meant as a far-fetched analogy or a metaphor. Nor is it a poetic turn of phrase. It is my earnest conviction that this illness of society has no other remedy than the undisguised recognition of the true and full nature of man, especially recognition of the no longer inaccessible method of the workings of the unconscious mental life; its prophylaxis is: a new education not based on dogmas but on insight, suited to the means to be achieved (*Zweckmässigkeit*)—an education to be worked out in the future.

XXIII

THE EFFECT ON WOMEN OF PREMATURE EJACULATION IN MEN[1]
(1908)

THERE is already an extensive literature dealing with the mental and physiological causes of premature ejaculation and describing the nervous conditions that accompany it. On the other hand there is little or nothing about its consequences for the nervous and mental life of the female sex. A thorough investigation on Freudian lines of the marital or sexual life of women suffering from anxiety hysteria will, however, lead to the conviction that states of anxiety, oppression, and restlessness are almost invariably to be traced back to lack of, or to incomplete, sexual satisfaction; and that the most frequent cause of this is premature ejaculation in the male. But, apart from the definitely pathological cases of premature ejaculation (which normally appear accompanied by several other signs of sexual neurasthenia), and apart from the fact that on the whole the male sex suffers from relative premature ejaculation in comparison with the female, even in favourable cases, where the friction has lasted long enough for the man, orgasm does not occur in the woman; the woman either remains completely anaesthetic or feels only a certain amount of libidinous excitation, but before she could reach the stage necessary for orgasm, the man finishes the act, and she is left unsatisfied.

Only the selfishness of the male, and of physicians who are generally males, has made it possible to overlook the fact that such a state of affairs, if it becomes stabilized, must lead at least to functional disturbances. We have for a long time been accustomed to grant the right to sexual libido and orgasms to the male alone. We have formed a feminine ideal, which we have allowed women themselves to accept, according to which they

[1] First published in Hungarian (under the title: *On the Significance of Premature Ejaculation*): *Budapesti Orvosi Ujság* (1908), in German: *Bausteine* II (1926). First English translation.

cannot admit or manifest sexual desire, but at most are allowed passively to tolerate it, with the result that, when libidinous tendencies manifest themselves in women, they are stamped as morbid or sinful.

The female sex, which has subjected itself to the male viewpoint in morals as in other matters, has so completely adopted this ideal of femininity that it holds the opposite attitude to be impossible for itself, even in thought. Often enough a woman suffering from severe anxiety, which questioning shows to be the result of nothing but unconsummated excitations, defends herself with vigour and righteous indignation against the insinuation that she is 'that kind of woman', to whom 'that sort of thing' is a matter of concern. Not only has she no desire for it, she generally maintains, but she regards 'the whole thing' as something indecent and distasteful, which she would gladly forego if only her husband did not demand it.

However, awakened and unsatisfied instincts cannot be disposed of by moral rules alone, and sexual desire which is consistently thwarted of satisfaction proceeds to live itself out in unpleasant female character traits and, in women suitably predisposed, results in anxiety neurosis, hysteria, or obsessional illness.[1]

If men gave up their selfish way of thinking and imagined what life would be like if they always had to cut the act short before their libidinous tension was relieved, they would gain some idea of the sexual martyrdom of the female sex, which is faced with the appalling dilemma of choosing between complete satisfaction and self-respect. They would then understand more easily why so large a proportion of women take flight from this dilemma into illness.

Looking at the matter from the teleological point of view, it is hard to believe that in the 'best of all possible worlds' it can be natural that there should be such a difference between the two sexes in the time required for the attainment of satisfaction in such an elementary organic function; and, indeed, closer investigation shows that it is not so much the organic difference

[1] Women's instinct that complete abstinence is less harmful to the nerves than unconsummated excitation is perfectly correct.

between the sexes which explains this 'dyschronism' in the sexuality of man and woman as the difference in the circumstances in which they live, in the amount of social pressure which rests on their shoulders.

Most men marry after a greater or lesser (generally greater) amount of sexual activity, and experience shows that in this field habit leads, not to an increase in the threshold of tolerance, but, on the contrary, to premature ejaculation. This acceleration of ejaculation is not inconsiderably accentuated in the majority of men by juvenile masturbation. That is how it comes about that men generally marry with a kind of restricted potency.

The female sex provides a great contrast to this. All sexual excitement is methodically kept away from girls, not only in reality, but also in fantasy; domestic education sees to it that the girl regards everything connected with sexuality as disgusting and contemptible. The consequence is that in comparison with the bridegroom the bride is, if not sexually anaesthetic, at any rate relatively hypaesthetic. Moreover, female masturbation has the opposite kind of disturbing effect on orgasm, i.e. tends to delay it.

I do not feel qualified to draw the sociological consequences from these facts and to decide whether the advocates of male chastity before marriage or the advocates of female sexual emancipation are in the right.[1] The mental hygienist would be more inclined to have sympathy with a course from which a diminution of female hysteria could be expected than with an alternative which would tend to extend it to the male sex as well.

I do not believe, however, that the only choice is between these two extremes. There must be a way of doing more justice to women's sexual interests than has been done in the past without destroying the social order founded on the family.

The first hesitant step in this direction is the early sexual enlightenment of women. Though many naïve non-understanding proposals have been made in this respect, they all contribute to

[1] I think women are wrong in regarding the political vote as the cure for all their ills. It would be more natural for them to demand a sexual vote.

a gradual break with the brutal practice which still prevails to-day of simply delivering over to her husband on her wedding day a terrified, unprepared woman entirely inexperienced in sexual matters.

So long as this state of affairs prevails we should not be surprised that the husband's relatively too quick ejaculation and the wife's relative anaesthesia leads to such conflict, and that as a consequence of the prevailing 'sexual pattern' happy marriages are so rare.

XXIV

STIMULATION OF THE ANAL EROTOGENIC ZONE AS A PRECIPITATING FACTOR IN PARANOIA[1]

(1911)

Contribution to the problem of homosexuality and paranoia

THE analysis of Schreber's autobiography[2] and the investigation of paranoiac patients[3] established the decisive role of homosexuality, generally warded off with the aid of projection, in the pathogenesis of this psychosis. Since then I have had the opportunity of observing a number of paranoiacs, and in every case without exception I have had no alternative but to interpret the symptoms as the consequences of a destroyed social sublimation of homosexuality. They were all to be regarded as individuals whose development from auto-eroticism to object-love had suffered disturbance, and who had thereupon, as a consequence of narcissistic fixation and subsequent accidental causes, regressed to the homosexual level, but had warded off this perversion, which was intolerable to their consciousness.

Let me now describe one of these cases.

A Suabian peasant[4] aged about forty-five, who had always lived a sober life, was brought to me because of his persecution mania. His wife explained to me that he had the fixed idea that every man who approached him was an enemy, wanted to poison him, pointed at him, wanted to ridicule him. If a cock crowed in the yard or a stranger passed him in the street, it all happened because of him.

I asked the man about his relations with his wife. I knew that delusions of jealousy were not confined to alcoholic paranoiacs.

[1] German original; *Zb. f. Psa.* (1911), 1, 557. First English translation.
[2] Freud, *Collected Papers*, Vol. III, pp. 390–472. London: Hogarth Press. 1933.
[3] Ferenczi, 'The Role of Homosexuality in the Pathogenesis of Paranoia' (1912), in *First Contributions*, p. 154. London: Hogarth Press. 1952.
[4] In the neighbourhood of Budapest there are a few villages inhabited by Germans. These Hungarian Germans are commonly known as 'Suabians'.

Both he and his wife answered unanimously that in that respect everything was in order; they were fond of each other, and had several children; true, since the beginning of his illness the man had refrained from sexual intercourse, but that was because he had 'other things on his mind'.

I went on to ask whether he took any interest in parish affairs, and, if so, whether there had been any change in this respect since the beginning of his illness. (I know from experience that those who later become paranoiacs, like true homosexuals, show an unusual amount of interest in social affairs and take an active part in them, but partially or completely lose this interest upon the outbreak of paranoia.) His wife answered with a vigorously repeated 'yes'. Her husband had been a parish councillor and had taken his duties very seriously, but since he had been ill he had taken no more interest in the parish.

At this point the man, who had hitherto listened quietly to all that had been said and had confirmed it, started getting restless, and in response to my questions confessed, after considerable pressure, that he thought I must obviously have been given secret hints by his wife; otherwise he could not see how I could possibly have guessed everything about him so correctly.

I then continued the interview with him alone, in the course of which he eventually admitted that I had been right about his jealousy too; he had not wanted to admit it in his wife's presence. He secretly suspected his wife in connexion with every male who came into the house. (In view of the sexual abstinence he had practised for many months, which was not really consistent with his being in love with his wife, I interpreted his jealousy as a projection of his own interest in the male sex.)

I next asked him when and in what circumstances this change in him and his environment had come about, whereupon he told me the following story. Some months previously he had been operated on twice in succession for an anal fistula. The doctor had done the second operation badly, he said, and for some time afterwards he had noticed 'noises in the chest' and had had attacks of feeling 'frightened to death' several times daily. Simultaneously he felt 'as if the fistula were suddenly climbing up into his stomach, and that he would be bound to die of it'. He had now got over this fear, but people now wished to declare him mad.

His wife and a friend who accompanied the couple confirmed what the patient said, and in particular made it clear that the delusional ideas had set in only after the paraesthesias and anxiety released by the operation had ceased. Subsequently he had accused the surgeon of having deliberately performed the operation badly.

In view of all that was known to me about the connexion between paranoia and homosexuality, I concluded that his intestinal illness and the resulting necessity for manipulation of his rectum by males (physicians) might have stimulated the patient's hitherto latent or sublimated homosexual tendencies by the resuscitation of childish memories. In view of the symbolic significance of unsheathed knives, the second operation in particular, which was carried out without an anaesthetic and in which the cutting instrument was introduced deeply into the rectum, seemed well calculated to revive the infantile idea of *coitus a tergo*.

Without very much beating about the bush, I asked the patient straight out whether in his boyhood he had not done forbidden things with other boys. This question obviously took him aback, and there was a long pause before he answered, and confessed rather shamefacedly that at the age of five or six he had played a remarkable game with another boy of the same age who was now one of his greatest enemies. This boy used to challenge him to play 'cock and hen'. He accepted, and always played the passive role in the game; he was the 'hen'. The other boy used to insert either his erect penis or his finger into his rectum; sometimes he would insert a cherry and then remove it with his finger. They had continued with this game until their tenth or eleventh year. Since then, however, he had known that such things were godless and disgusting, and he had never again indulged in them; in fact the idea of them had never again entered his head. He assured me repeatedly that he regarded such shameful actions with contempt.

Now this memory showed that our patient had lingered unusually long and intensely at the stage of homosexual object-choice, and had then energetically suppressed and partially sublimated it. Thus the brutal intervention in his anal erotogenic zone had been well adapted to reawaken the wish to repeat the infantile homosexual play which survived in his unconscious. But in the meantime the sexuality, which in the earlier stage had been childish play, had developed into the impetuous and dangerous drive of a strong, adult, man. No wonder, therefore, that the patient had tried to defend himself against giving abnormal (perverse) outlet to such large quantities of libido and had sought at first to convert them into paraesthesias and anxiety attacks and to project them from the ego into the outer world as delusional ideas. The same unconscious, passive-pederastic fantasy (the 'anal fistula climbing up into his stomach') underlay both the delusional ideas and the paraesthesias which had preceded the outbreak of those ideas. It is not improbable that this stage indicated an attempt to deal with the homosexuality by means of paraphrenia,[1] i.e. a complete turning away from men and a return to anal autoeroticism; and that the persecution mania broke out only with the 'return of the repressed', i.e. with the re-cathexis of the long-sublimated and then completely rejected male love-object. The 'crowing cock in the yard' to which the patient attributed a special place in his delusional ideas was identical with the 'greatest enemy' to whom he had played the hen in his boyhood.

As I had one conversation only with him, I was unable to confirm my suspicion that the fear of poisoning symbolized in his case, as in so many others, a wish to be made pregnant.

I had no choice but to be very sceptical about the prospect of a cure, but left open the possibility that when the anal fistula had completely healed and the physical conditions thus ceased to be so 'accommodating', the delusional ideas might partially or completely cease and that the patient might recover his capacity for sublimation (for intellectualized homosexuality, friendship community sense).

[1] Paraphrenia is suggested by Freud as a more suitable term than *dementia praecox* because it is without the latter's implications. Incidentally the pathology of the psychosis of paraphrenia is not sufficiently clarified to put out of court an alternative interpretation of the anxiety and the sensory stimulation phenomena as attempts at hysterical conversion.

XXV

ON THE ORGANIZATION OF THE PSYCHO-ANALYTIC MOVEMENT
(1911)

Address at the Second Congress of Psycho-Analysts, held in Nuremburg in 1910, when the author proposed the formation of an International Association of Psycho-Analysts

PSYCHO-ANALYSIS is still a young science, but its history is already rich enough in events to justify a momentary pause to survey the results attained and to weigh up its failures and successes. Such a survey should help us to apply our efforts more economically in future by abandoning ineffective methods for more fruitful ones. Drawing up such balance-sheets from time to time is as necessary in scientific workshops as it is in trade and industry. Congresses are generally nothing but Vanity Fairs, providing opportunities for self-display and the theatrical first production of scientific novelties, though their real task should be the solution of such problems of scientific policy.

Like all innovators and pioneers, we have had not only to work for our cause, but also to fight for it. Psycho-analysis, looked at objectively, is a pure science, the object of which is to fill in the gaps in our knowledge of the laws that determine mental events. This purely scientific question, however, touches so much on the raw the vital foundations of daily life, certain ideals that have grown dear to us, and dogmas of family life, school and church—incidentally disturbing so uncomfortably the contemplative ease of the nerve specialists and psychiatrists who ought to be the impartial judges of our work—that it is not surprising that we are met with empty invective instead of with arguments and facts.

We were thus, very much against our will, involved in a war, and it is well known that in war the muses are silent; but the

[1] First published in Hungarian: *Gyógydszat* (1911), in German: *Bausteine* I (1926). First English translation (abridged).

passions rage all the more vociferously for that, and it is held to be legitimate to use weapons not taken from the armoury of science. We suffered the same fate as the prophets of peace, who find themselves compelled to wage war for the sake of their ideals.

The first, what I should like to call the heroic, age of psychoanalysis was the ten years in which Freud had to meet entirely alone the attacks on psycho-analysis that were directed at him from all quarters and with no holds barred. He was first met with the well-tested method of complete silence; then came derision, contempt, and even slander. His only friend and his original fellow-worker abandoned him, and the only kind of praise that he earned was expression of regret that he should waste his talent on such bewildering aberrations.

It would be hypocritical to refrain from expressing our admiration of the fashion in which Freud, without troubling himself overmuch about the attacks on his reputation, and in spite of the deep disappointments caused him even by his friends, continued firmly to advance along the road that he had recognized to be the right one. He could say to himself, with the bitter humour of a Leonidas, that the shadow of being ignored and misunderstood at any rate gave him quiet in which to go on with his work; and so it came about that for him these were years in which imperishable ideas matured and books of consummate importance were written. What an irreplaceable loss it would have been if he had devoted himself to sterile controversy instead! The attacks made on psycho-analysis have in the great majority of cases not been worthy of notice.... The policy of non-reaction to unscientific criticism, the avoidance of sterile controversy, thus justified itself in the first defensive battles of psycho-analysis.

The second period was heralded by the appearance of Jung and the 'Zürichers', who associated Freud's ideas with the methods of experimental psychology and thus made them accessible to those who, though honourable seekers after truth, because of the awe in which they held scientific 'exactness', shrank back in horror from Freud's methods of investigation, which broke with all the traditional methods of psychological research. I know that kind of mentality from personal experience. I too came only later to see that the 'exactness' of pre-Freudian psychology was only a kind of self-deception, a cloak to hide one's own emptiness. It is true that experimental psychology is 'exact', but it can teach us little. Psycho-analysis is 'inexact', but it discloses unsuspected inter-relations and opens up layers of the mind hitherto inaccessible to research.[1]

New workers streamed into the new scientific field discovered by Freud just as they streamed in the wake of Amerigo to the new continent discovered by Columbus, and they too had to, and still have to, conduct guerrilla warfare, just as the pioneers in the New World did.... The lack of authority, discipline and leading strings served only to increase the independence essential in serving in such outposts. There was actually one type of human being who was won over by this 'irregular' type of work; I refer to people of artistic gifts, who were led into our camp partly because of their intuitive understanding of the problems with which we were concerned, but were also attracted by our rebellion against scientific scholasticism, and contributed not inconsiderably to the dissemination of Freud's ideas.

Disadvantages as well as advantages, however, gradually emerged from this guerrilla warfare. The complete lack of any central direction meant that in some cases particular scientific and personal interests got the better of and acted detrimentally to the common interest, what I should like to call the 'central idea'.... But psycho-analysis and analytic self-criticism might have convinced us all that only an exceptional individual can, without friends to help and check him, correctly recognize his own sometimes inopportune tendencies and inclinations and restrain them in the general interest; and that even in the scientific field a certain amount of mutual control can be only beneficial. . . . Another consideration is that, while a very valuable and talented section of society is attracted to us precisely because of our lack of organization, the majority, who are

[1] It cannot be admitted that only ponderable and measurable objects of experience, i.e. the results of observation of the experiments of the natural sciences, are to be regarded as reliable. Inner experiences, i.e. psychic reality (with which all introspective psychology is concerned), can also be the object of legitimate scientific inquiry.

accustomed to order and discipline, draw from our irregularity only new material for resistance. . . . The name of Freud inscribed on our banner is only a name, and gives no idea of the number of those who now concern themselves with the ideas which originated with him and of the work which psycho-analysis has already accomplished. Thus we lose even that measure of 'mass-effect' to which our numbers alone entitle us, even leaving out of account the specific gravity of individual personalities and their ideas. No wonder, then, that this new branch of science is still, so to speak, unknown to-day to laymen, to physicians untrained in psychology and, in a number of countries, even to professional psychologists; and that, when we are called into consultation by physicians, we generally have to lecture them about even the most elementary conceptions of psycho-analysis. . . .

The question I now wish to put is whether the advantages of our guerrilla warfare outweigh the disadvantages. Are we justified in expecting that these disadvantages will disappear of themselves without appropriate intervention? If not, are we strong and numerous enough to be able to organize ourselves? And, finally, what measures would be possible and advisable to make our organization useful, strong, and enduring?

I can answer the first question without hesitation by hazarding the opinion that our work would gain more than it would lose by the formation of an organization.

I know the excrescences that grow from organized groups, and I am aware that in most political, social, and scientific organizations childish megalomania, vanity, admiration of empty formalities, blind obedience, or personal egoism prevail instead of quiet, honest work in the general interest.

The characteristics of family life are repeated in the structure and the very nature of all organizations. The president is the father, whose pronouncements and authority are incontrovertible and sacrosanct; the other officials are the older children, who treat their juniors with superiority and flatter the father-figure, but wish at the earliest suitable moment to push him from his throne in order to reign in his stead. The great mass of members, in so far as they do not follow their leader with no will of their own, listen now to one agitator, now to another, follow the successes of their seniors with hatred and envy, and would like to oust them from the father-figure's favour. Organizations are the field in which sublimated homosexuality can live itself out in the form of admiration and hatred. Thus it seems that man can never rid himself of his family habits, and that he really is the gregarious animal, the ζῷον πολίτικον described by the Greek philosopher. However far he may roam both in time and space from his own family origins, he constantly and inevitably seeks to re-establish the old order, and to find his father again in an admired hero, a party leader, or a person in a position of authority over him; to find his mother over again in his wife; and to find his toys again in his children. Even in the case of us unorganized analysts, as I have been able to establish both in myself and in numerous colleagues, our intellectual leader is apt in dreams to condense with the father-figure. In our dreams we are all inclined in more or less concealed form to outsoar, to overthrow, our intellectual father, whom we esteem highly, but whom it is difficult inwardly to tolerate precisely because of his intellectual superiority.

Thus it would be doing violence to human nature were we to drive the principle of liberty too far and seek to evade the 'family organization'. For, though we analysts are now formally unorganized, we already live in a kind of family community, and in my opinion it would be right to give outward recognition to the fact.

Not only would it be right, it would also be expedient, for self-seeking tendencies are better kept in check by mutual control. The psycho-analytically trained are surely the best adapted to found an association which would combine the greatest possible personal liberty with the advantages of family organization. It would be a family in which the father enjoyed no dogmatic authority, but only that to which he was entitled by reason of his abilities and labours. His pronouncements would not be followed blindly, as if they were divine revelations, but, like everything else, would be subject to thoroughgoing criticism, which he would accept, not with the absurd superiority of the paterfamilias, but with the attention that it deserved.

Moreover, the older and younger children united in this association would accept being told the truth to their face, however bitter and sobering it might be, without childish sensitivity and vindictiveness. In the present state of civilization, i.e. in the second century of surgical anaesthesia, it can be taken for granted that we should endeavour to tell the truth without causing unnecessary pain. . . .

Such an association, which would be able to reach this ideal level only after a considerable time, would have excellent prospects of profitable work. In an association in which people can tell each other the truth, in which people's real capacities can be recognized without envy, or, more correctly, with natural envy held in check, in which no attention need be paid to the sensitiveness of the conceited, it will be impossible, for instance, for a man with a fine sense for details but ungifted in abstract matters to take it into his head to undertake the reform of scientific theory; or for another to wish to use as the background for the whole of science his perhaps valuable but entirely subjective trends; while a third will come to realize that the unnecessarily aggressive note in his writings serves only to increase resistance without advancing the cause; and a fourth will be convinced by the free exchange of opinions that it is absurd immediately to react to something new in a spirit of knowing better already.

These are more or less the types who appear in organizations in general, and also appear among ourselves; but in an organization of psycho-analysts it would be more easily possible, if not to eradicate them altogether, at least to hold them in check. The auto-erotic period of an organization's life would gradually give way to the more advanced stage of object-love, which would cease seeking and finding satisfaction in the titillation of intellectual erotogenic zones (vanity, ambition), and would seek and find it in observation of the object itself.

I am convinced that an association working on the basis of these principles will not only create favourable conditions for work among ourselves, but will also be in a position to gain us respect in the outside world. Freud's theories will always meet with great resistance, but since the second, 'guerrilla', period a certain diminution of the obstinate, negative attitude is unmistakable. If we set ourselves the unprofitable and disagreeable task of listening to the various arguments brought against psycho-analysis, we notice that those same writers who a few years ago ignored or excommunicated the whole thing now speak of the 'catharsis' of Breuer and Freud as a theory worthy of attention, or even brilliant; naturally they reject everything that has been discovered and described since the 'abreaction' period. Some are even so bold as to recognize the unconscious and the methods of investigating it analytically, but shrink back in horror from the problems of sexuality. Decorum as well as prudence keep them from such dangerous matters. Some accept the conclusions drawn by Freud's younger followers, but are as terrified of the name of Freud as if he were the devil incarnate; they completely forget that thereby they are committing the logical absurdity of *filius ante patrem*. The most usual and most contemptible way of accepting Freud's theories is that of rediscovering them and broadcasting them under new names. For what is the 'expectation neurosis' but Freud's anxiety neurosis sailing under false colours? Which of us does not know that the name 'phrenocardia', placed on the scientific market by an adroit colleague as his own discovery, is merely a new name given to a few of the symptoms of Freud's anxiety hysteria? And was it not inevitable that the use of the word 'analysis' should lead to the invention of the term 'psycho-synthesis', though its author forgot to pay attention to the fact that synthesis must naturally be preceded by analysis? More danger threatens psycho-analysis from such friends than from its enemies. We are threatened with the danger of becoming fashionable, so to speak, which would result in a notable increase in the number of those who call themselves analysts without being analysts.

We cannot take responsibility for all the nonsense that is served up under the name of psycho-analysis, and we therefore need, in addition to our own publications, an association, membership of which would offer some guarantee that Freud's own psycho-analytic methods were being used, and not methods cooked up for the practitioner's own purposes. One of the special tasks of the association would be to unmask the scientific looting to which psycho-analysis is subject to-day. Careful sifting of new members would make it possible to separate the wheat from the chaff. The association should be content with a small membership rather than accept or retain people who are not firmly convinced on matters of principle. Profitable work is possible only when agreement prevails on fundamental matters. It is undeniable that at the present time public association with a body such as I have in mind involves a measure of personal courage and a renunciation of academic ambition. . . .

I have already mentioned how wise it was of Freud to ignore the many senseless attacks made upon him at the time. But it would be wrong to adopt this attitude as the watchword of the future association. It is necessary from time to time to draw attention to the poverty of the counter-arguments used against us. This, in view of the weak foundation and the uniformity of the attacks on us, should not be an excessively difficult task.

The same logical, moral, and medical counter-arguments recur again and again, making it possible to draw up a regular catalogue of them. The logicians declare our views to be nonsense and self-deception. All the illogicalities and unintelligibilities produced in the unconscious of neurotics and brought to the surface by their associations are attributed to us.

Moralists shrink back in terror from the sexual subject-matter of our investigations and conduct a crusade against us, generally omitting in the process to recall anything that Freud has written about the taming and sublimation of the instincts laid bare by analysis. . . .

It is also interesting that people, though they habitually talk about the 'mendacity' and 'undependability' of hysterics, gladly swallow everything about analysis said by uncured patients with a still imperfect knowledge of the subject.

Many hold the view that the therapeutic effect of analysis depends on suggestion. Assuming, but not admitting, that that is the case, is there any reason why an effective method of suggestive therapy should be *a priori* rejected? The second counter-argument is that analysis 'does not work'. The element of truth in this is that analysis is unable to clear up all forms of neurosis, that it generally does not work quickly, and that putting right the personality of a human being that has developed askew since infancy often takes more time than his patience—and in particular that of his family—is willing to accept. Other critics say that analysis is harmful. By this they obviously mean the patient's sometimes violent reactions, which are, however, part of his cure, and are generally followed by periods of alleviation.

The final counter-argument is that analysts are out only for money; this obviously springs from the human tendency to fall back on abuse when the supply of objective arguments has been exhausted. This accusation is often brought up by patients, frequently just when they are about to give in to the weight of newly-acquired self-knowledge, in a last, desperate effort to remain ill.

The logical, ethical, and therapeutic outbursts of the medical profession are above all noticeably like the dialectical reactions which resistance produces in our patients. Just as the overcoming of the resistance of individual neurotics requires technical knowledge and steady work, so does group resistance (e.g. the attitude of the medical profession to the theories of analysis) require to be dealt with in a planned and expert manner and not, as in the past, to be left to chance. One of the chief tasks of an association of psycho-analysts, in addition to the development of our own science, would be to deal with the resistance of scientific circles. This task alone might justify the foundation of such a body.

If, gentlemen, you accept in principle my proposal that we should found an International Psycho-Analytical Association, nothing further remains for me . . . but to make concrete proposals. I propose the setting up of a central executive to support the formation of local groups in all centres of civilization, the organization of international congresses to meet annually, and, in addition to our *Jahrbuch*, the publication as soon as possible of a new official journal to appear at shorter intervals. . . . I have the honour to lay before you draft statutes for the association.

XXVI

EXPLORING THE UNCONSCIOUS[1]
(1912)

It is not the rulers, politicians, or diplomats, but the scientists, who decide the future fate of mankind. Those who hold power are, in fact, only executives, or even rigid opponents, that is to say, mere puppets of the powers liberated by the ideas of the scientists, and 'who knows', asks Anatole France somewhere, 'whether, somewhere in a little back room, some unknown research worker is not already engaged in a quest which one day will lift the world off its hinges?'

It is not only from the miracles of technique, from the ever-increasing harnessing of the forces of nature, that we may expect radical changes in the world, nor only from the experiments which attempt to make the life of the individual safer and more comfortable by a more equitable distribution of material goods, by better social organization; progress has a third possibility which is at least as promising, and this is the hope of developing man's physical and mental powers and his adaptability. This is the aim of individual and social hygiene, and of eugenics, that ever-expanding movement which has as its aim the improvement of the race. A conspicuous phenomenon of this movement, however, is its marked onesidedness. The workers engaged in it are not able to detach themselves from the bias of the exact and natural sciences, i.e. physics, chemistry, and biology, and to look for improvement *exclusively* from that direction, that is to say mainly from better selection and better protection of the progeny.

Unfortunately those mental phenomena which can be measured, expressed in mathematical formulas, and made accessible to experiment, make up such a minimal and pedestrian part of mental life that under the influence of this materialistic tendency psychology sank to the status of a subordinate province, of the physiology of the senses, and we may say has now for

[1] Published in Hungarian in 1912. German translation in *Bausteine* III. First English translation.

some decades remained sterile. The very complicated mental phenomena for whose study the only method is self-observation have not been considered by scientists as worthy of their attention; professional research workers have not condescended to occupy themselves with questions of the biology of character, of mental conflicts, of the ways of coping with transitory and permanent consequences of emotional experiences. Only the poets, biographers and autobiographers, and perhaps a few historians, were interested in this field, but of course they were not able to build up a real science. The poet's aim is not to teach, but to entertain; the historian's interest is, above all, in events, and the biographer examines the mental life of one individual only, and does not consider it his duty to abstract from his experiences generally valid laws.

The study of one of the mental illnesses, hysteria, led psychology back to its true task. The researches of Charcot, Möbius and Janet made it clear that this illness should be viewed as a very instructive 'experiment of nature', demonstrating that the human mind is far from being that unified and indivisible something that the word 'individual' makes us think of. It is in fact a most complex structure, of which consciousness shows only the exterior façade, while the true motor forces and mechanisms are to be found in a third dimension, that is, in the depth of the mind behind consciousness. It is true that these scientists fought shy of drawing these general conclusions from the phenomena of hysteria; they continued to believe that divisibility and disintegration of consciousness is to be found only in a pathologically affected mind, which perhaps is congenitally too weak for the necessary synthesis, for integrating the forces of the mind. They did not notice that hysteria only shows in an exaggerated and distorted form what occurs in every human being, although not in such a conspicuous way.

Almost contemporaneously with these studies in hysteria the theory of the indivisibility of consciousness was attacked from another side. This attack was led by Liébeault, Bernheim and the doctors of the Salpêtrière, who began to pay serious attention to the phenomena in hypnosis which until then had been looked upon as superstition and quackery. The state brought about by hysteria as a symptom of illness, the disintegration of the personality into two or more parts, could be produced deliberately by hypnotic experiments. In the Paris hospital where these experiments were performed the doctors literally 'bred' people who had two, or three, or even more, 'egos', 'egos' which did not know anything of the desires, intentions, and actions of the other ego components; the various 'egos' even represented personalities of entirely opposite characters and possessed completely separate memories.

It is characteristic of the inertia of the human mind that although these hypnotic experiments could be carried out not only on hysterics but also on normal people, science could not arrive at the self-evident conclusion that the disintegration of consciousness is not a scientific curiosity, not a teratological *lusus naturae*, but an essential quality of the human mind. So it came about that psychology, instead of investing a good deal of its energy in the study of these completely new problems of very wide perspective, obstinately continued its sterile psychophysical experiments, starting with the erroneous idea that the objects of psychology are exclusively phenomena associated with consciousness, and assuming *a priori* that the layer under the consciousness cannot be understood except physiologically. The experience obtained in hysteria and in hypnosis argued in vain against this conception. There remained unnoticed the empirical fact that, under the threshold of consciousness, there existed highly complicated abilities which—apart from the quality of consciousness—are of practically equal importance with the conscious ones. The attempt was made to cope with this contradiction either by degrading these complicated mental phenomena simply to 'brain functions', i.e. to the physiological level, or it was decreed in the face of the facts that the functions under consciousness must still possess some small amount of consciousness; science clung to the assumption of 'half consciousness' or 'under consciousness', even where the only reliable judge, i.e. the subject in question, neither knew nor felt anything of the existence of these functions. In short, it was again the facts which were worsted because they dared to get into conflict with petrified theories. *Tant pis pour les faits.*

This was the state of affairs when, in 1881, the Viennese physician, Breuer, was led by a talented patient to the conclusion that in hysterics it is possible, under certain conditions, to bring back to consciousness and to make conscious memories long submerged under the threshold of consciousness and causing disturbances from there. In addition to the fact that this procedure has proved its value as a therapeutic measure with neurotic patients, we must attribute to these events a very high importance for psychology in general. It was the first time that anyone had succeeded with a predetermined method in recognizing the content of the ideas hidden in unconsciousness, and the nature of the effects associated with them.

Amazingly enough, this discovery was not followed by a feverish investigation of the riddles of the unconscious mental world. For ten long years this case history lay untouched in the files of the Viennese physician, until at long last Freud recognized its general importance.

From that time on, the exploration of the underworld of the mind has been connected solely with the name of Freud. It was he who developed and perfected the method of analytic research into the healthy and the sick mind, thereby creating a new basis for our knowledge of mental life. Since Freud we have known that individual development of the human mind is not to be compared with the growth of a spherical surface, but to that of a tree, whose trunk when sawn through shows up the annual ring of each year lived through by the individual. In the unconscious layers of the mind live on all the uncivilized amoral instincts which we are wont to think of as long superseded, all the primitive complexes of childhood and youth. All these, as they are beyond the moderating, controlling, and directing power of consciousness, often disturb considerably the logical, ethical, and aesthetical harmony of the conscious 'ego', causing outbursts of passion, senseless or compulsive actions, mental illnesses, and much unnecessary worry and suffering.

Now let us return to our starting-point. Moderation of human tensions, decreasing mental burdens, prevention of psychiatric illnesses: these are no longer questions of an abstract science, but pointers in a new and hopeful direction, towards the development and thriving of mankind. Moreover, we can speak of 'freedom of thought' in the strict sense of the word only when thinking no longer moves merely on the surface of consciousness, when it is not subordinated to the directives of unconscious ideas; when thinking it is able also to take into consideration the deeply hidden ideas and tendencies in conflict with the present moral tenets, that is to say all the determinants hitherto unconscious, in order to have sovereign power to direct them purposefully to the welfare of the individual and of society.

The achievements of psycho-analysis to date in helping mentally ill persons justify the hope that the same research methods will be able to fathom the true causes of the many serious mental illnesses of our civilization and perhaps even to contribute towards their cure.

The not too distant future will moreover present us with a radical reform in the education of the human soul, and bring up a generation which will no longer sink into the unconscious natural instincts and desires, in conflict with civilization will no longer try to deny their reality and ward them off automatically, but will learn to tolerate them consciously and to direct them sensibly. So will be signified the end of an epoch characterized by hypocrisy, by blind adoration of dogmas and authorities, and by an almost complete lack of self-criticism.

XXVII

DIRIGIBLE DREAMS[1]
(1912)

THE 'dream in the dreams' as recognized by Stekel is the satisfaction of the desire that everything activated by the dream-thoughts may be untrue, unreal, that is, a dream. There are, however, dreams in which the dreamer is in a way aware that his thoughts are dreamlike. These dreams appear to need a different explanation of the way in which the dreamer becomes aware that he is dreaming. Many people who use sleep and dreaming as a flight from reality wish to prolong the sleeping state far beyond the physiological necessity for it; it is for this reason that, among other methods, they are inclined to cope with the arousal stimuli by working them into their dreams. Moreover, even when the arousal stimulus has been too strong and its reality can no longer be denied, that is, during the process of waking up, they still struggle with their 'inability' to get up and use every possible pretext to prolong their stay in bed.

One such patient reports to me quite frequently about his peculiar way of becoming aware that he is still dreaming in his sleep. In some of his dreams, which consist of several scenes, the change of scene does not happen as usual suddenly, in a surprising way, and without any obvious reason, but with a peculiar motivation: 'at this moment I thought to myself'—is the usual way he reports the transition between the two scenes—'this is a bad dream; the dream must be solved in a different way', and in the same moment the scene changed. The scene that followed brought in fact an acceptable solution.

This patient sometimes dreams three or four scenes one after the other which try to work through the same material, but with varying outcomes. All of them, however, are in turn inhibited in the decisive moment by the patient's becoming aware that he is dreaming and by his wish for a still better solution, until the last dream can be dreamt to its end uninhibited. This last

[1] German original: *Zb. f. Psa.* (1912), 2, 31. First English translation.

dream scene ends not infrequently with an emission. (Cf. Rank's opinion that all dreams are in reality wet dreams.) Occasionally, after the inhibition, the whole scene does not have to be newly created, the dreamer simply thinks to himself in the midst of his dream: 'this dream will end unpleasantly, and yet the beginning was so beautiful; I must dream it to its end in a different way.' And indeed the dream goes back to a certain point in the preceding dream scene and then corrects from that point the solution which has been recognized as unsatisfactory, without, however, changing in any way the scenery or the personalities in the corresponding first part of the dream.

In contradistinction to daydreams, which are also able to choose from various outcomes and possibilities, it must be stressed that these 'dirigible dreams', as I would like to call them, do not show the rational features of the fantasies produced in the waking state; they betray their close connexion with the unconscious by their ample use of displacement, condensation, and indirect representation. It must be admitted, however, that in these dreams closely knit 'dream fantasies' frequently occur.

We may add that these dreams are usually dreamt in the morning hours, and mainly by people who are bent on prolonging as far as possible their state of sleeping and dreaming. All this suggests that the occurrence of this peculiar mixture of conscious and unconscious thought processes may be explained by a compromise between the consciousness that has had sufficient sleep and wants to wake up and a desperate holding fast to sleep by the unconscious. Theoretically this kind of dream is important because it offers us the possibility of studying introspectively the wish-fulfilment tendencies of dreams.

Moreover, the insight into the motives of the scene-changes in these dreams may be used in general for explaining the connexion between several dreams dreamt in the same night. The dream elaborates from all sides the particular dream thought which occupies the mind, drops one dream-scene when there is a danger that the wish-fulfilment will fail, tries a new kind of solution, and so on, until finally it succeeds in bringing about a wish-fulfilment which satisfies, with a compromise, both instances of the mind.

It is unlikely that a similar mechanism is at work in cases in which the dreamer awakes because of the unpleasure character of his dream, only to drop off to sleep again and to go on dreaming 'as after brushing off a fly' (Freud). The following dream is a point in favour of this idea. It was dreamt by a man, now baptized and in a high position, coming from a very simple Jewish family. He dreamt that his dead father appeared at an elegant party and made the dreamer feel embarrassed because of his shabby clothes. This highly unpleasant situation woke up the dreamer for a moment; soon after he dropped off to sleep again and dreamt that his father was at the same party, but this time smartly and elegantly dressed.

XXVIII

ON THE DEFINITION OF INTROJECTION[1]
(1912)

Dr. A. Maeder[2] refers in one of his papers to my article on Introjection,[3] and on comparing this concept with that of exteriorization proposed by him, he concludes that the two mean much the same. If this is so, then we have to agree which of the two technical terms is to be dropped.

A repeated reading of both papers has convinced me that the identification of these two concepts can only be based on a misunderstanding of the ideas developed in my paper.

I described introjection as an extension to the external world of the original autoerotic interests, by including[4] its objects in the ego. I put the emphasis on this 'including' and wanted to show thereby that I considered *every sort of object love* (or *transference*) both in normal and in neurotic people (and of course also in paranoiacs as far as they are capable of loving) as an extension of the ego, that is, as introjection.

In principle, man can love only himself; if he loves an object he takes it into his ego. Just like the poor fisherman's wife in the fairy tale, on to whose nose a curse made a sausage grow and who then felt any contact with the sausage as if it were her own skin, and had to protest violently against any suggestion of cutting off the unpleasant growth: so we feel all suffering caused to our loved object as our own. I used the term introjection for all such growing on to, all such including of the loved object in, the ego. As already stated, I conceive the mechanism of *all*

---

[1] German original: *Zb. f. Psa.* (1912), 2, 198. First English translation.

[2] A. Maeder, 'Zur Entstehung der Symbolik im Traum in der Dementia praecox usw'. *Zentralbl. f. PsA.* (1910-11), 1, 383.

[3] S. Ferenczi, 'Introjektion und Übertragung', 1909. Reprinted in *First Contributions*, p. 35.

[4] (The word used in German is *Einbeziehung*, which means to pull in, to integrate, to incorporate, but as all these words have acquired a specific meaning during the development of analytic thinking, I had to choose a word in which nobody had a vested interest.—Translator)

transference on to an object, that is to say *all kinds of object love*, as *introjection*, as *extension of the ego*.

I described the excessive proneness to transference of neurotics as *unconscious exaggeration of the same mechanism*, that is, as addiction to introjection, while paranoiacs[1] tend to withdraw their love from the objects and, after its recovery therefrom, to project it again into the external world (addiction to projection). The true paranoiac could think of part of his own nose (his own personality) as a sausage and then cut it off and throw it away; but nothing could induce him to tolerate something foreign growing on to it.

I know full well, and in fact have pointed out in the paper quoted above, that the same mechanisms occur in normal people.[2] It is true that projection is mobilized also in certain cases of neurosis (for instance in hysterical hallucinations); and similarly in some cases of paranoia capacity for transference (introjection) is not completely lacking. In any case projection in paranoia and introjection in neurosis play so much more important a role than all the other mechanisms that we can regard them as characteristic of these clinical entities.[3]

Now let us turn to Maeder's exteriorization. As described by him, it means that individual organs of the body become identified with things in the external world and are then treated as such. (The paranoiac patient F. B. sees in the apples of the orchard duplications of his own genitals. Another thinks the water-pipes are his own blood-vessels.)

Maeder thinks that these are projections. According to my

---

[1] Unlike Dr. Maeder, I do not doubt the existence of paranoia without dementia.

[2] I could even add to the examples there given. One could, for instance, classify the metaphysical systems of philosophy as systems of projection and of introjection. The materialism which dissolves the ego completely into the external world marks the climax of projection; solipsism, which includes the whole external world in the ego, the maximum of introjection.

[3] According to recent experiences, paranoia is characterized, in addition to this pathognomic form, also by pathognomonic content (homosexuality). (S. Freud, 'Psychoanalytic Notes on an Autobiographical Account of a Case of Paranoia', 1911: *Collected Papers*, III, and Ferenczi, 'On the Part Played by Homosexuality in the Pathogenesis of Paranoia', 1911. Reprinted in *First Contributions*, 154.

way of thinking these cases must be explained as follows: the paranoiacs have perhaps in these cases attempted to project their pleasure in their own organs; they were only able, however, to achieve a *displacement* of this, subjectively preserved, interest. The ego can regard its own body as belonging to the external world, that is, objectively. In Maeder's exteriorization the interest is only *displaced* from one object in the external world (one's own organ) on to another similar one (the water-pipes, the fruit). We have known displacement for some time as a special case of the *mechanism of introjection*, to wit of *transference*, in the course of which, in place of the censured object, another similar one will be included in the sphere of interest, for the satisfaction of the 'free floating' libido. Maeder's 'exteriorization' is therefore not a process of projection, but of introjection.

In a really successful paranoid projection (for instance, in a delusion of persecution) one part of the mental personality itself (the homosexuality) is deprived of its connexion with the ego, deprived, so to speak, of its civic rights, and as it cannot be so simply removed from the world, it is treated as something objective, something alien. Such a transformation of the purely subjective into something objective may be referred to as projection. I think the 'exteriorizing' paranoiac, who has a kind of, though displaced, interest in the objects of the external world, and therefore can still introject, and, through such a detour, behave socially, must be regarded as not very far from the neurotic; for that reason he possibly offers somewhat more favourable therapeutic prospects.

Anyhow, Maeder's exteriorization must be considered not as projection, but as a special kind of introjection which incidentally occurs also in normal people,[1] and I propose to stick in the future to the notion of introjection which well describes all our past experiences.

---

[1] cf. reference to the mythical anthropomorphosis of inanimate objects in my paper *Introjection and Transference*, 1909. Reprinted in *First Contributions*, p. 35.

XXIX

A CASE OF 'DÉJÀ VU'[1]
(1912)

A PATIENT told me while under analysis of a dream she had had during her engagement; her fiancé had appeared with a short, English 'toothbrush' moustache. Immediately before reporting this dream she had told me how upset she had been by her fiancé's confession that men, unlike women, did not begin married life as 'virgins', but after sundry erotic experiences. When I asked her what her associations to toothbrushes were, and whether she had had any criticisms of her fiancé's oral hygiene, she confessed that sometimes he really had smelt of 'indigestion'. Taking all her associations together, I suggested that her sensitivity to this might have been accentuated by the disagreeable idea that her fiancé carried about with him the smell of other women. She then suddenly exclaimed: 'Everything that is happening at this moment has happened to me before. I've heard your voice saying exactly the same thing before, and all this furniture was arranged in exactly the same way! It has all happened to me before!' I explained to her that this was the well-known psychical experience of *déjà vu*, and that it might be a confirmation of what I had suggested. 'Yes, we (i.e. she and her sisters) knew all about it when we were children,' she said. 'We used to say that the reason why things sometimes struck us as so familiar was because we had met them before, when we were still frogs!' I drew her attention to the fact that, when she was still a 'frog' (an embryo), she had really been in most intimate contact with another woman's body (her mother's), and moreover in close proximity with organs and excreta the smell of which (as I already knew) were extremely repulsive to her. The patient thereupon produced some of her childish sex theories (the stork story with a frog pond, birth by the anal route, etc.), and a memory of the odour of her mother's body, which she had noticed when she had been allowed to get into her mother's bed.

[1] German original: *Zb. f. Psa.* (1912), 2, 648. First English translation.

I was able to use the dream, the *déjà vu* experience and the patient's associations as valuable confirmation of what I had long suspected to be her fairly strong (unconscious) homosexual fixation, which expressed itself in her consciousness, among other things, by an exaggerated aversion to female smells. The case simultaneously strengthened the impression I had formed on the basis of previous experience that there is a close connexion between *déjà vu* and dreams. Hitherto, however, I had found a connexion only between the *déjà vu* experience and a dream of the previous night, but this example showed me that such an experience could be connected with a dream that had occurred long before. If we also take into consideration Freud's original explanation, i.e. that the sensation of *déjà vu* generally signifies the memory of an unconscious daydream, we can draw the conclusion that *déjà vu* should be included among the '*passagère* symptom formations' and always means a confirmation from the unconscious.

My patient's childish theory on the matter is also interesting. It attributed the inexplicable sensation of familiarity with a new experience to a previous life, in which her soul had resided in the body of another animal (a frog). This is a confirmation of Freud's suspicion that such theories might exist.[1]

Moreover the doctrine of the transmigration of souls, which has been so obstinately believed in from time immemorial, can be regarded as a projection into mythology of the intuition which ever and again forces itself upon us that the human mind contains unconscious memory traces of phylogenetic development.

[1] Expressed in *The Psychopathology of Everyday Life*.

XXX

VARIA:[1]
ON THE GENEALOGY OF THE 'FIG-LEAF'
(1912)

THE choice of the fig-leaf for the concealment of the pudenda is to be explained by the symbolic identification of the genitals with the fruit of the fig. See the following couplet of Archilochus:

'Generous fig on the rock, food for many
crows; Pasiliphe opening her lap to strangers.'
(Quoted from Richard Nordhausen's *Ars Amandi*, p. 30.)

---

[1] German original in *Zb. f. Psa.* (1912), 2, 678. First English translation.

XXXI

VARIA:
METAPHYSICS .. METAPSYCHOLOGY
(1912)

'High in the heavens I sought the source
Of predestination, paradise and hell.
Then my wise teacher spoke: "Friend", he said,
"Kismet, paradise, and hell exist only inside you." '
(Apophthegm of Omar the Tent-maker (born 1025-1050,
died 1123).)

XXXII

VARIA:
PARACELSUS TO THE PHYSICIANS
(1912)

'... AND let it be no laughing matter to you, physicians, you know only a small fraction of the power of the will. For the will is a generator of spirits of a kind with which reason has nothing whatever to do.' (A premonition of the unconscious, which is inaccessible to reason.)

(Paracelsus, *Paramirum*, Treatise IV, chapter 81.)

XXXIII

VARIA: GOETHE ON THE REALITY VALUE OF THE POET'S FANTASY
(1912)

'It seems that, as we poets were put on short commons when the earth was divided up, we were granted the important privilege of being paid for our follies.'
(Letter to Schiller of 15 December 1795.)

XXXIV

A FORERUNNER OF FREUD IN THE THEORY OF SEX[1]
(1912)

DR S. LINDNER, a Budapest children's specialist, has died in his seventy-second year. He was one of the few whom Freud could look upon as a forerunner in the establishment of his theory of sex. Dr. Lindner's most important work was *Über Ludeln oder Wonnesaugen*[2] ('Thumb-Sucking'), published in the *Archiv für Kinderheilkunde* (1879), in which he reported his observations on the various sucking habits of infants and older children, embellished with many excellent illustrations. He specifically emphasized the erotic nature of this 'bad habit' and recognized its gradual transition to masturbation. Naturally nobody would believe him; as he vigorously defended his proposition against the mockers, he was held to be an eccentric. After the old gentleman had retired from medical practice, the writer had the privilege of drawing his attention to the triumphant resurrection of his theory in the works of Freud.

[1] German original in *Zb. f. Psa.* (1912), 2, 162. First English translation.
[2] Reprinted in the *Zeitschrift für Psychanalytische Pädagogik*, Vol. VIII, 1934.

XXXV

PHILOSOPHY AND PSYCHO-ANALYSIS[1]
(1912)

(Comments on a paper by Professor J. J. Putnam of Harvard University)[2]

THE distinguished professor of the Harvard medical school, in a paper motivated by the loftiest intentions and written with all the persuasiveness of honest conviction, argues warmly that psycho-analysis, the importance of which as a psychological and therapeutic method he unreservedly accepts, should be brought into relation with wider philosophical concepts.

All analysts will certainly accept and agree with a large part of what he says. The psychologist who makes it his task to deepen our knowledge of the human soul cannot afford to exclude from his field of observation those philosophical systems which humanity rightly holds in high regard, in which distinguished minds have set forth their profoundest convictions about the nature and meaning of the universe. Analysis having discovered permanent psychological truths, disguised in symbolic form, in those long-despised products of the popular mind, myths and fairy-tales, it is certainly to be hoped that new viewpoints and new discoveries will result from the study of philosophy and history. Also no psycho-analyst will deny that 'no form of investigation can thrive unless its natural relations with investigations of other kinds are carefully taken into account'. Psycho-analysis is not so immodest as to claim to be able to explain everything out of its own resources and, though we are still far from having exhausted all the things that can be explained analytically, we already have a rough idea where the

[1] Published originally in German: *Imago* (1912), 1, 519. First English translation.

[2] *Über die Bedeutung philosophischer Anschauungen und Ausbildung für die Entwicklung der psycho-analytischer Bewegung* ('On the significance of philosophical ideas and training for the development of the psycho-analytic movement'). Read to the third International Psycho-Analytic Congress, Weimar, 1911. Published in *Imago* (1912), 1, 101.

boundaries of our science lie, and where we must hand over the task of explanation to other disciplines, e.g. physics, chemistry, and biology.

Every analyst who has come into contact with the unconscious, i.e. the productive cambium layer of the mind in which all mental progress is prepared, will also unreservedly acknowledge that 'we know more than we can express', that 'the acquisition of knowledge is a voyage of discovery into one's own mind', and that it is the psycho-analyst's duty 'as far as possible to discover and to examine more closely thoughts and impulses (including religious thoughts and impulses)'. In short, if we wished to draw attention to all the things in Professor Putnam's paper with which we agreed, there would be nothing for it but to reprint a not inconsiderable part of it.

This extremely interesting and stimulating paper nevertheless contains observations which roused me to lively disagreement, which I shall not refrain from expressing, though I lack any philosophical training, while Professor Putnam has the advantage of a trained philosophical mind.

Professor Putnam wants psycho-analysts to subject, or at any rate adapt, their newly-gained knowledge to a specific philosophical outlook.

This idea seems to me to be dangerous to science in general, but particularly dangerous to psycho-analysis, which has not yet properly cleared up all the interconnexions even within its own field. Surely an off-season, like that in which game may not be shot, should be granted to a young science such as psycho-analysis, and a substantial delay should elapse before it is approached with the armament of metaphysics. The longer one postpones system-building and contents oneself with collecting facts and establishing their interconnexions, the greater is the prospect of making fresh discoveries. Premature system-building puts the investigator into a frame of mind unfavourable for objectively testing the truth, making him tend to ignore or minimize facts which do not fit in with the system.

It must also not be overlooked that psycho-analysis, like psychology in general, has the right, nay the duty, to examine and observe the circumstances in which mental products of all kinds originate, philosophical systems not excluded, and to show that the general laws of the mind are valid for them too. But how could psychology lay down the laws underlying the making of philosophies if it could be suspected of being itself part of a definite philosophical system at all?[1]

Science is to be compared with an industrial undertaking, the business of which is to create new values; a philosophical 'view of life', however, is nothing but a very rough balance-sheet which can be drawn up from time to time on the basis of our existing knowledge, particularly with a view to seeing where effort should next be applied. The continuous drawing-up of balance-sheets, however, would disturb the productive process and use up energies which could be better employed.

Philosophical systems are like religions; they are fictions, works of art. Unquestionably they contain many noble ideas, and their value should not and must not be disparaged. But they are in a category different from science, by which we understand the sum-total of those laws which, after they have been purged so far as possible of the fantasy products of the

[1] That it is neither impossible nor entirely unprofitable to consider from the psychological point of view the circumstances in which philosophical systems arise may be shown by an example. Psycho-analytic investigation of patients has led to the differentiation of two contrasting mechanisms of repression (i.e. the diversion of the conscious attention from the unpleasurable). Paranoiac patients tend to feel subjective mental processes producing unpleasure as effects upon them of the outer world (projection); neurotics, on the other hand, may feel processes in the external world (e.g. processes in other people) as intensively as their own: they 'introject' a part of the external world in order to ease certain tensions in their own mind. Now it is noticeable that there are philosophical systems which have close analogies with these contrasting mechanisms, which are unquestionably emotionally determined. Materialism, which denies the self, dissolving it completely into the 'external world', can be regarded as the completest conceivable form of projection; while solipsism, which completely denies the external world, i.e. absorbs it into the self, is the extreme form of introjection. (See Ferenczi, 'Introjection and Transference' (1909), reprinted in *First Contributions* and 'On the Definitions of Introjection' (1912) this vol., p. 316.) It is by no means improbable that a great part of metaphysics will turn out to be explicable in terms of psychology, or, as Freud says, will turn out to be metaphyschology. (Freud, *The Psychopathology of Everyday Life*.) Freud subsequently pointed to the partial analogy between philosophic and paranoiac system-formations (*Totem and Taboo*, Chapter II). Another part of philosophy may, however, turn out to be premonition of scientific truths.

pleasure principle, we must provisionally regard as being established in reality. There is only one science, but there are as many philosophical systems and religions as there are gifted people of varying intellectual and emotional trends.

The two disciplines, philosophy and psychology, obey different principles, and it is in the interests of both that they should remain apart. Psychology must reserve the right to deliver judgement on philosophy, and in return must not object to being adopted into various philosophical systems. But in its own field psychology must remain supreme, and must not allow its fate to be associated with that of any one of those systems.

The philosophical assumption to which psycho-analysis should adapt itself, according to Professor Putnam, is that the only real driving power in the universe is an independent driving force, a personality endowed with the highest intellectual and moral gifts—one might well say a divine personality—which allowed and still allows the 'physical world' to arise out of itself and develop as an expression of its inherent trends. Before the appearance of the most primitive bodies this spirit was both intelligent and moral, and in human beings it has not attained a full flowering of these characteristics. This sounds like an adaptation to biogenetics of the most ancient myths of creation, from which it is differentiated only by the fact that the creation of the world is not attributed to a single act, but to an infinite series of such acts, both in the past and continuing into the present. This system can, if you like, be called monistic, as it regards the physical world as a manifestation of the same spiritual force that created the world. But it is a monism which is extraordinarily like a dualism. That, however, is nothing against it; a dualistic universe is no more inconceivable than is a monistic universe, and both monistic and dualistic philosophies have an equal right to existence. But we do not see why any close, inner connexion should be established between psycho-analysis and the particular view outlined by Professor Putnam. The facts of psycho-analysis can be incorporated into any materialist or idealist, monistic or dualistic, system. They are quite compatible, for instance, with a philosophy which sees the essence and prime cause of the universe in a blind, non-intelligent, and non-moral urge, such as Schopenhauer's will. It is not inconceivable that a blind force, in itself aimless and meaningless, might lead to the development of highly intelligent creatures by the process of natural selection; there is nothing in our psychological experiences to conflict with such a view.

Another possible, and even desirable, philosophy from our point of view is agnosticism, which candidly acknowledges the impossibility of solving the ultimate problems, and is therefore not really a closed philosophical system at all. For, if Professor Putnam is right in maintaining that reason should not be used to deny the existence of reason, he overlooks the danger that lies in the temptation to over-estimate the role of consciousness in the universe and to succumb to a not entirely justified anthropomorphism. It can incidentally be regarded as almost a piece of good fortune for the sciences that there is nothing compellingly self-evident about any of these philosophical systems; for a final solution of the ultimate problems of life would destroy the impulse to search for new truths.

Professor Putnam rightly differentiates the contents from the functioning of the mind. But he adds that the mind, viewed from the standpoint of its means of functioning, is neither capable, nor in need, of development, and he expresses the opinion that the infantile mind and the unconscious (in the psychoanalytic sense) differs essentially from the conscious mind of the adult only in its contents, but not in its manner of functioning.

Psycho-analytic experience shows, however, that processes in the unconscious (and to some extent in the infantile mind as well) differ not only in content but also in manner of functioning from conscious processes.

The conscious psychical contents of a waking, normal adult are adapted to the categories of space, time, and causality, and are tested by reality. Consciousness is, in so far as unconscious factors do not intervene, logical. The psychical contents of an educated adult are also adapted to ethical and aesthetic standards.

In the unconscious, however, entirely different principles

prevail. The dominant principle is the averting of unpleasure, and temporal and causal standards hardly come into play. The psychical contents, torn from their logical connexions, arrange themselves in layers in a pleasure-space according to their specific pleasure-gravity, the most unpleasurable being farthest removed from the periphery of consciousness. Thus it comes about that logically heterogeneous elements, endowed with similar pleasure-tone and therefore associated, lie close up against one another or actually mingle; contradictions quietly tolerate each other in close juxtaposition; the remotest similarity is accepted as identity; the uncommonly 'light overflow of intensities' (Freud) makes possible the logically most senseless displacements and condensations; and the lack of the power of abstraction and of speech-symbolism permits thinking only in dramatized pictures. For anyone who has analysed dreams, jokes, symptoms, and neuroses there is no doubt that at that level of the mind ethical and aesthetic categories have little validity or none at all.

After all this it cannot be denied that it is at least possible that a psyche equipped with the faculty of consciousness represents a 'higher' form of mental development, not only in content, but also in manner of functioning; which implies simultaneously the possibility of the development of higher forms of mental activity from more simple and primitive ones.

The part of Professor Putnam's paper that touches psychoanalysis at its most sensitive spot is his attack on psychical determinism. For the greatest advance that we owe to analysis is the power that it has put into our hands of demonstrating that psychical events are subject to constant and unvarying laws, just as events in the external physical universe are.

That our acts of will are determined has been postulated many times in the course of the ages. But it was Freud's psychoanalysis which revealed the unconscious determining factors and thus enabled us to see that what are felt by the consciousness to be free acts of the will, as well as so-called casual ideas, are the inevitable results of other psychical processes, which in turn are strictly determined too. The psycho-analyst, whose daily experience clothes this determinism of the will in flesh and blood, owes to it the comforting feeling that in the mental field there is no need for him to leave the firm ground of scientific law.

Closer observation, however, leads to the conclusion that the apparently so great difference between this point of view and that of Professor Putnam rests partly on a difference in terminology. In places he identifies the conceptions of will and of undetermined will, which we sharply differentiate. Psycho-analysis certainly does not deny will (instinct). Far from being a biogenetic description which 'satisfies itself with tracking down the successive phenomena of a process of development with sufficient exactitude', it finds everywhere in the psyche trends, i.e. mental processes, which are closely analogous with our conscious will. Psycho-analysis has never suggested that 'the character of Hamlet was will-less'; it has suggested that Hamlet, as a consequence of his innate and acquired characteristics, was destined to exercise his will in a vacillating manner destined finally to lead to tragedy.

Professor Putnam also treats the *laisser-faire* principle wrongly, just as he does determinism. Modern political economists are right in teaching that 'ideologies', i.e. processes of the will and of consciousness, are highly important factors in national affairs. But that does not mean that these processes are free, i.e. undetermined. Determinism must not be confused with fatalism. The doctrine of the determination of the will does not say that we can do nothing or will nothing (*laisser-faire*) and that we must wait for the 'determinants' to do the work for us. It says only that when we activate what we subjectively feel to be our free will we cannot emancipate ourselves from the guidance of the determinate. The fact that we do not abandon ourselves to the *laisser-faire* principle but actively assume the direction of our destiny is not due to an act of free decision, but is the result of phylogenetic and ontogenetic determinants which protect us from succumbing to an idleness which would be deleterious to the self and to the species.

Professor Putnam cannot refrain from reproaching analysis with concerning itself onesidedly with the psychology of the unconscious, of children, savages, artists, neurotics, and psychopaths, and with applying the results to the healthy, sublimated activity of normal adults, while simultaneously neglecting the reverse process, namely, setting out to gain an understanding of the mind from man's most elevated mental achievements.

The facts as stated by Professor Putnam are not to be denied. But the question is whether the reversal of approach which characterizes psycho-analysis is really to be regarded as disadvantageous, and not as one of the most fruitful and praiseworthy advances in psychological method.

For centuries efforts have been made to gain an understanding of mental processes from the side of consciousness, by trying to force a way in through the categories of the conscious, cultivated human mind (logic, ethics, aesthetics). But it cannot be said that much has been attained. The commonest manifestations of mental life remained unsolved complexes and, in spite of assurances to the contrary, a sterile 'psychology of the faculties' prevailed. The reaction to this was the physical-psychological approach, which failed, however, to bridge the yawning chasm between relatively simple physiological processes and the complicated mental achievements of civilized man. Psychophysics broke down as soon as it attempted to leave the field of the descriptive physiology of the senses; alternatively—in striking contrast to the much-vaunted exactness of its methods—it found itself forced to take refuge in the most hazardous hypotheses.

Then came Freud's astonishing discovery of unconscious mental processes and of a method which enabled us to investigate the content and functioning of the unconscious. These discoveries were first made in the sick. But when Freud inserted into the gap between the biology of normal people and their conscious, mental awareness the latent mental processes that he had laid bare in neurotics, problems in face of which the psychology of the conscious had broken down, problems which psychophysics had not dared even to approach, were resolved without difficulty, as if by themselves.

The dream, jokes, parapraxes of normal individuals were recognized as psychical structures having a meaning and occurring in obedience to scientific law; the appearance of chance or arbitrariness attached to them vanished; the discovery of the unconscious led to the crystallizing out of a deeper understanding of the psychology of the artist and the writer, the subject-matter of mythology and religion, the psychology of peoples, and sociology. With the help of the unconscious it was possible to prove the existence of the biogenetic principle in the mental sphere.

The astonishing successes gained by the application of Freud's discoveries should persuade us, in my opinion, not to abandon so fruitful a method; but instead, taking its successes as pragmatic evidence of its correctness, to extend still further its field of application. In our view trying to explain the processes and functioning of consciousness by way of depth psychology is a more immediate, because more promising, task than following Professor Putnam's advice to approach from the side of consciousness, and to dig once more in shafts that have been abandoned because of their unproductiveness.

It is, of course, possible that the abundant stream of new knowledge that investigation of the unconscious is now yielding us may eventually run dry, and that psychological investigation will one day have to set out again from the angle of consciousness, or from that of physiology. But what I wish to emphasize is only that our immediate task is to continue with the building up of psycho-analysis independently of philosophical systems.

XXXVI

INTERPRETATION OF UNCONSCIOUS INCESTUOUS FANTASIES FROM A PARAPRAXIS (IN BRANTÔME)[1]
(1912)

BRANTÔME (1539–1614) tells the following anecdote among others in his *Vies des Femmes Galantes*: 'I remember a great prince whom I knew. Desiring to praise a woman whose love he had enjoyed, he said: "Elle est une très grande amoureuse, aussi grande que ma mère." Because of the ambiguousness of this phrase he added that he had not meant to say that the lady was as great a lover as his mother was, but that she was as big physically. Sometimes one says things one does not think, but often, without thinking, one says the truth.'

---

[1] German original in *Zb. f. Psa.* (1912), **3**, 53. First English translation.

XXXVII

TAMING OF A WILD HORSE[1]
(1913)

On April 29th, 1912, by permission of the Budapest mounted police, I attended a demonstration by Joseph Ezer, the Tolna blacksmith, who claimed to be able to tame the wildest horse at a single attempt. The newspapers had for some considerable time been full of stories about this man's extraordinary powers; he was said to be able to reduce the most refractory animal to docility by sheer transference of will, i.e. by suggestion, and a committee, consisting of police officials and senior cavalry officers, assembled in the yard of the police barracks for the purpose of testing the man's abilities on a particularly unruly animal. This was Czicza, a magnificent four-and-a-half-year-old thoroughbred mare belonging to a lieutenant of Hussars, which was unusable for any purpose whatever because, though a particularly fine animal in other respects, no one had been able to shoe her. She reared and kicked at the approach of any stranger, and even her usual groom had to approach her with caution. At most she would allow him to brush her back; if he made as if to touch her legs she reared and neighed madly. As she was otherwise perfectly sound and careered vigorously round the stud-farm, her condition was ascribed to 'nervousness' or 'wildness', and she had been written off for racing or stud purposes. The object now was to see whether Ezer with his mysterious skill would be able to humble Czicza's pride and fix shoes on her still-virgin hoofs.

Ezer turned up punctually. He was a short, stocky man of peasant-like appearance, aged about thirty. He seemed pretty self-confident and chatted unconcernedly with all the important personages who had gathered to see him. The mare, which was recognized by all the experts as an outstanding thoroughbred with a first-class pedigree (she was by Kisbéröccse, a well-known Turf winner, out of Gerjer), was then brought in by her

[1] German original: *Zb. f. Psa.* (1913), **3**, 83. First English translation.

usual groom. Czicza used to allow this lad to approach her, but any attempt to lay a hand on her legs caused her to lash out in all directions.

I saw at once that Ezer did not rely exclusively on the exercise of any exceptional mental powers. The performance started by his exchanging the mare's usual bridle for one he had brought with him. This had a number of heavy chain-rings immediately over the nose and ended in a long leading-rein. As I approached the performance with certain theoretical expectations (which I shall describe later), I prefer to quote a description of what followed by an unprejudiced reporter.[1]

'The blacksmith approached the mare, talking to her all the time, distinctly, even from a distance, but with extreme tenderness; he positively cooed. Simultaneously he took the leading-rein from the stable-boy's hands. "There, there, my beauty!" he said. "There's no need to be frightened of me, I shan't do you any harm! There, there, now! . . ." He made as if to stroke the animal's breast, but she reared and neighed. While her legs were still in the air he bellowed at her in such a ferocious voice that he startled us all. "You filthy brute, you!" he shouted, simultaneously tugging hard at the leading-rein.[2] The mare collapsed, terrified. She tried to rear and kick again, but as she did so she again heard the man's terror-striking voice and saw his intimidating look.[3] A moment later Ezer was again talking to her in the tone of a mother fondling her baby. "There, there, now; don't be frightened, darling!" he said, his face beaming with love and tenderness. "There, there, now, my beauty!" Slowly but surely, but without at any moment betraying the slightest hesitation, he placed the flat of his hand on the mare's neck, and from there he let it glide down to her forequarters. This caused her to rear again, almost vertically, making it look as if she were going to smash the blacksmith's skull in with her hoofs. But he sprang into the air with the mare, bellowing again and tugging at the rein, and once more this quietened her. The

---

[1] L. Fényes in the evening newspaper *Az Est* of 30 April, 1912.

[2] Which incidentally caused the chain-rings to strike a sharp blow on the animal's nose.

[3] Besides receiving a blow on the nose from the chain-rings.

first stage in Ezer's success was that the mare ceased neighing; she obviously realized that any noise she might make would be outdone by the man in front of her. After a quarter of an hour Czicza was trembling in every limb and sweating, and her flashing eyes gradually but perceptibly lost their gleam. After half an hour she actually allowed her legs to be touched, and the blacksmith was able firmly but gently to bend her knee and stroke it. She stood on three legs, as if bewitched, holding her fourth leg in the bent position the blacksmith gave it. So it went on for an hour. Whenever she threatened to become refractory, the blacksmith bellowed at her at the top of his voice, but so long as she behaved quietly he stroked her neck and cooed at her: "Oh, you poor thing, so you're sweating, are you? So am I! There's nothing to be afraid of, my beauty, I shan't punish you for that,[1] I know you're trying to be good! What a good little mare you are!" '

An hour later the blacksmith was hammering at one of the hoofs, and fifty minutes later Czicza was properly shod. True, she showed some signs of exhaustion, but she was quiet and obedient, allowed her legs to be stroked freely, and was led back to the stable.

According to the testimonials that Ezer produced, the effect on the horses he treated in this manner was permanent. They either ceased altogether to be unmanageable, or at least became much more tractable than before.

When the demonstration so admirably described by this keen-eyed journalist was over, I was asked whether thought-transference, hypnosis, or suggestion had played a part in it. I replied that there was no need to talk of any extraordinary phenomena so long as the facts of the case could be explained by already familiar scientific and psychological laws. It seemed to me that they could be so explained, for the following reasons.

The psycho-analytic explanation of the results and the working of hypnosis and suggestion had enabled me to trace back all such phenomena to the lifelong survival in the individual of the

[1] The blacksmith penalized only the mare's deliberate movements, not her unavoidable reflex actions.

element of infantile obedience.[1] I had been able to show that there are two ways of inducing hypnosis: by love and by authority. The loving method (i.e. affectionate stroking and monotonous appealing, lulling talk, etc.) I called maternal hypnosis; hypnosis induced by authority (compelling, authoritative, loud-voiced commands, taking by surprise, etc.) I called paternal hypnosis.

Whether a person remained susceptible to one or other of these types of influence, or to both, depended on the history of the first four years of his life, and on his relations with his parents in particular.

Thus an adult's susceptibility to hypnosis depended, not on any special aptitude on the part of the hypnotist, but on his own innate or acquired (i.e. phylogenetically or ontogenetically acquired) susceptibility to being deprived of his own will by love or by fear, i.e. by the educative methods to which he became accustomed in infancy. Claparède was of the opinion that this explanation went much deeper than others.[1] In the course of his very complete treatment of the subject he mentions, among other things, numerous examples from natural history to show that certain animals (frogs, guinea-pigs, chickens, etc.) have a liability, no doubt explicable by the theory of evolution, to succumb to hypnosis on receiving a sudden shock.

By staring at and gently stroking the breast and arms of an untamed female baboon the same writer was able to reduce it to a state of complete passivity and cataleptic rigidity.

He believes this sudden docility can be explained as an instinctual reaction, possibly as an attitude of orgasm expectation, and finds support for this theory in the view put forward by Freud and myself, namely, that suggestibility depends on a sexual dependence on the suggester.[2]

[1] 'Cette théorie va bien plus profond que les autres, en cherchant à expliquer comment cette hypersuggestibilité est déclenché, par quels mécanismes particuliers des actions aussi puissantes que celles que l'on rencontre dans l'hypnose peuvent se réaliser, quel est le véhicule affectif qui va faire accepter au sujet la pilule de la suggestion donnée.' Prof. Dr. Ed. Claparède, 'Interprétation psychologique de l'Hypnose', *Journal für Psychologie und Neurologie*, 1911, Vol. XVIII, No. 4.

[2] Claparède, 'Etat hypnoïde chez un singe', *Archives des Sciences physiques et naturelles*, Genève, Tome XXXII.

Morichau-Beauchant[1] and E. Jones[2] also agreed with my views on this matter, on the basis of their experiences with human beings.

There is no reason why these conclusions should not be applied to the suggestive technique of the blacksmith Ezer. He seems to have been led on his own to using a clever combination of the two possible methods of inducing submission, namely, gentleness and terror, and taming an otherwise untamable animal by a combination of paternal and maternal suggestion. This combination, because of the psychological effectiveness of opposites, made a particularly deep impression on the animal, and it is easy to believe that the subsequent effect of such a profound experience may be as lasting as certain experiences in infancy are in human beings.

True, this kind of training is at most appropriate in the case of the domesticated animals, for whom the primary virtue is obedience. A human being, however, subjected to such excesses of love and terrorization, runs the risk of permanently losing the capacity of independent action. People readily susceptible throughout their lifetime to transferred paternal or maternal suggestion and a large proportion of neurotics are recruited from children who are 'trained' in this manner.

There is no way of deciding *a priori* whether this violent method of training is disadvantageous to a horse's character or health.

---

[1] R. Morichau-Beauchant, Professeur à l'École de Médecine de Poitiers, 'Le 'rapport affectif' dans la cure des Psychoneuroses,' *Gazette des hôpitaux du 14 novembre* 1911.

[2] Professor E. Jones (University of Toronto). 'The Action of Suggestion in Psychotherapy', *Journal of Abnormal Psychology*, Boston, Dec. 1910. Vol. 5, p. 217.

XXXVIII

ON THE GENESIS OF THE JUS PRIMAE NOCTIS[1]
(1913)

IT seemed to me *a priori* probable that the feudal lord's right to deflower his female serfs was a relic of patriarchal times, when all the women of the household were at the disposal of the head of the family. The equivalence of father-priest-god makes it possible to quote the following religious practices in support of this view: 'In the neighbourhood of Pondicherry the bride sacrifices her virginity to the idol. In some parts of India priests take the place of God. On the first night of his marriage the King of Calicut leaves his bride to the most respected priest of his kingdom.' (H. Freimark, *Okkultismus und Sexualität*, p. 75.) In our immediate neighbourhood, in Croatia, some fathers are said still to preserve the right to sexual intercourse with their daughters-in-law until their sons, who marry very young, grow up. I find a neuropathological parallel to these religious and racial practices in the mostly unconscious fantasies of many neurotics, in which the father is postulated as predecessor in sexual intercourse.

---

[1] German original in *Zb. f. Psa.* (1913), III, 258. First English translation.

XXXIX

REVIEW[1] OF 'DIE PSYCHISCHE BEDINGHEIT UND PSYCHOANALYTISCHE BEHANDLUNG ORGANISCHER LEIDEN'

By Georg Groddeck

(1917)

It will certainly not have escaped the attentive reader of psycho-analytic literature that we consider the unconscious as the layer of the mind nearest to the physical; a layer that commands instinctual forces which are not at all, or only to a much lesser extent, accessible to the conscious. Psycho-analytic case histories tell of intestinal disturbances, catarrhs of the throat, anomalies of menstruation, etc., which have developed as reactions to repressed wishes, or which represent such wishes disguised and unrecognizable to the conscious mind. Although the paths linking these phenomena to normal and pathological physiology have always been left open (here I refer, for instance, to the repeatedly stated identity of the mechanism used in hysteria and when expressing emotion), psycho-analysis has confined itself mainly to the study of the physical changes in hysteria conditioned by mental processes.

Dr. Groddeck, in this pamphlet, is the first to make the courageous attempt to apply the results of Freud's discoveries to organic medicine, and this first step has already led him to such surprising results, new points of view and fresh perspectives, that at least the heuristic value of the step appears beyond any doubt. We have therefore no justification whatever for rejecting out of hand anything from Groddeck's statements which might startle us now. What he describes is mostly not hypothesis, but fact. He reports that in a great number of purely organic illnesses, such as inflammations, tumours, and constitutional anomalies, he has succeeded in demonstrating

[1] German original in *Zeitschr. f. Psa.* (1917), 4, 346. First English translation.

that the illness has developed as a defence against unconscious 'sensitivities', or that it is in the service of some other unconscious tendencies. He has even succeeded through psychoanalytical work, that is through making such tendencies conscious, in improving, even curing, very severe organic illnesses such as goitre, sclerodermia, and cases of gout and tuberculosis. Groddeck is far from assuming the role of a magician, and he states modestly that his aim was merely to create, through psycho-analysis, more favourable conditions 'for the *it* by which one is lived'. He identifies this '*it*' with Freud's unconscious.

Such facts, one might say facts in general, cannot be rejected out of hand on any consideration whatever. Their validity depends exclusively on whether or not—if re-examined under identical conditions—they can be proved. Moreover, there is no theoretical reason for declaring such processes impossible.

Dr. Groddeck is a practitioner who did not start with psychoanalysis, but came upon our psychotherapy by chance in his search for a useful treatment of organic illnesses. This explains the far-reaching differences between him and ourselves, both in theory and, particularly, in the meaning attributed to some of the processes and mechanisms in question. There is, however, sufficient agreement to raise the hope that the barrier separating the two series of observations will soon be cut through. Also from the psycho-analytical side some observations have been made public which appear to be remarkably near to Groddeck's theses.

The sober way, free from all 'finalistic' philosophizing, in which Groddeck treats the teleology demonstrable in the organic (a teleology which is determined causally) must be stressed. In this way he happily avoids the rocks on which Adler's research foundered after a promising beginning.

Further, we must respect this author who, in his great love of truth, in the service of science does not hesitate to expose several weak points and shortcomings of his own physical and mental organization. We eagerly await further communications from Groddeck, particularly case histories and results.

XL

REVIEW[1] OF 'DER SEELENSUCHER'
EIN PSYCHOANALYTISCHER ROMAN

By Georg Groddeck

(1921)

In German literature Groddeck must be known to many as a physician full of temperament who had always held scientific obscurity in horror, and who, like the original Schweniger, looked at men and things, illnesses and cures, with his own eyes, described them in his own words, and did not allow himself to be forced on to the Procrustean bed of conventional terminology.

Some of his writings appear to be similar to some psychoanalytical theses. In his first period, however, the author turned against the Freudian school, as he had done against every other. Eventually his fanaticism for truth proved stronger than his hatred of 'scholarly erudition', and he publicly admitted that he had been mistaken when he had fought against the creator of psycho-analysis, and, what is still more unusual, he unmasked *coram publico* his own unconscious, in which he revealed a tendency that drove him, out of pure envy, into opposition to Freud. It is not surprising that Groddeck, even after openly confessing his adhesion to psycho-analysis, did not follow the customary course of one of Freud's pupils, but went his own way. He had little interest in mental illnesses, the proper field of analytical research; even the words 'psyche' and 'psychic' sounded false to his monistically-tuned ear. Quite consistently he thought that if he was right in his monism, and if the teachings of psycho-analysis were correct too, then psycho-analysis must prove valid also in the field of organic phenomena. With confident courage he turned the analytic armoury against organic diseases, and he soon reported on case histories which proved the correctness of his surmises. In many cases of severe organic illness he recognized the action of unconscious *intentions*,

[1] German original in *Imago* (1921), 7, 356. First English translation.

which, according to him, played a prominent part in the causation of all human suffering. To his way of thinking, bacteria are always and everywhere present; when and how man avails himself of their services depends on his unconscious will. Even the development of tumours, haemorrhages, inflammations, and so on may be fostered, even provoked, by such 'intentions', so that Groddeck finally came to consider these tendencies as a *conditio sine qua non* of every illness. According to him the central motive of these latent, illness-causing tendencies is always the sexual instinct; the organism easily and willingly becomes ill if thereby it can satisfy its sexuality or escape a sexual unpleasure. And in the same way as psycho-analysis cures illnesses of the mind by making conscious hidden urges and overcoming resistances to repressed tendencies, so Groddeck says he has influenced the course of severe organic illnesses by methodical analytic therapy.

I have no knowledge whether other physicians have examined these remarkable therapeutic results and have proved or disproved them, and so for the time being I cannot say definitely whether we have to do here with a really new therapeutic method of genius or with the suggestive power of a single extraordinary medical man. On no account, however, could the consistency of the author's arguments or the sincerity of his main idea be doubted.

Now this research worker has prepared for us a new and not unimportant surprise; he presents himself in his latest book as poet and novelist. I do not believe, however, that his main aim in doing so was to acquire literary fame; the novel offered him a suitable medium for getting off his chest the latest consequences of his new ideas about illness and life, men and institutions. As probably he has very little faith in the capacity of his contemporaries to accept something new and unaccustomed, he finds it necessary to mitigate the strangeness of his ideas with the help of a comic and thrilling plot, that is to say to bribe his readers with a premium of pleasure.

I am no literary critic and do not presume to judge the aesthetic value of this novel; I believe, however, that it cannot be a bad book which succeeds, as this does, in holding the reader from beginning to end and in putting difficult biological and physiological problems in a humorous and even comic form, and in presenting with gentle humour crudely grotesque and deeply tragic scenes which, taken by themselves, would have been repugnant.

He wittily represents his hero, Müller-Weltlein, the 'Seelensucher',[1] as a genial fool, and the reader can never be certain when he is revealing the results of his genius or of his folly. In this way Groddeck-Weltlein is able to ventilate many things which he could not either in a scientific book or in a seriously meant fantasy without challenging the whole world. The indignant bourgeois would immediately call for the strait jacket; but as the mocking author has already donned it himself, even the guardians of public morals have no choice but to put a good face on it and laugh. Moreover, many a physician, thinker, and philosopher will find in this book the beginnings of a philosophy freed from the shackles of traditional mysticism and dogmatism and the rudiments of a re-evaluation of man and institutions. The educational value of the book lies in the fact that the author, like Swift, Rabelais, and Balzac in the past, has torn the mask from the face of the pious, hypocritical spirit of the age and has exposed the cruelty and lust hidden behind it while at the same time comprehending its inevitability.

It is almost impossible to give a brief report of the content of this novel. The hero is a middle-aged bachelor whose ordered solitude, spent in contemplative reading, is disturbed by the sudden emergence of a widowed sister and her marriageable young daughter. What really happened between the hero and the daughter we are never explicitly told; we can hardly even guess from the vague hints given us. In the beds of the house vermin—bed-bugs—make their home, and in their extermination the master of the house eagerly helps. In the chase after these bloodthirsty parasites the hero becomes crazy,[2] that is to say, he frees himself of all the shackles imposed by tradition,

---

[1] Both 'soul searcher' and 'searcher for souls' would be equally correct translations. (Ed.)

[2] The German word is 'verrückt', which might perhaps be translated as thrown out of balance'. (Ed.)

inheritance, and education. He becomes 'changed', even changes his name and becomes a vagrant. At the same time, however, his money and his old connexions secure him the entry into the highest of the high strata of society; wherever he arrives he makes good use of his fool's liberty to cast the truth into people's faces, and in this way the reader comes to hear truths which even Groddeck would not dare to utter except with the fool's cap on his head. We see and hear our Müller-Weltlein in the police cell, in a low-class skittle alley, in the general ward of a hospital, in a picture gallery, at the Zoo, in a fourth-class railway compartment, at a street-corner meeting, at a feminist congress, among hard-boiled prostitutes, tricksters, and blackmailers, and even at a drinking bout with a Prussian royal prince.

Everywhere he speaks and behaves as a real 'enfant terrible', notices and comments on everything, admits consciously and openly to the unavoidably childish basic quality of the adult, and ridicules all the boastful and swaggering hypocrites. The chief motive of his folly remains all the time the bed-bugs, obviously a remnant of the traumatic event hinted at in the beginning of the book, and he never wearies of repeating its many-sided symbolism. Moreover, like a child he finds real pleasure in every sort of symbolic equation wherever he can discover one, and in their discovery he becomes a real champion. Symbolism, which psycho-analysis has considered rather tentatively as one of the factors leading to the formation of ideas, is for Weltlein deeply rooted in the organic, perhaps even in the cosmic, and sexuality is the pivot round which the whole world of symbols revolves. All the work of man is only plastic representation of the genitals and of the genital act, of that archaic prototype of all longing and endeavour. The world is dominated by a magnificent unity. The dualism of body and soul is a superstition. The whole body thinks; thoughts can find expression in the form of a moustache, a corn, even of excreta. The soul is 'infected' by the body, the body by the contents of the soul; and in fact it is not permissible to talk of an 'ego'. One does not live, but one 'is lived' by a 'something'. The strongest 'infections' are the sexual ones. He who does not want to see eroticism becomes myopic; he who cannot 'smell' eroticism catches a cold. The preference for the erotogenic zone may manifest itself in the formation of one's features, in, for instance, double chin. The priest is clerically 'infected' by his cassock; it is not the woman who knits a stocking; on the contrary, knitting knits the whole female sex into a pathetic pettiness. The highest human achievement is giving birth; the spiritual efforts of man are but ridiculous attempts at imitating it. The desire for children is so general—both in man and woman—that 'no one becomes fat except because of an unsatisfied longing for a child'. Even illnesses and injuries are not merely sources of suffering, out of them wells also the 'nourishing power of completion'.

Of course Weltlein feels most at home in the nursery where he plays with the children with gusto, and finds sympathetic pleasure in their still naïve eroticism. On the other hand, it is against the scientists and especially the physicians that he battles most vigorously. Their stupid limitation is the favourite target for his mockery. Even psycho-analysis is not spared entirely, although the fine irony with which it is treated is sheer affection compared with the cruelty with which the 'school psychiatry' is exposed in the stocks of ridicule. It is with sorrow that we hear of the catastrophic end of this laughing martyr. He is killed in a railway disaster—but even after death he flaunts his cynicism; his head cannot be found, and his identity can be established only from intimate details of his body, the task, remarkably enough, being attempted only by—his niece.

This then is an extremely condensed account of the contents of this psycho-analytic novel. It is certain that Groddeck-Weltlein 'will be interpreted, commented on, torn to pieces, maligned, and misunderstood to death', as Balzac said of Rabelais in the *Contes Drolâtiques*. But in the same way as Gargantua and Pantagruel have been preserved for us, perhaps a future epoch will see that justice is done for our Weltlein.

XLI

DISCUSSION ON TIC[1]
(1921)

THE courtesy of the president enables me to participate, at least by correspondence, in this interesting discussion. Every reader of the paper which is now being discussed must concede that Dr. van Ophuijsen points out the obvious when he calls attention to the incompleteness of this presentation, and especially of the definition of tic. As I expressly said, my formulation was intended only to serve as a preliminary orientation and to bring into prominence such problems as might arise from it. Thus it will have entirely fulfilled its purpose if it is successful in eliciting other points of view, as, for instance, the interesting contribution to the discussion by Abraham.

I admit that according to Abraham's experiences a higher valuation should be placed upon sadistic and anal-erotic impulsive components in the genesis of tics than I credited to them in my paper, but I may add that I did not overlook them. His 'conversion on a sadistic anal plane' is an original point of view and is also important theoretically. I cannot refrain, however, from calling attention to the points which remain unshaken, even after accepting Abraham's propositions.

1. Tic, even in Abraham's formulation, is just as contiguous to obsessional neurosis and hysteria as to catatonia.

2. The fundamental relationship of tic to catatonia (Abraham says 'resemblance') remains (as a localized motor defence in contradistinction to generalized catatonia).

3. The analogy between tic and the traumatic neurosis permits us to classify this type of neurosis between the narcissistic

[1] (In June 1921 Dr. J. Harnik opened a discussion in the Berlin PsA. Society on Ferenczi's paper on Tic (reprinted in *F.C.* 142). Among others Abraham and van Ophuijsen took part in the discussion (Report in *Int. Journal of PsA.*, 2, 477). This is Ferenczi's contribution read at the meeting by Abraham. Ed.)

German original: *Int. Z. f. Psa.* (1921), 7, 395. English translation: *Int. J. of PsA.* (1921), 2, 481.

and the transference neuroses. The intermediary position, as is well known, is also characteristic of the war neuroses.

4. The termination of the 'maladie des tics' in catatonia is a definitely established fact (see the reports of Gilles de la Tourette) even if it is not a very frequent occurrence.

I hope that the consideration of the 'regressions of the ego', to which the work of Freud on *Group Psychology* and the analysis of the ego points the way, will cause the still remaining differences in the theory of tic to disappear. In my work on the 'Developmental Stages of the Sense of Reality' (1913)[1] I have already expressed the opinion that in order to define any neurosis it will be necessary to state the ego-regression as well as the libido-regression characteristic of it. As a result especially of the observations made on psycho-neurotic tic, I now believe that the regression of the ego is far more extensive in this form of neurosis than in hysteria or obsessional neurosis (obsessional neurosis regresses to the 'omnipotence of thought', hysteria to 'magic gestures', tic to the plane of defence reflex). Future observations should determine whether the forcible suppression of a tic can provoke only 'tension states' or true anxiety also.

[1] Reprinted in *First Contributions*, p. 213.

XLII

PSYCHO-ANALYSIS AND THE MENTAL DISORDERS OF GENERAL PARALYSIS OF THE INSANE[1]

(1922)

THE problem of the mental disorders of general paralysis can be approached psycho-analytically from various angles, but to me the most appropriate point of departure seems to be the relation between mental states and physical illness. What descriptive psychiatry has to teach us about the matter can be summed up in a variation of the old catch-phrase *mens sana in corpore sano*. We are told that there are mental disturbances which appear as the direct consequences of physical illness or damage; but pre-Freudian psychiatry leaves us entirely in the dark about *how* the two are connected. On the other hand, it is only since the 'introduction of narcissism'[2] that psycho-analysis has taken an interest in the question. One of the observations that led Freud to regard narcissism, an individual's libidinous relationship to his own ego, as a universal phenomenon and not, as it had hitherto been regarded, as an odd perversion, was human behaviour during periods of physical illness.[3] A sick man withdraws his interest and his love from the objects of his environment and transfers them more or less exclusively to his own self or his diseased organ: he becomes 'narcissistic', i.e. his illness causes him to regress to a stage of development through which he once passed in infancy. Following up this idea, the author of this paper described the clinical picture of *patho-*

[1] Originally in German as Chapter III of a book written jointly with S. Hollós in 1922. English version: 'Psycho-analysis and the Psychic Disorders of General Paresis', Nervous and Mental Diseases Publ. Co., New York. 1925. New English translation.

[2] Freud, 'Narcissism. An Introduction', *Coll. Pap.*, Vol. IV. German original 1914.

[3] Freud acknowledges that it was the author who suggested this idea in a private communication.

neurosis,[1] i.e. a particular narcissistic neurosis which may appear as the consequence of disease or damage to vital organs or parts of the body felt as especially important to the ego, above all the erotogenic zones. The theory of the pathoneuroses culminates in the proposition that quantities of libido can be accumulated not only in the ego in general, but also in the diseased organ itself (or in its representative in the mind), and that a role should be attributed to these quantities of libido in organic healing and regenerative tendencies. This assumption has been confirmed by certain observations on the traumatic neuroses of the war period.[2] It was established that a shock accompanied by a simultaneous severe wound left behind either no traumatic effect or one very much smaller than a similar shock unaccompanied by physical injury. The only explanation of this apparent paradox is the assumption that when there is a simultaneous wound the narcissistic libido mobilized by the trauma, the libido which psycho-analysis postulates as the cause of the traumatic neurosis, is used up in part 'pathoneurotically', is bound to the damaged organ, and is thus unable to float freely and generate neurosis. Two more points can also be mentioned in this connexion: (i) that disease of or damage to the erotogenic zones can lead to severe psychotic illnesses—in the author's view the puerperal psychoses, for example, are really pathopsychoses of this type; and (ii) that, as Freud himself points out, severe narcissistic psychoses of purely psychogenic origin, e.g. melancholias, often unexpectedly disappear as a consequence of an intercurrent organic illness which binds the excessive libido.[3]

All these facts, though they are apparently remote from our theme, are quoted here because we are about to hazard an attempt to represent at any rate some of the mental symptoms

---

[1] Ferenczi, 'On Pathoneuroses'. German original 1916. English version in *Further Contributions*, p. 78.

[2] *Psycho-Analysis and the War Neuroses*. London, 1921. German original, 1919.

[3] Jelliffe has advanced similar conceptions independently. See discussions in New York Neurological Society, *Journal of Nervous and Mental Disease*. See also Jelliffe and White, *Diseases of the Mental System*, 1915, 1917, 1920, 1923.

of general paralysis as *a cerebral pathoneurosis*, as a neurotic reaction following injury to the brain, or alternatively damage to its functioning.

No one of course would dream of underrating the significance and the primordial role of the purely physical symptoms of paresis—the paralyses and irritations in the motor, vegetative, and sensory spheres. It is also agreed that a large proportion of the disturbances of the mental functions must be regarded as pathological deficiencies or as the effects of pathological irritation, i.e. as the direct effects of the organic process. All we are adding is the suggestion that another, and perhaps no less important, part of the mental symptomatology corresponds to the mental effort to cope with the quantities of libido mobilized by the cerebral lesion.

At this point the reader uninitiated into the latest psychoanalytic literature will certainly ask in astonishment what an illness of the brain has to do with libido; for—surely he will say to himself—the brain is no 'erotogenic zone', injury to which could provoke a pathoneurosis in the above-mentioned sense. This objection, however, can be easily met. For in the first place we believe, in accordance with our theory of sexuality, that excitation of or shock to any physical organ whatever must also involve the excitation of sexuality; and in the second place we have special reason to assume that the brain and its functions enjoy a particularly high degree of narcissistic-libidinous cathexis and that a particularly high value is subjectively attached to them. For just as in the course of development the independent satisfaction of the peripheral erotogenic zones is for the most part renounced in favour of the leading (genital) zone, with the result that the latter assumes primacy over all others, so does the brain go through a parallel development until it becomes *the central organ of the ego functions*.[1] 'Perhaps the most significant result of organic evolution, aiming as it does at division of labour, was that it achieved the differentiation of particular systems of organs on the one hand for the control and distribution of external stimuli (the mental apparatus) and on

[1] Schopenhauer describes the intellect and its organ, the brain, as the opposite pole to sexuality and its organ.

the other of special organs (the genitals) for the periodical discharge of quantities of sexual excitation accumulated in the organism. The organ for the distribution and control of stimuli becomes ever more intimately associated with the instincts of self-preservation while the genital . . . becomes the central erotic organ.'[1] But while the sexual character of the genitals, the executive organs dedicated to object-love, is obvious, the narcissistic-libidinous undertone which accompanies all our higher mental activity in the form of a non-rational 'self-respect' or 'self-awareness' can only be inferred from certain psychopathological processes.

We may now conjecture that, when the metaluetic cerebral affection attacks the central organ of the ego-functions, it not only causes pathological deficiencies but also acts in the fashion of a trauma and produces a disturbance of balance in the economy of the narcissistic libido which also finds expression in the mental symptoms of general paralysis.

This conjecture has, of course, no claim to credibility unless it can contribute to the understanding of the individual symptoms of the illness as well as of its course as a whole. Let us therefore re-examine the typical stages of general paralysis in its light.

By and large we can still adhere to the pattern laid down by Bayle a hundred years ago when he said that the typical course of general paralysis is its initial depression, manic excitement, formation of paranoid delusions, and terminal dementia.

General paralysis often begins with symptoms which give the patient the impression that he is suffering from 'neurasthenia'; a general impression arising from a number of signs of reduced mental and physical prowess. This is the only stage of the illness which is characterized exclusively by pathological deficiencies, and it is this stage which frequently passes unnoticed; for patients generally come under medical treatment only at a later stage, characterized by secondary compensatory phenomena. Of the numerous symptoms of this *'neurasthenic'* period we may

[1] Ferenczi, 'The Phenomena of Hysterical Materialization'. German original, 1919. English translation in *Further Contributions*, p. 89.

emphasize the very frequent diminution of genital libido and potency. Relying on our experiences with other illnesses, particularly with traumatic neuroses, we may confidently regard this symptom as a sign of withdrawal of libidinous interest from the sexual objects; and we shall also be prepared to find that the quantity of libido withdrawn from objects will reappear elsewhere.[1]

We do not have to wait long for confirmation of our expectation. In the depressive forms of general paresis this initial stage is often followed immediately by the most curious *hypochondriacal sensations* all over the body. Patients complain that they have a stone in their stomach, that their head has become an empty hollow, that they are pestered by worms all over them, that their penis has been nibbled off, etc. Now we adhere to the Freudian view which regards hypochondria as a *narcissistic actual-neurosis*, attributable as such to the painful effects of an accumulation of narcissistic libido in the bodily organs. To this it is necessary to add only that hypochondrias occur not only in individuals whose organs are anatomically unharmed (as is the case in the usual neurotic hypochondrias), but also in association with real injuries and illnesses when the quantity of libido mobilized as 'counter-cathexis' of the organic process exceeds the level required by the curative tendencies and has to be dealt with mentally. But that is exactly the situation in pathoneuroses; thus the flaring up of the hypochondriacal syndrome in the depressive forms of general paralysis is a by-no-means negligible argument for the pathoneurotic foundation of paretic mental disorders.

In many cases the initial neurasthenic-hypochrondriacal stages remain latent and, as Hollós in particular points out, patients generally come under treatment when they have reached a euphoric stage in which they are excessively active, with restored libido and potency. But this euphoria and intensified

[1] The assumption that the disturbance of potency is of purely anatomical origin, resulting from degenerative processes in the nervous centres of erection and ejaculation or in the conduction paths, is countered by the subsequent states of lasting excitation or even remission in which potency in the male and the corresponding sexual sensitivity in the female may return in all their youthful vigour.

interest in the outer world, not least in the objects of sexuality, is only an attempt to over-compensate narcissistic-hypochondriacal unpleasure by frantic object-cathexis. In reality one gets clear glimpses from time to time of the hypochondriacal undertone beneath the exaltation that results from the intensification of the patient's physical functioning, so that it is not difficult to unmask this euphoria as '*hypochondria with a plus sign*'.

The symptoms of these two preliminary stages which, as we have said, do not necessarily develop manifestly in every case, are mainly confined to the organic-physiological sphere and involve the psyche only to the extent that the latter reacts with exaggerated unpleasure to the pathoneurotic hypochondria and with pleasure to the successful euphoric over-compensation. These two initial stages ought to be isolated as a paralytic actual-psychosis from the subsequent psychotic superstructure, which is generally confined to the mental sphere.[1]

Thus the paralytic actual-psychosis is made up of symptoms which can be traced partly to a draining away of libido from, or alternatively a frantic re-cathexis of, objects, and partly to a pathoneurotic-narcissistic increase of libido provoked by the organic lesion.

Generally the patient's euphoric mood does not last long. When the signs of mental and physical insufficiency increase and multiply, and when finally the simplest and most obvious functions of the ego and of the organism are affected, and dysarthria, sphincter paresis, etc., as well as intellectual degeneration appear, a real *paretic melancholia* develops, accompanied by sleeplessness, self-reproaches, suicidal tendencies, loss of appetite, and emaciation; a melancholia sometimes differentiated from psychogenic melancholia only by the presence of incurable physical signs of a cerebral disease.

There is no reason why psycho-analytic theory, which enabled Freud to be the first to explain the mechanism and mental

---

[1] According to Freud, psychogenic hypochondria (in schizophrenia) arises when narcissistic libido which cannot be dealt with psychically attaches itself to an organ. In pathoneurotic hypochondria narcissistic libido insufficiently bound by the organic process has to be dealt with psychically.

economy of psychogenic melancholia,[1] should not be applied to the melancholia in general paresis.

Psychogenic melancholia, according to this theory, is a narcissistic psychosis; its symptoms are the mental expression of the great injury and loss of libido which the patient's ego has suffered by the loss of devaluation of an ideal with which it had completely identified itself. The depression is unconscious mourning over this devaluation; the self-accusations are really accusations directed at someone else; the suicidal impulses conceal murderous impulses directed against the previous love-object, or alternatively against that part of the self which is identified with that object. Another part of the symptoms is to be explained by a regression of the libido to archaic levels of organization (oral eroticism and sadism).

Freud leaves open the question whether there are only such 'identification melancholias', or whether there are other melancholias resulting from direct injury to the ego itself.

My view is that in paretic melancholia we are faced with a psychosis of the latter kind as a consequence of direct injury to the ego; that its symptoms, the depression, the self-reproaches, the suicidal tendencies *all refer to a part of the self which has lost its previous skills and powers as a consequence of the cerebral illness*; and that this loss deals a shattering blow to the patient's self-respect and esteem. The paretic melancholia *is mourning the loss of his once-accomplished ego-ideal*.

So long as the pathological symptoms affected only some of his peripheral organs, the patient managed to extricate himself from the calamity by means of a pathoneurotic hypochondria, or alternatively by a reactional euphoria—in other words, using only 'actual-neurotic' methods. But when the ravages extended to the most highly prized activities of the ego and invaded intellect, morality, aesthetic sense, the patient's awareness of such decay necessarily involved a feeling of impoverishment relating to the whole of the amount of narcissistic libido which, as we indicated above, is associated with the higher mental functions.

Part of the amount of libido withdrawn from objects can

[1] Freud, 'Mourning and Melancholia', in *Coll. Pap.*, Vol. IV.

attach itself to the ego, and such an expansion of the ego can act as a protection against illness; physical mutilation, the loss of limbs or sense organs, by no means necessarily leads to neurosis. So long as the libido is satisfied by the value of one's mental activities, any physical defect can be borne with philosophy, humour, or cynicism, or even with pride, defiance, arrogance, or scorn. But what is there left for the libido to cling to when it has long since been withdrawn from objects, can take no pleasure in the performances of a physical organism which has become infirm and useless, and is now driven from its last refuge, the self-respect and esteem of the mental ego? That is the problem which confronts the poor paretic, the problem with which he has to struggle in his melancholic phase.[1]

Some 'micromanic' paretics continue with this mourning work to the day of their death, but the majority of patients manage to rid themselves of the mourning by means of a *manic-megalomanic reaction* mechanism, or less often by a *hallucinatory wish psychosis*.

The observations in the preceding section[2] mostly show us the patient occupied with this defence work, i.e. in a manic-hallucinatory state; for it is only in this stage that a large proportion of patients are referred to mental hospitals. While the 'actual-psychotic' and depressive melancholic phases often remain latent or pass quickly, being euphemistically explained away by those in the patient's environment as 'moods', the noisy and persistent symptoms of paretic megalomania make it no longer possible to doubt the severity of the mental illness.

---

[1] That the body ego is more easily abandoned, i.e. is less highly valued, than the mental ego is shown by the everyday psycho-analytic observation that female patients who have no hesitation in allowing their genitals to be examined by a gynaecologist often hesitate for weeks before telling the psycho-analyst anything about their sex life. *Il y a des choses qui se font, mais qui ne se disent pas.* Also a catatonic in a state of *flexibilitas cerea* allows anything to be done to his body, which has become as indifferent to him as has the outer world; the whole of his narcissism has been withdrawn into his mental ego, the citadel which is still defended after all the outer and inner forts have been lost. Cf. 'Psycho-analytic Observations on *Tic*' in *Further Contributions*.

[2] I.e. the preceding chapter (written by J. Hollós) of the book as part of which this paper was written. (Ed.)

In our psycho-analytic interpretation of the manic-megalomanic symptoms of the mental disorders of general paresis we are, in short, following Freud's theory of psychogenic mania, according to which the latter is a triumph over melancholic mourning attained by the dissolution in the narcissistic ego of the ego-ideal which has been altered by identification (and is mourned and hated because of its devaluation).[1]

In the case of psychogenic mania we already understand this process; the patient needs only to give up his identification with an outside object (person) for the 'counter-cathexis', mobilized to cope with the mourning for this person, to be free to be used in the mania; the narcissistic ego, undisturbed by the demands of the ideal, is able to feel happy again. But what happens in the case of paretic melancholia? Can an individual free himself from integral parts of his own ego after they have been devalued by his illness? The fact, mentioned in a footnote above, that in certain cases of catatonia the body can be 'totally sequestrated'[2] from the ego appears to justify the expectation that such a process may go still deeper and apply even to parts of the mental ego. According to the view put forward here, this happens in general paralysis with the aid of *regression to earlier stages of ego-development*.

At this point it is necessary to recapitulate briefly the course of development of the ego in so far as it has become comprehensible to the analyst. A child is born into the world justifiably expecting a continuation of that complete omnipotence which it enjoyed in the womb, when all its wants were satisfied and it was protected from all unpleasure. The attentive care lavished on the new-born infant permits it to preserve the illusion of this omnipotence if it adapts itself to certain conditions imposed by

---

[1] See Freud's observations on this subject in 'Mourning and Melancholia' and *Group Psychology and the Analysis of the Ego*.

[2] The word 'sequestrate' is used here in the sense of 'segregate', 'seclude', 'keep away from general access'. In organic medicine this term is widely used to denote a state where a diseased part of the body has been treated as if it were alien and, consequently, where the healthy, coherent parts have succeeded in isolating it completely. In this paper an attempt is made to extend the use of this term to describe similar processes in the mental sphere. (Ed.)

its environment, which at first are very insignificant. Thus there develops the stage of hallucinatory omnipotence, which is succeeded by that of omnipotence by means of magic signs or gestures. It is only after these stages have been gone through that there comes dominance of the 'reality principle', the recognition of the limitations imposed upon one's wishes by reality.[1] However, adaptation to civilized life demands even more abandonment of narcissistic self-assertion than is required by the recognition of reality. An adult's environment requires him, not only to act in accordance with the dictates of reason, but also to display such qualities as attentiveness, adroitness, cleverness, wisdom; in addition it imposes moral and aesthetic standards, and even puts him in situations in which sacrifices are demanded of him, or in which he is expected to behave with heroism. This whole development from the stage of the most primitive narcissism to the accomplishments demanded (at any rate theoretically) by society takes place, not spontaneously, but under the continuous influences of education. If we extend Freud's ideas on the role of ideal-formation in ego-development[2] to the whole of this process of development, the education of children and young people can be described as a continuous series of identifications with educators who are taken as ideals. In the course of this development ego-ideals and the deprivations and renunciations demanded by them occupy a larger and larger space and constitute, according to Freud, the 'ego-nucleus', which behaves as the 'subject', criticizes the rest of the ego, which has remained narcissistic, and sets up the institutions of conscience, censorship, reality-testing, and self-observation. The acquisition of every new skill or capacity signifies the fulfilment of an ideal and, apart from its practical utility, yields narcissistic satisfaction, increased self-respect, the restitution of ego-stature lost by the unfulfilled demands of one's ideals.

The libido directed to outside objects has also, of course, to

---

[1] Ferenczi, 'Stages in the Development of the Sense of Reality', *First Contributions*, p. 213.

[2] Freud, *Narcissism, An Introduction*, and *Group Psychology and the Analysis of the Ego*.

submit to a certain degree of education, though a less severe one, and to learn to renounce at any rate the crudest infringements of sexual morality (incest and some of the perversions). Object-love too has to become 'ego-syntonic' and must subject itself to the points of view of utility and narcissistic self-respect.

Now when essential products of this development are destroyed as a consequence of paretic brain disease, when self-observation reveals to the ego-nucleus the loss, not only of valuable physical skills, but also of supremely important mental faculties, the ego-nucleus reacts to the loss of self-esteem by an outbreak of the paretic melancholia briefly described above. When the pain of this becomes intolerable—as it does in the great majority of cases—the way lies open for the patient's narcissism *to regress to stages of development which in spite of their primitiveness were once ego-syntonic*. If the patient succeeds in giving up the ideals imposed on him by his education to civilization and in activating regressively memories of primitive-narcissistic forms of activity and ways of achieving satisfaction, his narcissism again finds a safe sanctuary and the progressive decline of his true value can no longer affect him. As the destruction caused by the paretic process goes deeper and deeper, gnawing away, so to speak, at the successive annual rings of the tree of life and limiting the patient to ever more primitive functions, the narcissistic libido follows regressively in its wake; this it can do because there was a childish and before that an infantile past in which the individual, in spite of his helplessness, was able to feel contentment, and more, actual omnipotence.

Thus the manic-megalomanic phase of general paralysis (which often appears to be the primary phase) is a step-by-step regression of the narcissistic libido to superseded stages of ego-development. From the psycho-analytic viewpoint *paralysis progressiva* is in reality *paralysis regressiva*.

Thus stages are successively reached which are characterized by the reactivation of childish and eventually infantile methods of reality testing and self-criticism, of ever more naïve forms of fantasies of omnipotence, distorted by rudiments of the healthy personality (as demonstrated by Freud in the case of schizophrenic megalomania) and interrupted from time to time by lucid intervals of depression in which the ravages which have taken place are at any rate partially recognized by the patient's self-observation.

The course of development of paretic psychosis which we have outlined here is most evident in *cyclic* cases. In these, deep melancholic depressions provoked by the mental effort to deal with the progressive advances of the degenerative process alternate with states of manically intensified self-confidence, i.e. with periods of successful self-cure. The depressive state is the 'end of the world'[1] confronting the ego-nucleus as it becomes aware of the devaluation of the ego as a whole, while the various rebirths in the manic, exalted state show us that, with the aid of regression to still more primitive situations of self-satisfaction, the ego has succeeded in overcoming the trauma of libido impoverishment and finding its way back to a lost self-complacency.[2]

We find here another confirmation of Freud's prediction that analysis of the psychoses would reveal in the field of ego-psychology mechanisms of conflict and repression among the components of the ego similar to those already discovered between ego and object in the transference neuroses. The 'process of sequestration', the way in which damage to the ego is rendered inoperative in the manic phase, is fully analogous to neurotic repression, to the way in which a situation of frustration by an object is made unconscious. This of course can happen only with the aid of 'recompenses' (Tausk), i.e. compensations for lost happiness in the present provided by regression to an earlier happiness.

If one considers the symptoms of paretic megalomania from this point of view, they become at any rate more intelligible. One can understand why a patient whose sickly body ought to be as pitiful a sight to himself as it is to others not only feels perfectly well but discovers a panacea against all possible illnesses and grants mankind the gift of eternal life; for at the

[1] 'Weltuntergang' (Ed.).
[2] Dr. Hollós is of the opinion that destructive processes in the brain, loss of tissue, result in impoverishment of the libido, while regenerative processes lead to an increase of libido in the organism.

mental level to which his ego has regressed the mumbling of magic words or a few magic rubbing movements are sufficient to enable him to do this. Though he may have only one tooth in his head, his capacity for hallucinatory or delusional regression enables him to feel himself equipped with several rows of magnificent teeth. In spite of his obvious impotence he can pride himself on being the creator of all mankind; to fulfil this miracle he has only to regress to the extragenital sexual theories of his infancy. His enormous loss of mental values causes him no more pain, for he has found compensation in archaic oral and anal satisfactions (over-eating, messing himself with faeces).

If hallucinatory magic is unable to ban awareness of his decay, he simply projects all the disagreeable facts 'on his partner' or sequestrates the whole of his physical existence from his ego and takes 'it' (his sick body) to be a sick Christian, while he himself is the King of the Jews, able to fling vast sums of money about and go about things on a colossal scale. As Hollós has observed, some patients become in turn counts, princes, kings, and finally God himself. Every real loss is accompanied by an advance in imaginary importance.[1]

A patient may still have the intellectual capacity to add his age when he entered the institution to the number of years that he has since spent in it; but the satisfaction of his ego is more important to him than any mathematical calculation, and if he is asked how old he is he will accordingly state his age before his decay began; the evil years of his illness simply do not count. He is like the girl in Wordsworth's beautiful poem who continued to insist that 'we are seven', though her brothers and sisters were lying in the cemetery.

Simultaneously with the decline in the level of personality all the superseded stages of eroticism and of libido organization are revived in turn: tendencies to incest, homosexuality, exhibitionism, scopophilia, sado-masochism, etc. It is as if the

[1] Since the observations of Groddeck, who demonstrated psycho-analytically the strength of psychological influences on men's feeding habits, the way in which paretics put on weight, which is such a characteristic symptom of their condition, can be regarded as a physical expression of their trend to 'ego-expansion', i.e. of their narcissism. Cf. the expression: 'He's inflated with pride'. In Hungarian a conceited person is said 'to grow fat on flattery'.

whole process which in the course of development led to the 'polarization' of instinctual cathexes between the centre of the ego (the brain) and the genitals has been undone step by step and as if the ego, cleansed by education of such 'naughty' impulses, were once more flooded with eroticism. Thus the more the patient degenerates, the more uninhibited and omnipotent he becomes, and he dies in the euphoria of a helpless but blissful child.[1]

The analogy shown here between paretic and psychogenic manic-melancholia can be taken still further if we remember Freud's words in the Introduction to *Group Psychology and the Analysis of the Ego:* 'In the individual's mental life someone else is invariably involved, as a model, as an object, as a helper, as an opponent, and so from the very first the psychology of the individual is at the same time social psychology as well—in this extended but entirely justifiable sense of the words.'

The essential point in psychogenic melancholia is mourning over the loss of an ego-ideal accepted as a compelling model, or, in other words, hate impulses against parts of the ego which are in the process of being identified with the object; while general paralysis destroys one by one all the successfully accomplished identifications the sum-total of which signified the attainment of the patient's ego-ideal.

---

[1] A. Stärcke, in his book *Psychoanalyse und Psychiatrie*, Wien, Int. Psa. Verlag, 1921, expresses surprise that a clinical psychiatry has not yet been based on my *Stages in the Development of the Sense of Reality* (1913). This paper may perhaps count as a first attempt in that direction. Incidentally Stärcke says himself that in the psychoses 'palaeopsychic layers which otherwise lie deeply buried and can normally be reached only by painful excavation . . . lie open in the light of day'.

It can be no accident that many intimate connexions exist between lues and libido. Not only the primary effects but also the secondary efflorescences attach themselves for preference to the erotogenic zones (mouth, buttocks, genitals), though the tertiary infiltrations no longer show this localization. In general paresis the spirochetes seem to have re-established the connexion and to have settled in the 'narcissistic zone'. In this context there should also be remembered an observation made long ago by Freud, who pointed out that severe neuroses, or in other words disturbances in the economy of the libido, occur very frequently among the offspring of syphilitics. Freud also occasionally drew attention to the striking difference in the course of lues in the male and female sex, which points to a dependence of the virulence of this illness on sexual chemistry.

As is demonstrated in the case of the hallucinations, personifications, etc., which sometimes become apparent in the psychoses, these identifications and ideals must, like the earlier stages of development, be regarded as relatively independent, coherent complexes within the ego which may regain their independence in dream or in psychosis. In any case the progressive 'process of sequestration' in general paresis can be compared with the mechanism of projection and regarded as the opposite process to the gradual 'introjection of ideas', i.e. to what, in the light of analysis, we take ego-development to consist of.

Even the final stage of general paralysis, that of complete 'imbecility', is not just a direct consequence of destruction of nervous tissue; in the effort to maintain the ego-content and, to a certain extent, its integration, the paretic's mind holds out to the last, and by achieving infantile and perhaps fatal regression persists in the 'sequestration' of what is painful to it to the limit of unconsciousness.[1]

However, a satisfactory psycho-analytic theory of general paresis must also make more intelligible to us the various clinical courses that illness may take. The principal types are the melancholic (micromanic); the manic (megalomanic); and simple imbecility. The psycho-analytic theory of the pathogenesis of the neuroses, in which both constitutional and traumatic factors are allowed for, offers us a general aetiological equation, and general paresis can surely be no exception to this rule. The 'choice of neurosis', the selection of the kind of neurosis in which a mind in distress takes refuge, is always dependent on both of these two factors. It is at this point that the endogenous factor so often mentioned in the literature fits in organically in the aetiology of general paresis. The individual constitution of the ego and the libido, the individual's weak points, the places at which fixations took place in his development, cannot be a matter of indifference to the course of the pathological process, to the way in which the psyche reacts to the brain injury. We may assume *a priori* that in an already strongly

[1] '*bis zur Bewusstlosigkeit*'. An untranslatable pun in the German original. (Ed.)

narcissistic individual general paresis will assume another colour, psychosis will take a different course, from that which it would take in an individual of the 'transference' type; that in the process of regression in an individual with an oral-erotic or sadistic-anal-erotic fixation the predominant symptoms will be different from what they would have been if the primacy of the genital zones had been fully established. Also the patient's past, the ego-development on which he can look back, the cultural level he has attained, the ideals he has fulfilled, cannot be irrelevant to the manner and intensity of his pathoneurotic and psychotic reactions. It will be the task of future investigations to demonstrate in detail the influence of ego-character and sexual character on the symptomatology of general paresis.

In the meantime something can already be said about the connexion between the trauma and the choice of psychotic symptoms. By that is meant, not the significance of the patient's pathological-anatomical state, though a time may come when we shall receive some enlightenment on that, but on certain *temporal* and *topographical* factors connected with the onset of the illness.

Just as an unexpected death leads to more intense grief or a sudden disappointment in a narcissistically loved object calls forth a more deeply melancholic mood, so one could expect a cerebral process which comes on tempestuously to evoke a more violent pathoneurotic reaction and to stimulate the psyche to a noisier work of compensation than a cerebral disease which sets in imperceptibly and progresses only slowly. In the latter case we should expect a simple process of increasing imbecility, for the traumatic factor which might have led to the mobilizing of large amounts of narcissistic libido and could have provoked paretic melancholia and mania is absent.

In addition to this temporal factor there is also a topographical factor that must be taken into account, not for the time being in the sense of anatomical or histological localization, but in the sense in which Freud speaks of topography in his *metapsychology*.[1] The violence of the melancholic reaction to the cere-

---

[1] See Freud's metapsychological papers in *Coll. Papers*, Vol. IV, and in particular his reference to the subject in *Group Psychology and the Analysis of the Ego*.

bral disease, as well, of course, as the manic counter-reaction, must, in the light of Freud's metapsychology, be regarded as dependent *on the degree of the difference in tension between the ego-nucleus and the narcissistic ego.* If in the general destruction the ego-nucleus (and its functions of self-observation, conscience, etc.) is relatively spared, the catastrophic decline of the various mental and physical faculties is bound to involve violent psychotic reactions. But if in the general mental collapse the faculty of ego-criticism is simultaneously destroyed, the illness is more likely to present the picture of simple imbecility.

Thus the noisy, megalomanic paretic does not deserve to be characterized, as he is by the textbooks, as 'completely uncritical'. That would be a more appropriate description of the purely imbecile paretic; for the striking symptoms of the micromanic or the megalomanic are in reality the product of his highly sensitive self-criticism. A proportion of paretics exhibiting manic and melancholic symptoms are actually capable of recovering from the mental shock and of continuing to live for years, either normally or with only minor mental defects; surely a definite proof that their psychotic symptoms were of a 'functional' nature. Alternatively the ego-nucleus, after at first being relatively spared, may itself be attacked by the pathological process, in which case the manic-melancholic stage is followed by that of imbecility. Diminution of criticism by the ego-nucleus leads to the disappearance of the tension between the latter and the narcissistic ego-remnant which gave rise to the work of compensation, with the result that the individual who has now really become 'completely uncritical' is able to calm down and experience the subsequent progressive decline of his faculties without any particular emotion.

There is another clinical picture of general paresis which, though less common, deserves special attention from the theoretical point of view. I refer to the *'agitated'* or *'galloping'* form. This sets in violently, with tremendous restlessness, meaningless speeches, outbursts of rage, etc., and soon degenerates into a hallucinatory anxiety delirium in which the patient raves and shouts incoherently, destroys everything within reach, dances about, makes brutal attacks on the attendants, and is unable to concentrate his attention in any way whatever.[1] 'Personifications' take place in the patient and give him the most remarkable orders, which he faithfully carries out, etc. These patients generally die very quickly, often only a few weeks after the onset of the mental disturbance, of the exhaustion which is the consequence of the uncontrollable pressure of activity.

As pathological anatomy has so far failed to provide us with an explanation of this special form of general paralysis, we are justified in calling on psycho-analysis to make the attempt. Once more this provides us with an approach based on Freud's metapsychological topography. In the great majority of cases, as we have seen, the process of deterioration begins at the 'periphery of the ego', i.e. with a breakdown of physical functions, and gradually or step by step it attacks the higher mental faculties. But an ego-nucleus continues to hold the whole together, and the unity of the personality, if at a regressively lower level, is maintained. The ego-nucleus is able to save itself from complete dissolution by counter-cathexes and reaction-formations; the libido-cathexes of the 'sequestrated' ego-elements and identifications can be taken over in good time into the 'ego-nucleus' which become more and more narcissistic. In the exceptional cases in which the disease (whether psychotopographically or histologically) starts by destroying the ego-nucleus and its functions, we may assume that the agglutinant which cemented the separate parts of the personality together has been attacked and dissolved, with the result that the individual 'identifications' and 'personifications' which had no time to surrender their libido cathexes are able to act in a completely anarchical fashion, independently from, and without the slightest regard for, each other, leading to the picture of galloping general paresis described above.

The theoretically interesting point about this explanation, assuming that it is correct, is that, by carrying further Freud's parallel between the psychology of the individual and that of the group, we have been able to arrive at a plastic conception of the 'organization' which is the individual mind. In the in-

[1] See the case quoted in Bleuler's *Lehrbuch der Psychiatrie*, Berlin, 1916, p. 243.

dividual as in the group mind we can identify the force which welds the parts into a whole as the libido, and more particularly the narcissistic libido. In the individual, as in certain group organizations, there exists a hierarchy of different levels of agencies, but the effectiveness of the organization as a whole depends on the existence of a leader who is superior to the whole hierarchy. In the individual mind this leadership is assumed by the *ego-nucleus*, and if it is eliminated, leaving the remainder intact, a degree of confusion may arise in the individual corresponding to the phenomenon known to us in group psychology as *panic*. With the dissolution of the libidinous ties between the various parts of the ego and the ego-nucleus, the tie cementing to one another the elements previously subordinated to the ego-nucleus is dissolved also, because, in Freud's view, the only motive for co-operation between them was the emotional relationship to their joint leader. This analogy is certainly made more probable by the fact that a tremendous amount of *anxiety* is generally released in hallucinatory confusion. When a 'panic' of this kind breaks out, it is as if all the mental energy that had been 'bound' in the course of development had been suddenly released and changed into 'free-floating' energy.

An attempt should of course be made to explain non-paretic cases of anoia in the same way. On the other hand this 'plan of the organization of the individual mind' may show the way to the explanation of the hitherto inexplicable *tendency of the mind to unification*, and even of the fundamental fact of the association of ideas. The compulsion to unify two separate psychical contents may really originate in deference to a libidinous relationship to a third 'leading' complex, the 'ego-nucleus'.

It is time, however, to break off these speculations about a stereochemistry of the mind and to return to our main theme. It can definitely be said that many of the psychotic phenomena of progressive paralysis, as well as the course of the illness as a whole, are not inaccessible to psycho-analytic explanation, and that the attempt to explain them psycho-analytically leads to ranges of ideas which hold out the promise of a solution of difficult problems of psychiatry and psychology. If the degree of understanding that a theory makes possible is taken as the measuring-rod of its truth-content, the opinion may be hazarded that psycho-analysis, which has hitherto claimed to be able to grapple only with the 'functional' psychoses, has now earned itself a place in organic psychiatry as well.

XLIII

FREUD'S 'GROUP PSYCHOLOGY AND THE ANALYSIS OF THE EGO'[1]

Its contributions to the Psychology of the Individual[2]

(1922)

LOOKING at scientific advance as a whole, we see that direct, rectilinear advance keeps coming to a dead end, so that research has to be resumed from a completely fresh and often entirely unexpected and improbable angle. I once had occasion [in 1915] to point to one such surprising event when, in reviewing Freud's *Three Essays on the Theory of Sexuality*[3] a purely psychological work, I had to describe it as an important advance in biology, i.e. in one of the natural sciences, an advance which that discipline would never have been able to make out of its own resources.

The value of this 'utraquism' (as I propose to call it) of a correct scientific policy is demonstrated, not only in the two great alternative possible approaches to knowledge, the objective (in the natural sciences) and the subjective (in psychology); it is also true within the field of psychology itself. Scarcely had we got used to the idea that the basis for unravelling the complex phenomena of the group mind (art, religion, myth-formation, etc.) had been provided by the findings of the psychology of the individual, i.e. of psycho-analysis, when our confidence in it was shaken by the appearance of Freud's recent work on 'group psychology'; which showed us the converse, namely that the investigation of the processes of group psychology was capable of solving important problems of individual psychology. In the following pages I propose to draw attention to the most

[1] German original 1921. English translation: London, Hogarth Press, 1922.
[2] See *Further Contributions*, p. 253.
[3] Published in German: *Int. Z. f. PsA.* (1922), 8, 206. First English translation.

important respects in which Freud's dissection of the group mind throws light on the normal and pathological psychology of the individual.

Freud disposes of the idea, automatically assumed by other writers on the subject, that group psychological phenomena take place only in a 'group', i.e. in the presence of a large number of individuals. On the contrary, he demonstrates that the same emotional and intellectual phenomena can appear within a small group of persons, e.g. in the family, or even in relations with a single other person, i.e. in a 'group of two'. This viewpoint enables us fundamentally to alter our views on one of the most remarkable and, from the standpoint of the psychology of the individual, most significant processes, namely hypnotism and suggestion.

Previous authors have tried to understand group phenomena by using the idea of suggestion without being able to explain the nature of suggestion. Freud, however, points out that it is in fact group phenomena and their historical development which help us to explain what occurs between two individuals in the process of suggestion. He traces the disposition to hypnosis back to its source in primitive humanity; in the primal horde the eye of the feared father-leader, who disposed of the power of life and death over every single one of its members, exercised over them throughout their lifetime the same paralysing effect, inhibiting all independent action, all independent intellectual activity, that the eye of the hypnotist still exercises over his subjects to-day. The effectiveness of hypnosis is due to this fear of the hypnotist's eye; all other methods of inducing it (monotonous sounds, fixing the eye on a single spot, etc.), are only subsidiary devices which have the effect of diverting the subject's conscious attention in order the better to bring his unconscious under the hypnotist's sway.

In contrast to Bernheim's hitherto generally accepted view that hypnosis is only a form of suggestion, we must now adopt Freud's view that the fundamental phenomenon to which we must look for an explanation of suggestibility is susceptibility to hypnosis. But this susceptibility is not, as we have previously supposed, merely a residue of infantile fear of the strict father;

it is also the return of emotions felt by primitive man in the presence of the dangerous leader of the horde. Thus group psychology provides a phylogenetic parallel to the ontogenesis of susceptibility to hypnosis. If we have regard to the central position of suggestion and hypnosis in the pathology and therapy of the neuroses, in education, etc., we shall immediately see that a fundamental revision of our previous views on the subject will have a perceptible effect throughout the field of normal and pathological psychology.

The second vital innovation for which the psychology of the individual has to thank this research into group psychology is the discovery of a new stage in the development of the ego and the libido. The transference neuroses, which were the original point of departure of psycho-analysis and for a long time its only subject-matter, of course enabled Freud to make a practically complete reconstruction of the phases of development of the sexual instinct. Meanwhile the second factor in the formation of neuroses, the ego, remained a compact mass, incapable of being analysed into its component parts, about the structure of which it was possible to form only the most hypothetical ideas. Some light was thrown on this darkness by the study of the narcissistic neuropsychoses and of normal love life; but it was Freud's research into group psychology which first enabled him to establish a real 'stage' in the development of the ego. The primary narcissism of the child and of humanity is succeeded by a higher ego-stage, which consists in the separating out from the former of an 'ego-ideal', the pattern which one sets up inside oneself and against which one subsequently measures all one's actions and qualities. This ego-ideal takes over the important functions of reality testing, of the moral conscience, of self-observation and dream-censorship; it is also the force at work in the creation of the 'unconscious repressed' which is so important in the formation of neurosis.

There is a libidinous process which runs parallel with his stage of ego-development and henceforward must be inserted as a special phase of development between narcissism and object-love (or, more correctly, between the still narcissistic oral and sadistic-anal stages of organization and true object-love). This process is identification. In this phase external objects are not really incorporated, as in the cannibalistic phase, but are 'incorporated' in an imaginary fashion, or, as we term it, introjected; that is to say, their qualities are annexed, attributed to the ego. The establishment of such an identification with an object (a person) is simultaneously the building of a bridge between the self and the outer world, and this connexion subsequently permits a shifting of emphasis from the intransitive 'being' to the transitive 'having', i.e. a further development from identification to real object-love. But a fixation at the stage of identification makes possible a regression from the later phase of object-love to the stage of identification; the most notable examples of this occur in certain pathological processes no less than in certain hitherto not understood phenomena of the group-mind. The establishing of this new stage of ego and libido development obviously opens a broad perspective, and will certainly bring nearer an understanding of many insufficiently understood phenomena of psychopathology and the psychology of the individual.

Though in this work Freud was primarily concerned with the dynamics of the group mind, he could not help making further contributions to certain aspects of the theory of the neuroses which in previous works he had left incomplete. Out of the fullness of his offerings I shall quote only a few examples.

Previous clinical-analytic investigation had already established that homosexuality in males generally appeared as a reaction to a previous excessively strong heterosexual trend. We now learn from Freud that this reaction is simultaneously a regression from object-love to identification. Woman as an external love-object is given up, but in compensation is reconstituted in the ego by way of identification and put in the place of the ego-ideal; thus the male becomes feminine and seeks out another male, thereby re-establishing the original heterosexual relationship, but in reverse.

Freud's theory of the libidinous nature of the social tie between the individual and a leader and between an individual and his fellow-men grants us some insight into the pathogenesis of paranoia. Freud has now for the first time enabled us really to understand why so many people succumb to paranoia as a result of offences to which they have been subjected in social life. As a consequence of a social insult the libido, which was previously socially bound, is set free; it would like to express itself in a crudely sexual, generally homosexual form, but such an outlet is intolerable to the exacting standards demanded by the ego-ideal; and the way out of the acute dilemma is found in paranoia. The earlier social binding still finds expression in the feeling of being persecuted by compact groups, communities, or associations (Jesuits, Freemasons, Jews, etc.). Thus paranoia turns out to be a disturbance, not only of the (homosexual) tie with the father, but also of social 'identification' (which is in itself a-sexual).

Freud's solution of this problem of group psychology provides new support for the previously elaborated metapsychology of melancholia; this psychosis too turns out to be a consequence of substituting for the ego-ideal the object which has been outwardly given up, because of hatred; the manic phase of cyclothymia, however, turns out to be a temporary rebellion of the primary-narcissistic ego-residue against the tyranny of the ego-ideal. We can see that the exploitation of the new phase of ego and libido development has made a promising beginning in psychiatry.

Hysterical identification differs from the above in that, among other things, the (unconscious) incorporation of the object is only partial and is restricted to certain characteristics of the latter.

Our view of normal love-life must be revised in important respects in the light of the new insights. The difference between uninhibited and aim-inhibited sexual impulses turns out to be even more important than had previously been supposed. The latency period, which brings about this inhibition of aim, of course also acquires increased significance.

The correct evaluation of aim-inhibited sexual impulses led Freud to a new conception of the dynamics of neurotic illness; according to the new description, the neurotic conflict is played out between the sexual trends which are inhibited in aim in accordance with the demands of the ego-ideal (trends acceptable to the ego) and direct sexual trends (trends unacceptable to the ego). To a considerable extent the processes of libido-cathexis in falling in love also appear in a new light as a result of Freud's research into group psychology. The feeling of shame actually appears to be determined by a phenomenon of group psychology. It appears to be a reaction to the disturbing effect on the expression of the heterosexual instinct, which is always a-social, of being brought before the public eye.

Returning to our point of departure, let us in conclusion draw attention once again to the group-psychological factors involved in every psychotherapy which make the study of this paper of Freud's essential to everyone concerned with the healing of sick minds. For in dealing with the patient the physician is the representative of the whole of human society. Like a Roman Catholic priest, he has the power to loose or bind; through him the patient learns to render inoperative the former 'conscience' which made him ill; and it is by virtue of his authority that the patient is enabled to overcome his repressions. It is thus not least physicians who owe a debt of admiration and thanks to the author of this work. For in certain processes of group psychology he has provided an explanation of the effectiveness of psycho-therapeutic measures which has made intelligible to them the working of a tool that they use daily.

BIBLIOGRAPHY

THIS bibliography is designed to supplement those already published in *Bausteine zur Psychoanalyse* Vol. IV (Bern, Hans Huber, 1939; since 1948 Imago Publ. Co., London) and *Further Contributions to Psychoanalysis* (London, Hogarth Press, 1926, 2nd ed. 1950). It consists of the Ferenczi papers that have been translated into English. For those papers which have not yet been so translated, the reader is referred directly to the two earlier bibliographies.

As far as possible, the papers are chronologically arranged under the dates of their original publication. The numbers on the left side of each page refer to the numbering of the papers in the *Bausteine zur Psychoanalyse* bibliography, while the numbers enclosed in brackets are those which appear in the bibliography of *Further Contributions to Psychoanalysis*. In brackets and following the abbreviations for collected works or journals, the Roman numerals indicate volume numbers, the Arabic page numbers.

KEY TO ABBREVIATIONS

C.   A Collection which first appeared as *Contributions to Psychoanalysis* (Boston, R. G. Badger, 1916) and subsequently as *Sex in Psychoanalysis* since the second American edition of 1916, and then as *First Contributions to Psychoanalysis* (London, Hogarth Press, 1952). The page references in this bibliography refer to the two later publications.

F.C. *Further Contributions to Psychoanalysis*, London, Hogarth Press, 1926, 2nd ed. 1950.

Fin. Final Contributions to the Problems and Methods of Psycho-Analysis. London, Hogarth Press, 1955.

J.   International Journal of Psycho-Analysis.

R.   The Psychoanalytic Review.

Q. The Psychoanalytic Quarterly.
Trans. Psycho-Med. Soc. Transactions of the Psycho-Medical Society.
Brit. J. med. Psychol. British Journal of Medical Psychology.
Indian J. Psychol. Indian Journal of Psychology.

SÁNDOR FERENCZI

1908

57 (33b) The effect on women of premature ejaculation in men (*Fin.* 291)

60 (30) Actual- and psycho-neuroses in the light of Freud's investigations and psycho-analysis. (*F.C.* 30)

61 (31) Analytical interpretation and treatment of psycho-sexual impotence in men. (*C.* 11)

63 (38) Psychoanalysis and education (*Fin.* 280); *J.* 1949 (XXX, 220)

1909

65 (34) The analytic conception of the psycho-neuroses. (*F.C.* 15)

66 (37) On the psychological analysis of dreams. (*C.* 94)

67 (36) Introjection and transference. (*C.* 35); *R.* 1916 (III, 107)

1911

75 (41) On obscene words. (*C.* 132)

77 (42) Stimulation of the anal erotogenic zone as a precipitating factor in paranoia. (*Fin.* 295)

78 (43) The psycho-analysis of wit and the comical. (*F.C.* 332)

79 (45) On the organization of the psycho-analytic movement. (*Fin.* 299)

80 (46) On the part played by homosexuality in the pathogenesis of paranoia. (*C.* 154); *R.* 1920 (VII, 86)

1912

83 (47) Dirigible dreams. (*Fin.* 313)
84 (48) On the definition of introjection. (*Fin.* 316)
85 (49) On transitory symptom-constructions during the analysis. (*C.* 193)
86 (50) A case of *déjà vu*. (*Fin.* 319)
87 (51) On the genealogy of the 'fig-leaf'. (*Fin.* 321)
88 (52) Metaphysics = Metapsychology. (*Fin.* 322)
89 (55) Paracelsus to the physicians. (*Fin.* 323)
90 (56) Goethe on the reality value of the poet's fantasy. (*Fin.* 324)
91 (57) Dr. S. Lindner; a forerunner of Freud's in the theory of sex. (*Fin.* 325)
92 (58) Symbolic representation of the pleasure and reality principles in the Oedipus myth. (*C.* 253)
93 (59) Philosophy and psycho-analysis. (*Fin.* 326)
94 (61) Suggestion and psycho-analysis. (*F.C.* 55). The Psycho-analysis of suggestion and hypnosis. *Trans. Psycho-Med. Soc.*, London, 1912 (III, Pt. 4)
95 (53) A striking picture of the 'unconscious'. (*F.C.* 350)
96 (54) The interpretation of unconscious incest fantasies from a parapraxis (Brantôme). (*Fin.* 335)
97 (61a) Exploring the unconscious. (*Fin.* 308)
100 (60) On onanism. (*C.* 185)

1913

103 (81a) On psycho-analysis and its judicial and sociological significance. A Lecture for Judges and Barristers. (*F.C.* 424)
104 (71) Taming of a wild horse. (*Fin.* 336)
105 (62) To whom does one relate one's dreams? (*F.C.* 349)
106 (63) On the genesis of the *jus primae noctis*. (*Fin.* 341)
109 (81b) Belief, disbelief and conviction. (*F.C.* 437)
111 (65) Stages in the development of the sense of reality. (*C.* 213)
112 (69) On eye symbolism. (*C.* 270)
113 (66) The grandfather complex. (*F.C.* 323)

114	(67)	A little Chanticleer. (*C.* 240)
115	(72)	A transient symptom: the position during treatment. (*F.C.* 242)
116	(73)	Obsessional etymologizing. (*F.C.* 318)
117	(74)	The symbolism of bed-linen. (*F.C.* 359)
118	(75)	The kite as a symbol of erection. (*F.C.* 359)
119	(76)	Paraesthesias of the genital region in impotence. (*F.C.* 312)
120	(77)	Flatus as an adult prerogative. (*F.C.* 325)
121	(78)	Infantile ideas about the female genital organs. (*F.C.* 314)
122	(79)	Childish ideas of digestion. (*F.C.* 325)
123	(80)	The cause of reserve in a child. (*F.C.* 327)
125	(68)	On the ontogenesis of symbols. (*C.* 276)

1914

135	(82)	Some clinical observations on paranoia and paraphrenia (*C.* 282)
136	(83)	On the nosology of male homosexuality. (*C.* 296)
137	(87)	Obsessional neurosis and piety. (*F.C.* 450)
138	(88)	On the feeling of giddiness at the end of the analytical hour. (*F.C.* 239)
139	(89)	Falling asleep during the analysis. (*F.C.* 249)
140	(90)	The psychic effect of the sunbath. (*F.C.* 365)
141	(94)	On embarrassed hands. (*F.C.* 315)
142	(85)	Rubbing the eyes as a substitute for onanism. (*F.C.* 317)
143	(93)	Vermin as a symbol of pregnancy. (*F.C.* 361)
144	(86)	Dread of cigar and cigarette smoking. (*F.C.* 318)
145	(92)	The 'forgetting' of a symptom and its explanation in a dream (*F.C.* 412)
146	(84)	On the ontogenesis of an interest in money. (*C.* 319)
147	(91)	Discontinuous analysis. (*F.C.* 233)

1915

159	(96)	Psychogenic anomalies of voice production. (*F.C.* 105)
160	(99)	The dream of the occlusive pessary. (*F.C.* 304)

161	(100)	The scientific significance of Freud's *Three Contributions to the Theory of Sexuality*. (*F.C.* 253)
162	(101)	*Nonum prematur in annum.* (*F.C.* 419)
163	(108a)	Hebbel's explanation of *déjà vu*. (*F.C.* 422)
164	(97)	The analysis of comparisons. (*F.C.* 397)
165	(103)	Two typical faecal and anal symbols. (*F.C.* 327)
166	(104)	Spectrophobia (*F.C.* 365)
167	(106)	Pompadour-fantasies. (*F.C.* 351)
168	(105)	Talkativeness. (*F.C.* 252)
169	(107)	The fan as a genital symbol (*F.C.* 361)
170	(108)	Polycratism. (*F.C.* 423)
171	(109)	Restlessness towards the end of the hour of analysis. (*F.C.* 238)
172	(110)	Micturition as a sedative. (*F.C.* 317)
173	(111)	An anal-erotic proverb. (*F.C.* 365)
174	(98)	On supposed mistakes. (*F.C.* 407)

1916

186	(112)	*Contributions to Psychoanalysis* (since the 2nd ed. *Sex in Psychoanalysis*), Boston, Richard Badger.
187	(115)	Interchange of affect in dreams. (*F.C.* 345)
188	(116)	Significant variation of the shoe as a vagina symbol. (*F.C.* 358)
189	(113)	Two types of war-neurosis. (*F.C.* 124)
190	(114)	Composite formations of erotic and character traits. (*F.C.* 257)
191	(117)	Silence is golden. (*F.C.* 250)

1917

193	(118)	Pollution without dream orgasm and dream orgasm without pollution. (*F.C.* 297)
194	(120)	Dreams of the unsuspecting. (*F.C.* 346)
195	(119)	Disease- or patho-neuroses. (*F.C.* 78)
196	(121)	On the psychical consequences of 'castration' in infancy. (*F.C.* 244)
197	(122)	The compulsion to symmetrical touching. (*F.C.* 242)
198	(123)	*Pecunia—olet.* (*F.C.* 362)

206 Review of Groddeck, G.: 'Die psychische Bedingtheit und psychoanalytische Behandlung organischer Leiden. (*Fin.* 342)

1919
210 (126) Technical difficulties in the analysis of a case of hysteria. (*F.C.* 189)
211 (130) Sunday neuroses. (*F.C.* 174)
212 (128) Thinking and muscle innervation. (*F.C.* 230)
213 (131) Disgust for breakfast. (*F.C.* 326)
214 (132) Cornelia, the mother of the Gracchi. (*F.C.* 318)
215 (133) On influencing the patient in analysis. (*F.C.* 235)
216 (127) On the technique of psycho-analysis. (*F.C.* 177)
217 (129) Nakedness as a means of inspiring terror. (*F.C.* 329)
218 (134) (with Karl Abraham, Ernst Simmel, Ernest Jones). *Psychoanalysis and the War Neuroses.* London, Int. Psa. Press, 1921.
219 (135) On the psychogenesis of mechanism. (*F.C.* 383)
220 (136) The phenomena of hysterical materialization. (*F.C.* 89)
221 (136) An attempted explanation of some hysterical stigmata. (*F.C.* 110)
222 (136) The psycho-analysis of a case of hysterical hypochondria. (*F.C.* 118)
224 Psychoanalysis and criminology (*F C.* 434)

1920
226 (137) Supplement to 'Psychogenesis of mechanism'. (*F.C.* 393)

1921
232 (139) Psycho-analytical observations on tic. (*F.C.* 142); *J.* 1921 (II, 1)
233 (141) The symbolism of the bridge. (*F.C.* 352); *J.* 1922 (III, 163)
234 (138) The further development of the active therapy in psycho-analysis. (*F.C.* 198)

235	(140)	Discussion on tic. (*Fin.* 349); *J.* 1921 (II, 481)
236	(142)	General theory of the neuroses. *J.* 1920 (I, 294)
238		Review of Groddeck, G.: 'Der Seelensucher'. (*Fin.* 344)

1922

239	(143)	(with S. Hollós) *Psycho-analysis and the psychic disorder of general paresis.* New York, Washington, Nervous and Mental Disease Publ. Co. 1925. (*Fin* 351.)
242	(149)	Bridge symbolism and the Don Juan legend. (*F.C.* 356); *J.* 1922 (III, 167)
243	(145)	The psyche as an inhibiting organ. (*F.C.* 379)
244	(146)	Freud's 'Group Psychology and the Analysis of the Ego'. (*Fin.* 371)
245	(148)	Social considerations in some analyses. (*F.C.* 413 and 417); *J.* 1923 (IV, 475)

1923

249	(154)	Ptyalism in an oral erotic. (*F.C.* 315)
250	(155)	The sons of the 'tailor'. (*F.C.* 418)
251	(156)	'Materialization' in Globus hystericus. (*F.C.* 104)
252	(157)	Attention during the narration of dreams. (*F.C.* 238)
253	(158)	Shuddering at scratching on glass, etc. (*F.C.* 313)
254	(159)	The symbolism of the Medusa's head. (*F.C.* 360)
255	(160)	Stage fright and narcissistic self-observation. (*F.C.* 421)
256	(161)	An 'anal hollow-penis' in woman. (*F.C.* 317)
257	(162)	The dream of the clever baby. (*F.C.* 349)
258	(163)	Washing-compulsion and masturbation. (*F.C.* 311)

1924

264	(164)	(with Otto Rank) *The Development of Psycho-Analysis.* New York, Washington, Nervous and Mental Disease Pub. Co. 1925.
265	(165)	On forced fantasies. (*F.C.* 68)
268	(165c)	*Thalassa: a Theory of Genitality.* New York, Psychoanalytic Quarterly, 1938, 2nd imp. Q. 1933–34 (II, 361–403; III, 1–29, III, 200–22)

1925
269 (166) Psycho-analysis of sexual habits. (*F.C.* 259); *J.* 1925 (VI, 372)

1926
271 (168) Contra-indications to the 'active' psycho-analytical technique. (*F.C.* 217)
272 Organ neuroses and their treatment. (*Fin.* 22); *Medical Review of Reviews* (XXXVI, 376)
273 (169) To Sigmund Freud on his 70th birthday. (*Fin.* 11); *J.* 1926 (VII, 297)
274 (171a) Freud's importance for the mental hygiene movement (*Fin.* 18); *Mental Hygiene*, 1926 (X, 673)
275 (170) The problem of the acceptance of unpleasant ideas —advances in knowledge of the sense of reality. (*F.C.* 366); *J.* 1926 (VII, 312)
276 *Further Contributions to the Theory and Technique of Psychoanalysis.* London, Hogarth Press, 2nd ed. 1950
277 (171) Review of Rank, O.: 'Technique of Psycho-Analysis', Vol. I, *J.* 1927 (VIII, 93)
278 (171b) Present day problems in psycho-analysis. (*Fin.* 29); *Archives of Psycho-Analysis*, 1927 (I, 522)
280 (171c) Gulliver phantasies. (*Fin.* 41); *J.* 1928 (IX, 283); *R.* 1932 (XIX, 227)

1928
281 (174) The adaptation of the family to the child. (*Fin.* 61); *Brit. J. med. Psychol.* 1928 (VIII, 1)
282 (175) The problem of termination of the analysis. (*Fin.* 77)
283 (176) The elasticity of psycho-analytical technique. (*Fin.* 87)

1929
286 (178) Male and female. *Q.* 1936 (V, 249); Masculine and feminine. *R.* 1930 (XVII, 105). Included in *Thalassa* No. 268

287 (179) The unwelcome child and his death-instinct. (*Fin.* 102); *J.* 1929 (X, 125)

1930
291 (183) The principle of relaxation and neocatharsis. (*Fin.* 108); *J.* 1930 (XI, 428)

1931
292 (184) Child analysis in the analysis of adults. (*Fin.* 126); *J.* 1931 (XII, 468)

1933
293 (185) Freud's influence on medicine. In 'Psycho-Analysis To-Day', ed. by S. Lorand. Covici-Friede Publ. New York, 1933. (*Fin.* 143)
294 (186) Confusion of tongues between adults and the child. (*Fin.* 156); *J.* 1949 (XXX, 225)

POSTHUMOUS PAPERS

296 (188) Some thoughts on trauma. (Included in *Notes and Fragments*, 1920 and 1930–33)
298 (190) More about homosexuality (*c.* 1909). (*Fin.* 168)
299 (191) On the interpretation of tunes which come into one's head (*c.* 1909). (*Fin.* 175)
300 (192) Laughter (*c.* 1913). (*Fin.* 177)
301 (193) Mathematics (*c.* 1920). (*Fin.* 183)
302 (194) Epileptic fits—observations and reflections (*c.* 1921). (*Fin.* 197)
303 (195) Contribution to the understanding of the psychoneuroses of the age of involution (*c.* 1921–22). (*Fin.* 205)
304 (196) Paranoia (*c.* 1922). (*Fin.* 213)
308 (200) Notes and fragments (1920 and 1930–32). (*Fin.* 216); *J.* 1949 (XXX, 231); some parts printed in *Indian J. Psychol.* 1934 (IX, 29)

ADDENDA

1920
1. Open letter. *J.* 1920 (I, 1)

1927
2. Introduction to Freud, S.: 'Inhibition, Symptom and Anxiety', Stamford, Conn., Psychoanalytic Institute.
3. Introduction to Freud, S.: 'The Problem of Lay-Analysis', New York, Brentano's.

OBITUARIES OF SÁNDOR FERENCZI

SIGMUND FREUD, *J.* 1933 (XIV, 207)
M. BALINT, *Indian J. Psychol.* 1934 (IX, 19)
M. EITINGON (in German), *Imago* 1933 (XIX, 289)
P. FEDERN, *J.* 1933 (XIV, 467)
E. HITSCHMANN (in German), *Psa. Bewegung* 1933 (V, 205)
I. HOLLÓS (in Hungarian), *Gyógyászat* 1934 (XX)
E. JONES, *J.* 1933 (IV, 463)
S. RADO, *Q.* 1933 (II, 356)
E. SIMMEL (in German), *Imago* 1933 (XIX, 296)

APPRECIATIONS

I. DE FORREST, *J.* 1942 (XXIII, 120)
C. THOMPSON, *J.* 1943 (XXIV, 64)
FERENCZI NUMBER, *J.* 1949 (XXX, No. IV)

INDEX

Explanatory Notes

1. List of abbreviations:
   I = 'First Contributions to Psycho-Analysis' (Bibl. no. 186)
   II = 'Further Contributions to the Theory and Technique of Psycho-Analysis' (Bibl. no. 276)
   III = 'Final Contributions to the Problems and Methods of Psycho-Analysis' (this volume)
   D = 'The Development of Psycho-Analysis' (Bibl. no. 264)
   T = 'Thalassa: A theory of Genitality' (Bibl. no. 268)
   W = 'Psycho-Analysis and the War Neuroses' (Bibl. no. 218)
2. Square brackets contain:
   (a) in Roman letters: synonyms of a heading or terms closely related to it in meaning
   (b) in italics: references to related terms which have been listed separately.
3. Round brackets contain:
   apart from plural endings of the heading, explanations of terms.
4. Quotation marks indicate:
   (a) original terms or original use of a term
   (b) titles of publications.
5. Dashes have been substituted for headings in the case of compound terms or to avoid possible misunderstandings.
6. Roman figures and capital letters refer to volumes, Arabic figures to pagination within a volume.
7. Arabic figures in italics refer to:
   (a) starting page of a chapter or section in which the subject is dealt with,
   (b) passages which contain basically informative or original material about the subject.
8. Adverbs and conjunctions have been disregarded in the alphabetical order.
9. Sub-headings are arranged in alphabetical order, except for definitions which precede them.
10. No discrimination is made whether or not the term referred to appears in the main text, in a whole chapter or in a footnote.
11. Particular applications of a term are generally listed under the term in question, but in a few cases very frequently used compounds have been listed separately.
12. Adjectives, as far as possible, do not appear as separate entries.
13. Cross-references from one heading to another follow the principle of:
    (a) accumulating kindred material as far as possible—and
    (b) preferably under a main heading which dominates more than one sub-heading.
14. Possible inconsistencies of the index are mainly due to problems

caused by divergencies between the various translators and by the fact that the present indexer felt obliged to take into consideration as far as possible the work of her predecessors and their principles of selection (i.e. the published indices of Vols. I, II, and T, and those of Vols. D and W which existed only in manuscript).

ABANDONED [Deserted], feeling of being, III 137-8, 219, 227
ABASIA [*see also Motor disturbances*], II 134, 135, 138
ABRAHAM, K., I 47, 50, 61, 155, 313; II 134, 323; III 33, 210; T 5-6
ABREACTION [*see also Catharsis*], I 25, 29, 224; II 36; D 48; W 10, 16, 20
  in catharsis and analysis, D 25
  in conversion, II 102
  in imitation magic, III 266
  by laughter, III 181
  in tic, II 53, 153
ABSENT PERSONS, analysis of, III 59
ABSOLUTION, see Confession
ABSORPTION, *see* Psycho-analytic treattion, absorption; Trance
ABSTINENCE [*see also Alcoholism*], I 14, 38, 186
  during analysis [*see also Psycho-analytic treatment; Psycho-analytic technique*], II 202, 206, 271-2, 275-8, 289; III 37
  & anxiety, II 279
  marital, II 275
ABSTRACTION [*see also Logical relations; Thinking; Thoughts; Screening;* III 190, 195
  & details, III 275
  in mathematics & mental life, III 187
ABSURDITY (Absurd—), *see* Comic, Dream(s), Jokes, Laughter, Wit
ACCEPTANCE [*see also Compensation; Unpleasure*], II 366, III 80
ACCESSIBILITY, of the repressed, II 401
ACCIDENTS, railway —, W 8
'ACCIDENTS', importance of, in technological discovery, II 395
  as material in analysis, II 40
ACCOMPLICES, communion of, III 179
ACCUMULATIO LIBIDINIS, III 257
ACCUSATION, self-, *see* Self-accusation
  of the physician, *see* Patient(s)
ACQUIESCENCE and over-acquiescence, III 277
ACQUIRED CHARACTERS [*see also Heredity*], T 68
'ACTING-OUT' [*see also Abreaction; Action; Psycho-analysis; Psycho-analytic technique; Trance*], II 181; III 233-4
ACTION(s) [ACT(s)], freedom of, *see* Freedom; Patient(s)
  inhibition, unequal, resulting in — [*see also Inhibition*], II 381, 405
  limitation of, and repression [*see also Repression*], III 75

  obsessional, *see* Obsessional actions
  squandering through —, III 188
  & thought [thinking] [*see also Thinking; Thought(s)*], II 187, 232
  voluntary; bad habits, as intermediate between instinct and —, II 286
'ACTIVE THERAPY' Active technique, Activity, *see* Psycho-analytic technique, active
ACTUAL NEUROSES, II 16, *30-55*
  psychoses, III 356
  general paralysis as —, III 353
  hypochondria as —, III 355
ADAPTATION [Adjustment] [*see also Education; Identification*], II 375; III 62-3, 66-7, 221, 249; T 104; W 19
  alloplastic & autoplastic, II 163; III 221; T 92-3, 104
  & character, III 66-7
  & death (definition), III 243
  & devouring, II 229-30
  of the family to the child, II *61-76*
  as interrupted destruction, III 225
  new personality through, III 225
  onto — & phylogenesis of, II 37, 375
  organic, inflexibility of, II 375
  'pleasure of', *see* Pleasure of adaptation
  & regression, II 376
  instead of self-reconstruction, III 221
  & splitting [*see also Fragmentation; Splitting*], III 220
  & superego formation, III 229
  in the unwelcome child, defective, III 106
ADDICTION to alcohol, *see* Alcoholism
  to unpleasure, in masochism, III 244
ADJUSTMENT, *see* Adaptation
ADLER, I 148, 231; II 211-12, 449; III 25
ADMIRATION, in homosexuality, I 176
  in masochism, III 244
  of the opponent, III 225, 244
  & self-destruction, III 225
'ADOPTION' of neurotic patients, III 124-5
ADULT(s) [*see also Maturity; Parents*], I 72; II 330; III 156-7, *163*, 263
  child analysis in the analysis of, III 122-3, *126-42*, 136
  & children, *see* Child(ren); Parents
  flatus, as prerogative of, II 325
  hypocrisy towards child, III 133, 163
  incestuous tendencies & tenderness [*see also Incest; Incestuous*], III 121
ADVICE [*see also Psycho-analyst; Psychoanalytical technique*], II 184, 197, 235, 237

INDEX

AESTHETICS [Aesthetic pleasure] [*see also Art*], I 305, 325; III 225
AETIOLOGY [Aetiological factor(s) of neurotic & psychotic diseases] [*see also Constitution; Heredity; Predisposition*], I 37, 39, 50, 52
  hereditary explanation of, II 24, 49, 53–4, 248; III 67
  hypersensibility and mistreatment, role of, III 120–1
  social advancement of family, role of, II 417
  traumatic explanation of, II 24, 36–7, 52, 248; III 110; D 48
AFFECT(S) [*see also Abreaction; Emotion(s); Transference*], I 39, 44–5, 50, 63, 256, 272, 277, 305, 314, 315; D 38
  of analyst, *see* Psycho-analyst, affects
  discharge of
    genital excitement & conversion as, III *218*
    increased, by fragmentation, III 230
  in dreams, II 345
  excessive, & 'petite hystérie', III *218*
  & idea(s), II 216
  negative, in paranoia, I 155
  in neurosis, II 345
  'squandering' of, and introjection, III 218
  in symbol formation, I 280–1
AFFECT HYSTERIA [*see also Affect(s); Hysteria*], III 218
AFFECTION [*see also Emotion; Incest; Love; Tenderness*]
  lack of, in mother, III 227
  between lovers, & the sex act, III 257, 267
  between men, I 317
AGE, OLD [Age of involution], as contraindication for analysis, III 278
  cynicism & maliciousness in, III 205
  dementia, *see* Dementia senile
  of involution, III *205–12*
  love in, III 206–8
  masturbation in, III 205, 208
  object-cathexes, abandonment of, in, III 205–7
  sexual differences and bisexuality in, T 106–7
  Swift on —, III 211
AGGRESSION [Aggressiveness; Aggressivity] [*see also Aggressor; Destruction; Lust-murder; Murder; Murderous; Rage; Revenge; Ruthlessness; Sadism; Seduction; Self-destruction*]
  & abstinence, II 277
  & anxiety, III 219
  in coitus, T 35
  & discharge of tensions in the infant, III *219*
  disclosed by comparisons, II 398
  forced fantasies of, II 72–3
  & frustration (oral), III 219

  irritation, as unconscious —, III 32
  in jokes, II 339–40
  male, I 302, T 105
  & myth, T 266
  object relations of child disturbed by adult —, III 227
  & obscene words, I 141
  in paranoia, III 32
  of patient, *see* Patient(s), aggressiveness; Psycho-analytic treatment, aggression
  in repression and resistance similar, III 237
  in women, III 34, 205
AGGRESSOR [*see also Identification; Infantile sexual trauma; Seduction*], III 224–5, 228, 244
  assimilation of, by pretraumatic personality, III 228
  displacement of unpleasure on to, III 244
  identification with, III 163–4, 244
AGORAPHOBIA, II 34, 58
'AHA'-EXPERIENCE, III 269
AICHHORN, August; III 39, 128
ALCOHOLISM [Alcoholic indulgence], I 130, 162,; III 43
  a case of, I 157–63; II 113, 245
  & homosexuality, I 161–2, 315; III 212
  & manic exaltation, III 181, 209–10
  & neurosis, I 163
  & paranoia, I 157–62; III 212
  & self-destructive tendencies, III 104
ALEXANDER, III 102
ALGEBRA [*see also Arithmetic; Mathematics*], III 183, 186, 187, 190, 192
ALGOLAGNIA, *see* Masochism
'ALIENATING OVER', of pains, III 265 [*see also Regression*]
ALLOPLASTIC, *see* Adaptation
ALTRUISM, III 224–6, 248, 251–3
AMBISEXUALITY [Amphierotism] [*see also Bisexuality*], I 107, 184, 296, 302, 303, 312, 314
AMBITION (Ambitiousness), I 59, 117, 207; III 262–3
  & urethral erotism, I 208; III 33
AMBIVALENCE [Ambivalency] [*see also Defusion*], I 246–7, 260; II 372, 409–10
  & laughter, III 180
AMENTIA and reality, III 31
AMNESIA (infantile), I 77, 177; III 62, 71, *278–9*
AMNESIA (retroactive), I 77; II 130; W 7
  as defensive mechanism against memory of trauma, III 231
AMNIOTIC [*see also Intrauterine*], fluid & sac, T 50, 56–7
AMORALITY, *see* Morality
AMPHIBIA, origin of coitus in, T 63–4
  development from fishes, T 100

AMPHI-EROTISM [*see Ambisexuality, Bisexuality*]
AMPHIMIXIS [*see also Displacement(s)*]
  of auto-erotism, II 172
  in children, T 13
  and coitus, T *15*
  in ejaculation, T *1*
  erotic [of erotisms], T 5, 14, 97-8
  theory of, II 263-4; T 10-11
  & voyeurism, T 13
AMPUTATED WOMEN, desire for, II 361
ANAESTHESIA [Analgesia] (psychogenic), I 42, 75, 147; II 98, 112-15
  sexual, *see* Frigidity
  stigmatic & traumatic, II 114-15
  as symbol for 'death', III 139
ANAESTHETIC(S) [*see also Drugs*], narcotics, use of, during analysis, II 28-9
  shocks in trance compared to —, III 239
ANAGOGIC INTERPRETATION, D 36-7
ANAL [*see also Anus; Rectum*], I 208, 209, 329
  auto-erotism, *see* Anal erotism; Auto-erotism
  character [*see also Anal erotism*], II 257, 264, 266
  '— children', II 307, 408
  erotogenic zone, *see* Erotogenic zone(s),
  anal fantasies & stammering, II 251
  habits, *see* Habits
  orgasm, *see* Orgasm, anal
  '— penis', II 314-15, 317; T 9
  sphincter, *see* Sphincter, anal
  symbols, eggs & vermin, as, II 327-8
  symptoms, typical, II 327
  technique in impotence, T 6
ANAL EROTISM [Anal character; Anal satisfaction(s)] [*see also Constipation; Coprolalia; Coprophilia; Defaecation; Retention; Urethral erotism*], I 16, 108, 134, 310, 317, 322, 328-31; II 172, 258, 261-2, 266, 270, 302, 328, 347, 420-1; III 363
  & aesthetics, I 325
  in ageing women, III 205
  & avarice, I 320; II 248, 257; III 33
  & bowels, II 82, 94
  & castration complex, II 248
  & comparison, II 397, 398
  & counting, economizing, III 188
  in general paralysis, III 363
  & hate, sadism, III 33
  & masochism, II 47
  & money, I 320; II 362-4
  & object homo-erotism, I 307, 317
  in proverb, II 365
  & smell and odours, II 362-4
  & speech, II 251
  & sphincter play, II 204
  & sublimation, I 324-5
  & tics, III 349
  unsublimated, I 328
  & urethral erotism, II 263; T 11
ANALGESIA, *see* Anaesthesia
ANALOGY [Analogies], *see* Comparison(s)
ANALYSAND, *see* Patient(s); Training analysis
'ANALYSING, COMPULSIVE —', III 98-9
ANALYSIS, chemical, psycho-analysis compared to —, D 34, 65
  lay, *see* Lay analysis
  psycho-, *see* Psycho-analysis
  'wild' [Analyst, 'wild'], *see* 'Wild' analysis [analyst]
'ANALYSIS, GROUP —, & THE ANALYSIS OF THE EGO' (Freud), review of —, III 371-6
'ANCESTORS, EATING UP THE —', and super-ego formation, III 229
ANDREAS-SALOMÉ, L., I 326
ANGER, *see* Rage
ANGINA PECTORIS NERVOSA, I 26
ANIMAL(S), III 183, 224-5; T 69
  autotomy in, II 160; T 9, 63
  'dying', feeling of, projected on to lifeless thing or —, III 221
  as father-figure, I 248
  homosexuality non-existent in —, III 173
  hypnosis of, maternal & paternal, III 339
  imitation of, III 265-6
  fragmentation process in, III 229-230
  narcissism in, II 375
  obedience in, *see* Animals, hypnosis of; Animals, taming
  play of, I 238
  self-castration in, T 30
  sex in, T 26-7, 29, 31-2
  small—, & Gulliver fantasies, III 50
  as symbols for penis, III 53
  taming of a wild horse, III 336-40
  unicellular —, symbiosis in, T 62
ANIMALCULISTS, T 65
ANIMISM, I 227-8, 275; II 256, 393
ANOREXIA, *see* Appetite, loss of
ANOIA, non-paretic, III 369
ANTENATAL, *see* Intrauterine
ANTHROPOLOGY, *see* Ethnology
ANTHROPOMORPHISM, I 49
ANTIPATHY [Aversion] [*see also Sympathy*], I 43, 54, 64, 65, 82, 86; III 95
ANUS [*see also Anal; Rectum*], erotogenicity of, & patho-neuroses, II 85
  pruritus of, II 269
ANXIETY [*see also Anxiety hysteria; Castration Fear; Panic*], I 30, 74, 82, 113, 115, 272, 306; II 134, 161, 162; III 24, 264; (definition), III 249
  (definitions, different, by Freud), III 36
  & abstinence, II 279
  & aggressivity, III 219
  & anal & urethral constriction, II 268

& birth trauma [*see also* Birth trauma], I 220; II 354; III 64; T 39
& coitus, T 39, 43
'courage for madness without—', III 251
-delirium in agitated paralytics, III 367-8
-dreams, I 17-18, 107, 273 [*see also* Nightmares]
& ego-psychology, III 36
& exacerbation of pain (& other symptoms), III 27
& forgiveness, III 179
& frustration, II 35; III 218, 219, 253
& Gulliver fantasies, III 43
hysterical, *see* Anxiety hysteria
of hypochondriacs, II 58, 118
& inability to adaptation in situation of unpleasure, III 249
infantile, II 331; III 66; D 10
& libido, II 300, 331; III 253
& lust-murder fantasies, II 278-9
& masochism, III 244
& paranoia, III 249-50
pavor nocturnus, II 111
& protection of instinctual energies, T 64
& real tasks, III 264-5
release of, and self-destruction, III 249
& repetition, D 4
stage fright, II 421-2
states, I 209; III 233
& trauma, III 249-50
virginal, II 35
& war neuroses, W 19
ANXIETY HYSTERIA [*see also* Anxiety neurosis], I 72, 74, 90, 163; II 277; III 156-7
active technique in, II 196, 209, 236
psycho-analysis of, II 201
in war neurotics, II 133-5, 139; W 19
ANXIETY NEUROSIS [*see also* Anxiety hysteria], I 14, 18, 34, 46, 107, 275; II 14, 32-4, 107, 130, 195, 277, 300; III 24, 217; (definition), II 253
& coitus interruptus, II 35; III 24, 217
& ejaculatio praecox, II 35
retardata, II 277; T 7
a case of —, II 353
& Gulliver fantasies, III 43-4
& libido, II 34-5, 275; III 217, 253
& neurasthenia, II 34; III 253
& rage, III 253
APHONIA and infantile sexual trauma, III 246
APHORISTIC WRITINGS, III 271
APPARATUS, mental, *see* Mind
APPETITE [*see also* Hunger], II 326; III 356; T 211
self-destructive tendencies in loss of —, III 103
APROSEXIA, I 186

ARITHMETIC [*see also* Algebra; Mathematics], II 183, 186, 188, 192
ARK, as uterus symbol, T 49
ART [*see also* Aesthetics; Artist(s)], I 305; II 116, 214, 389
& anal character, II 419-21
artistic endowment, & hysteria, II 104
production & narcissism, II 420
ARTIFICIAL PRODUCTS, collecting of, I 326
ARTIST(s), antipathy against psychoanalysis, III 87
ASCETISM, *see* Abstinence
ASCHAFFENBURG, W., W 7, 16
ASEXUAL CHARACTER, of children (alleged), III 71
of social 'identification', III 375
A-SOCIAL CHARACTER of the heterosexual instinct, III 376
ASSIMILATION, of aggressor, *see* Aggressor
of superego, *see* Superego
ASSAULT, SEXUAL [*see also* Infantile sexual trauma]
& repetition compulsion, II 140
& tics, II 226; III 349
ASSOCIATION(s), I 19, 20, 25, 44, 51, 98-100, 114, 116, 117, 119, 143, 197, 202, 205, 211, 229, 317; II 29, 40, 177, 181, 183, 221, 284, 289, 426; III 188
'being dead', represented in, III 223
collecting of, D 28-9
condensation as physiological analogy to, III 256
dematerialization in, III 223
dispersal in —, II 61
experiments, Jung's, II 38; III 111
free, *see* Psycho-analytic rule(s), fundamental
musical, III 175-6
resistance, II 178-9
ASTASIA [*see also* Motor disturbances], II 134, 135, 138; W 19
ASTHMA, bronchial [*see also* Lungs; Respiration], III 25, 103, 278
ATAVISM in war neuroses, W 20
ATOMIZATION, *see* Split
ATTACK(s) [*see also* Convulsion(s); Epilepsy; Hysteria; Trance]
during analysis [*see also* Trance], III 130-2, 139-40, 156-7; 261
hysterical [*see also* Hysteria], III 119, 233-4,
& 'professional hypocrisy' of the analyst, III 158-9
sexual, *see* Assault, sexual
ATTENTION [*see also* Concentration], II 230, 231-2, 401-2; III 23
& censorship, II 400-1, 404
diversion from actual reality, in analytical process, II 233, 238
inhibition of, *see* Inhibition
ATTITUDE, *see* Behaviour
AUTARCHY [*see also* Egoism], III 252

AUTHORITY, II 438; III 71
AUTO-EROTISM [see also Egoism; Masturbation; Narcissism], I 64, 155, 208, 209, 233-6, 294, 298, 321; III 68-9; T 11, 86
& amphimixis, II 172
& genitalization of parts of the body, II 172
regression from object-love to, II 309
in sleep, T 74
AUTO-HYPNOSIS [AUTO-SUGGESTION] [see also Trance], T 59, 71, 82-5
AUTOMATISM, I 37, 76; II 299; III 177
AUTOMATON, misused children, behaviour analogous to, III 162-3
as organ-projection, II 390
AUTOPLASTIC ADAPTATION, see Adaptation, autoplastic [see also Reality]
AUTOSYMBOLISM [Autosymbolic, Functional phenomenon], I 217; III 135, 194, 221, 247-8
ego memory system, as reproduction of the, III 221
& historical representation, III 221
& mathematics, III 183
of resistance, in post-traumatic mental processes, III 234
AUTOTOMY (Autotomic tendency) [see also Body; Masochism; Scratching; Sequestration], II 160; III 202; T 9, 63
adaptation, autoplastic, preceded by, III 220
& origin of life, T 70
& repression, T 83
sex act as —, T 30
AVARICE [see also Anal eroticism; Money], I 320, 328; II 248, 257; III 33
AVERSION, see Antipathy; Disgust
AWAKENING [see also Nightmare; Trance], III 223, 232-3, 236

BABINSKI REFLEX, in sleep, T 75-6
BABY [Babies], see Child(ren); Childhood; Infant(s); Newborn
'BAD LIAR', III 262
BADNESS & seriousness, III 179-80
BASKET, dream-figure, I 123
BAUER, W 8
BAYLE on general paralysis, III 354
BEAURAIN, I 276
BED-LINEN, symbolism of, II 359
BEETLES, fear of, I 272
BEHAVIOUR, 'intelligence' producing correct physical and psychical —, III 230-1
'BEING dead [Dying]', feeling of, see Dead; Dying; Split
'BEING' & 'having', III 374
BELIEF, see Conviction
BELLES-LETTRES, & psychology, I 18
BERGSON, on laughter, III 177, 182
BERNHEIM, I 58, 67; III 372

'BESIDE ONESELF', feeling of getting —, III 222-3
'BESITZ.', meaning of, I 138, 326
BIOANALYSIS, I *82*, 93, 102; II 276, 370, 375, 377
BIOGENESIS [Caenogenesis], T 45-6, 103
BIOLOGY [see also Adaptation; Biological]
physiological changes, expressed in psychic processes, II 98
& psycho-analysis, II 104; D 36, 65; T 84, 87
of 'utility' & of 'pleasure', II 103; T 83
BIOLOGICAL [see also Biology]
aspects of death, T 67, 95
bisexuality, I 184, 296
censorship, see Censorship, biological
model of superego formation, III *227-31*
role of the cerebrospinal system, III 255-256
significance of sphincters, II 267-8
situations, repressed, reappearing in symbols, T 87
theory of functional psychoses (cellular changes), III 19
unconscious, the —, T 83, 85
BIRNBAUM, W 7, 12
BIRTH [see also Birth fantasies; Birth trauma; Confinement; Pregnancy], I 220
incompleteness of — (Freud), T 73
as recapitulation of retreat from ocean, T 45
symbolism, II 44-5; III 36; T 42-3
BIRTH FANTASIES [Birth theories] [see also Birth; Birth trauma], II 307, 399; III 36, 55-6
& examination dream, III 47
Rank on, II 296
BIRTH TRAUMA [Birth shock], III 47, 64-5
& anxiety, see Anxiety
& castration complex, III 45-7
coitus as denial of, T 40
as a substitute for sexual trauma, III 45-6
theory of — (Rank), II 223, 296; III 36-37, 45, 47-8, 54, 58, 64
BISEXUALITY [see also Ambisexuality], I 21, 184, 296; T 23, 102-3, 107
mutual co-ordination & domination, III 257
in myth, I 262
in old age, I 107
BITING, in dream, I 19
BJERRE, P., II 211; T 78
BLADDER [see also Micturition; Urethral], I 207; II 264
BLASPHEMIES, I 151
BLEULER, I 218
BLINDING [see also Eye(s)], I 248, 263-4; III 52
BLOOD, idiosyncrasy against, I 305
BLUSHING, III 48

BODY [see also Organic; Somatic], III 44
  ego & mental ego, III 358
  feeling of being bodily dead, III 222
  & genitals, II 269; III 36, 46–7
  'leap from psychic to —', in hysteria, II 90–1, 100, 173
  maternal, see Intrauterine; Mother, body of; Womb
  parts of — [see also Organ]
    genitalized, I 273–5; II 82, 85; III 48
    'permitted —', as substitutes, III 219
  sensations, see sense-perceptions
  'sequestration', in catatonia, III 358–9
BONHÖFFER, W 9, 12, 13, 15
BOOKS, obsessive fear of, case, II 50
'BOTANIC method' of sex education, III 69–70
BOUGH, broken, as symbol, T 48
BOWEL(s) [see also Anal erotism; Constipation; Defaecation; Diarrhoea; Digestion; Excrements], II 82, 94, 265–6
  & facial tic & masturbation, II 271
BOY(s) [see also Child], I 305; III 58, 104, 161–2
BÖLSCHE, T 46, 62
BRAIN [Cerebral] [see also Intelligence; Mental; Pathoneurosis;
  anatomy of, & mental disease, II 17–18
  as counting machine, see Counting machine
  as 'erotogenic' zone, III 353
  & genitals, II 99; III 353–4
  haemorrhage as emission, III 255
  metaluetic affection, traumatic effect of, III 354
  pathology of, & mental disease, I 58–9, 63; II 17–18; III 18–20, 353–4, 362
BRANTÔME (quotation on incestuous fantasies), III 335
BREAKFAST, children's disgust for, II 326
BREAST [see also Sucking], I 147; III 218–19
BREATHING [see also Odour; Respiration; Smell]
  on penis, orgasm by —, II 227
BREATHLESSNESS [see also Asthma], hysterical, & infantile sexual trauma, III 246
BREUER, Joseph, Dr., I 29; II 36, 153; III 109, 143, 145, 184, 218
BRIDGE as symbol, II 352–3, 356
BRILL, A. A., Dr., III 41
BROODING, philosophic, case of, II 49–50
BRUTALITY [Brutal force], absurd and naïve, III 225–6
  of another ego, motherliness as appreciation of —, III 226
BULL, dream of, I 108
BURIAL, presence at own —, as symbol, II 357
'BURSTING', III 237

CAENOGENESIS, see Biogenesis
CALCULATION [Calculus], see Counting
CALUMNY, against doctor, see Psycho-analyst(s); Patient(s)
CANNIBALISTIC [see also Oral], fantasies, I 249; III 375
CAPITALISM, I 326
CARDIAC PAINS, see Heart
CASE HISTORIES
  'active technique', II 202–7
  alcoholism & paranoia, I 157–63
  anxiety-hysteria, I 74
  anxiety neurosis & ejaculato retardata, II 353
  asthma, III 111–12
  castration complex, II 78–80, 86; II 244
  child analysis technique, III 129
  convulsions, II 46–7
  dementia praecox, I 179–83, 285
  fainting, II 210, 356
  family-romance, II 413
  fear of dark, III 218
  Ferenczi's housekeeper, I 157
  fluctuation of resistances, III 246–8
  forgotten appointment, III 77–8
  globus hystericus, II 43
  grandfather, aggressiveness of, III 227
  Gulliver fantasies, III 46–7
  homosexuality, II 79; III 168
  hyperaesthesia, in war neurotic, II 140
  hypnotism (3 cases), I 72–6
  impotence, psychic, I 13
  infantile sexual trauma reappearing in dream, III 241–2
  involution (depression), III 207
  'a little Chanticleer', I 240–52
  masochistic orgasm, III 248–9
  obsessive fear of books, II 50
  paranoia, I 285
    subsequent to castration, II 78–9, 86
    with 'two voices', II 105–7
  paraphrenia, II 78–9
  recurrent double (self-repeating) dreams, III 239
  screen memory, III 219
  symptoms emerging during analysis, III 139
  'the wise baby', III 136
  washing compulsion, II 43
  word-memories, repressed, II 73
CASE HISTORIES, FRAGMENTS OF:
  B. III 227, 246–9, 258, 259
  C. III 168
  Dm. III 227, 249, 250, 263–5
  G. III 261–3
  H. III 227
  I. III 250
  S. III 227, 228, 250, 273
  T. III 168
  Tf III 224, 261–3, 267
  T.Z III 227

U. III 249, 263-4, 272-3
CASSIERER, W 7.
CASTRATION [see also Autotomy; Mutilation], I 34, 185, 186, 192, 200, 243, 247, 250, 264, 266, 270
  blinding as symbol for — (Oedipus myth), III 52
  Gulliver fantasy, as substitute for, III 45-7
  homosexuality, caused by, II 79
  paranoia, subsequent to, II 78-9, 86
CASTRATION COMPLEX [see also Castration fantasy; Castration fear; Castration threat], II 244, 278, 313; III 45-9; D 17, 33-4
  abandonment of —, as sign of termination of analysis, III 84
  a case of, II 78-80, 86
  & defects in one's children, II 120
  & father's occupation, II 419
  & female genitals, II 80, 307, 314-15, 361
  & narcissism, II 248
  & scratching on glass, II 313
CASTRATION FANTASY (fantasies), II 313-14; III 36, 45-9, 52-3
CASTRATION FEAR, I 34, 185, 247, 270-1; II 313, 419; III 35-7, 122
  & myth, I 266
  in old persons, III 207
  & shortsightedness, I 270-1
CASTRATION, SELF- [see also Autotomy], III 49; T 30, 40, 67
CASTRATION THREAT, I 243, 250-1; II 307, 313; T 107
  Ferenczi on —, III 34
  Freud on —, III 33
  & masochism, II 88
CATALEPSY, I 69; II 163-4, 402; T 78
CATALYSIS, analysis as, I 39
'CATASTROPHE'-theory of coitus, II 279
CATASTROPHES, GEOLOGICAL, and development, I 237; T 61-3, 69, 70, 101-2
CATATONIA [Catatonic] [see also Paraphrenia; Schizophrenia], I 284-5, 291, 294-5; II 163-5, 173
  & ego-hysteria, II 163, 173
  & obscene words, II 161, 165, 171, 226
  'sequestration' of the body in, III 358-9
  & tics, II 146-7, 162; III 349
CATHARSIS [see also Abreaction; Psychoanalytic technique, active], I 29; II 402; D 25, 37
  & 'active technique', differences, II 199, 212, 216
  & analytical therapy, II 37, 199, 499
  fractional, D 38
  neo —, III 156-8, *223-4*, 232-3
  & frustration principle, III 111-14

spontaneous, III 223, 232
  & suggestion, III 243
  in trance state, see Trance
CATHEXIS [Cathexes] (of libido), III 356; D 10
  of the analyst, III 98
  in coitus, T 38
  counter —, III 251, 264, 359
  defensive, III 224
  & falling in love, III 376
  object —, see Object-love
  'polarization' of, III, 364
  re-, in paralytic actual psychosis, III 356
  in war neuroses, II 141; III 352
CAUSALITY, lacking in dreams, I 124-5
CAUSATION, knowledge about, III 221
CENSOR(SHIP) [Censuring instances], [see also Superego], I 25, 93, 103-5, 109, 111, 113, 117, 127-9, 136, 210; II 37, 54, 380-2; III 187
  (definition), I 104
  biological, T 89
  & comparisons, II 400-4
  in dreams, see Dreams
  & inhibited thought, II 231
  lack of, in paranoia, III 212, 215
  through laughter, III 179
  in politics & erotic literature, II 405
  relaxation of, in doctor's presence, I 403
  after split of the ego, III 241-2
'CENSURE-POISON', I 162
CEREBRAL, see Brain
CEREBROSPINAL SYSTEM, III 255-6
CEREMONIALS, obsessive, rooted in childish activities, II 284
CEREMONIOUSNESS, III 33
CESSATION, see Disappearance, of symptoms; Psycho-analysis, termination
CHAIR, broken, dream-figure, I 110-11
CHANTICLEER, Little, I *240-52*
CHANTING, as holding off of death, III 274
CHARACTER [see also Character traits; Personality; Superego; Trauma], I 37, 44, 47, 141, 145, 148, 150, 202, 206, 207, 237; II 212, 263, 290, 363; T 68
  (definition), III 66
  & adaptation, see Adaptation
  -analysis [see also Ego-psychology; Psycho-analysis; Psycho-analytic technique], III 32-5, 80-2, 85
  use of 'active' technique in, II 211, 214-15, 263, 266, 291
  development & oral gratifications, III 219
  & erotic traits, II 257
  & inheritance, III 67; T 68
  as obsessional symptom, III 66
  & Oedipus Complex, I 258-9
  & organic illness, II 82
  & psychosis, II 212, 215, 291

-regression, II 363
  during analysis, *see* Psycho-analytic process
  -synthesis after analysis, III 80–1
  & toilet training of the child, III 66
CHARACTER-TRAITS [*see also Character*], II 257, 266, 418; III 104
  anal, urethral, etc, *see* Anal-; Urethral-, etc.
  & tics, II 152–3; III 81
CHARCOT, I 58, 83; III 67; W 11
CHEMISTRY, physiological & psychoanalysis, D 65
CHEMITAXIS [Chemotaxis], II 88
CHILD(REN) [*see also Adults; Child analysis; Childhood; Education; Father; Infants; Infantile; Mother; Parents*], I 77, 107, 215, 276–7, 325–6; II 284, 325–7, 427, 443; III 71, 83–4, 120–1, 132; T 13
  & acquisition of knowledge, passive, III 269
  adaptation of family to, III 61–76
  & anal interest, [*see also Dirt*] I 321; III 67–8
  auto-erotism & 'bad habits' of, III 68–9
  bisexuality of, *see* Bisexuality
  colds of, III 102
  & the comic, III 171, 182
  & duplicity of moral standards, III 73
  ego of, I 48; III 72–3
  egoism of, III 226
  & exhibitionism of parents, II 320–1
  genital analogies used by, I 279
  gratifications of adults or children different, III 166–7
  guilt feelings in, III 70–1, 163
  & hypocrisy of environment, III 133
  incestuous tendencies, *see* Incestuous; Oedipus complex
  living in the present, III 279
  love needed by, III 268
  micturition, as libido reward [*see also Micturition*], II 317
  mistrust in, III 71
  monism of, I 48; II 366
  motor character of [*see also Motility; Motor*], I 148
  & narcissism of adults, II 330
  negativism in, II 367
  neurotic [*see also Child analysis*], I 240–52; III 66, 71
  Oedipus-situation in the eyes of, III 268
  & omnipotence, *see* Omnipotence
  & his parents, *see* Father; Mother; Parents
  passionate adult love, superimposed on child [*see also Love, over-passionate*], III 163–5
  precocious, *see* Infant prodigies
  & primal scene, *see* Coitus, observation & comments by the child
  seduction of [*see also Infantile sexual trauma; Seduction*], III 161–3, 230, 241, 245–8
  sexuality of, I 26–7, 32, 108, 279; III 68–71
  signals used by —, to secure satisfaction, I 223–4
  superego formation in, III 72–3
  symbols for, II 318, 361; T 49–50
  tics, contagious, in, II 165
  traumata, suffered by, *see* Infantile sexual trauma; Seduction; Violation
  & ununderstanding adults, III *156–7*, 167
  unwelcome [unwanted], III *102*
  visual character of, I 148
  want of tenderness, III 104, 121
  'without milieu', II 320–1
CHILD ANALYSIS [*see also Child, neurotic; Education*], III 38–9, 61–2, 66, 69, 278–9
  active technique in, II 46
  in the analysis of adults, *see* Adults
  'pre-treatment' for (A. Freud), III 106
CHILDHOOD [*see also Child, etc.*], I 23, 26, 28, 41, 50, 60, 70–2, 76, 79–81, 104, 106–8, 110, 111, 147, 179, 185, 197, 208, 216–19, 231, 256, 273–5, 296, 297, 307, 315, 320; II 76;
  affects & transference in, I 63
  hypocrisy experienced in, III 133
  libido development in, II 331
  masochistic impulses in, I 107, 249
  memories (Childhood memory; Childhood reminiscences) [*see also Cover memories*], I 33, 70–1, 84, 90, 101, 108, 110; 264–5
  incompletely lived out, III 262–4
  neurosis, behind every neurosis, D 18
  sadistic impulses in, I 107, 246
  shame & psychosexual inhibition, I 31–2, 33
  wish fantasies & Gulliver fantasies, III 44
CHIROMANCY, III 274
CHOKING, in dream, I 87, 90
CHOREA, II 18
CIGAR, symbol, II 357
CIRCULATORY disturbances, nervous, self-destructive tendencies in, II 103
CIRCUMCISION, II 228, 244–9
CIVILIZATION, II 389; III 67–8, 140–1, 166
CLAIRVOYANCE [Clairvoyant], III 243
CLAPARÈDE, Ed., III 339; T 79
CLAUSTROPHOBIA [*see also Hysteria*], I 51; II 357
CLEANLINESS [*see also Toilet training*], I 322, 325, 328; III 33, 67–8

CLIMACTERIC, III 206
CLIMBING UP TOWER, feeling of, III 222
CLITORIS (Clitoric erotism) [*see also* Genital(s); Masculine; Masculinity; Woman]
CLOACA, coitus through the, T 52-3, 59
CO-EDUCATION, III 73-4
COHABITATION, *see* Coitus
COITUS (Sexual Act) [*see also* Conjugation; Copulation; Ejaculation; Impotence; Orgasm; Potency; Unicellular(s)*], I 13-16, 19, 23, 29, 89, 108, 135, 158-61, 166, 168, 180, 191, 250, 263, 266, 269, 271, 274, 301, 308; T 60-72, 73-80
aggression in, II 279; T 35
alloplastic technique in, T 74
& amphimixis, T *15*
& anxiety, II 35, 279; III 24, 36, 216-7,
as autotomy & self-castration, T 30, 40
biological nature of, T 57, 63-4, 75, 100
& birth symbolism, III 36, 44-5
'catastrophe' theory of, II 279
cloacal, T 52-3, 59
& consciousness, T 35-6
& defaecation, T 6
without ejaculation, II 277
as denial of birth trauma, T 40
emotions, during & after, I 187-8; III 182, 208-9; T 33-4, 56;
epileptic fits, as surrogates, III 203
fantasied, of the impotent (Freud on —), II 269
-fantasies of father as predecessor in sexual intercourse, III 341
& fertilization, T 60, 63
Freud's conception of, T 53
& genital friction, T 28-30
identifications in, T 18
infantile theories of, III 51-2
interruptus or reservatus, II 35; III 24, 217
introjection in, T 74
& mother-fantasies, I 146; III 36
nervous process in, I 189-90
nocturnal emission & masturbation, III *216-17*
observation and comments by the child, III 65-6, 167, 268
& orgasm, *see* Orgasm
physiological nature of, II 103; T 37, 74
pleasure & unpleasure in, T 34-5, 38
posture, T 75
processes of sexual act, analysis of, T *28*
as punishment for Don Juan type, II 358
regression in, T 18, 73, 74
respiration in, T 34-5, 56, 75

rhythmicity, T 35
& scratch-reflex, T 30
& sleep, T 36, 73
stimuli (external), excluded in, T 74
symbols, III 36, T 42-5
unorgiastic, III 271
COLDS, III 102, 104
COLLECTING, I 326; D 28-9
COMA [Comatose], *see* Dying; Hypnotism; Sleep; Trance; Unconsciousness
COMIC(AL) [*see also* Automatism; Joke(s); Laughter; Ridicule; Wit], II 342-3; III *178*, 225, 268
(definition), II 342-3; III 177-8
COMMAND-AUTOMATISM(S), post-hypnotic, I 76
COMMUNICATIONS, *see* Empathy; Imitation; 'Mitteilen'; Patient
COMPARISON(S) [Analogies; Metaphors; Similes], II *397*
aggression in, II 398
& anal erotism, II 397, 398
during analysis, II *184*, *397*, 400
of dying, *see* Dead; Death
of the ego, III 222
genitals, childish analogies to, I 279
of neurosis, II 398; III 228
psychic conditions in making, II 400
similes distinguished from symbols, I 277-8
of trance, *see* Trance
in transference, I 42
COMPENSATION(S), II 369; III 362; W 8
& acceptance of unpleasant ideas, II *366*, 369
'Recompenses' (Tausk), III 362-3
COMPLEX(ES) [*see also* under individual headings], I 25, 29, 36, 39, 42, 43, 45, 51, 52, 56, 57, 59, 60, 62, 64, 67, 72, 80, 83, 86, 88, 91, 96, 112, 118, 125, 128, 129, 135, 143-8, 177, 198, 212, 235, 258, 265, 267, 271, 293, 321, 329; D 31, 34-5, 51
breeding of, II 37-8; D 33
& free associations, II 38
in the 'healthy', I 12
repressed —, are always sexual, II 41-2
COMPULSION [*see also* Obsession(al)], I 25, 77, 237, 306, 318
to dance, II 161
neurosis, I 46, 185, 218, 234, 235, 303, 306, 312, 318
to occupy hands, II 316
repetition —, [*see also* Repetition] II 102
to seduce men, III 227
of symmetrical touching, II *242*
washing —, II *311*
'COMPULSIVE ANALYSING', III 98-9
CONCENTRATION [*see also* Attention; Thinking], II 401-4

CONCEPTION & UNIFICATION (in logic), III 191
CONCEPTS, I 121, 276
CONCERT TICKET, dream figure, I 109
CONCRETIZATION, in dreams, I 121
CONDENSATION, I 100, 113, 115, 118, 126, 266, 276; III 188, 192-4; T 82
& association, III 256
CONDITIONALISM, I 232
CONDITIONED REFLEXES, III 63
CONFESSION, & analysis, contrasted, II 216
CONFIDENCE, disappointed, in neurotics [*see also Patient(s)*], III 270
CONFINEMENT [*see also* Birth], disgust at, III 218
CONFLICT(s) (*see also* under the appropriate subjects), mental, I 12, 32, 56, 96; D 10
dealing with, in alloplastic or autoplastic way, III 227
CONFUSION [*see also Senseless*], III 221
of tongues, III 156
CONGENITAL between adults & child [*see also Constitution; Heredity; Predisposition*]; I 27, 28, 148, 319, 320
CONGESTION, in the head, III 234
& infantile sexual trauma, III 241, 246
CONJUGATION [*see also Coitus; Unicellular(s)*], T 58, 62
CONSCIENCE [*see also Censor(ship); Super-ego*], I 23, 122, 177, 301
CONSCIOUS [*see also Instances, psychic, the Conscious*]
reaction against unconscious wish-fulfilment, I 18
superstructure, corresponding to cerebrospinal system, III 256
CONSCIOUSNESS, I 16-19, 21, 35, 43, 48, 53, 65, 66, 112, 113, 140, 147, 152, 175, 195, 199, 210, 212, 277, 301, 311
& concentration, II 404
& censorship, II 380
& inhibition, II 381
loss of –, III 118-19, 230-1, 236, 241
passive character of, II 380
reduction of, in coitus, T 35-6
CONSONANTS, *see* Vowels and consonants
CONSTIPATION [*see also Anal eroticism; Bowels; Defaecation; Digestion; Digestive disturbances; Excrements*], I 208, 329; II 94-5; III 25, 210; T 6
CONSTITUTION [*see also Body; Congenital; Heredity; Predisposition*],
ego & libido, as the weak points of, III 365
& homosexuality, III 173
nervous, of the offspring of syphilitics, III 364
neurasthenic, III 217
urethral-erotic, II 268

CONTEMPLATION [*see also Thinking*], II 372
CONTEMPT (Contemptuous), *see* Grimace;
CONTRADICTION, indirect, I 203
CONTRA-INDICATIONS, *see* Psycho-analysis; Psycho-analytic technique
CONVERSION(s) hysterical [Hysterical conversion in general] [*see also Hysteria; War neuroses*; and under the various symptoms], I 46, 154, 185, 200, 225, 235; II 82, 91, 99, 223, 438, 444
(definition), II 90
& abreaction, II 102; III 218
active therapy seldom necessary, II 209
& bodily representations
of fantasies, II 89-90, 101, 173
of genital impulses, II 85, 89, 102, 173
breathlessness as, III 246
convulsions as, II 46-7
in digestive tract, II 92
& displacements [*see also Displacements*], I 275; II 102, 241, 268; T 82
as exhaustion, II 241
female proneness to, T 25
Freud's views on, II 35-7
& giddiness, II 241; III 221
'idiom', II 100
& inheritance, III 218
innervation changes in, *see* Muscle
& leap from psychic to bodily, II 90-1, 100, 173, 232
& materialization [*see also Materialization*], I 10-11; II 89
& obesity, III 228-9
& onto & phylogenesis, III 218
pains, *see* Pain(s), hysterical
'physical approach' in, II 173
as regression, III 261
as repetition, III 221
of repetition into recollection, III 124
repression in, II 102-3
& skin sensibility, disturbances of, II 111
stigmata, II 110; III 218
& symbolism, II 89, 100-1
& traumatic neuroses, II 156
& war neuroses, II 128, 131; W 19
CONVICTION [*see also Doubts; Incredulity; Scepticism*], I 231; II 437-50; D 45
in analysis, *see* Psycho-analysis, aims; Psycho-analytic technique; Psycho-analytic technique, active; Transference
lack of
in obsessional neurosis, II 228, 436, 444
in paranoia, II 26-7, 438
CONVULSIONS [*see also Attack(s); Epilepsy; Hysteria*], case of, II 46-7

INDEX

CO-ORDINATION, mutual, III 257
COPROLALIA [Coprophemia], I 150
  & tic, II 146, 152, 165, 171, 196, 226
COPROPHAGIA, II 47, 325-6; T 14
COPROPHEMIA, see Coprolalia
COPROPHILIA [see also Anal erotism], I 38, 66, 143, 150, 305, 307, 323, 325, 328, 329
COPULATION, [see also Coitus; Conjugation], T 58
CORNELIA, mother of the Gracchi, II 318
CORNS, I 272
CORPSE, see Dead; Death
CORPULENCE [Corpulent], see Fat [Fatness]
COUGHING, I 210; III 26
COUNTER-CATHEXIS [see also Cathexis; Libido], III 251, 264, 359
COUNTER-RESISTANCE [see also Resistance], III 124
COUNTER-TRANSFERENCE [see also Patient; Psycho-analyst(s); Transference], II 186-8, III 124,
  negative, II 180; III 95, 159, 272
COUNTING [Calculation; Reckoning], II 370, 375, 378; III 183, 275
  as holding off of death, III 274
  'reckoning', double meaning of the word, II 378
COURTSHIP, I 31; T 30-3, 103
COVER-MEMORY [Screen memory] [see also Memories], I 22, 62, 76; II 38, 39
COVETOUSNESS [Greed], I 45, W 8
COWARDICE, I 15, 17-20, 200
CRAMMING & forgetting, III 263
CRAMP(S), I 200; II 170; III 48
  & expressive gestures, III 180
CREDULITY [see also Convictions; Doubt(s); Incredulity]
  & scepticism, III 263-4
CRIME [see also Totemism], II 431, 432, 435; III 203
CRIMINAL PSYCHOLOGY [Criminology], analytic, II 431-2, 434; III 39
CRUELTY [see also Aggressiveness; Masochism; Sadism], I 19-20, 78, 79, 107, 119, 245, 246, 248, 249, 307; III 226
'CRYPTAMNESIC rediscovery', II 394
CRYPTOGRAPHY, II 404
CRYSTAL-GAZERS, II 402
Cs [the Conscious], see Conscious; Consciousness; Instances, psychic
CULPABILITY, see Guilt; Crime
CULTURE, see Civilization
CUNNILINCTUS, I 180
CUPBOARD, dream-figure, I 122
CURE FINISHING, see Psycho-analysis, termination
CURIOSITY, I 74, 116, 122, 144, 176, 250, 273, 275, 276

CURSES, I 151
CUTTING INSTRUMENTS, II 248, 353, 418
CYCLOTHYMIA, see Mania; Melancholia
CYNICISM [see also Grimace; Irony], III 132, 205

DALY, C. D., on menstruation, III 122
'DAMAGE', III 251
DANCING, II 161
DANGER, re-creation & conquest of, T 42
DARKNESS, fear of, III 218
DARWIN, C., III 62, T 31, 50-1, 69
DAUGHTER, see Child; Girl; Oedipus complex; Parents
DAY-DREAMS [see also Dreams; Fantasies], I 43, 102
DAY'S RESIDUES, see Dream(s)
DEAD [see also Death; Dying]
  feeling of being —, III 222, 226, 243-4
  man, dream of —, I 123
  as resistance, III 237
DEATH [see also Dead; Death instinct; Dying], I 152; III 244, 254; T 67, 94-5
  & adaptation, III 243
  as existence, continued in toto, III 48
  'holding off', III 220, 274
  laughter as disguised longing for, III 177
  less dreaded than mutilation, III 48
  maniac delusions about, III 274
  & masochism, III 243-4
  partial, III 223, 226, 245
  symbolism, III 202
  tic, as holding off of —, III 274
  & trauma, III 243-4
  utero-regressive trends in, [see also Womb] T 95
DEATH INSTINCT [see also Autotomy; Death; Destruction; 'Dying'; Life & death instinct; Self-destruction], 66, 89; II 376; III 220, 251, 268-9; T 25, 94
  as 'cause of being', II 377
  & epilepsy, III 102-3
  & Eros, see Life & death instinct
  Ferenczi's views, III 16
  Freud's views, III 16, 30
  & unwelcome child, III 102-7
DECEPTION, automatic, see Mendacity [see also Fantasy]
DECISION(S), see Patient, Volition, Will
DEDUCTION & INDUCTION, see Logical relations; Thinking
DEFAECATION [see also Anal erotism; Bowels; Constipation; Digestion; Excrements], I 320-1; II 101, 263-4, 271
  & coitus, T 6
  delayed, & feeling of 'eternity', II 270
DEFEAT, see Defence; Ego

INDEX

DEFENCE [Defence reaction] [*see also Identification; Resistance;* and under individual headings], III 230–1, 256, 265
  inability to —, after shock, III 253–4
  by laughter, II 336–7
  & muscles, III 230, 234
  overpowered by aggression & enjoyment of unpleasure, III 224
  self-destruction, after exhaustion of, III 224, 228
  as self-preservation, III 220, 222–3, 228, 230, 265
DEFIANCE of children after sexual attack, III 163
DEFICIENCY [Defectives], *see* Idiots
DEFLORATION, II 89; III 341
DEFUSION, II 279, 370–2, 378–9
DEGENERATION, *see* Aetiology
DÈJA-VU, II 87, *422;* III *319–20*
DEJECTION, *see* Depression
DELIRIUM, III 236, 244, 268–9
DELUGE, the, T 48–50
DELUSION(S) [*see also Hallucination(s); Illusions; Omnipotence*]
  grandiose [*see also Megalomania*], I 155, 165, 217, 270, 286, 288; III 250
  of guilt (depressive), III 210
  of jealousy, I 63–70, 161–3
  maniac; of holding off of death, III 274
  in paranoia, I 292–3; III 32, 212–13, 250
  of persecution, I 48, 157, 170, 175, 176, 179, 183, 286, 288, 290, 293, 294; III 32, 250 375
DEMATERIALIZATION [*see also Fragmentation; Split*], III 220, 223
DEMENTIA PRAECOX [*see also Catatonia; Paraphrenia; Schizophrenia*], I 47, 130, 154, 155, 163, 234, 294; II 22
  cases of, I 179–83, 285
  libido withdrawal in, II 22, 153
  self-curative tendencies in, II 87
DEMENTIA, SENILE [*see also Age, old*], II 25–7; III 210–11
DEPRESSION [Melancholic depression] [*see also Grief; Melancholia; Mourning*], I 30
  (definition) III 210
  after coitus, III 208–9
  ego ideal in, III 31
  in general paralysis, III 354, 356–8, 361–2
  after laughter, III 182
  after masturbation, III 208–9
  & neurasthenia, III 210
  object love in, III 209–10
  in old persons, III 206, 210
DEPTH, *see* under the particular heading
DESERTED, feeling of being, *see* Abandoned, feeling of being

DESICCATION, T 49, 50, 58, 62, 63
DESIRE, *see* Longing; Sexual desires; Wish
DESTRUCTION [*see also Aggression; Death instinct; Rage*], III 219, 226
  self-, *see* Self-destruction
DETAILS, sense for, III 275
  overestimation of, D 29
DETERMINISM, psychic, I 100, 195, 232, 258; II 39, 87
DEUTSCH, Felix, III 39
DEVELOPMENT [*see also Maturity; Ontogenesis; Phylogenesis;* and under the various headings]
  differentiation & integration in, T 92
  without fertilization, II 377
  & geological catastrophes, I 237
  in onto — & phylogenesis, I 237–8; II 99
  precocious, *see* Infant prodigies [*see also Homoerotics*]
  repetition of, in analysis, D 19
  of sex relations, T 102–3
  sexual [of sexuality] [*see also Sexual; Sexuality*]
    autoplastic & alloplastic periods in, T 23–4
    defective, & infantile sexual traumas, III 163
    feminine [of female sex], II 89; T 24–6, 103–4
    omnipotence fantasies in, I 233–4
    & psychoneuroses, & perversion, T 26
    in puberty, III 68
    regression to womb in —, T 20, 38–9
  of speech, & projection, I 50
DEVOURING [*see also Cannibalism; Incorporation; Introjection; Oral*]
  & adaptation, III 228–30
  the ancestors, & superego formation, III 229
  mutual, III 230
  & obesity, III 228–9
'DIALOGUES OF THE UNCONSCIOUS', II 109
DIARRHOEA [*see also Bowels; Defaecation; Digestive disturbances*], I 208; III 24–5
DIDACTIC ANALYSIS, *see* Training analysis
DIFFERENTIATION & integration, alternation of, T 92
DIGESTION [Digestive] [*see also Anal; Bowels; Constipation; Defaecation; Diarrhoea*], II 92, 325;
DIRT [*see also Anal; Money; Underwear*], I 179, 320, 324; II 362–5; III 68
'DISADOPTION', III 278
DISBELIEF, *see* Incredulity [*see also Conviction; Scepticism*]
DISCHARGE [*see also Affect; Coitus; Conversion; Emission; Epilepsy; Libido; Motor; Orgasm*], III 217, 219

DISCOVERIES (technological) [see also Machine(s); Mechanical; Mechanism; Tools], II 386-9, 395
DISEASE [see also Patho-]
hysteria, II 82
narcissism, II 83-4, 86
symbols in dreams, I 112-13
DISEASE(s)
mental, see Neurosis; Psychoneurosis; Psychosis
organic, see Organic disease(s)
DISGUST, I 65, 144, 151, 167; II 326; III 218
for breakfast, in children, II 326
at food, T 66
at genitals, female, II 307, 314-15; III 218
DISINTEGRATION, see Death; Split of the ego
DISORDER [Disorderliness], ambivalent attitude to, III 178
DISPERSAL, associative, II 61
DISPLACEMENT(s) [see also Conversion; Transference], I 49, 56, 60, 120, 154, 202, 210, 264, 271, 272, 276, 316, 318, 323; II 5, 49-51, 82, 267; T 82
of affect & ideas in obsessional neurosis, II 21, 23, 50, 243
from below upwards, I 275, II 85, 101, 102, 112, 117, 171, 172, 360; T 11
to body organs, II 82; T 210
to body surface, III 48
& cerebrospinal system, III 256
from clitoris to vagina, II 89, 228
in dreams, I 118-19
of evacuation tendency, II 263-4, 271
'of expression', I 193, *209-11*
& facial tic, II 271
of genital sensations [see also Conversion], T 82
repression as, III 222, 255-6, 264
of sphincter constriction, see Sphincter
& transference, I 39
of unpleasure on to others, III 244
DISPOSITION, see Congenital; Predisposition
DISSATISFACTION, see Frustration
DISSOCIATION, in brain, I 58-9, 63
DISTINCTIONS, child's inadequate, I 276-7
DISTORTION, I 18; III 231, 264
DISTRUST and disbelief, II 439; III 104
DOCILITY, I 308; III 339
DOCTOR, see Psycho-analyst, Physician
(definition), III 148
DOG, dream-figure, I 119
DOMINATION, and mutual co-ordination, III 257
DON JUAN legend & bridge symbol, II 356
DON-JUANISM [Don Juan type], I 316; II 358

'DORA', Freud's patient, sexual hunger in, I 66
DOUBT(s) [see also Confidence; Credulity; Incredulity; Scepticism], III 83, 223, 232, 268, 272-3
DREAD [Terror], see Fear [see also Anxiety; Panic; Shock]
DREAM [Dreaming], I 42, 94-119, 123-31, 191, 192, 196, 201, 245, 246, 255, 261-4, 269, 272, 280, 320; II 96, 345, 394 [see also Dream(s), interpretation of]
(definition), III 213, 238
-books, I 95, 124
Freud's theory, I 97-113, 130-1, 140; III 20, 336-7
revision of, III *238-43*
role & significance in analysis, I 129-30; II 40
traumatolytic function of, III 240
DREAM(s) [Dreaming] (Dreaming function), I 18, 43, 99-103, 110-15, 118-21, 124-8; II 345; III 43-5
& censorship, I 103, 127
& childhood memories, I 71, 106, 108
day-, see Day-dream(s)
'day's residues' in, III 238; T 78;
& day-time associations, II 394
defiance, mockery & scorn concealed in, II 309
& 'déjà vu', II 422-3
dematerialization in, III 223
destruction, partial, of personality, in III 226
dirigible, III *313-15*
& erotomania, III 213
exhibitionism in, I 105-6
& fantasy [see also Fantasy], I 19, 126
forgetting of, I 127
'forgetting of a symptom', its explanation in a —, II *412-13*
& hallucinations, I 140; II 98, 232
-images, I 116-18, 140; III 241-2
& imitation, II 266
& materialization, II 96-7
-narration, II 238, 349
negation in, I 125
& omnipotence, I 223
& orgasm & pollution, II 276, *297*
& perversions, I 105
primary & secondary, III 239, 241-2
regression in, II 232; T 78
& repression, I 97, 107
self-repeating (double), on different levels, III 239
symbols, see Dreams of [Dream symbols] [see also Symbol(s); Symbolism]
symbolism [see also Dream(s) [Dreaming] (Interpretation); Dreams of (Dream symbols)]
& anxiety dreams, I 17-18, 107, 273; II 139
autosymbolism, III 135, 221

death symbolism, III 223
hunger & thirst dreams, I 112-13
& hysterical symbolism, II 100-1
importance of, II 352
micturition symbolism, I 110-11
'occupation-dreams', II 298
pollution dreams, II 276, 297, 300
sexual dreams, I 19; III 47, 213; T 78
temporal sequence in, I 125
& trance, III 242
transvalutation in, I 118, 119
& trauma, III 238, 240-1
typical dreams, I 106
as wish fulfilment, I 101, 109-10; II II 301; III, 213, 239
theory modified, II 238-41
& wit, I 115; II 335-7
DREAM(s) [Dreaming] (Interpretation of), I 95; III 221, 238-43; D 24
(definition) III 20
difficulties of, I 116, 125; II 346, 352
of healthy persons, I 128-9
of homo-erotics, I 309; III 168-9
of paranoiacs, III 213-15
self-analysis of dreams, I 129
of war neurotics, II 132, 139
DREAM(s) OF [Dream symbols] [see also Dream (definitions, theories, views); Dream(s), interpretation; Dream(s) symbolism; Fantasy; Symbol(s); Symbolism]
analyst, I 40
biting, I 19
bridges, II 353
broken chair, I 110-11
bull, T 108
bundle, III 228
choking, I 87, 90
coitus, II 276, 297, 300, 302
concert ticket, I 109
cruelty, I 19-20, 107
cupboard, I 122
dead man, I 123
death of nephew, I 109, 118
defaecation, II 101
dog, I 119
enveloping great person, III 228
examination, I 19; III 47
eyes, I 273
falling, I 123
fat woman, I 17, 21
'frater', I 107
growth, III 228
hollow, III 44-5
horse, I 89, 116
house, I 123, III 44
hump, III 228
landscape as Gulliver fantasy, III 44
laughing, II 345
monstrosities, I 115
nakedness, I 105, 170-6
newspaper, foreign, I 114-15

nose, I 40
park, I 121
pessary, II 304
pulverization, III 223
rescue, III 44
robbers, I 108
shooting, I 123
sitting, I 123
slave-market, I 105-6
water, T 101
weapons as symbols, I 19
'the wise baby', see Wise baby
DREAMS (SEVERAL), dreams within —, II 412
series of, III 239-41
two in the same night, III 55
variety of meanings, I 124
DYNAMICS, of neurosis, III 375-6
DRINK, idiosyncrasies against certain kinds of [see also Alcoholism; Oral erotism], III 218
DROWNING [see also Suffocation], III 274
DRUGS [see also Addiction; Alcoholism], II 28-9; III 161-2
DUBOIS' method of therapy, II 27, 200, 446
DUELS, students', I 315
DUMMY [see also Oral erotism; Thumbsucking], III 219
DWARFS, III 43, 47
'DYING' (feeling of dying) [see also Dead; Death], III 138, 221, 237, 243-4
partial, and intellectual achievements, III 245
DYSARTHRIA, in general paralysis, III 356 [see also Speech]
DYSPRAXIA, see Motor disturbances

EARTH, I 326; T 47, 49
EATING (up), see Appetite; Devouring; Hunger; Incorporation
ECHOLALIA, & tic, II 146, 157, 164, 165
ECHOPRAXIA & tic, II 163
ECLECTICISM [see also Philosophy] in scholars, III 78
ECONOMIZING and mathematics, III 188
'ECONOMY'
in dealing with things; & intelligence, III 228, 231
of suffering, III 118
EDDA-saga, I 262
EDUCABILITY of children, through suggestion, III 269-70
EDUCATION [see also Adaptation; Identification], II 265, 428; III 75-6, 359-361
& analysis, see Psycho-analytic technique; Re-education; Sublimation
& command-automatisms, II 92, 265, 283
Freud on, II 215
frustration principle in, III 115-16

as limitation of actions, III 75-7
oral gratifications in, III *219*
& parents [*see also* Child; Parents], II 266, 446
pregenital, II 265
& relaxation, III 115-6, *236-8*
in school, III 69-70, 73-4
sex —, 'Botanic Method', III 69-70
& sphincter-morality, II 267
& suggestion, II 57; III 269
as superego 'intropression', III 279
tactless —, of infants, III 219
& understanding, III 62
as unlearning of supernormal capacities, II 283
EDUCATOR(s) [*see also* Adults; Child(ren); Parents], III 83
EGGS, as anal symbol, II 327-8
EGO [*see also* Fragmentation; Personality; Split; Superego]
analysis [*see also* Ego psychology], II 112; III *371*; D 19
& anxiety, III 36
body- [*see Body*]
boundaries of, III 246
brain as the central organ of the, III 353
of the child [*see also* Child(ren)], I 48; III 72-3
-consciousness, I 48
destructive tendencies in, *see* Death instinct; Masochism; Self-destruction
development of, I 217-18; II 164; III 359-60
divisions of, II 285
& external world [*see also* Environment; Reality & ego], I 227-9; II 164, 366, 274, 441; III 244, 257-258; T 48
in general paralysis, III 353-4, 357, 359-67
-hysteria, catatonia & tic as, II 173
& id, II 285; III 72-3, 112-13; D 49-50
-ideal [*see also* Superego], II 418; III 31, 33, 357, 360, 373-5; D 9, 21
identification of, with one's genitalia [*see also* Identification], II 86
'-indebtedness' in neurasthenia, III 253
instincts, & reality [*see also* Ego & external world; Reality*]*, I 233
intact parts of, III 224-6
libidinal, *see* Libido
'-memory-system', II 155-6, 158, 160, 173, 355; III 221
narcissistic, *see* Genitalia
'non-existence' of (in Groddeck's novel), III 347
-nucleus, III 225, 362, 368-9
'nursing' part of the split-off —, III 226, 237-8

objectivation of [*see also* Objectivation & Subjectivation], III 266
penis, as a miniature —, T 16
-psychology [*see also* Character], III 30-37, 151, 185-6, 373
in psychoses, I 47; III 357, 362
& reality, *see* Ego & external world; Reality
sensitivity [*see also* Hyperaesthesia; Paraesthesia], III 23, 32, 65, 120-1; W 18-19
sequestration of the —, III 357-9
shrinking & widening of, I 48
split of, *see* Split
'superiority' after defeat, III 225-6
'-syntonic', III 360-1
in war neuroses, II 141
EGOISM (Egoistic) [*see also* Ego], I 325; II 373; III 221, 224-8, 253
& altruism [*see also* Self-sacrifice], III 252-3
& intelligence, III 243, 245
& love, III 248
& melancholia, *see* Melancholia, egoistic-subjective
of parents [*see also* Parent(s)], III 273
& split of the ego, *see* Split
surrender of, III 220-1, 224-7, 243-6
EHRENFELS, von, I 22
'EINFÄLLE' [*see also* Idea(s)], III 184
EITINGON, M., III 39
EJACULATION [Emission, pollution] [*see also* Coitus; Impotence; Potency]
amphimixis in, T *1*
anal & urethral components in, III 217; T 7
cerebral haemorrhage instead of, III 255
coitus without, II 277
& dream [*see also* Dream], II 276, *297*
involuntary [precocious, premature, Ejaculatio praecox], I 13, 191; II 35, 277, 289-302; III 23, 46-7, 216-17
effect on women, III 24, *291-4*
retarded (Ejaculatio retardata), T 7
as a sacrifice, III 217
spermatorrhoea in, II 270
ELASTICITY [*see* Flexibility; '*Nachgiebigkeit*'; Pliability]
of psycho-analytic technique, *see* Psycho-analytic technique
ELECTRICAL TREATMENT [Electrotherapy] [*see also* Psychotherapy, non-analytical], I 55; II 28, 140-1; III 144
'ELEMENT analyses' & 'Complex analyses', D 34-5
ELLIS, Havelock, III 144
EMACIATION, III 103, 356
EMBARRASSMENT [*see also* Exhibitionism; Shame; Surprise], I 273; II 202, 315-16

EMBRYO [Embryonic state, Foetal; Foetus] [*see also Intrauterine*]
lesions of, III 65
'Organanlagen', & displacement facilities in, III 265
as parasite, T 85
protective arrangements for, I 64
EMISSION, *see* Ejaculation
EMOTION(S) [*see also Affect(s); Affection; Affectivity*], I 35, 65, 74, 109, 186, 195; III 181, 209-10, 231
during coitus, T 33-4, 56
excessive, during analytic treatment, III 236
materialization in the expression of, II 96
outbursts of, III 33
repeated in hysterical symptoms, III 221
tail, as organ for expression of, T 92
unconscious, expressed by organic illness, III 256
EMPATHY, role of, in analysis [*see also Psycho-analyst*], III 89-90, 92, 99-100
EMPRESS, as mother-symbol, III 51
ENCOURAGEMENT in analysis, *see* Psycho-analytic technique
'ENDLESS ANALYSIS', III 86
ENDOCRINE SYSTEM, III 255-6
ENDURANCE, of pain, *see* Pain
ENGRAM, *see* Memory traces
ENURESIS [*see also Bladder; Sphincter(s); Urethral*], II 171, 262; III 217; T 77
ENVIRONMENT [*see also Adult(s); Aggressor; Child(ren); Ego; Social*], I 24, 50, 66; III 73, 102, 225, 266
ENVY, *see* Jealousy; Penis envy
EPILEPSY [Epileptic(s)], I 75, 224
(definition) III 203
aggressiveness in, III 201-4
ambulatory automatism in, III 199
& death instincts, III 102-3
fits in III, *197-204*
EQUILIBRIUM, egoistic, III 221, 224-5
ERBEN, W 14-15
ERECTION, I 13-14, 23, 200, 273, 285, 295; II 269
explanation of, T 28
repressed, I 295
spinal rigidity or cramp as surrogate for, III 48
symbols of, II 360
& unpleasure elimination, T 29
EROGENOUS, *see* Erotogenic
EROS, *see* Death instinct; Life & death instinct; Life instinct
EROTIC [*see also Libido [Libidinous]; Sexual; Sexuality*]
amphimixis, *see* Amphimixis, erotic
development, & perversion, T 26
reality sense, development of, T 20
EROTICISM, *see* Erotism

EROTISM(S) [Eroticism] [*see also Auto-erotism; Erotogenic zones*], II 191, 265, 389
(definition), T 5, 98
& amphimixis, T 5, 97-8
'hierarchy of,' III 209
muscle-, *see* Muscle-erotism
organ-, III 25-6
parental, T 24
EROTOGENIC ZONE(S) [Erogenous zones) [*see also Erotism; Pregenital* & under special headings], I 15, 90, 108, 189, 276, 320; II 87, 228; III 295-8; T 5
& analysis, D 34-5
brain as [*see also Brain*], III 353
clitoris as [*see also Clitoris*], II 89, 206, 228
foreskin as, II 227
genital [*see also Genital; Genitality; Penis; Phallic; Sexual; Vagina*]
primacy of, I 85-6, 90, 99; II 265, 270; III 33, 121; T 9, 15-16, 22-3
injury to; II 84, 86
muscles as, II 172
respiratory, III 202
skin as, *see* Skin
& spirochetes, III 364
EROTOMANIA [*see also Sexual hunger*], I 288; II 78; III 213-15
ERRORS, *see* Mistakes, Symptomatic acts
'ERSCHÜTTERUNG', *see* Shock
'ESPRIT D'ESCALIER', I 20
'ETERNITY', feeling of, II 270
ETHNOLOGY [*see also Primitive man*], I 153; III 39
ETYMOLOGIZING, obsessional, II 318
EUPHORIA, III 355-7, 364, 368
EVACUATION, *see* Defaecation; Micturition [*see also Retention; Spitting; Vomiting*]
EVIL, recognition of, results from two negatives, II 368
EVOLUTION, *see* Bio-analysis; Development; Ontogenesis; Phylogenesis
EXAGGERATION [Exaggerated; Excessive] [*see also Hyper-; Over-; Super-*]
of hysterical parents, I 36-7, 39
ridicule, as expression of, III 170-1
of tasks, III 271-2
EXAMINATION(S)
dream of, I 19; III 47
medical & transference, I 40-1
EXCESSIVE, *see* Exaggeration; Hyper-; Over-; Super-
EXCITEMENT [Excitation], I 195, 207
[*see also Sexual excitement*]
EXCREMENT(S) [Faeces] [*see also Anal erotism; Bowels; Constipation; Coprophagia; Coprophilia; Defaecation; Diarrhoea; Digestion*], I 326, 329
affection of the child for his, III 67-8

closing of eyes at, I 134
experiments with, II 261
introjection of, I 322
& money, [see also Money] T 320, 329
retention of, & 'strength', II 251
safeguarding of, T 60
'stool-hypochondria', I 32
symbols for, I 321-3
as toys, I 321-2
EXCRETION [Excretory function] *see* Defaecation; Micturition
EXECUTION(s)
dream-figure, I 119
somatic relaxation at, I 209
EXHAUSTION, I 200-1, 271; III 241
after masturbation & orgasm, II 33, 266
& self-destruction, III 224
EXHIBITIONISM [Exhibitory tendencies], I 16, 105-8, 167, 172, 177, 313; II 85, 315-16, 318; III 205
& facial injury, II 85
fear of mirrors as flight from, II 365
in general paralysis, III 363
in Gulliver fantasies, III 51
narcissism as, II 329-30
obscenity as, I 150
in old people, III 205
of parents, II 320-1
& penis envy, II 122, 204
pride in children as substitute for, II 320-1
EXPERIENCES, *see* Child; Childhood; Infantile sexual trauma & other respective headings; Shock; Trauma
'EXPRESSION DISPLACEMENTS', in analysis, I 193, *209-11*
EYE(s) [*see also* Blinding], I 134, 273; T 76
& masturbation, I 186, 188; II 317
paternal, & sun, II 247
psychosis after operations on, II 84
symbolism of, I 264, *270, 271, 276, 280*
'EYE ANIMALS', primates as, T 71

FACE, as representing genitalia, I 273
FACULTIES traumatically acquired [*see also* Infant prodigies; Intelligence], III 262-3
FAECES, *see* Excrements
FAINTING [*see also* Unconscious; Unconsciousness], II 210, 356; III 26, 118, 121, 138; W 16, 17; T 87
FAIRY TALES & omnipotence [*see also* Omnipotence], I 238-9
FAKIRISM, III 251
FALLING, dream of, I 123
FAMILY [*see also* Child; Parent(s)]
adaptation of, to the child, III *61-76*
analysis, II 49
-physician & psycho-analysis, D 64-5
real existence of —, as group, III 252
'romance' [*see also* Heroes], II 413-7
FAN as symbol, II 361

FANTASIES [Fantasy] (function) [*see also* Day-dream(s); Dream(s); Imagery; Image(s); Imagination], II 76-9; III 79, 268
automatism in, II 299
autosymbolism in, III 135
& castration anxiety, III 36
freedom of, in the child; III 72, 75
homosexual, I 91, 92, 170, 176
in hysteria, II 89-90; III 79
in masturbation [*see also* Masturbation], III 216
& mendacity, III 78-9
in paranoia, III 298
partial destruction of the self, represented by —, III 226
as pathogenic factor, III 120-1,
& pleasure principle, I 255
of the poet (Goethe on), III *324*
& precocious ejaculation, III 217
& the split of the self [*see also* Split], III 135
& symptom formation, D 49
& thinking, III 192
in trance, III 223, 232, 259
wish-, of children, III 44
FANTASIES [Fantasy] (Contents)
of aggression, I 19-20, 107; II 72-3
anal, II 251, 298
birth-, II 296; III 36
cannibalistic, I 249
castration, *see* Castration
coitus-, *see* Coitus
of father, as predecessor in sexual intercourse, III 341
of father's eye, as sun, II 247
of fire extinguishing by micturition, III 51-2
forced-, *see* Psycho-analytic technique, 'active'
of grandeur, *see* Delusions
Gulliver —, II *41-60*
of hatred suffered in intrauterine life, III 227
of hypnotic suggestions, I 91-2
incestuous, *see* Incest
of incorporation, III 48-9
lust-murder, II *278-9*
masturbation —, I 189; II 190-1; III 266
Pompadour —, II 351
of pregnancy, I 90; III 246-7
of rape, I 200
of rescue, *see* Rescue
of revenge, I 308
of seduction, II 73-4
sexual [*see also* Incest], I 14
of teasing (passive), II 75
of womb [*see also* Intrauterine; Womb], III 36, 44-7, 268-9
FAT
meat, obsessive fear of [*see also* Fatness], II 50

INDEX

woman, I 17, 21; III 218
FATE, projection on to, I 259
FATHER [see also Child(ren); Parents; Paternal], I 77, 90, 247; III 33, 48, 303-4
  complex [see also Complex(es)], I 70, 75, 78-80
  -hypnosis, see Hypnosis, paternal
  hypnotic power of, in the primal horde, III 372
  -ideal, difficulty in detaching from father's person, II 418
  identification with, I 77; II 122, 265, 267; D 17, 21
  loss of, I 152; III 58, 227
  occupation of, & castration fear, II 418-19
  as predecessor, fantasied, in sexual intercourse, III 341
  'revenants' of, I 41, 260
  -symbols, I 248, 264; II 246-7, 365
  yielding to, III 34
FATIGUE, in neurasthenics, III 23 [see also Exhaustion]
FATNESS [see also Fat], hysterical, III 228-9
  & introjection of mother figure, III 227-8
  organic aspects of, III 229
  paretic, III 363
FAUSER, W 8
FEAR [Dread; Obsessive fear; Phobia; Terror] [see also Anxiety; Castration; Panic; War neurosis], II 134, III 233
  of beetles, I 272
  of books, II 50
  of darkness, III 218
  of fat meat, II 50
  & hypnosis, I 69-71; III 224-5
  of incest & masturbation, I 185
  of madness, III 249, 251, 268
  of mice, II 109
  of micturition in public, II 49
  of mirrors, II 365
  of movement, I 148-9
  of nakedness, II 329
  of needles, I 270
  of novels, I 50-1
  in patient, see Patient(s)
  pavor nocturnis, I 107, 245; II 111
  physical symptoms of [see also Trembling; War neuroses], W 11
  of privies, I 50-1
  of salt, II 50
  of smoking, II 318
FEDERN on catatonia, II 147
FEELING, see Affect(s); Emotion(s); Unconscious feeling
FEINDEL, E., on tics, II 148
FELLATIO & voice, II 108
FEMALE [Feminine], see Girl; Woman [Women]
'FEMME ENTRETENANTE', III 217

FERENCZI (personal notes)
  on being an 'enfant terrible' of psycho-analysis, III 127
  case of housekeeper's paranoic husband, I 157-63
  dreams (drinking cool water, drowning), III 274
  having no dreams, III 258
  hypnogogic images, III 258
  on naïveté of own outlook, III 142
  views on death instinct, controversial with Freud's, III 251
FERTILIZATION, II 377; T 60, 61, 63, 68
FETISHISM, foot —, I 16, 22
FEUDAL, right of lord to defloration, III 341
FEVER, III 27, 268-9
'FIG LEAF', the, III 321
FINGER [see also Thumb], symbol for penis, III 50
FIRE [Incendiarism], II 258; III 51-2
FISH(ES), T 49-50, 100
FIT(s), see Attack(s); Epilepsy; Hysteria
FIXATION [see also Regression], I 27, 31, 58, 179, 205, 207, 208, 211, 224, 234, 236, 258, 294, 307; III 278
  & hate, III 123-4
  in homo-erotics, I 304
  incestuous, I 24, 25, 26, 33, 81; T 61
  infantile & analytic [see also Patient(s); Psycho-analyst; Transference], I 87; III 27, 278; D 12-13
  mutual, see Mutual fixation
  & omnipotence, I 216
  to organ erotism & hypochondriac constitution, III 217
  to patient, indications of [see also Counter-transference], II 188
  -points, I 235-6; II 90, 368
  resistance to, I 252
  traumatic, in war neurosis, W 15
'FLASHLIKE' solutions, III 263
FLATULENCE, III 25
FLATUS, I 134, 143; II 284
  as adult prerogative, II 325
FLEXIBILITAS CEREA [see also Catatonia], II 163; III 254
FLEXIBILITY [see also Pliability, Rigidity], developed by fragmentation, III 220
FLIESS, W 1, 184, 190, 296
FLIGHT [see also Anxiety; Defence; Fear; Trauma; Responsibility],
  from complexes, I 45
  of ideas, see Thoughts, flow of
  from the present, III 268-9
  from responsibility, III 262, 272
  from unpleasure, II 22-3, 239; III 249
FOETUS, see Embryo, Intrauterine
FOLK SOUL [see also Popular views], operation of, I 265
FOOD, reactions to, I 38, 66; III 218; W 19

FOOT, as penis-symbol, I 263
-fetishism, I 16, 22
'FOR EXAMPLE' [see also Comparison(s); Psycho-analytic process]
'FORCED FANTASY', see Psycho-analytic technique, active
FORE-PLEASURE, III 217; T 15
not purely psychological, I 188, 190
FORESKIN, I 30; II 227-8
FORGETTING [see also Memory disturbances], I 16, 72, 100, 127, 149; II 20, *412*; III 263
(definition) II 20, 37-8
FORGIVENESS, III 178-9
FORMULAS, belief in, I 231
FORSTER, W 13
FORSYTH, D III 202
FOSTER-MOTHER, fixation on, I 26-7
FOWLS, case of boy afraid of, I *230-52*
FRAGMENTATION [see also Split of the ego]
& adaptation, III 220-5, 236
'bursting', symbol for, III 237
explosion of the head, symbol for, III 221
'falling to pieces', symbol for, III 234
& hypersensitiveness, III 220
as immediate effect of trauma, III 230
plasticity developed by, III 220
'FRATER', dream of, I 107
FREEDOM [see also Limitation], I 44-5; III 81
of action, reduced to absurdity by patient, II 224
FREIMARK, H., III 341
FREUD, Anna, III 38, 69, 106, 122, 128
FREUD, Sigmund,
on 'active technique', II 196, 223, 224, 236, 271, 293
on affect & idea (reciprocity of), II 216
on analysis & education of children, II 215
on the analyst's unconscious, II 189, 401
on anxiety & free floating libido, II 236; III 218
appreciation of, II 30, 41; III *11-17, 18-21, 126-7, 143-55*
'Beyond the Pleasure Principle', III 16
on blending of aetiologies, II 53
on building up of psychical systems, II 155-6
on the censuring instance, III 241
on coitus, T 53
on complexes, D 31
on conversion, III 218
on counter-transference, II 180
on denial of satisfactions in analysis, II 201-2
'The Ego and the Id', D 49-50
on ego-development, II 164
on fantasied coitus of the impotent, II 267
a forerunner of — (Lindner), III *325*
on frustrated curiosity in children, II 327
on Group Psychology, III 15, 364, 371-6
'Hemmung, Symptom & Angst', III 35
on hysteria, as a negative perversion, III 68
on incompleteness of birth, T 73
& the instincts, II 158, 271; T 62, 93-7
on interpretation of dreams, I 99-113, 140; II 336-7; III 127, 144, 152, 238
on materialism & mechanism, III 252
on masculinity complex, T 106
on memory & bad experiences, III 244
'Mourning & Melancholia', III 357
'On Narcissism', II 215, III 205, 211
on negation, II 368-79
on obsessional doubt, II 274
on Oedipus complex, T 104
'pansexuality' alleged, of his teachings, III 151
on perfection, II 382
on pollution, II 298
'The Predisposition to Obsessional Neurosis', III 205
pre-Freudian & post-Freudian periods in psychiatry, III 13-14, 18-20
on primary process, II 369
on psychic shock, III 19-20
'Psychopathology of Everyday Life', I 49, 200
racial origin of, III 155
on reality testing, II 370-1
'Remembering, Repeating & Working Through', D 3
on repetition, II 217
on repression, III 237
on resistance, D 40
on self-destruction, III 30
on sexuality, II 52; T 68
on similarity of internalized stimulus to instinct, II 158
on stages of development, II 373
on stammering, II 251
on suggestion, II 200
on thoughts, II 232
'Three Contributions to the Theory of Sexuality', II 52, *253*
'Totem & Taboo', III 15
on traumatic neurosis, T 66
'Wit & its Relation to the Unconscious', II 332, 336-7; III 15
FREUDIAN, see Freud; Psycho-analysis
FREUND, W 8

FRICTION, genital, in sex act, T 28-30
FRIENDSHIP, male, mutual, I 315
FRIGIDITY, III 34, 104
  caused by ejaculatio praecox, III 24
  male [see also Paraesthesia], II 312-13
FRINK, III 263
FRUSTRATION, II 197, 211, 213, 225
  & anxiety, II 35; III 218, 219, 253
  effect of, on the child, II 327; III 164, 219, 327
  principle, in analysis [see also Cathexxs; Psycho-analytic technique; Relaxation], II 75, 201-2, 297; III 115, 123
  trauma of first oral —, III 219
'FUNCTIONAL' phenomena (Silberer) see Autosymbolism
FUNDAMENTAL RULE(S), see Psychoanalytic rule(s)

GAIT, see Posture
GALOSHES, as symbol of vagina, II 358
GAS, smell of, I 324
GAUPP, W 7, 9, 11-12, 13, 14, 15
GENERALIZATION(S), resistance through, II 184
GENITAL(S) [Genitalia; Genital organ(s)] [see also Erotogenic zones; Libido; Sexual], III 49, 70-1; T 5-43
  & brain, II 99; III 255, 353-4
  childish analogies of, I 279
  & conversion, II 99
  female [see also Clitoris; Uterus; Vagina], I 156; II 307, 313-15, 361; T 57
  identification of, II 86, 204, 269; III 49; T 37, 60
  lesions of and pathoneuroses, II 86
  male [see also Penis], I 89; T 50
  & narcissistic ego, II 85-6
  & nose, I 190-1
  paraesthesia of, in psychic impotence, II 312-13
  & personality, II 204; III 49
  re-direction of libido to, & disappearance of symptoms, II 197
  symbols of, I 264, 271, 273, 280, 361; III 44-5
GENITALIZATION (definition), II 85, 102
  of auto-erotism, II 172
  of body, II 82-5, 90, 102, 171-2, 269; III 255
GENITALITY [see also Erotogenic zones;] II 171, 173, 197; III 121, 218; T 16, 69
  amphimixis theory of, II 263-4; T 5, 15
  feminine [see also Woman], II 89, 171-2; T 5, 102-6
  friction in, see Friction
  function of, II 263-4; T 5-44
  phylogenesis, theory of, III 243, 246; T 5, 97, 44-72, 99-105
  primacy, see Erotogenic zones

& symbolism, T 87-8
& urethral erotism, T 5
GENITOFUGAL & GENITOPETAL flow of libido, see Libido
GENIUS [see also Infant prodigies; Progressive faculties; Talent], III 184, 187
GERM-CELL [Germ plasm], T 46, 65, 68-9, 90
GESTURE(S) [see also Grimace; Omnipotence; Posture]
  development of, I 42, 151, 217, 234, 235, 241
  expressive, III 180-1
  in hysteria, [see also Hysteria] I 225-6; II 90
  language of, D 3
  magic, I 225; II 90, 217
  as masturbation equivalents, II 282
  as memory traces of childhood, III 264
  speech as substitution for, I 229
GIANT(S) [see also Gulliver], III 43, 48; T 70
GIDDINESS [see also Vertigo], I 199; II 34, 241
  at end of analytic session, II 239
GIGANTIC, see Giant(s)
GILLES DE LA TOURETTE, on tics, II 146
GIRL(s), III 104, 161-2
GLOBUS HYSTERICUS, see Hysteria; Spasm(s)
GOD, development of idea of, II 429
GOETHE, I 259-60; III 324
'GOLDEN'
  age, I 106
  silence, II 250
GOLDSCHEIDER, W 7, 11, 16
GRANDFATHER, II 323; III 227
GRASSET, on tics, II 166
GRATIFICATIONS [see also Frustration; Libido; Sexuality, and under particular headings], I 138; III 354, 360; T 77-8
  adult and childish, difference between, III 166-7
  countermanding, in analysis, II 272
  emotional & intellectual, through insight, III 236
  in hastening of unpleasure, III 244
  micturition in children, as libido-reward, II 317
GRAPHOLOGY, III 82, 274
GREED, see Avarice; Covetousness; Hunger
GRATITUDE, expressions of, and encouragement, III 270
GRIEF [see also Depression; Mourning], II 61
GRIMACE(S) [see also Gesture(s); Tics], III 267-8
GRODDECK, G., II 225, 375; III 84, 344-348
  on therapy of organic diseases, III 39, 123, 342-3

GROSS, Otto, I 39; III 209
'GROTESQUE', III 267-8
GROUP
  delusion of persecution by —, in paranoia, III 375
  education, see Walden school
  enjoyment, III 178
  -leader, III 371-6
  -mind, II 428
  psychology [see also Individual; Infection, psychical], II 405; III 178-9, 369, 371-6
  real existence of —, problem of (Roheim), III 252
GROWTH,
  bio-analytical faculty of, II 376, 377; III 264-5
GULLIVER-FANTASIES, III 41-60
GUILT [see also Crime; Punishment; Sin],
  feeling, D 4, 10-11
  in the child, III 70-1, 163-4
  in depression, III 210
  & egoistic & altruistic obligations, III 253
  introjection of, see Introjection
  & laughter, III 178
  motiveless, I 17
  & neurasthenia, see Neurasthenia
  in old age, II 206-7
  social, III 253
GYPSIES & obscenities, I 153

HABITS, II 259-97
  bad, II 282-3; III 68-9
  metapsychology of, II 284-8
  and repetition compulsion, II 285
  sexual [see also Sexual; Sexuality], II 259, 260, 271-8
  sleeping, T 70
  & symptoms, II 281
  training, see Toilet training
HAECKEL, A., T 45-6, 55, 103
HAEMORRHAGE, cerebral, as emission, III 255
'HALF-CURED' patients [see also Healing; Patient(s), incompletely cured], return to analysis of, II 233
HALL, Stanley, III 41, 74
HALLUCINATION(S) [see also Delusion(s); Dream(s); Fantasies; Nightmares; Omnipotence], I 21, 44, 96, 137-9, 141, 145, 149, 156, 189, 204, 205, 214, 221-3, 291; II 95, 98-9, 369
  in analysis [see also Psycho-analytical process; Trance; Trauma], I 193, 204-5
  compensatory in masochism, III 244, 248-9
  distorted childhood memories in, III 264
  in fantasies, see Fantasies
  formation of, II 95
  hypnagogic, see Hypnagogic images

negative, III 121
  of omnipotence [see also Omnipotence], III 213-14, 221-3, 359-60
  organic, sleep as, T 78
  in paranoia, I 291; III 212-13
  in psychoses, III 43, 358, 365-8
  suggested, in trance, III 259 [see also Trance]
  & trauma, see Trauma
HAMBURGER, W 15
HAND(S) [see also Grip], I 185; II 315-16
HANGING, somatic concomitants of, I 209
HATE [Hatred] [see also Aggression; Aggressor; Maliciousness], I 19, 21, 36, 39, 41, 42, 44, 48, 49, 63, 78, 175, 182, 246, 247, 258-60, 287, 297, 306; III 33
  & confessions & absolutions, III 261
  fixation less strong through love than through —, III 227
  fantasy of having suffered intrauterine, III 227
  object-, see Object-love & object hate
  & resistance, III 157-8
  traumatic appearance of, III 166-7
  after trance, III 157
HASTENING of unpleasure, gratification in, III 244
'HAVING' and 'being', III 374
HAUPTMANN, W 10, 12
HEAD, 'cut-off —', as symbol for split of the ego, III 135, 221
  'explosion of the —', as symbol for fragmentation, in hysteria, III 221-2
  genitalization of, III 255
  Medusa's, II 360
  'lost —', as symbol for unconsciousness, III 221
  pain & congestion in, III 234
  'splitting open', II 123
  tics, II 170
HEADACHE(S), III 23, 26, 139, 210, 234
HEALTH, III 26-7
  striving for, & trauma, III 230-1
HEALTHY persons, see Normal persons
HEART, I 26, 27, 198, 199; III 24-8
HEBBEL, Friedrich, & 'déja vu', II 422
HELPFULNESS, III 136, 206, 230
HEMI-ANAESTHESIA, see Anaesthesia
HEREDITY [Inheritance] [see also Aetiology; Constitution; Predisposition], T 66
  of acquired characters, I 319; II 287; III 67; T 68
  of conversion symptoms & stigmas, III 218
  organic, II 287
  pseudo —, & psychic impotence, I 28
HEROES [see also Family romance] as 'revenants', I 260
HERTWIG, R., T 56-7

HESITATION, & anal erotism, II 420-1
  between duty & suicide, II 329
HETEROSEXUALITY [see also 'Sexuality]
HIBERNATION & menstruation, T 77
HICCOUGH, I 211
'HIERARCHY OF EROTICISMS', III 209
HISS, III 278
HISTORICAL REPRESENTATION, & autosymbolism, III 221
HOARDING OF LIBIDO [see also Libido], III 253
'HOLDING OFF', see Death; Unpleasure
HOLIDAYS, & neuroses, II 175-6
HOLLÓS, I., II 210; III 198, 355, 358, 362, 363
HOLLOW, in dream as Gulliver fantasy, III 44, 45
'-penis', anal, II 317
HOMO-EROTISM [Homo-erotics] [see also Homosexual(s); Homosexuality] (male)
  fixation to, I 304
  object —, I *296-318*; II 108
  subject —, I *296-318*
HOMOSEXUAL(s) [see also Homo-erotism; Homosexuality], I 91-2, 200, *296-318*
  acts with little boys, III 161-2
  dreams, III 168-9
  fantasies, & sleep during analysis, II 250
  heterosexual love in, III 168
  identification in, III 374
  mother-fixation in, III 168-9, 171-3; T 48
  & nakedness, I 170, 176
  obsessions, in analysis, I 209
  Oedipus complex in, I 297, 303
  relations to parents of, III 168-9
  transference in, I 43, 161, 309
  traumatophilia of, I 305; II 139-40
  & women ('chivalry' in —), I 176
HOMOSEXUALITY [see also Homo-erotism; Homosexual(s)], I 169, 175, 291, *296-317*; II 247; III *168-74*, 212
  (definition) III 171
  active & passive, see Homo-erotism, object, subject
  & alcoholism, I 161-2, 315; III 212
  analytical therapy of, I 302, 305-6, 309, 311-12
  female, III 263
  in general paralysis, see Paralysis, general
  & heterosexuality, III 168, 174-5
  & insults in social life, III 375
  'intermediate stage' theory, I 311
  male (see also Homo-erotism), I 296-318; III 48, 58, 374
  & neurosis, I 20-1
  & paranoia, I *154*; II 79, 105-6, 359-60; III 212
  & persecutory delusions, I 170
  & position during analytic session, II 242

'primary', III 171
'third sex'-theory, III 173
  traumatic sources of, III 226
HOPE, III 223, 232; W 8
HOPELESSNESS, III 223, 232, 277-8
HORDE, primal, III 252, 372
HORSE, analyst identified in dream with, I 86, 116
  taming of a wild, III *336-40*
'HOT' feeling in homosexuals, III 48
HOUSE, in dream & fantasy, I 123; III 44
HOUSEKEEPER, case of author's, I *157*
'HOUSEWIFE-PSYCHOSIS', II 257
HUG-HELLMUTH, Hermine von, III 127
HUMANITARIANISM & neurosis, I 38
HUMOUR & wit, II 344
HUMP as symbol for neurosis, III 228
HUNGER [see also Sexual hunger] & appetite, I 112-13; III 228, 276, T 41,
HYDROTHERAPY, & transference, I 55
HYGIENE, mental, III *18-21*
HEALING [see also Psycho-analysis; Psycho-analytic method; Psycho-analytic treatment; Psychotherapy]
  'half-cured' patients, II 233; III 98-9
  process of physical & libido, II 88, 376
  remembering as a final factor of, D 26
  self-healing, attempt(s) at, II 310, III 86
HYPER- [see also Exaggeration; Over-, Super-
  aesthesia [-Sensibility,-Sensitivity]; [see also Ego-sensitivity], I 14, 188; II 138
  in war neurotics, II 132, 138-40, 142
  in tic-cases, II 145, 152, 417
  cathexis of injured organ, II 81, 89
  performance, intellectual, see Genius; Infant prodigies
  sensibility [Hypersensitiveness; Hypersensitivity], see Hyperaesthesia
HYPNAGOGIC, images (Ferenczi's own), III 258
  hallucinations, I 21
HYPNOSIS [Hypnotism] [see also Psychotherapy, non-analytical; Suggestion], I 54, 55, 58, 64, 67-77, 80, 83-8, 305; II 91, 163, 446
  & 'administration of ideas', I 58-9
  & analysis, I 59; II 27-8, 65-6, 397; III 110, 134, 149
  & antipathy, I 86
  as 'artificial hysteria', I 83
  'being startled' -feeling in, I 68-9
  childhood, return to, in, I 70, 71
  concentration in, II 402
  courtship, analogy with, T 32-3
  fantasies of homosexuals (passive), I 91-2
  & group psychology, III 372

innervation changes in, *see* Innervation
& love, I 69–71, 91–2; T 78
maternal & paternal, I 70; II 163, 402, 448; III 338–40; T 32, 78, 106
& neurosis, I 83–4, 86
& Oedipus situation, D 62
& orgasm expectation, III 339
in primal horde, paternal, III 372
projection in, I 60
repressed infantile impulses in, I 63
a return to infantile submission, II 443
& sleep, T 77
susceptibility to [*see also* Suggestibility], I 85–6; III 372–3
technique of, I 68–70
as therapy [*see also* Hypnosis & analysis], I 67; II 447; D 61
& transference, I 58, 60, 67, 72–6; II 237

HYPOCHONDRIA [Hypochondriac(s); Hypochondriasis], I 14, 30, 82, 270, 271, 282–3, 328
& 'active' technique, II 121, 189
as actual psychosis (Freud), III 355
anxiety, in hysterical, II 118
& 'déja vu', II 87
euphoria, as over-compensation of, III 356
in homosexuality, II 108
hysterical, II *118*, 123, 262
masturbation in, III 208
& neurasthenia, III 208
& organ libido, III 217
& pathoneuroses, II 83
& psychoses, II 87; III 355–7
reality of anxiety in, II 58
& split of the ego, *see* Split of the ego
& stool, I 32
'superstructures' on, II 124
& transference, II 121, 124

HYPOCRISY [*see also* Acceptance of unpleasant ideas; Education; Self-sacrifice], II 336–7; III 80, 133
professional, III 158–60

HYSTERIA [*see also* Anxiety hysteria; Attack, hysterical; Conversion], I 35–8, 46, 54, 66, 73, 75, 86, 108, 130, 133, 143, 177, 185, 194, 196, 210, 211, 234; II 21, 27, 42, 48, 85, 100, 114, 425, 444; III 22, 43, 140
& actual neuroses, II 34
aetiology, *see* Aetiology; Hysteria, formation of
affect-, III 218
'artificial-', hypnosis as (Charcot), I 83–4
& artistic talent, II 104
compensation-, W 8
in children, *see* Child(ren)
disease-, II 82
'ego-', II 173
fixation points of, I 235–6; II 90
formation of, II 36–7, 90, 99, 110; D 48; W 12
genital sources of, II 99, 173
genitalizations in [*see also* Conversion; Genitalization]
& heredity, III 218
& hypochondria, *see* Hypochondria
identification in, *see* Identification
infection, psychical, in, I 37
& infantile sexual trauma, III 241, 246
& infantilism, psychic, III *260–1*
as a negative of perversion (Freud), III 68
& neurasthenia, III 22
& obsessional neurosis, differences, II 48–9, 444
& patho-neuroses, II 86, 88, 172
& pleasure principle, II 103, 116
predisposition to, in normal persons, I 83
self-destructive tendencies in, III 202
& simulation, III 78
surprise, representation of, in, III 221
symptoms [Hysteric(al) symptoms] [*see also* Conversion; Displacement]
confusion, feeling of, III 221
'dying', feeling of, III 221
gestures, I 225–6; II 90
globus hystericus, II 43, 92, 93, 104–5, 117, 268
'idiom, hysterical', II 100
kleptomania, I 39
pain, [*see also* Trance], III 241, 246
'petite', I 46–7; III 218
reappearance of, II 21–2; III 118–19
as repetition, III 221
simulation [*see also* War neurosis], III 78
self-destructive tendencies, III 202
spasms, *see* Spasm(s)
& tics, II 72–3
traumatic origin of [*see also* Aetiology], II 36–7; III 110, 221; D 48
unconsciousness in, III 221
& war neuroses, II 127, 131; W 14, 20
& will (lack of), III 255
in women, greater incidence of, II 25

IBSEN, H., I 20, 21; II 59
ICE AGE(s) [*see also* Deluge], I 237; T 70–1, 104
ID, II 285, 375; III 30–1, 35, 72–3
IDEA(s) [*see also* 'Einfälle'; Thought(s); Unpleasant ideas; Unpleasure], I 58–9, 319–20; II 22; III 365
IDEAL, *see* Ego-ideal, Super-ego
IDENTIFICATION(s) [*see also* Fixation(s); Superego formation], I 52, 117, 176, 191, 275–7, 280, 326; II 229; III 364, 368

with the aggressor, III 163-4, 244
with the analyst [*see also Patient(s)*], III 158
of the body, with genitalia, *see* Identification, with genitalia
with child (one's own), II 122
in coitus, T 18
contemptuous, accompanied by reaction formation, III 267
& education, *see* Education
with father [*see also Identification with parents*], I 77; II 122, 265, 267; D 17, 21
with genitalia, II 85, 260, 269; III 204; T 60
hysterical, I 37; II 45; III 375
as imitation, permanent, III 267
& infantile sexual trauma, III 162
maniac, III 375
masculine, III 248-9
in masochism, III 224
'-melancholia', III 357
of mother, *see* Mother
with mother, [*see also Identification with parents*], II 307; D 17
mutual, T 17
new faculties arising from, III 164-5
& object-love, *see* Object-love
in paranoia, III 375
with parents [*see also Identification with father; Identification with mother*], I 77; II 167, 265, 267, 269
regression in homosexuality from object-love to, III 374
of sexuality with oral activity [*see also Oral erotism*], I 38
symbolic, of objects with bodily organs, I 275
wish-fulfilling, III 267-8
IDENTITY, ideational & perceptual, I 138, 223
IDIOSYNCRASIES [*see also Disgust*], II 38, 66; III 218
IDIOTS [*see also Imbecile*]
talent, mathematical, in, III 184, 189, 192, 195, 275
tics in, II 152
IDLENESS, *see* Laziness
IGNOTUS, I 18
ILLNESS
mental, *see* Mental disease(s)
organic, *see* Organic disease(s)
ILLUSIONS [Illusionary deceptions] [*see also Alcoholism; Delusions; Gulliver fantasies*], I *193*, 205-6; II 96
IMAGE(s)
composite, I 117
erotic, retained as word pictures, I 137-8
& fantasy, *see* Fantasy
hypnagogic, *see* Hypnagogic images
obscure, latency of, I 149
& speech, *see* Speech

IMAGERY, mimicry of, I 141, 145
IMAGINATION [*see also Fantasy*], I 139, 148
IMAGO, parental [*see also Identification; Transference*], D 21
IMITATION [*see also Mimicry*], I 37, 225, 229, 241, 245; II 164-5
& dream, III 266
identification & superego formation as permanent —, III 267
-magic & language, III 266
in neurosis, I 37
& physical resemblance, III 267
IMPARTING, *see* Empathy; Identification; Imitation; 'Mitteilen'
IMPOTENCE [*see also Ejaculation; Frigidity; Potency*]
general [*see also Exhaustion*], III 221
sexual [physiological, organic], I 22, 26, 28, 31-4, 61, 114, 123, 161; III 355, 363
sexual (psychic), I *11*, 19-20, 27-34, 51, 61; II 53, 132, 142; III 104, 354-355; T 6
anal & urethral, II 264; T 6-7
analytical therapy of, I 12; II 214, 261
& birth anxiety, II 354
& bridge-symbol in dreams, II 353
& constipation, II 94-5
dreams of & in, *see* Dream(s)
fantasied coitus in, II 269
& homosexuality [*see also Homosexuality*], II 94-5, 106-8, 244; III 173
& inhibition of obscene words, II 227
& mimicry, III 267
obsessive ideas in, I 17
paraesthesia of genitals in, II *312-13*
in paranoia, II 106, 360
& social advancement, II 417
'two voices' in, case of, II 108
& the unconscious, I 15, 17, 24-5, 33, 60
& the 'Zuhälter'-type, III 217
IMPOVERISHMENT FEELINGS [Impoverishment of libido] [*see also Exhausting; Libido*], II 22, 153; III 210, 217, 357, 362
IN-PATIENT TREATMENT, psycho-analytic, *see* Psycho-analytic in-patient treatment
INACCESSIBILITY in psychosis, I 291
INCENDIARISM, *see* Fire
INCEST [*see also Incestuous; Oedipus complex*], I 31, 33, 34, 61, 80, 87, 107, 136, 148, 185-6, 259, 293, 294; -barrier III 34-5
& the scientist, I 252-3
INCESTUOUS [*see also Fixation*]
affection of adults, masquerading as tenderness, III 121
fantasies, I 146; III 335

seduction of children by relatives, III 161–3
tendencies, III 33, 363
INCONTINENCE & sphincter tension, II 268
INCORPORATION (oral) [*see also Devouring; Introjection*], III 48–9, 375
INCREDULITY [*see also Conviction; Credulity; Doubt; Scepticism*], repressed, I 202–3; II 438–9, 445–6; III 268
INDISCRETION, III *271*, 273
'INDIVIDUAL PSYCHOLOGY', *see* Adler; Inferiority feeling
INDIVIDUAL(s), III 371–4
INDIVIDUALISM & QUANTUM THEORY, III *257–8*
INDIVIDUALITY, *see* Personality
INDIVIDUATION & the psychic instances, III 183
INDUCTION & DEDUCTION [*see also Logical relations; Thinking*], D 47
INDULGENCE PRINCIPLE [*see also Abstinence; Frustration; Relaxation*], II 297; III 114–15, 123
'INERTIA', resistance as, III 258
INFANT(s) [*see also Child(ren); Infantile; Infantilism; Newborn*], III 65, 219, 261
acceptance of reality by, II 370
discharging of tensions through aggressivity, III *219*
omnipotence feelings in [*see also Omnipotence*], III 359–360
prodigies [*see also Trauma*], III *262–3*, 271–2
self-destructive tendencies of, in form of glottal spasms, III 103
INFANTILE [*see also Child(ren); Childhood; Childish*, and under the respective headings], I 19, 20, 23, 25–9, 31, 65, 70, 71, 73, 82, 84, 86–9, 91, 93, 107, 108, 111, 143–6, 151–3, 175, 176, 185, 199, 200, 206, 207, 211, 224, 257, 258, 274, 277, 305, 308, 325
flight from responsibility, III 262
impulses & hypnosis, I 63
phobias, III 66
play of organs, III 26
sexual theories, *see* Infantile theories
sexual trauma, III 136, 230
defiance & guilt feelings after, III 163
forced fantasies of, II 76
& hysterical symptoms, III 241, 246
& identification, III 162
immediate reactions to, III 162
insignificant amount of, II 77
& intelligence formation, III 245
occurrence of, III 161
& pain as hysterical symptom, III 241, 246

paralysing effect of [*see also Inhibition*], III 162
perversion as an outcome of, III 163
& psychoneuroses, II 52, 54
reappearance of, [*see also Trance*], III 241–2
& underdeveloped sexuality, III 163
sexual wishes, I 15, 26, 32
theories, I 136, 307; II 50, 93, 314, 317, 325, 327; III 51–2
traumata (other than birth-trauma & sexual trauma), III 65, 121
INFANTILISM [Infantility] [*see also Child (ren); Childish(ness); Infant; Infantile; Naiveté*], II 152–3, 344; III 166
& anxiety concerning real tasks; III *264-5*
hysteria as [*see also Hysteria*], III *260–1*
& idleness, III 272
of organ-eroticism, III 26
INFECTION, psychical, in hysterics, I 37
INFERIORITY, feeling, I 28, 146, 231
& flight from responsibility, III 272
sexual, *see* Sexual inferiority
INFLEXIBILITY, *see* Elasticity; Flexibility; Rigidity
INHERITANCE, *see* Heredity
INHIBITION [*see also Act(ion); Activity*], I 20, 114, 125, 133, 136, 144, 147, 149, 201, 235, 261, 317; II 372, 380–1
of attention, II 231, 405
economy of, in wit, II 334
in latency period, III 375
of laughter, by the presence of strangers, III 178
of memory, motility & perceptions, III 240
psyche as organ of, II 379
sexual, I 27–33; III 375
by shock [*see also Motor disturbances*], III 239–40, 244
of thinking [thoughts], II 230–1, 240, 404; III 231, 240
in trance, by reappearance of trauma with shock-effect, III 239, 240
unequal, as essence of all action, II 381, 405
verbal [*see also Speech; Stammering*], I 135–6
& will-power, II 405
INNERVATION, *see* Muscle innervation
INJURY [Injuries], II *81–7*, *147*; W 8
amount of, producing masochism, II 280
auto-erotism, caused by, T 86
in childhood (sexual & traumatic), *see* Child; Childhood; Infantile sexual trauma; Seduction

ego-, I 223; II 83, 88, 141
& hyper-cathexis, II 81
libido disturbed by, II 81, 87
non-existent in case of hypochondria, II 83
in social life, & homosexuality, III 375
'INNOCENCE, primeval', III 84
INORGANIC tendencies in the organism, III 229
INSATIABILITY, see Hunger Sexual hunger
INSECURITY [see also Helplessness], III 223, 232
INSIGHT [see also Self-observation; Self-perception] & emotional & intellectual gratification, III 236
INSINCERITY, see Lie(s); Mendacity
INSOMNIA, see Sleeplessness
INSTANCE(s), censuring, see Censor(ship) psychic [see also Conscious; Mental mechanisms; Preconscious; Psychic system; Unconscious] (definition) II 197
the Conscious [Cs], III 183, 186-187, 189, 191, 222, 249, 255
& censorship, II 380, 382
inhibitory function of, II 380
& individuation, III 183
& mathematics; III *183-94*
the Preconscious [Pcs], I 64; II 304, 374, 382; III 183, 186-187
& unpleasure, III 264
the Unconscious [Ucs] [see also Id; Unconscious; Unconsciousness], I 18, 22, 31, 36, 37, 40-3, 53, 55, 58, 60-2, 65, 71, 72, 82, 86, 97, 107, 129, 138, 227, 262, 265, 276, 278; II, 20, 304; 350; III 186-187, 192, 251, 256, *265-7, 308-12*
biological, T 83, 85
'dictionary' of, given by Freud, III 148
& impotence, I 15, 17, 24-5, 33
language of, III 265-7
overpowering by, II 46
Paracelsus on, III *323*
of patient & physician [see also Patient(s)], III 148
role of, III 183
INSTINCT(s) [see also Death instinct; Libido; Life instinct, and under the particular headings], II *158*, 271; III 80, 225
defusion of, II 370, 377-9
education of, in analysis, D 19
& habit, II 286
& incompleteness of birth (Freud), T 97
& introspection, III 184
& mathematics, III 184
mutual neutralization of, II 372
play-, T 41
of self-destruction, II 376

socialization of, II 19, 382; III 68
& voluntary action, II 286
INTEGRATION
of the medical profession, see Medical profession
Man, as microcosmic —, III 252-3
mathematical, see Mathematics
& splitting of the ego, III *270-1*
INTELLECT, see Intelligence
INTELLECTUAL [see also Intelligence]
achievements & the feeling of 'dying', III 245
degeneration in general paralysis, III 356
faculties, see Thinking
gratifications through insight, III 236
knowledge, see Knowledge
pleasure in laughter, III 225
precocity in homo-erotics, I 307
super-performances, III 245
INTELLECTUALIZATION in analysis, III 38
INTELLIGENCE [Intelligent; Intellect; Intellectuality] [see also Brain; Genius; Intellectual; Knowledge; Logical relations; Mental; Progressive faculties; Thinking], III 228-31, *243-6*
(definition), III 246
aim of (preservation of unified personality), III 228
& correct behaviour, III 230-1
& egoism, III 243, 245
of the id, II 375
& genitality, T 71
lack of, in aggressor, III 225
male & female [see also Intuition], T 106
& sexuality, Schopenhauer on, III 353
& suffering, III 243-6
& superego formation, III 228
traumatic origin of, III 165, *243-6*
& unified personality, III 228
'INTER-RELATION' in mathematics & mental life, III 187
INTERCOURSE, see Coitus
INTERPRETATION(s), see Psycho-analysis; Psycho-analytic interpretations; Psycho-analytic method; Psycho-analytic technique
INTERRUPTION of the analysis & improvement, III 260
INTESTINES, see Bowels; Stomach
INTOXICATION & trauma, III 274
INTRAUTERINE [see also Mother; Omnipotence; Womb], I 83, 232, 238; T 78
happiness, III 359
'-hatred', III 227
& inorganic repose, orgasm as, T 63
life, I 218-22; T 73, 75
'play' with phylogenetic possibilities, III 265

regression, T 18, 20, 38-9, 95
theory of epilepsy, III 198-9
INTROJECTION, I 35, 49-53, 57, 226, 322; II 373, 406; III 227-8
(definition), I 47-8; III *316-18*
in coitus, T 74
of faeces, I 322
of guilt feelings, III 162-3
& habit formation, II 286
of ideas, sequestration as reverse process of, III 365
& narcissism, III 212, 373-4
& object-love, III 373-4
primitive machines as introjections, II 390
'squandering of affect' in, III 218
& transference, I *35*
'INTROPRESSION' of the super-ego in education, III 279
INTROSPECTION, see Self-observation
INTROVERSION
& musical faculty, II 378
& psychology, II 378
INTUITION [Intuitiveness] [see also Empathy; Intelligence], I 302; II 442; III 243
INVERSION
in childhood memories, III 264
sexual [see also Homo-erotism; Homosexuality], I 299-306, 309, 311, 313; III 171
of words or relationships, expressing ridicule, III 170
INVOLUTION, age of, see Age, old
IRONY [see also Comic; Cynicism; Grotesque; Wit], II 309, 343-4; III 170-1, 181
IRRESPONSIBILITY, see Childish(ness); Flight; Play
IRRITABILITY [Irritation], III 32; T 93, 94
ITCHING [see also Stimulus], II 87, 113, 269; T 38

JEALOUSY [see also Paranoia], I 44, 65, 74, 80, 159-66, 168; III 33, 212
delusions of, I 63-70, 65-6, 161-3
penis-, see Penis
JENDRASSIK, L., W 13
JEWELS as symbols, II 318, 321-2
JOCASTA, I 262
JOKE(s) [see also Aggression; Cynicism; Irony; Wit], I 115, 137, 141; II *339-43*
JONES, Ernest, I 93, 251, 307, 325; II 236, 323; III 74, 102, 104, 340
JUNG, I. G., I 13, 47, 51-2, 61, 78, 82, 83, 87, 177, 278; II 38, 211, 258, 389, 421, 449; III 111, 260, 264; D 36
JUDGMENT, see Objectivity
JURISPRUDENCE [see also Law], II *424*
JUS PRIMAE NOCTIS, III *341*

Kapp, E., on mechanical construction, II 389
KARSCH-HAACK, I 299
KELLER, I 304
KINDNESS, III 251, 270
KISSING, III 212, 219
KITE as erection symbol, II *359*, 360
KLEIN, Melanie, III 38, 69, 75, 127-8
KLEINPAUL, I 49-50, 151, 229; III 176
KLEPTOMANIA, I 39
KNEIPP, I 172
KNOWLEDGE [Knowing] [see also Ignorance; Intelligence; Thinking], I 236, 277; III 221, 269; D 22, 45
unfelt & unconscious feeling, split of the ego into, III 237
of the Universe, III 252-3
KOLNAI, II 216
KOVÁCS, V., on tics, II 271
KRAFFT-EBING, III 144

LABOUR, rhythmicity in, T 35
LAMAISM, III 274
LAMARCK, T. [Lamarckism] [see also Bioanalysis], III 62; T 50, 90-1, 94
LANGUAGE [see also Imitation magic; Obscene words; Psychoses; Speech; Words], III 265-7
LAP(s), female, I 156
LATENCY
of obscure images, not absolute, I 149
period, I 144-9, 233, 236, 308; II 161, 272, 417-18; III 33, 375
& ice age, I 237; T 104
LATENT DREAM-CONTENT, see Dream(s)
LAUDENHEIMER, W 13
LAUGHTER [Laughing] [see also Comic; Joke(s); Wit], II 232, 336-7; III *177-82*
(definitions), III 179-80
& the comic of brutal force, III 225
excessive, in dream, II 345
inhibited by the presence of strangers, III 178
& laughing at, II 336; III 177-8, 182
& love, III 179, 181
as motor discharge, II 232, 234; III 180-1
obsession as a reverse process of, II 432
physiological explanation of, III 180-2
at senseless struggle, III 226
& smiling, III 179
at unpleasant thoughts, II 336
LAW [see also Jurisprudence], respect for, II 430
LAY ANALYSIS, III 39, 42; D 66
LAZINESS, II 419-21; III 104, 272
& the pleasure in the mechanical, III 177

LEADER [see also Group psychology]
 & ego-nucleus, III 368-9
 & individual, III 374
LEARNING & play, see Play
LECANOSCOPY, see Crystal-gazers
LEFT SIDE, & anaesthesia, II 115-16
LEG [see also Cramp], I 186-8, 284, 285, 294
LESSING, II 317
'LIAR, a bad —', III 262 [see also Lie; Mendacity]
LIBIDO [Libidinal; Libidinous] [see also Cathexis; Object-love; Organ libido, & under the respective subjects], I 25; II 82, 200; III 49, 70-1, 354-6; D 6, 12; T 21
 accumulation of, II 160-1; 195; III 253, 257
 & anxiety, II 34-5, 275, 277, 300, 331; III 218, 253
 development of, in the child, see Child
 & discoveries (technological), II 389
 distribution, II 83; III 205, 224-7; T 86
 exchange of, III 253
 free floating, & anxiety, III *218*
 frustration of & anxiety, III 218, 253; D 9, 12
 genitopetal & genitofugal flow of, T 38
 -impoverishment [see also Impoverishment], II 22, 153; III 208, 217
 increase, local, II 83, 160-1; III 354-6
 injury, disturbing —, II 81, 87, 376
 instincts (libidinal) [see also Instincts; Pleasure principle]
 & lues, III 364
 & motility, II 230
 protonarcissistic, & hypochondria, III 217
 squandering of, II 195; III 188
 re-direction to genitals, & symptoms, II 197
 re-education of, D 16
 & self-destructive pleasure, III 224-7
 & sympathy, I 64, 65
 '-theory' period of, in psycho-analytical movement, III 185
 'thesauring' ['hoarding'] of, III 253
 vicissitudes of, III 173
 in war neuroses, II 141; III 352
 & wit, II 403
 withdrawal of [see also Depression; Melancholia, & under the various illnesses], I 45-6; II 22, 153; III 219
LIÉBAULT, III 198
LIEPMANN, W 12
LIE(s) [Lying] [see also Liar; Mendacity], III 70, 72, 79-80, 82, 262
LIFE [see also Organic; Psychic life, etc.], T 62, 70, 93-5
 continued in toto, death as, III 48
 & death instincts [see also Death instinct], II 337, 367; III 105, 220, 225, 252
LIFELESS thing, see Impersonal; Object
LILIENSTEIN, W 7
LIMITATION of action, & repression, III 75
LINDNER, S., on sucking, I 170; II *325*
'LITTLE HANS', III 71
LOCALITY, mental, see Instances; Mind; Locke, on intuition & proof, II 442
LOGIC, III, 183, 186, 188, 191, 196
LOGICAL RELATIONS [Logical functions], I 124-5; II 187; III 187, 263
 abstraction, III 187, 190, 195, 275
 affirmation, II 368, 378, 379
 causation (knowledge about), III 221
 deduction & induction, D 47
 & symbolism, I 178, 280
LOGICIAN, III 190 [see also Logic; Logical; Philosophy]
LOGORRHOEA, II 165
LONELINESS, see Abandoned
LONGING [see also Wish], III 104, 123, 262
 for death, disguised as laughter, III 177
 to return to womb, see Intrauterine; Mother; Womb
LOVE [see also Affection; Fixation(s); Hate; Incest; Longing; Object-love; Sympathy; Tenderness], III 179, 206-9, 376
 amount & character of, needed, III 164
 falling in —, libido-cathexis in, III 376
 & hatred, I 155; III 123-4
 heterosexual, intensity in homosexuals, III 168
 & hypnosis, analogy between, I 90-2; T 78, 106
 & laughter, III 179, 181
 mutuality in, III 248
 in the newborn, passive, III 219
 over-passionate, III 163-5, 227
 withdrawal of & split of the ego, III 219
LUES [Luetics] see Syphilis
LUNGS [see also Asthma; Respiration], diseases of, III 27-8
LUST-MURDER [see also Defusion; Sadism], II 278-9
LYING, see Lie(s); Mendacity
MACH, Ernst, II 383, 387, 393
MACHINE(s) [Machinery] [see also Discoveries; Mechanical; Mechanism; Tools], II 386-90, 393
MADNESS [see also Psychosis and under the various headings], II 311; III 246, 249
 'courage for —', III 251, 268

MAEDER, I 155–6; III 203
MAGIC [Magical] [*see also Imitation magic; Omnipotence*], I 222, 225, 230
MALE, *see* Man
MALICIOUSNESS [*see also Hate*], II 371, III 205
MALINGERING, *see* Simulation
MAN [Mankind], III 187–93, 252–3; T 85
MAN [Male; Men] [*see also Adult(s); Homoerotism; Homosexual; Sexual differences; Woman*], II 24–5; III 364; T 105–6
  childishness in, III 263
  dependence in, III 58, 217
  Don Juan types of, II 358
  egoism of, III 226
  reality principle in, I 262
  termination of analysis, signs in, III 84
MANIA [Manic; Maniac] [*see also Delusion; Depression; Euphoria; Melancholia; Paranoia*], I 38–9; II 403; III 31, 181, *355–62*
  & alcoholism, III 181, 209–10
  'doubting-', II 438
  & ego-ideal, III 31, 375
  & exaltation, III 209–10, 355
  megalo —, *see* Megalomania
  object libido, defective in, III 209–10
MANKIND, *see* Man (Mankind)
MANN, L., W 16
MANNERISMS & tics, III 81
MARRIAGE [Marital life] [*see also Coitus; Family; Love; Orgasm; Sexuality*], I 302; II 272–5; III 24–5
MASCULINE [Masculinity] [*see also Man; Sexuality; Woman*], II 219; III 248–9; T 106
  giving up of —, as sign of termination of analysis, in women, III 84
MASOCHISM [Masochist; Masochistic] [*see also Anal erotism; Sadism, Sadomasochism*], I 16, 75, 81, 107, 108, 249, 271; II 88, 280; III 33, 166, 244, 249, 363; T 25
  & addiction to unpleasure, III 244
  & anal erotism, II 47, 280
  & analysis, 'active' & 'passive', *see* Psycho-analytic technique
  cutaneous envelope as the seat of, II 88
  & death, III 243–4
  & hallucinations (compensatory), III, 244
  & hypnotic pliancy, I 80–1
  & masculine identification, III 248–9
  nature of pleasure in, II 280
  & orgasm, III *248–9*
  & pleasure in self-destruction, III 224–7, 244
  & reality, II 376
  & scratching, II 87
  & tic, II 160

MASS TREATMENT & ANALYSIS [*see also Psycho-analysis*], III 149
MASSAGE, & transference, I 55
MASTURBATION [Onanism] [*see also Auto-erotism*], I 13, 23, 32, 50, 73, 122, 168, *186*, 192, 198, 250, 251; II 33, 75, *170*, 194, 195, 247, 300, 316; III 23, 216–217
  & analysis, I 208–9; II 214
  bad habits, as equivalents for, II 282
  & constipation, T 6
  converted into coitus, III 216
  disposition to, III 217
  -equivalents, II 192, 282
  excessive —, causal factor in neurasthenia, II 32
  exhaustion & 'after pains', II 33; III 266
  & eyes, I 186, 188; II 317
  & fantasies, III 216, 266
  'without fantasies', II 298; III 216
  fear of, I *185*
  & genital primacy, T 22–3
  giving up of, II 53; III 216
  & guilt feeling, II 32; III 253
  in hypochondria, III 208
  & impoverishment feelings, III 208, 210
  larval form of, II 189, 190, 195, 205, 317
  & neurasthenia, II 32, 33, 53; III 23, 208, 253
  & nocturnal emission & coitus, II 276–7; III 216–17
  in old persons, III 205, 208
  & prayer, II 299
  & primal scene, III 266
  'pulling off', symbol for —, II 276
  regression to, III 272
  & tic, II 144, 160, 170, 173, 271
  & urethral erotism, III 217
  per vaginam, I 187
  & washing compulsion, II *311*
MATERIALIZATION [*see also Conversion*], II *89*, *104*, *110*, 172–3
  (definition) II 96, 104
  hysterical, II *89*, 96; T 10–11
MATERIALISM [*see also Philosophy*], & mechanism (Freud), III 252
  psychology undervalued by, III 146–8, 153–4
MATHEMATICIAN, introspection in, III 183–4, 187
MATHEMATICS [*see also Algebra; Arithmetic; Counting*], III *183–96*
  & autosymbolism, III 183
MATTER, double meaning of word, T 70
MATURITY [*see also Development; Infant prodigies*], in homo-erotics (sexual & intellectual), I 307
  & hypnosis, II 56
  precocious, after trauma, III 165
  sleep, diminution of need in, T 77

McCurdy, III 198
Mechanical [see also Discoveries; Machine(s); Mechanism; Tools],
construction, E. Kapp & H. Spencer on, II 389
pleasure in the —, & laziness, III 177
as substitution for lost omnipotence, III 177
Mechanism,
Mach on, II *383*, *393*
& materialism, Freud's views on, III 252
mental, see Mind, Mental mechanism(s) [see also under the respective subjects]
of tools, machines, etc., see Discoveries; Machines [Machinery]; Mechanical; Tools
Mechanotherapy, see Psychotherapy, non-analytical
Medical [Medicine] [see also Physician; Psycho-analysis; Psycho-analyst; Psychotherapy]
jurisprudence, see Jurisprudence
profession
hypocrisy in, III 158–60
integration of, III 14–15
& reluctance to appreciate psychoanalysis, III 152
Medicine, see Medical
Medusa Head, as erection symbol, II 360
Megalomania [Delusion of grandeur; Grandiose delusion] [see also Omnipotence], I 117, 155, 165, 219, 231, 285; II 22, 105; III 215, 250, 272, 361, 365–7
euphoria, capacity for, in, II 368
& humour, II 344
Meige, on tics, II 148
Melancholia [Melancholic] [see also Depression; Mania], III 202, 210, 356–7, 365
disappearance of, in course of organic illness, III 352
& ego-ideal, III, 31, 375
egoistic-subjective ['-egoistica'], & identification [see also Identification], III 253
object libido, defective in, III, 209–10
respiration in, III 181
Melusina Legend, T 46
Memories [Reminiscences] [see also Child, Cover-memory], I 16, 75, 90, 100, 134, 137, 149, 196, 204, 242; II 73
Memory [see also Remembering], III 77–8, 194–5, 260–1; D 9
for details, III 275
images, I 22, 118, 120, 137, 139
inhibited by shock, III 240
'mnems' [Engrams], II 287; III 264; T 66

& partial reproduction of traumatic event, III 264
repetition converted into —, through relaxation, III 124
-system, see Ego-memory-system [see also Psychical systems],
traces, I 15, 32, 138, 219, 255, 303; II 158, 377; III 264
& unpleasure (Freud), III 244
Men, see Man [Men]
Mendacity [see also Liar; Lie(s), (Lying); Simulation], III 77–9
giving up of, in last phase of analysis, III 78–9
in money questions, I 45
of parents, III 70, 72
Mendelism & repression, T 87
Menstruation [Menstrual cycle], III 122; T 57, 77
Mental, see Mind
Mereshkovsky's 'Peter & Alexis', I 78
Metabolism in sleep, embryonic state & coitus, T 75
Metaphysics [see also Metapsychology], III 322
Metapsychology [see also Mind], I 49; III 98, *145–8*, *185*, *322*
of habits, II *284*
Meynert, III 31
Method(s), psychological, criticized, III 63, 74–5
psychotherapeutical, see Psychoanalysis; Psychotherapy, nonanalytic
Mice, fear of, II 109
Micromanic paresis, see Paresis
Micturition [Urination] [see also Bladder; Urethral erotism], I 20, 31–2, 90, 110–11, 192; III 24; T 5
during analysis, desire or need for, I 206–7; II 260–1
in children as libido-reward, II 317
-fantasies of Gulliver, III 51–2, 54, 55
fear of, in public, II 49
fire extinguishing by, as infantile theory of coitus, II 258; III 51–2
as sedative, II 317
Migraine (see also Headache), III 26
Mimicry, I 141, 145; II 165; III 267
& analysis, III 82
autoplastic reaction as, III 163
as regression, I 164
Mind [Mental] [see also Brain; Intelligence; Instances; Psychic(al)], I 105, 266; II 267, 370; III 194, 322, 364
dynamic-economic-topic construction of, III 221–3
diseases [Disturbances],
heredity in the aetiology of, see Aetiology;
Heredity
organic causes of, II 17–18; III 362
& sexuality, II 21, 52

418 INDEX

& social advancement, II *417*
-ego & body-ego, III 357-9
hygiene movement, III 18-21
levels, II 374
locality, & displacement of energy, III 222
mechanism(s) [*see also Instances*], II 374; III *221-3*
paralysis, & intellect, III 244-5
MIRRORS & exhibitionism, II 365
MISERLINESS, *see* Avarice; Money
MISFORTUNE as counter-indication for analysis, III 278
MISTAKES [Errors; Erroneous performances; Parapraxes; Slips], cases, II *407-10*; III *335*
 childhood elements in, I 71
 & symptomatic acts [*see also Symptomatic acts*], II 411-12
MISTRUST, *see* Distrust
'MITTEILEN', III 266
MIXED NEUROSES, *see* Neuroses, mixed
'MNEM', *see* Memory
MODESTY, exaggerated, II 239
MOHR, W 16
MONASTERISM & masturbation, II 170
MONEY, I 45, *319-32*
 'Besitz', meaning of, I 138, 326
 filth equated with, I 320; II 362-5
 interest in [*see also Avarice*], & anal erotism, I 320, 329; II 248, 257, *362*; III 33
 & intestinal disorders, I 329
 matters, in psycho-analysis, *see* Psycho-analytic technique
MONISM, I 48; II 16, 366, 383
MONOSYMPTOMATIC NEUROSES, III 25
MORAL
 masochism, *see* Masochism
 standards, *see* Standards
 principle, *see* Principle(s)
MORALIZING, as 'therapy', II 27, 235, 446, 449
MORALITY, II 25; III 80, 179-80
 ambiguous (double code), imposed upon the child, III 73
 semi-physiological groundwork of mental —, II 267
MÖRCHEN, W 9
MORICHAU-BEAUCHANT, R., III 340
MORO, E., W 21
MOTHER [*see also Intrauterine; Parent(s); Womb*]
 & aggressiveness [*see also Hatred, maternal*], III 227, 255
 body of, and death symbolism, III 202
 breast of, thumb equalled with, III 219
 -child relation, & relaxation & security feeling after orgasm, III 257
 -complex (example), I 74-5
 'enveloping' as symbol for assimilation, III 228

-figure, introjection of, III 227-8
-fixation [*see also Mother & son*] & maternal hatred, III 227
 foster —, I 26-7
 hatred in, *see* Hate
 & homosexuality of son, III 168-9, 171-3; T 48
 '—' hypnosis, *see* Hypnosis, maternal
 identification of oneself with [*see also Mother-symbols*], I 77; II 265, 267, 307; D 17
 of analyst with, I 74
 incestuous fantasies of coitus with, I 146
 '—', origin of word, T 70
 as provider, III 58-9, 217
 & son, I 51, 176; III 58, 227
 symbols for, [*see also Mother, identification*] III 51; T 47, 49
 woman (cook, provider) & the 'Zuhälter', III 217
 '—'s womb' [*see also Regression; Womb*]
 fantasies about, III 36, 44-7, 268-9
MOTHERLINESS [*see also Maternal; Tenderness*]
 in response to brutality of, III 217
 another ego, III 226
MOTILITY [*see also Motor*], II 230, 382
MOTOR [*see also Motility; Movement; Muscles; Paralysis*],
 discharge, laughter as, II 232, 234, 334
 tic as, II 160, 165, 172
 disturbances [*see also Abasia; Astasia; Inhibition; Stammering; Trembling*], III 240, 255; W 15
 elements, III 222
 invested in obscene words, I 141
 functions, & attention, II 232
 type, I 148; II 161, 230
MOURNING [*see also Depression; Grief*], II 61; III 85, 357-8
MOUTH, *see* Oral
'MOUTH-POLLUTION', II 43, 315
MOVEMENT(s) [*see also Motility; Motor*]
 dread of, I 148-9
MUD & analerotism, I 322-5
MURDER, lust-, *see* Lust-murder
MURDEROUS TENDENCIES [*see also Aggression; Destruction; Paranoia; Rage*]
MUSCLE(s) [Muscular],
 clonuses & tonuses [*see also Epilepsy*], III 180-1
 & defence, III 230, 234
 -erotism, II 172; III 48
 innervation [*see also Motility; Motor-disturbances*], II 48, 91, 128, 230
 relaxation, & free association, II 231, 282 [*see also Neocatharsis; Psychoanalytic technique; Relaxation*]
MUSICAL [*see also Dance; Rhythm*]
 associations, III 175-6
 faculty & introversion, II 378

INDEX

& mathematical talent, III 189, 193
MUTHMANN, I 12
MUTILATION [*see also* Autotomy; Castration], death less dreaded than, III 48
MUTISM, *see* Catatonia
MUTUAL [Mutualism; Mutuality]
 devouring & adaptation, III 230
 domination & co-ordination, III 257
 fixation & transference, I 87
 forgiveness & the comic, III 178
 identification in sex act, T 17
 in love, III 248; T 106
 neutralization of instincts, II 372
 regard, origin of, III 251
 transference, & incestuous fixation, I 87
'MÜNCHHAUSEN'S METHOD', II 27
MYOPIA, I 270-1
MYTH(s), I 266

NAECKE, I 297
'NACHGIEBIGKEIT' [*see also* Elasticity; Indulgence; Pliability; Trauma], III 114
NAÏVE [Naïveté], II 342-3; III 128-9, 182, 226
 encouragement to, in analysis, III 123
NAIL-BITING & masturbation, II 170
NAKEDNESS, I 105, 170, 176; II 329
NARCISSISM [*see also* Auto-erotism; Egoism; Narcissistic; Omnipotence], I 167, 205, 233, 289, 297-8, 301, 302, 305; II 85, 172, 239, 248, 282, 406, 420; D 9
 in the age of involution [*see also* Age, old], III 205, 209
 & analysis, *see* Psycho-analytic treatment
 of analyst, D 41
 in dementia praecox, I 234
 disease-,—*see* Disease-narcissism
 in general paralysis & libido increase, III 354-6
 in neurosis, II 106, 417
 object-love at the expense of, II 377
 in paranoia, II 81, 87, 106
 in patho-neuroses, II 81, 248
 in primitive organisms, II 375
 & procrastination, II 419; III 272
 proto-, *see* Libido
 regression in physical illness to, III 351
 resistances due to, D 9
 secondary, *see* Secondary narcissism
 & shock, III 230
 & social advancement, II 417
 & split of the ego, III 135, 226, 237, 246 [*see also* Split]
 & stage fright, II 421-2
 & tic, II 144, 151, 161, 171, 283; III 81

transferred to child, II 330
 & traumatic neurosis, II 156; W 17, 18-19
NARCISSISTIC [*see also* Autoerotism; Egoism; Narcissism; Omnipotence]
 ego, *see* Ego, narcissistic [*see also* Split of the ego]
 neuroses, & transference neuroses, III 349-50
 psychoses, I 234; II 87, 106; III 353-6
 '-split of the self' [*see also* Split of the ego], III 135
NARCOTICS, use of, in therapy, II 28-9
NAUGHTINESS(ES) [*see also* Aggression; 'Bad habits'], during analysis, II 216; III 83-4, 132
NECROPHILIA, Pfeifer on, II 279
NEEDLE, I 30, 270
NEGATION [*see also* Negativism], II 367, 374, 376
 in dreams, I 125
 & neurosis, II 369
 in organic pathology, II 375-6
 & pleasure principle, II 379
 of reality, *see* Reality
 in transference, II 368
NEGATIVISM [*see also* Negation], I 80, 87, 291; II 367
 in persecution mania, II 439
 primary process of, II 367
 transitory, in child, II 367
NEOCATHARSIS, *see* Catharsis; Psychoanalytic technique, active
NEPHEW, death of, in dream, I 109, 118
NEURALGIA, I 190
NEURASTHENIA [Neurasthenic(s)], I 34, 130, 186-91; II 31, 276-7; III 22-4, 210, 253; T 26
 aetiology, II 18, 31, 32; III 217
 & anxiety neurosis, II 34; III 253
 & depression, III 210
 as ego-indebtedness, III 253
 exhaustion in, II 275; III 23
 in general paralysis, III 354
 & hypochondria, III 208
 & hysteria, III 22
 inadequate discharge, as alleged cause of—, II 275
 & involuntary emission, III 23
 & masturbation, II 32-3, 53; III 23, 208, 253
 & obsession, II 35; III 23
 'one-day —', II 186, 190
 & urethral erotism, III 217
NEUROSIS [Neuroses] [*see also* Neurotic(s); Psychoneuroses, and under the respective subjects], I 23, 32, 41, 45-7, 51, 77, 82-5, 98, 111, 122, 130, 154, 186, 192, 213, 216, 231, 255, 307, 312, 317, 318; II 16, 21, 30, 52, 345; III 19-20, 35, 85-6; D 18

aetiology of [see also Aetiology; Constitution; Heredity; Predisposition], II 24, 32; III 110, 120, 364
  & alcoholism, I 163
  & anal activity, II 264
  'artificial —', analysis as, D 12
  & birth trauma, Rank on, II 223
  of children, see Child
  choice of, I 184, 234–5; III 365–6
  comparisons & symbols used by patients for, II 398
  of covetousness, see Covetousness
  dementia praecox compared to, I 47
  dynamics of III, 375–6
  the ego in, I 47
  & excessive libido discharge, III 217
  fixation points of, I 236
  & habits, II 281
  hypnosis, analogy with, I 83–4
  inability in —, to be hypnotized, I 86
  mixed, II 52; III 85–6
  monosymptomatic, III 25
  & object-homo-erotism, I 303, 313
  & obscene words, see Obscene words
  paranoia compared to, I 48
  pathogenesis of, I 28, 129
  perversion as a negative of, II 368
  physio-, II 18, 32
  secondary functions of, I 86
  & sexual life [sexuality], I 86; II 32; III 24–5
  stages of, I 211–12
  stimulation phenomena in hypnosis & —, I 84
  substitution in, I 155, 193
  'Sunday —', II 174
  symbols in, II 398; III 228
  & transference, I 36, 155
  & traumata, see Infantile sexual trauma; Trauma
  two periods of development, D 18
  & urethral activity, II 264
  wish constituent of, I 235
  in women, more frequent, II 25
NEUROTIC(S) [see also Neurosis], I 38, 48; II 413; III 81, 85, 123–4
NEW
  ideas & reality testing, I 257; II 54
  pleasure & unpleasure in the —, III 275
NEWBORN [see also Child; Infant], behaviour of, I 220; III 198–9
  disgust at, III 218
  feeling of being deserted, in, III 219
  love of, III 219
  monism of, I 18
  'omnipotence' of, I 213–14, 221–3; III 359–60
  passivity of, III 219
  pleasure & unpleasure of, III 199
  self-destructive tendencies, caused by frustration, in, III 219
  sleep of, III 198; T 73

split of the ego in, III 219
NEWS, good & bad, effects on health, III 26–7
NEWSPAPER as a dream-figure, I 114–15
NIETZSCHE, I 70
NIGHTMARE(S), I 113; III 24, 44, 157
  as repetition of the traumatic events, III, 233, 236
  in trance, III 233–4
NONNE, W 10, 13, 15, 16, 17
'NONUM PREMATUR IN ANNUM', II 419–21
NORMAL [Normal person(s)]
  dreams of, I 128–9
  grief & mourning in, II 61
  hypnotism of, I 83, 85
  hysterical predisposition in, I 83
  introjection in, I 52
  orgasm in, III 267
  projection in, I 49
  & psychoneurotics, I 61
  repression in, III 19–20
  scopophilia in, II 300
  & unpleasure, reaction to, II 22–3; III 228
NOSE, in dreams, I 40; II 101
  & genitalia, I 190–1
  idea of misshapen, in case of neurosis, II 283
  as oral substitute, III 219
NOSOLOGY, see under the respective headings
NOVELS, phobia of, I 50
NUNBERG, H., on catatonia, II 173
NURSERY TALES, the Oedipus complex in, T 48
'NURSING' part of the self (split-off), III 226, 237–8
NUTRITIONAL FUNCTIONS [Nutrition], II 271, T 85–6

OATHS, I 151
OBEDIENCE, I 32, 71, 76–7, 80, 81, 93
  & maternal & paternal hypnosis, III 340
  of patient, as repressed criticism, III 158
OBESE [Obesity], see Fat; Fatness
OBJECT(S) [see also Ego & external world; Impersonal]
  anthropomorphism of, I 49
  'dying', feeling of, projected into, III 221
  -erotism, I 234
  identification, symbolic, with bodily organs, I 275
  'maliciousness' of, II 371
  words treated as, II 442
OBJECT-LOVE, I 49, 65, 67, 74, 77, 185, 208, 234, 298, 300, 302, 306, 315, 321
  analytic, III 98
  & conversion symptoms, II 173, 197

defective, in manic-depressives, III 209–10
'ego-syntonic', III 360–1
& hate, I 49
& identification, III 374
introjection preceding, III 373–4
& narcissism, II 377; III 205–7
& obedience, I 77
passive stage [*see also Tenderness*], III 163–4; T 21
regression from, II 309; III 205–7, 374
OBJECT-HATE, see Object-love, first, & -hate
OBJECT-HOMO-EROTISM, see Homo-erotism; Homosexuality
OBJECTIVATION & SUBJECTIVATION, III 265–6
OBJECTIVITY [*see also Negation; Reality sense*], II 372–3, 444; III 63, 263
development of, II 373, 439, 440, 441
OBSCENE WORDS [*see also Obscenity*], I *132–53*; II 73, 182, 226–7, 403
& aggression, I 141
evocative power of, I 137
& impotence, II 227
in obsessional neurosis, II 226
orgasm, achieved only by use of, II 227
repressed wishes expressed in, II 403
& sphincter activities & speech culture, II 226, 251
& tics & catatonia, II 161, 165, 171, 226
OBSCENITY [*see also Obscene words*], I 105, 132–8, 140–5, 149–53, 160
OBSESSION(AL) [Obsessive] [*see also Compulsion (Compulsive)*], I 54, 150, 152, 271, 316; II 21, 23, 48–51, 232, 243, 284, 419, 430, 444, 450
actions, differentiation from tics, II 51, 174
fear, see Fear
ideas, I 17, 25, 51; II 232
homo-erotism (object-), I 306–7
& laughter as reverse process of, II 432
symptoms, in analysis, I 209
thought, see Obsessional idea
OBSESSION(AL) NEUROSIS, I 46, 185; II 21, 35–6, 48–9, 430–1, 444; III 662
(definition) II 21, 444
in ageing women, III 205
analysis of, II 48–9, 209, 221
fixation points in, I 235–6
& homosexuality, I 209, 306–7
& hysteria, II 48–9, 444
increasing, apparently, II 444
in men, commoner, II 25
lack of confidence & conviction in, II 228, 438, 444
& neurasthenia, III 23
obscenity in, II 226

& omnipotence, see Omnipotence
& piety, II 450
& postponing of projects, II 419–21
& religion [*see also Religion*], II 450
& taboo, II 430
therapy of, II 48
OBSTINACY [Stubbornness] [*see also Anal erotism*], II 258; III 33; T 22
& active therapy, II 262
OBVIOUSNESS, feeling of, I 216–17
OCEAN [Sea], T 45, 47, 56
OCCUPATION
'-cramps', & tics, II 170
-delirium, Tausk on, II 170, 298
of father, & neurosis, II 418–19
'-pollution', II 298, 300
OCCUPATIONAL THERAPY, II 28
ODOUR(s), see Smell
OEDIPUS COMPLEX (Oedipus conflict) [*see also Complex(es)*] *Oedipus myth*], I 26, 41, 91, 136, 235, 258, 259, 307, 310; II 50, 111; III 33–5, 71–2; D 54; T 104
female, III 34–5
in homosexuals, I 297
in individual development, T 104, 105
inverted, I 303
& masturbation, II 214
negative, D 17
in nursery tales, T 48
reactivation by active technique, II 267
situation, III 268; D 17–18, 54, 62
wish, T 19
OEDIPUS MYTH [*see also Oedipus complex*], I 26, 259, 267
in analysis, II 428–9
Schopenhauer on, I 253–4
symbolism in, I *253*, 259, 261–4; III 52
OESOPHAGUS, as symbol, II 101
OKEN, on coenogenesis, T 45
OMNIPOTENCE (fantasy of), I 77, 215–17; III 250
a case of, II 105
in the child, II 366; III 359–60
of doctors, III 27
in dreams, I 223
in fairy tales, I 238–9
in the foetus, I 218–19; III 359
in general paralysis, III 361–2, 364
by magic gestures, thoughts, & words, I 225, 230; II 373
magical-hallucinatory period of, I 213–14, 221–3; III 360
& the mechanical. III 177
& obscene words, I 231
of parents, III 27
& pleasure principle, II 366
regression to, I 231; III 361
in sexual development, I 233–4
sleep as regression to, I 222–3

stages of, III 359-60
surrender of, II 367, 373, 400
unconditional, period of, I 219
ONANISM, see Masturbation
ONTOGENESIS [see also Development; Phylogenesis]
autoplastic stage in, II 97
development in, I 237-8
of ego-consciousness, I 48
of genitality, T 5, 23
of interest in money, I *319-31*
of knowledge process, I 277
of neurotic regression, II 137, 138
& phylogenesis, II 97, 99, 254, 374-5; T 19
of psychical mechanism, I 38; II 374
of symbols, I *276-81*
of war neuroses, W 16
OPERATION
dream of, I 40
nervous phenomena after, III 26
persecution mania after rectal, II 80
OPHUIJSEN, van, III 349
OPPENHEIM, on traumatic neuroses, W 6-7, 14
OPPONENT, see Aggressor
OPPOSITE, in childhood memories, III 264
OPTICAL, see Visual
OPTIMISTS & PESSIMISTS, I 232
ORAL
activity, identification of sexuality with, I 38
character, see Oral erotism
erotism [see also: Cannibalistic; Erotogenous zones, oral; Sucking], I 16, 108, 189; II 315; III 33, 219
frustration, see Frustration, oral
gratification, III 219
incorporation, II 370
nose as — substitute, III 219
satisfaction, in general paralysis, III 363
ORDER & pleasure, III 178
ORGAN(s) [see also Body, parts of],
differentiation & evolution of, II 99
erotism [see also Organ libido], II 103; III 25-6
formation of, & volition, T 100
libido [see also Hypochondria; Organ erotism], II 124; III 217; T 86
neurosis, III 22-8, 256
projection, II 166, 389-90
sense —, see Sense organs
subordinated to pleasure principle, II 103, 152
'unemployable', T 92
ORGANIC [see also Body; Somatic]
adaptation, see Adaptation, organic
analogies for the psychic, II 377
causes of mental disease, II 17-18; III 362
destructive processes in the brain,

causing libido impoverishment, III 362
difficulties, erotism as pleasurable overcoming of, II 265
disease(s) [see also Narcissism; Regression, & under the respective headings],
& disease narcissism, II 83-4
disappearance of melancholia & narcissistic psychoses as consequence of, III 352
dream symbolism of, I 112-13
& endocrine system, III 256
& libido (re-)distribution, II 82; T 86
negation & adaptation in, II 375-6
as pathoneuroses, see Pathoneurosis
displacement into the —, through repression [see also Conversion; Displacement; Repression], II 264
evolution & retrogression, T 88-9
groundwork of mental morality, II 267
individuality, T 82
pathology, see Organic diseases
repression, T 83
senses & sensations, see Sense(s); Sensation(s)
sexual inferiority, I 28-9
ORGANIZATIONS, scheme of, III *256-7*
ORGANISM [Organic life], I 237; III 229, 251; T 61, 83
ORGASM [see also Coitus], III 257, 267; T 35-6, 39, 42-3, 60, 99
anal, II 270
by breathing on penis, II 227
dream —, & pollution, II 297
'effortless reality' through, III 267
expectation of, hypnosis as, III 339
identification of whole personality with genitals in, III 204
as intrauterine & inorganic repose, T 63
masochistic, III *248-9*
masturbatory, & exhaustion, III 266
obscene words as condition of, II 227
relief after, compared with mother-child relation, III 257
& sleep, T 73
'ORGASTIC POTENCY' (Reich), III 121
ORLOVSKY, W 17
ORTVAY, T 87
'OUTLET', III 249, 251
OVER-ACQUIESCENCE, see Acquiescence
OVER-COMPENSATION of hypochondria with euphoria, III 356
OVER-DETERMINATION, I 197; T 84
OVER-EATING, in general paralysis, III 363
OVERPASSIONATE LOVE, see Love, overpassionate
OVER-SENSITIVENESS, see Hyperaesthesia

INDEX 423

PAEDERASTIA, *see* Homoerotism; Homosexuality
PAIN(s) [Painful] [*see also Suffering; Unpleasure; (Unpleasant)*]
  'alienating over' of, III 265
  & analysis, II 201, 287; III 236
  & anxiety, III 27
  in eyes, after masturbation, I 186, 188
  flight from, II 22–3, 239; III 248–249
  frightened awakening after sudden, III 233
  in the head [*see also Head; Headache*], III 234
  in the heart [*see also Heart*], I 26, 27, 198, 199
  in the spine (in neurasthenia), III 23
  as hysterical symptom, & infantile sexual trauma, III 241, 246
  infant's first experience of, II 370
  & intelligence, III 243–6
  lessening of, by fragmentation, III 230
  monism of child kept from, II 366
  symbols of, III 222
  toleration of, III 90, 276–7
  in trance, *see* Trance
  turning away from, symbolized by 'getting beside oneself', III 222
PAINTER, 'replacement in', I 51
PALINGENESIS [*see also Biogenesis*], Haeckel on, T 45–6, 103
PALPITATION, *see* Heart
PAN-EROTISM, *see* Pansexuality
PANIC [*see also Fear; Shock; Stage-fright*]
  & general paralysis, analogy between, III 369
PANGENESIS, T 16, 69
PANSEXUALITY
  alleged, of Freud's doctrines, III 68, 151
  in Groddeck's 'Seelensucher', III 347–8
PARACELSUS, on the unconscious, III 323
PARAESTHESIA [*see also Anaesthesia*], I 14, 19, 34, 186, 198, 284; II 44–5, 87, 101; III 118, 139–40; T 16–17
  in the genitals [*see also Genital*], II 74, 246, *312–13*
  and impotence, II 312–13
PARALLELISM, psycho-physical, II 16
PARALYSIS [*see also Paralysis, general, of the insane*], I 75, 84, 130, 195, 196, 200
  mental, *see* Mental paralysis
  sensory, with inhibition of perception & thinking, III 240
  traumatic [*see also Shock; Trauma*], III 162, 239–241, 244
PARALYSIS, GENERAL, OF THE INSANE [*see also Paralysis*], III *351–70*
  as actual psychosis, III 353, 355–8
  choice of symptoms in, III 365–6

  destruction of identifications in, III 364
  ego-nucleus, role of, in, III 362, 368, 369
  & hypochondriac sensations, III 355
  mania in, III 355, 358–9, 361–4
  narcissistic libido increase in, III 354–6
  & omnipotence feelings, III 364
  & panic, III 369
  projection in, III 363
  '—, regressiva', III 361
  'sequestration' in, III 361
  stages of, III 354, 358
    euphoric, III 355
    hallucinatory, III 358
    'imbecility', III 365
    'neurasthenic', III 354
  & temporal & topographic factors in, III 366–7
  & vicissitudes of the ego, III 359–69
PARANOIA [*Paranoic; Paranoiac(s)*], I 26–7, 32, 47, 65, 130, 154–7, 159, 167, 170, 175–9, 183, *184*, 233–4, 289–94; II 94–5, 247, 438; III 32, *213–5*, 250
  (definition) II 81
  & alcoholism, I 157–63; III 212
  & anal erotogenic zone, II 80; III 295–8
  & analysis, I 294; II 26–7; III 215
  & anxiety, I *282*; II 78, 79, 86; III 249–50
  & homosexuality, I 94–5, *154*, 247, 297; II 79, 359–60; III 212
  narcissism in, II 81, 87, 106
  & neurosis, I 47–8; II 105
  & paraphrenia, I 285
  & projection, I 48, 154–5, 169, 175, 184, 233, 293; II 22, 53, 80, 438
  rationalization, in, I 126
  & reality, III 31
  self-observation in, III 213–14
  sex incidence of, II 25
  & sexual hunger, I 48, 184
  'social identification', III 374–5
  system-formation, I 293–4
  & tics, II 146
  'traumatic', II 81
  'two voices', a case of, in, II 105–7
PARAPHRENIA [*see also Dementia praecox; Schizophrenia*], I 234, *282*, 292, 294, 298; II 78–9, 86–7, 153, 403; III 211
PARAPRAXES, *see* Mistakes
PARASITE, man as lifelong — (*see also 'Zuhälter'*), T 85
PARENT(s) [Parental] [*see also Educators; Family; Father; Mother; Obedience*], I 40, 42, 60–5, 69, 77, 81–4, 87, 91, 93, 102, 116, 135, 136, 143, 151, 265, 266, 273, 274, 276, 281, 307, 308, 310; III 71

awe of, I 20, 80; III 27
& children [*see also* Child], II 266, 320–1; III 27, 161–3
'-complexes' [fixations], I 60–1, 67, 252; III 27
egoism of, III 273
erotism of, T 24
identification with, *see* Identification
imago [*see also* Superego; Personality], II 266, 286; D 21
dissolution of, II 100–1
'impeccability' of, III 268
lies of, III 70, 72
'omnipotence' of, III 27
understanding, lack of, in, III 62
PARESIS [Paretic(s)] [*see* Paralysis, General, *of the insane*]
PARK, dream-figure, I 121
PARTIAL
'death', *see* Death, Dying
pain [pain-fragments] leading to greater adaptability, III 230
reproduction of traumatic event [*see also* Memory], III 264
surrender of personality, in adaptation, III 243
PASSAGÈRE, *see* Transitory
PASSION(s) [*see also* Emotion(s); Exaggerated; Love; Over-; Super-], I 45–7; III 137–8, 156–67
PASSIVITY (Passive) [*see also* Homosexuality; Masochism; Woman], I 302
of analyst [*see also* Psycho-analyst], II 75, 182, 224, 238, 290, 291, 401
castration tendencies, *see* Castration, self-
character of consciousness, II 380
incorporation, *see* Incorporation
induced by shock, in trance, III 239
in love life, III 163–4, 219
'pleasure in —', III 224–7
'PAST, PULL OF THE —' [*see also* Present], III 268–9
PATHOGENESIS, *see* under the respective headings
PATHO-HYSTERIA, II 82–3
PATHOLOGY, organic, negation & adaptation in, II 375–6
PATHONEUROSIS [Pathoneuroses], *see also* Organ neuroses II 78–9, 82–3, 145, 247; III 256, 351–2; D 35
analytic treatment of, III 39, 123, 342–3, 344–5
cerebral, III 352–3
circulatory disturbances [*see also* Heart], III 103
of digestive system, *see* Digestion
ego-identification with injured organs in, II 83, 88
& genital lesions, II 86
& hyper-cathexis of injured organs, II 81
& hypochondria, differences between, II 83
& narcissism, II 81, 248
& respiratory system, *see* Asthma; Respiration
& sympathetic system, III 256
& tic, II 147
& traumatic neurosis, II 83
PATIENT(s) [Analysand] (Personal aspects), [*see also* Physician; Psychoanalytic situation; Psycho-analyst(s); Resistance; Transference]
& 'active therapy' [*see also* Psychoanalytic technique, active], II 64, 225, 228–9, 293–6, 448–9
& analyst [*see also* Transference], D 40–1
childishness of [*see also* Child analysis in the analysis of adults], II 132–3, 186
communications, subjective reality of, III 235
confidence of, III 232–3, 270
criticisms by [*see also* Patient(s) doubts], III 158, 235, 242, 247, 261; D 13
& decisions, II 183
doubts of [disbelief, distrust] [*see also* Patient(s) criticisms], III 89, 91–93, 222, 232–3, 235, 261, 268
'dying', feeling of, III 138
escape, tendency to, III 233, 234, 246–8
freedom of [*see also* Relaxation] in analysis, I 44–5; II 181, 224
generalizations by, II 184
grip, intensity of, III 233
'half-cured —', II 233; III 98–9
hatred of, *see* Transference, negative
hopes of, III 91–2, 222–3, 233–4
identifications by [*see also* Identification; Transference], I 74; III 158
initiative of, II 289; III 235
knowledge, theoretical, of no therapeutic use during analysis, D 22
mendacity of, I 45; III 77–9
& misuse of fundamental rule, II 177
narcissism of, D 42
questions put by, II 183–4
relation of, to physician [*see also* Transference], III 148; D 40–1
renunciation (final) of analysis as source of gratifications, III 85
& resistance, *see* Resistance
revocation & repudiation by, of confessed material, III 233; D 11
self-analysis of, attempts at, II 310; III 83, 98–9
submissiveness of, as repressed criticism, III 158
suggestibility of, alleged, II 235; III 27
suicidal tendency of, III 238, 247

testing by, the analyst's patience & goodwill, III 83, 90
turning from past, Jung on, II 211
PAVOR NOCTURNUS [see also Anxiety; Fear], I 107, 245; II 111
PCS [the Preconscious], see Instances, psychic, the Preconscious; Preconscious
PECULIARITIES, II 316; III 81
PEDAGOGIC MEASURE, see Education, Re-education
PEDANTRY, I 148-9; II 258, 261-2; III 33
PEDERASTY, see Homosexuality
PENIS [see also Castration fear; Genital; Phallus], I 89; II 227-8; III 49
'anal', see 'Anal penis'
body, as substitute for, III 46-7
as 'comical appendage', III 268
as ego (miniature), T 16
-envy [jealousy], II 122, 204; III 34-5, 46; T 106
& personality, III 49
& primal struggle, T 50
primal —, tooth as, T 22
symbol(s), I 263, 294; II 272; III 36, 50, 53, 56; T 49-50
PERCEPTION [see also Projection; Self-perception; Sense perception], II 382; III 275
PERCEPTUAL IDENTITY, see Identity
PERFUMES, I 324-5
PERIGENESIS, T 46, 61, 69
PERIODICITY [see also Menstruation], in sleep & coitus, T 79
PERSECUTION [Persecutory delusion(s)] [see also Paranoia], III 32, 250
by groups (alleged), III 375
'-mania', II 80, 439
PERSEVERATION, I 237
'PERSONAL EQUATION', in analysis, III 88-9
PERSONALITY [see also Character; Ego; Patient(s); Superego-formation]
'adjusted', III 225
'being torn to pieces', see Split of the ego
'dead part' of, III 226
disintegration [dissolution] of [see also Death instinct; Psychosis], III 220, 254
fragmentation of, see Fragmentation
& the genital organs, III 49
identification of genitalia with, III 204
'beside itself', W 222-3
partial destruction of, III 226, 243
plurality of — (zoological analogy), III 222
organic & psychic, T 82
pretraumatic, III 228
reconstruction of [see also Psycho-analytic method; Psycho-analytic technique], II 225

splitting of, see Split
superficial, emerging from atomized ego, III 226
topical view of, III 222-3
'torn in pieces', feeling of, III 221-2
unification of, III 220, 222, 228
whole —, analysis of, D 30
PERVERSION(S) [Perversities; Perversity], I 107, 108, 132, 144, 150, 178, 180, 181, 298, 299, 313
& early genital level, III 121
& epilepsy, III 203
& erotic development, T 26
& hysteria, II 47-8; III 68
& infantile sexual trauma, III 163
& infantilism, III 166
& neurosis, II 47, 52, 368
& tenderness, III 166
PESSARY, dream of, II 304
PESSIMISM, I 232, III 104-5
'PETIT MAL', III 203
'PETITE HYSTÉRIE', see Hysteria
PFEIFER, on necrophilia, II 279
PFISTER, on cryptographia, II 404
PHALLIC [Phallus] [see also Penis] stage, III 33-5
PHANTASY, see Fantasies
PHILOSOPHY [Philosophic] [see also Brooding; Introversion; Thinker; Thinking; Thought], I 292-3; III 78, 147, 252
& psycho-analysis, III 326-34
PHOBIA, see Fear
PHRENOLOGY, II 17; III 189
PHYLOGENESIS [see also Development; Ontogenesis], I 238, 277
autoplastic stage in, II 97
of conversion, see Conversion
& fertilization, T 61
of genitality, T 44-72, 97, 102, 103-5
of group phenomena, III 372-3
'intrauterine play', with possibilities of, III 265
neurotic regression, a model of, II 137, 138
& ontogenesis, T 19
of reality sense, I 236
of symbols, I 319; II 356
PHYLOPHAGY, T 85
PHYSICIAN (Doctor) [see also Psycho-analyst(s)],
& analyst, difference between, D 7
family —, & analysis, D 64-5
'omnipotence' of, III 27
& patient [see also Transference], 'a dialogue between two unconscious minds', III 148
PHYSICS & psycho-analysis, II 393
PHYSIOGNOMY & psycho-analysis, III 81-2
PHYSIOLOGY, see Biological; Biology; Organic; Somatic, and under the respective headings

PHYSIO-NEUROSES, II 18, 32
PIÉRON, on sleep, T 74–5
'PIÉTINER SUR PLACE', III 258
PIETY, see Religion
PINEL, III 150
PLAINS, feeling of moving in endless, III 222
PLASTICITY, see Adaptation; Flexibility; Personality; Pliability
PLAY
  '-analysis', see Child analysis
  in animals, I 238
  with erotic organ functioning, III 26
  & expression, III 130–2
  & growth, III 264–5
  -instincts, T 41
  'intrauterine —', with phylogenetic possibilities, III 265
  with language & words [see also Speech, Word(s)], III 265
  & learning, III 269
  longing for irresponsibility, III 262
  & reality, III 272
  & repetition compulsion, T 40
PLEASURE [Enjoyment] [see also Frustration; Gratification; Instincts; Libido; Pleasure principle; Unpleasure],
  'of adaption', III 225–6
  aesthetic, see Aesthetic pleasure
  'altruistic', see 'Altruistic pleasure'
  & anxiety, concentrated in coitus, T 43
  in comparisons, II 406
  & counter-cathexis of unpleasure, III 251
  in defence situation, [see also Masochism] III 265
  & fertilization, T 68
  fore-, see Fore-pleasure
  & laughter, III 179, 225
  masochistic, see Masochism
  in the mechanical & laziness, III 177
  of the new, III 275
  & order, III 178
  organ-, see Organ-erotism
  -organs & hysteria, II 103
  '— in passivity', III 224–7
  & perception, III 275
  physiology of, T 83
  in rediscovery & repetition, II 406–7
  & security-feeling, III 178
  of self-destruction [see also Libido; Masochism; Self-destruction], III 224–7
  in smell, I 305, 322, 324
  in superiority (intellectual) over brutal opponent, III 225
  & unpleasure, see Unpleasure & pleasure
PLEASURE-PRINCIPLE, I 223, 232, 255, 331 [see also Pleasure]
  (definition), III 191
  & 'active therapy', II 211, 218

as 'controller-in-chief' of action, II 19, 136
development from, I 217–18, 232
& negation, II 379
& omnipotence, II 366
& other principles of mental life, III 31
psychogenetic stage of, I 214
resolution of, I 213
in self-sacrifice, III 224, 226
& sexuality, I 233
& sphincters, see Sphincter(s)
subordination of organs to —, in hysteria, II 103
symbolized by Jocasta [by the woman], I 262, 269
thoughts rarely independent of, II 99
in tic cases, II 152
toleration for actions against, III 276
PLEXUS SYMPATHICUS [see also Reflex system], III 256
PLIABILITY (Pliancy) [see also Character; Flexibility], I 80–1; II 163
PLOUGH, as symbol, T 48
POET(S) (Poetic), I 266; II 403–4; III 324
POLARITY, II 99, 367
POLLUTION, see Ejaculation
POLYCLINICS (Psycho-analytic), D 58
POLYCRATISM, II 423
POLYGAMY [see also Don Juanism; Marriage], I 302
'POLYMORPHOUS-PERVERSE' [see also Perversion; Sexuality, infantile], stage, I 298
POMPADOUR fantasies, II 351
POPULAR VIEWS
  of dream-theories, I 95
  of evaluation of masturbation, III 23
  wisdom of, and science, I 94
POSITION, see Posture
'POSTHUMOUS ANALYSIS', III 59
POST-NATAL, see Newborn
POSTPONEMENT, in obsessional neurosis, II 419–21
POST-TRAUMATIC
  autosymbolism, see Autosymbolism
  fragmentation, III 230
  hatred, III, 157–8, 166–7, 261
  homosexuality, see Homosexuality
  intelligence, III 165, 243, 244–6
  maturity, see Maturity
  personality, III 228 [see also Death; Dead; Dying]
  progressive faculties, see Progressive faculties
  split of the ego, III 162, 164–5 [see also Split]
POSTURE, II 131, 242; III 81
  intrauterine, T 75, 78
  in sleep & coitus, T 75
  upright, I 322
POTENCY [see also Ejaculation; Impotence],

boasts regarding, I 159-60, 163
false superperformance, II 264; III 272
hallucinatory, in general paralysis, III 363
of homosexuals, III 173
& libido squandering, II 195
'orgastic —' (Reich), III 121
reduced, II 132; III 354
PRAYER, [see also Religion]
automism in; II 299
PRE-ANALYTIC THERAPY, see Psychotherapy, non-analytic
PRECONSCIOUS [see also Instances, psychic, the Pre-conscious]
attention, diversion of, in analysis, III 232-233
fear & impotence, I 31
memory-material, D 9
results from selective activity of censorship, II 404
superego, III 100-1
& unpleasure, III 264
PREDISPOSITION [Disposition] [see also Aetiology; Constitution; Heredity], I 28, 33, 65, 209; II 115, 130; W 13-14
& effectiveness of trauma, II 52, 115, 130, 156
& localization of symptoms, II 42
PREGENITAL [see also Erotogenic zone(s)],
amphimixis, T 11-12
education, see Child(ren); Education
& genital erotism, II 265, 270
identification, II 265
PREGNANCY [see also Birth; Confinement],
disgust at, III 218
imagined, I 90, III 246-7
manias in, I 38-9
sickness in, II 93, 95
symbols for, II 101, 305, 361
PRENATAL, see Intrauterine
PREPUCE, see Foreskin
PRESENT
child, living in the —, see Child(ren)
flight from the —, III 268-9
& past, III 279
PRESENTATION, I 42, 121, 124, 125, 131, 239
PRESERVATION, tendency of, in organic life, I 237
PRE-TRAUMATIC PERSONALITY [see also Personality; Post-traumatic], III 228
PRE-TREATMENT (A. Freud), III 106
PRIDE, in one's children, & exhibitionism, II 320
PRIMAL [Primary, Primeval, Primordial],
catastrophes & ice ages, T 70
father, see Father
'— homosexuality', III 171
horde, see Horde
'— innocence' (Groddeck), III 84

penis, tooth as, T 22
process, II 336, 367, 375
projection, see Projection
repression, II 77
scene, III 65-6, 167, 266
& secondary process, II 369, 375
PRIMITIVE MAN (Primitive peoples) [see also Ethnology; Popular Views], I 314, 331; II 387
PRINCIPLE(s)
of pleasure, reality & morals (Freud), [see also Pleasure principle; Reality principle], III 31
of knowledge about the Universe, III 252-3
PRISONERS OF WAR, & neuroses, W 9
PRIVATION(s), see Abstinence; Frustration
PRIVIES, phobia of, I 50-1
PROBLEM(s), II 183-4; III 263
'-children' [see also Bad habits; Child; Naughtiness (es)]
PROCESS(ES) [see also under the respective headings]
mental, see Mind [Mental] processes
primary & secondary, see Primary process; Secondary process
procreative [see also Coitus; Genital; Sexual], T 38-9
psycho-analytic, see Psycho-analytic treatment
PRODIGIES, see Infant prodigies
PROFESSION(s), see Occupations; Medical profession
PROFESSIONAL HYPOCRISY, see Hypocrisy, professional
PROGRESSION [Progressive faculties] [see also Genius; Infant prodigies; Intelligence; Trauma] & trauma, III 165, 243-6, 262-3
PROHIBITION(s), see Abstinence; Education; Frustration; Psycho-analytic rules; Psycho-analytic technique, active
PROJECTION(s), I 92, 154, 177, 183, 216, 232, 233
of the disliked, III 212
on to fate, I 259
of feeling of 'dying' into animals & objects, III 221
in free association, II 180
in general paralysis, see Paralysis, general
of homosexuality, see Homosexuality
Kleinpaul on, I 49-50
of the mathematician, III 194-5
of memory, III 260-1
Oedipus myth as, I 259
organ —, self-acting machine as, II 390
in paranoia, see Paranoia
of perception (distorted), I 175
period of, I 227; II 373, 439, 441

primal, I 48; II 441
of sexual hunger, I 48
in sleep, T 74
& speech development, I 50
PROPHYLAXIS, I 29, 34; II 30
PROSTITUTE, being kept by, III 217
PROTECTION, through ambivalence, II 372
PROTOPSYCHE, regression to, II 97
PROTONARCISSISTIC LIBIDO, see Libido
PROVERB, anal-erotic, II 365
PRURITUS ANI, see Itching
PSYCHE [see also Mind; Soul]
   as organ of inhibition, II 379
   projection phase, I 227
   proto-, regression to, II 97
PSYCHIATRY [see also Psychotherapy],
   analytic, see Psycho-analysis; Psycho-analytic method, movement
   non-analytic [see also Psychotherapy, pre-analytic], III 18–20
   organic, see Anoia; Brain; Functional psychoses; Organic diseases; Paralysis, general
   'pre-Freudian & post-Freudian epoch of psychiatry', III 13–14
PSYCHIC(AL) [see also Mind; & under the respective headings]
   forces & analysis, II 213, 266
   'leap from' —, to body, II 90–1, 100, 173
   life [see also Mind, Mental life], regressive tendency of, T 83
   organic analogies for the (see also Organic; Somatic), II 377
   processes & physiological changes, II 98
   shock, Freud's theory, III 19–20
   system(s) [see also Ego; Id; Superego], II 99, 155–6; III 183
PSYCHO-ANALYSIS* (as Science) [see footnote and also Patient(s)], I 105; II 21, 24, 57, 390; III 29–40, 68, 110, 235; D 2, 14, 31, 45–6, 50, 57; T 96–7
   & animism, II 256
   & chemical analysis, D 34
   of comparisons & symbols, II 397–407
   & criminology, II 431–2, 434; III 39
   & education [see also Child analysis; Education], III 37–8, 74, 80, 134, 280–90; D 14, 19, 34–5
   & ethnology, I 153; III 39
   experiments in, II 197
   & the family physician, D 64–5
   & graphology, III 82
   & group analysis, review of Freud's work on [see also Group(s)], III 371–6

& introspection, III 63–4
lay-analysis, see there
& mass treatment, III 149
& medicine, D 50–1
& mimicry, III 82
& money matters [see also Money], I 45; III 92–3
'pan-sexualism' of, III 68, 151
the 'personal equation' in, III 88–9
& philosophy, III 326–34
& physiognomy, III 81–2
& physiology, see Biology, organic
& psychiatry, II 53
& religion, II 429
rules, see Psycho-analytic rule(s)
& science, I 256–7; II 393; D 65
social aspect of, II 216
& talent research, III 186
time factor in, see Psycho-analytic treatment, duration; termination
training —, see Training analysis
'wild', see 'Wild' psycho-analysis
PSYCHO-ANALYST(S) [see also footnote on this page and Counter-transference; Patient; Psychologist(s); Transference], I 40–4, 54, 74, 89, 116; III 124, 233; D 23, 29–30
   activity of [see also Psycho-analytic technique, active], II 75, 215, 220–91
   admission of blunders, III 94–5, 159
   alternating between critical scrutiny & fantasy, II 189
   analysis of the —, see Training analysis
   'analytic object love', III 98
   attitude of, to patients [see also Counter-transference; Patient], II 64, 177, 188, 215–16, 235–7; III 91–5, 233, 261–2
   as catalyst, D 8
   change of, D 41
   & contact with patient, III 89, 114, 233
   contradiction & dissatisfaction displayed, III 233
   contra-indications not observed, II 53
   coolness of, III 95, 129, 159–60
   dangers of counter-transference [see also Counter-transference], III 95, 124, 159; D 34
   emotions of [see also Counter-transference], II 186; III 98
   empathy of, III 89–92, 99–100
   goodwill of, III 90, 114, 233, 236
   holiday of, II 235
   'humility' of, III 94–5, 233–4, 235
   identification of the patient with, III 158
   indiscretion of, helpful, III 271, 273

* NOTE. The general heading 'Psycho-analysis' was broken down as follows: Psycho-analysis (as science); Psycho-analyst; Psycho-analytic interpretations; — method; — movement; — rules; — session; — situation; — technique; — technique 'active'; — treatment (process).

lack of energy & sympathy, alleged, III 261
'lay' —, see Lay-analysis
narcissism of, D 41
objectivity of, III 263
'omnipotence', parental, seen in, III 27
passivity of, see Psycho-analytic technique
patience of, II 53; III 94-5, *233-8*
& physician, difference between, D 7
pressing the termination of the analysis, III 84-5
professional hypocrisy of, III 158-60, 272-3
psychological difficulties of, II 189
reaction to patient's reactions, III 89
as 'revenant' (Freud), I 41
role of, D 7
sadism in, II 220
sex of, & transference, I 43
sleepiness of, II 180
sympathy of, II 186; III 161, 259, 270, *278*
tact of, III 82, 89, 99-100
& teacher-pupil relation, III 37-8, 113; D 38-9
truthfulness of, II 180
verbosity of, III 96
'wild', see 'Wild' analysis

PSYCHO-ANALYTIC INTERPRETATION [*see footnote on page 428 and also Interpretation(s)*], II 199, 352; III 20, 96; D 24
anagogic, D 36-7
analyst's scepticism in his own, II 70
autosymbolism & hysterical representation in, III 221
of dreams, easy with 'unsuspecting' difficult with 'warned' people, II 346
economy in, II 199; III 96
fanaticism for, D 29-30
instead of repression (after repetition), III 261
premature, D 23
squandering with, III 96
timing of, III 89-90, 96

PSYCHO-ANALYTIC METHOD [*see footnote on page 428* and also under the particular headings], I 130; II 29; III 152; D 7, 26
(definition) II 29-30; D 6
with absent people, III 59
the 'accidental' as material in, II 40
achievements & results, III 148-9; D 5
child analysis, see Child
child analysis with adults, III *126-42*
contra-indications, II 278
& conviction, I 193-4; II 64, *437-49*
dangers, alleged, I 53
depth of analysis, III *276*

as derivation of psychic formations from infantile experience, II 385
'descriptive', D 28
with difficult, stagnant or 'dried-up' cases, II 196, 212; III 128-9
failures, II 53, 220
& hypnosis & suggestion [*see also Abreaction; Catharsis; Hypnosis; Suggestion*], II 27-8, *55*, 200
& 'active therapy' [*see also Catharsis*], II 69, 212, 224, 266, 291
comparison, I 59; II *55-67*, 184, 197, 235, 237, 447-8; III 110, 149
historical relations between, II 65-6
problems of possible use of suggestion in (after) analysis, III 255, 269-70
& inpatient treatment, III 124-5
& other methods compared [*see also Psychotherapy, non-analytical*], I 11; II 25-9, 61, 256; III 90-2, 110, 149
& outpatient treatment, D 58
as repetition of individual development, II 272; D 19
replacing repression by repetition, III 261
revision, incessant, of, III 97-8
sincerity essential in, III 117
'social' aspect of therapy, II 216
superannuated techniques in, D 28
as symbol interpretation, II 352
as synthesis, III 80-1
turning the patient away from his past, II 211
two phases of therapy in, II 200

PSYCHO-ANALYTIC MOVEMENT [*see footnote on page 428*]
criticisms against, by Ferenczi, D 28-44
by Groddeck, III 348
by opponents, I 53
future tasks of, III 185-6
history of, II 30-8, 425-6; III 109-11, 143-55, 373
epochs in, III 184-6, 373
free association method in, III 145
hypnosis, renounced, II 37
inhibitions in development, D 28
libido-theory period in, III 185
Oedipus complex, discovery of, D 54
traumatic-cathartic period of, II 37, 199, 449; III 184
organization of, III *299-307*
separatists in, III 152

PSYCHO-ANALYTIC RULE(S) [principles] [*see footnote on page 428*]
of abstinence
of satisfactions, frustration, privation [*see also Psycho-analytic technique; gratification; Psycho-analytic technique, active*], II 201-2, 260, 271-2, 275-6, 278-9; III 37, 217

& transference love [*see also Psycho-analyst, attitude to patient; Psycho-analytic technique, passivity; Psycho-analytic technique, silence*], II 290
appointments, keeping of, II 200–1; III 77
of conduct, *see* Psycho-analyst(s); Transference
'fundamental —' [Free association(s)] I 22, 99, 110, 129, 193, 194, 202, 204; II 38, 40, 42, *177–83*, 201, 401; III 115, 145, 232; D 48
abuse of, II *177–83*, 207
in active therapy, II 68–77
& differentiation of thinking & doing, II 181
& 'forced fantasies', II *68–77*
& incomplete sentences, II 181
& relaxation, II 282; III 115, 258
& senseless material, II 77–8
& silence, III 129, 258
& withholding of help by analyst, II 182
& writing, uselessness of, II 182
of kindness [*see also Psycho-analyst*], III 270
of objective attitude [*see also Psycho-analyst*], III 263
of passivity, *see* Psycho-analytic technique
of relaxation [*see also Neo-catharsis; Psycho-analytic technique, active*], II 290; III *108–25*
& silence, III 89, 129, *258–60*
of training analysis [*see also Training analysis*], III 88–9
of truthfulness & sincerity, II 180; III 117

PSYCHO-ANALYTIC SESSION [*see footnote on page 428*]
coma in, *see* Trance
disillusionment at end of, II 240
gestures during —, as masturbation equivalents, II 282
giddiness at end of, II 239
homosexual fantasies during, II 242, 250
masturbation during, I 208–9
micturition during, II 260–1; T 206–7
movements during, II 281–2
posture during, II 242–3
restlessness at end of, II *238*
shame, feeling of, after II 241
shock-effect of end of, III 114
silence in, II 179, *250*
sleep during, II 79–80, 179, 249–51
sleepiness during, I 199–200; II 179
trance during, *see* Trance

PSYCHO-ANALYTIC SITUATION [*see also footnote on page 428 also Patient(s); Transference*], absence of associations in, II 179
limits of compliance in, III 236
& parental 'omnipotence', III 27
rules abused in, II 69, 177, 179, 181
& teacher-pupil relation, III 108–109, 113
& trance, *see* Trance

PSYCHO-ANALYTIC TECHNIQUE [*see footnote on page 428 and Patient(s)*], II 38, *177*, 181, 199, *288*; D 6, 46–7
activity in, *see* Psycho-analytic technique, active
applied, *see* under the respective headings
at the beginning of treatment, II 219
of child analysis applied to adults [*see also* Child analysis], II 186; III 106, *126–42*
by comparisons, II *184*, 400
& compliance, III 236
& conviction, I 193–4; II 448–9
dangers of disregarding technical rules, II 219
of discontinuous analysis, II *233–5*
education, III 37–8
efficacy of, II 213
elasticity of, III *87–101*
encouragement in, II 27; III 133–4, 158, 265, 266, 268, 270, 271, 360, 361
ineffective in cases of anxiety, III 264
to naïveté, III 123
versus suggestion of contents, III 243
at end of analysis, II 109
failures in, II 53, 220
fantasy & critical scrutiny in, II 189
& free associations, *see* Psycho-analytic rule(s), fundamental
frustration principle [*see also Psycho-analytic rule(s), abstinence; Relaxation*], III 112, 114
& generalizations, II 184
& graduation of sympathy, II 186
& gratification [*see also Psycho-analytic rule(s), abstinence*], II 272
indiscretion in, III 271, 273
& money question [*see also Money*], I 45
& narcotics during treatment, II 28–9
of *passagère* symptoms, *see* Transitory symptoms
passivity in, II 182, *199*, 224, 228, 238, 290–1, 401; III *108–25, 156–67*; D 43
popular or technical terms used in, I 132
& questions & problems of patients, II *183–4*
regulation of habits, anal, urethral & sexual, II *259–78*, *260–71*, 286
relaxation in, *see* Catharsis, neo-; Psycho-analytic technique, active

INDEX

with sceptics, II 445–6; III 268
& silence, II 179, 288, 290; III 89, 129, *258–60*
& speed of initiation, II 180
success with, endangering thoroughness, II 233
suggestion in [*see also Psycho-analytic method & other methods*], II 235; III 243, 255, *269–70*
teachability [*see also Training analysis*], III 87
& termination of analysis, *see* Psychoanalytic treatment, termination
of trauma-analysis & sympathy, III *278*
traumatic factors of pathogenesis emphasized in, III 156
& 'working through' III 82–3
writing down to be avoided, II 182

PSYCHO-ANALYTIC TECHNIQUE, 'ACTIVE' [*see footnote on page 428 and also Abreaction; Catharsis; Relaxation*], II 75, *177*, 184, 196, 198, 228–9, 233, 259, *288*; III 37–8, 96–7; D 2, 4–5, 34, 49, 55
abstinence principle extended [*see also Psycho-analytic rule(s), abstinence*], II 201, 202, 206, 260
& 'acting out' in trance, III 233–4
aggressive features of, II 215
applied to [*see also Psycho-analytic technique active, indications*]
anxiety hysteria, II 196, 209, 236, 260
character analysis, II 214–15, 220, 263, 291
conversion hysteria, II *189*, 209
hypochondria, II 121, 189
impotence (psychic), II 214
masturbation (positive indication for), II 191, 214
neuroses of children, II 210
obsessional neurosis, II 209, 210, 221, 228
psychotic cases, II 291
repetition compulsion, II 217, 224
tic, II 282
war neuroses, II 210
in association technique, II 68
at the beginning of treatment not advisable, II 219
& catharsis, differences [*see also Catharsis*], II 212
at close of treatment, II 209
commands & prohibitions in, II 68, 75, 191, 196, 206, 214, 220–1, 235–6, 260–1, 266
contra-indications of, II 69, 208, 217
dangers of [*see also Psycho-analytic technique, active, conditions for use of, — contradictions of, — misuse of*], II 213–14, 220

& 'dried up' (stagnant) cases, II 196, 212; III 128–9
& education, III *236–8*
an experimental method, II 197, 261
failures, II 53, 220
'forced fantasy' method, II *68–77*, 207, 289
frustration principle, revision of, III 112, 114
further development of, II *198*
Groddeck on, II 225
indications for, II 70, 198, 208, 213–14, 270, 289, 292, 294
misuse of, III 99–100
& nutritional functions, II 271
Oedipus complex reactivated by, II 267
pain in, II 287
— tolerance strengthened by, II 280, 287
& pleasure principle, II 211, 218
promoting non-active procedure, II 228
relaxation technique [*see also Catharsis; Relaxation*], II 199, 212, 226; III *108–25*, 128–9, 160, 236
& repetition tendencies, II 217; III 37, *124*
repressed inclinations rendered fully conscious by, II 205
& resistance, II 63, 218; III 37–8
& 'sexual anagogy', II 274
& speeding up of analytical work [*see also Psycho-analysis, termination*], II 213, 289
sphincter-exercises, *see* Sphincter experiments [Exercises]
& suggestion-therapy, differences between [*see also Psycho-analytic method & other methods*], II 60, 62–3, 69, 184, 197, 200, 212, 224, 235, 237, 266, 291, 447–8; III 70
theory of (importance, meaning, metapsychology, etc.), II 213, 223–4, 287, 292; D 14, 55
& transference, *see* Transference

PSYCHO-ANALYTIC TREATMENT (Process) [*see footnote on page 428 and also under the various illnesses & symptoms*], I 209; II 368; III 232–3, 236; D 15–18, 22, 38–9, 54
absorption during [*see also Trance*], III 232–3,
aims of, II 292, 448–9; III 100–1; D 62
as 'artificial neurosis', D 12
breaking off, while transference undissolved, II 233
comparisons emerging during, II *184*, 397
duration of, II 223; III 91–2, 148–9; D 13–14, 52–3
emotional transports during, III 236

432   INDEX

emotionalization or intellectualization of the, III 38
'endless' [interminable], III 86
'for example' during, II *184*
frustration(s) [privation] during [*see also* Abstinence; *Psycho-analytic rules, abstinence*], II 75, 260, 271, 277, 289
& gratification [*see also* Gratification; *Relaxation*], II 272; III 85
homo-erotic fantasies & sleep during, II 250
hysterical attacks during, III 118, 129, 261
& latency period, II 272, 418
narcissism of patient during, II 215; D 42
'naughtiness' developed during, II 216
new material, access to, during III 82–3
obscene words, during, I 132, 142
pain during, III 90, 236
the 'personal equation' in, III 88–9
pliancy [elasticity] during, II 163, III *87–101*
problems of patient during, II *183–4*
psychosis, transitory, during, III 86
& reality, II 234, 366; III 233
reappearance of symptoms in, III 118–19
regression during, I 207–9
& repetition(s), D 3–5, 11
  hallucinatory, of traumatic experience [traumatogenic situation], I 193, 204–5; III 156–60, 223, 224, 232–3, *268*
  interpretation, instead of repression of —, III 261
  & resistances, *see* Resistance
rigidity during, II 281
simulation during, III 78
speed of, II 213, 220, 289
suicidal tendencies during, III 238, 247
superego transformation in, III 98, 100–1
& sympathy, III *278*
termination of, II 123, 221, 296; III 77–86, 277–8; D 14
  with active technique [*see also* Psycho-analytic technique, active], II 189, 209, 213, 221, 223, 289, 293
  breaking off (sudden), III 114
  conditions towards end of, II 209
  depreciation in the last phase of, D 13
  'endless analysis', III 86
  & fantasies, III 277–8
  frustrations in the last phase of, II 75
  & 'half-cured' patients, II 233
  reality as substitute for transference towards, II 369
  renouncing analysis, as a source of gratifications at, III 85
  signs of III 78–9, 84–6, 120
  time-factor in, II 221, 223, *294*; III 37–8, 83–6, 112
  weaning from analysis, II 293
trance during, *see* Trance
transference in, *see* Transference
transitory symptoms during, I *193–212*; II 213, 216, 282; III 118, 129, 156–7; T 7
words, resistance to use certain, II 182, 442
& 'working through', II 220, 290; III 82–3, 97
PSYCHOGENESIS [*see also* under the various headings], I 214; II 390; W 7, 10, 12
(PSYCHO)GNOSIS, III 263
PSYCHOLOGICAL TACT, *see* Tact
PSYCHOLOGIST(S) [*see also* Psycho-analyst(s)], I 256; III 190–1
PSYCHOLOGY, I 18; II 19, 378; III 146–8, 153–4
PSYCHONEUROSIS [Psychoneuroses, Psychoneurotic(s)] [*see also* Neurosis, and under the specific headings] I 11, 14, 16, 20, 24, 32, 34, 46, 52, 54–7, 60, 76, 83–5, 97, 99, 104, 128, 130, 152, 163, 186, 187, 282, 313; II *15*, 30
of the age of involution, *see* Age, old
& infantile traumata, II 52
& normal persons, I 61
& parental fixations, I 61
& sexual development, T 26
PSYCHO-PHYSICAL PARALLELISM, *see* Parallelism
PSYCHOSIS [Psychoses, Psychotic(s) (in general) [*see also* Madness; Organic; *Psychoneuroses*; and under the particular headings]
actual —, III *353*
analysis of, I 294; II 26–7; III 18, 215
ego-psychology of, *see* Ego-psychology
fixation-points of, II 368
hallucinations in [Psychoses, hallucinatory], III 43, 358, 367–8
inaccessibility in, I 291
language in, III 20
narcissistic, I 234; II 87, 106; III *353*
as pathological self-cure, III 86
puerperal, II 86; III 352
& reality sense, III 31
& split of the ego, III 121 [*see also* Split]
transitory, III 86, 121
wish-fulfilment in, I 223
'PSYCHOPATHOLOGY of Every Day Life', I 49, 200
PSYCHO-SEXUAL, *see* Sexual
PSYCHOTHERAPY (non-analytic) [*see also*

Psychiatry; Psycho-analysis; Psychoanalytic movement, history], I 27, 67, II 157; 34; III *18*, 27; D 8, 31, 36-7
compared with psycho-analysis, *see* Psycho-analytic method
by diet, I 27
Dubois's method of, II 27, 200, 446
electrotherapy in, II 28; 140-1; III 144
hydrotherapy in, I 55
by hypnosis, *see* Psycho-analytic method
mechanotherapy in, I 55
by medicaments, II 28-9
moralizing in, II 27, 235, 446, 449
occupational, II 28; III 91
pre-Freudian & post-Freudian, III 13-14
sanatorium treatment in, II 28, 36
by suggestion, *see* Psycho-analytical method
superstitions as cures, III 27
symptomatic cures, *see* Symptom
& transference, I 53-7; II 186
PSYCHOTRAUMA, *see* Trauma
PUBERTY, I 24, 27-30, 122, 135, 146, 149, 272, 308; II 316; III 68; T 97
'PUBLIC OPINION', III 267
PUERPERAL PSYCHOSIS, II 86; III 352
'PULLING OFF', II 205
PULVERIZATION, *see* Fragmentation; Split of the ego
PUNISHMENT [*see also Crime; Guilt; Sin; Trauma*], I 199, 264, 274; II 51, 74, 431
exhibitionism as means of, II 331
need for, in masochism, II 280
passionate, III 165
sadistic elements in, II 436
sexual act as, in Don Juan type, II 358, 431
& superego-formation, III 73
& talion, I 199, 264, 274
trauma of, *see* Trauma
PUTNAM, J. J., Dr., III 41
PYROMANIA, *see* Fire; Micturition; Urethral erotism

QUANTITY, in analysis, D 39
QUANTUM THEORY, & individualism, III *257-8*
QUESTIONS of patients [*see also Patient(s)*], II *183*

RAGE [*see also Aggression*]
& anxiety neurosis, III 253
& asthma, III 278
& neurasthenia, III 253
& oral frustration of the infant, III 219
in paralytics, III 367-8
in repression & resistance similar, III 237

& war neuroses, W 19
RANK, Otto, I 191, 264, 265-7, 278, 416; III 36-7, 56, 102, 112
on analysis (termination), II 221, 296
on analytical situation, II 225
birth-trauma theory, II 223, 279, 294, 296; III 37
on dreams, II 301, 302
RAPE, *see* Violation
RAPTURE, *see* Delirium of rapture
RATIONALISM [*see also Philosophy, rational*], I 293, 323
RATIONALIZATION
in dreams, I 126
in paranoia, I 293
REACTION(s)
adaptive & reactive, III 226
of the analyst, *see* Psycho-analyst
-formation, I 36, 51, 53, 56, 66, 88, 148, 231, 247, 251, 310, 315, 324, 331; II 382, 417, 427; III 267
REALITY [*see also Adaptation; Ego & external world; Negation; Reality sense; Unpleasant ideas*], III 31, 187, 232-3
acceptance of, I *213*; II 368, 370, 373, 377-9; III 260; D 10
& anxiety in hypochondria, II 58
contact with [*see also Reality-sense*], II 76, 90, 234; III 31
effortless, in orgasm, III 267
& ego [*see also Ego & external world*], I 233; III 187
erotic —, II 371; T 20
of family as a group, III 252
& fantasy, III 79, 259
& introspection, III 187
& masochism, II 376
negation of, II 367-8; III 233
& paranoia, *see* Paranoia
& play, III 272
principle, I *213*, 232, 255-6, *261-9*, 331; III 31, 195
psychical, III 79, 235
resistance against, III 260
& sexuality, I 233
subjective, of the patient's communications, III 235
-testing, I *213*, 256-7; II 371, 411
& transference, II 369
& 'unreality', III 235
REALITY SENSE [*see also Objectivity; Reality*]
adaptation as condition for, III 221
cerebrospinal system, as organ of, III 256
development of, I *213*, 236; II 378-9
erotic, T *20*, 53-4, 70
& narcissism, II 377
& primal repression(s), III 270
projection phase of, II 439-41
& psychoses, III 31
& split of the ego [*see also Split*], III 270

& successive repressions, I 236-7
in trance state, III 223, 232, 259
REAPPEARANCE OF TRAUMA, see Repetition; Trauma
REASSURANCE, see Patient, Psychoanalytic technique; Transference
RECAPITULATION (biological) [see also Biogenesis; Phylogenesis; Repetition], T 46, 103
RECIPROCAL, see Mutual
RECKONING, see Counting
RECOLLECTION, see Memory; Remembering
'RECOMPENSES', see Compensation; Gratification
RECTUM [Rectal] [see also Anal], II 80, 264
REDISCOVERY [see also Remembering], II 394, 406-7
RE-EDUCATION [see also Education; Psycho-analysis & education], III 37-8, 74; D 16
REFLEX(ES) [see also under the respective headings], I 15; III 63, 256; W 21
REFORM MOVEMENTS & neuropaths, I 38
REFUSION, T 90
REGENERATIVE TENDENCIES, see Health
REGRESSION [Regressive] [see also Fixation; Intrauterine], I 137, 145, 153, 205-7, 209, 224, 225, 234-7; II 81; III 361; T 52-9, 83-4, 103-4
& adaptation, II 376
character—, see Character-regressions
conversion as, II 137-8; III 261
in death, T 95
in illness, III 351
in infant prodigies, III 262-3
to masturbation, see Masturbation
& nutrition, T 86
from object-love to self-gratification [see also Auto-erotism; Gratification; Narcissism; Object-love], II 309
to omnipotence, I 222-3, 231
& organic evolution, T 88-9
& phylogenesis, II 137, 138; T 88-9
to protopsyche, II 97
as sequestration of the mental ego, III 359
tendency to, in organic life, I 237; T 83
thalassal, T 52-9, 73
& thinking, II 232
in 'unemployable' organs, T 92
in war neuroses, II 137
& words, I 140
REICH, W., II 264, 276; III 121
REIK, Theodor, III 39
REJUVENATION, T 66-7
RELAXATION [see also Psycho-analytic technique, active; Tension], II 226, 282; III 108, 115

after orgasm, III 257
after trance, III 223, 234
RELIGION [Religious feelings; Piety] [see also Ceremonials], II 44, 203, 424, 429; III 206
& blasphemies, I 151
in guilt-laden, passionate adults, III 163
& obsession, II 284, 299, 450
in women, III 182
REMEMBERING [see also Cryptamnesia; Cover-memories; Déja-vu; Memories; Memory; Re-discovery], III 124; D 3, 26
REMINISCENCES, see Memories
RENUNCIATION
to analysis, II 233; III 85
to guilt feelings, D 10
as hypocrisy, III 80
to knowledge, III 221
to narcissism, see Narcissism; Reality, uncompensated, II 376
REPETITION (Repeating) [see also Recapitulation]
in analysis, D 3-5, 11
& anxiety, D 4
-compulsion, II 140; III 102
& active therapy, II 72, 217
& habit, II 285
& play, T 40
& proneness to sexual assault, II 140
of gratification, I 138
& guilt, D 4
hallucinatory, see Trance; Trauma; Traumatic experience
instinct of, & day's residues, III 239
pleasure in, II 406; T 40
of trauma, in analysis, III 37, 124, 261
day's residues as symptoms of, III 238
in hysterical symptoms, III 221
in nightmares, III 233, 236
tendency greater during sleep, III 240
in traumatic neuroses, III 238
REPLACEMENT, I 51, 202
REPOSE, see Tranquillity; Intrauterine; Inorganic
REPRESENTATION, I 83, 138, 148, 195, 205, 213, 223, 228, 229, 262, 267, 276, 277
REPRESSION(S) [see also Libido; Wish(es)], I 16, 22-3, 24, 33, 40, 56, 82, 90, 100, 107, 134, 148, 204, 210-13, 235, 248, 255, 258, 259, 262, 272, 296, 302, 305, 313, 314, 317, 322; II 37, 153, 156, 403-4, 417, 425; III 19, 20, 237, 255-6; T 87
& 'active' technique, II 205
& autotomy, T 83

in concentration & making comparisons, II 404
as displacement of mental energy, III 222
in education, II 428
failure of, resulting in laughter, III 180
& fantasy life, II 77
of hatred, III 261
& hemi-anaesthesia, II 114
& hypnosis, I 63
& hypochondria, II 120
& hysteria, II 21-2, 42, 102-3
of incredulity, I 202-3
of indifferent material, II 403
& limitation of action, III 75
& materialization, II 97
& Mendelism, T 87
of the not-loved, III 212
& 'omnipotence', I 216-17
as organ of outlet, III 251
organic, T 83
into the organic, III 264
as 'permanent alienation', III 265
primal, II 77, 121-2, 443; III 131, 135, 270
in puberty, II 316
& 'sequestration', III 362
successive — & reality sense, I 236-7
& suppression, III 265
& symbolic equation, I 275, 280
& symptoms, II 114, 120
technological discoveries & tools as consequences of, II 389
tenderness as outcome of, III 121
universality of, III 19-20
unwisdom of, II 59
REPUDIATION, *see* Patient; Revocation
REPULSION, *see* Disgust
RESCUE, dream of, III 44
RESERVE in child, cause of, II 327
RESIDUES, day's, *see* Dream
'RESIDUARY PHENOMENA' (Freud), III 211
RESISTANCE(s) [*see also Defence*], I 57, 62, 63, 85-7, 133-6, 252, 256; II 123, 182, 252, 297; III 37-8, 82, 89-92, 110, 114-15, 123, 223; D 4, 9, 15, 38
in associations, II *177*
& autosymbolism, III 246-8
& active technique, II 63, 218; III 37-8
catharsis by overcoming, III 223
by falling asleep, II 249
& feeling of 'dying', III 237, 243-4
fluctuation of, III *246-8*
by generalizations, II 184
hatred as, III 157-8
& hopes, III 91-2
indulgence as a factor against, II 297; III 114-15, 123

as 'inertia' against external influences, III 258
lack of, in trance, III 239
to new ideas, II 54
'objective', III 117
period [phase], III 93-4; D 9
to reality, III 260
to reality-testing, I 256
by silence, II 179
by talkativeness, II 252
& timing of interpretations, III 89-90
after trance, III 232-4
transference —, II 45
RESPECT, I 26, 63, 65, 72, 135
self-, *see* Self-respect
RESPIRATION [Respiratory] [*see also Asthma; Lungs*], III 103, 202
during coitus, T 34-5, 56, 75
& laughter, III 180-1
in mania & melancholia, III 181
murmuring & suffocation, III 274
in sleep, T 75
RESPONSIBILITY
feeling of, lessened in doctor's presence, I 43-4
flight from, III 262, 272
RESTLESSNESS
at end of analytic session, II *238*
& concealed masturbation, II 191
in paralytics, III 367
while thinking, II 230-2
RETENTION [*see also Anal erotism; Evacuation; Sphincter(s); Urethral erotism*], II 251, 261-2; III 217, 253
RETROGRESSION, *see* Regression
RETURN OF THE REPRESSED, I 231, 317, 323; II 20, 21; T 89, 91-2
'REVENANT', I 41, 260
REVENGE, I 308; II 431; III 32
REVERSAL, *see* Inversion
REVOCATION, in analysis, III 233; D 11
RHYTHM(ICITY)
in coitus & labour, T 35
producing compulsion to dance, II 161
RICKMANN, J., III 138
RIDICULE, *see* Comic; Laughter; Irony; Wit; Words
RIGIDITY [*see also Elasticity; Flexibility*], I 291; II 281; III 230
cataleptic, & foetal posture, T 78
of character in unwanted children, III 104
spinal instead of erection, III 48
RIKLIN, Fr., I 238
ROBBER(s), dream of, I 108
ROBERT, W., on dreams, II 394
ROHEIM, Geza, II 228; III 39, 252
ROMANCE, *see* 'Family Romance'
ROTATION, delusion of, III 221, 222
RUBBING, of eyes & masturbation, II 317
RULE, fundamental, *see* Psycho-analytic rule(s)

RUMBLING, intestinal, in analysis, I 211
RUTHLESSNESS, *see* Aggressiveness; Cruelty; Sadism

SACHS, Hans, I 227, 278; II 403; III 57; W 8
SACRIFICE, II 429-30
  self-, *see* Self-sacrifice
SADGER, J., I 61, 179, 297, 307; II 236; III 172
SADISM [Sadistic] [*see also* Aggression; Anal erotism; Destruction; Lust-murder; Masochism; Murderous tendencies; Rage], I 16, 107-8, 271, 307; II 428, 436; III 33, 248, 363; T 22
  of the analyst, II 220
  & civilization, III 166
  & coitus anxiety, *see* Coitus anxiety
  comparisons indicating —, II 400
  & hatred, III 33
  & obscene words, II 226
  & tic, II 160; III 349
  & vermin killing, II 328
SAFETY, *see* Security
SALAMANDER, T 47, 53
SALIVATION, excessive [Ptyalism] [*see also Secretion; Spitting*], II 42-3, 315
SALT, obsessive fear of, II 50
SANATORIUM '-disease', II 28
SAND as faeces symbol, I 323
SARBÓ, J., W 8
SATISFACTION, *see* Gratification; Instinct(s); Libido; Orgasm
SAVINGS, faeces as, I 321
SCEPTICISM [*see also* Conviction; Doubt(s); Incredulity*], II 447; III 104, 263-4
  analyst's in his own interpretations, II 70
SCHIZOPHRENIA [*see also* Catatonia; Paraphrenia*], II 123, 146; III 31, 356
SCHMIDT, W 10
-SCHOOL, III 69-70, 73-4
SCHOPENHAUER, I 253-4, 259-62, 269; III 353
SCHUSTER, W 7, 9, 12, 14, 16
SCIENCE, III 63, 74-5, 88; D 65
  (definition) III 87-8
  & popular wisdom, I 94
  & psycho-analysis, I 256-7; III 185-6
  & reality principle, I 232, 255-6
SCOPOPHILIA [Voyeurism], I 16; II 300-1; III 363
  & amphimixis, T 13
  obscenity as, I 150
  in old people, III 205
  'peeping mania', I 177
SCORN [*see also* Defiance; Rage*], in dreams, II 309
SCOTT, Walter, III 57
SCRATCHING
  & coitus, T 30
  on glass, & castration, II *313*
  & itching, reciprocity of, II 87
  & masochism, II 87
  -reflex, II 160
SCREEN-MEMORY, *see* Cover-memory
SCREENING, III 187, 189, 190, 191, 193, 195
SCRIBBLING, & the repressed, II 404
SEA, *see* Ocean; Sickness
SECONDARY
  elaboration, I 126
  functions of neurosis (Freud), I 86
  narcissism (a case of —) [*see also Split*], III 227
  process(es), II 369, 375
SECURITY [Safety] feeling [*see also Stability*]
  in analysis, III 232-3
  lack of, after trance, III 223, 232
  necessity for, in pleasure, III 178
  after orgasm, compared with mother-child relation, III 257
SEDATIVE(s), *see* Anaesthetic(s); Drugs
  micturition as, II 317
SEDUCTION(s) [Rape, Violation] [*see also Child; Parent; Trauma, sexual*],
  of boys by mature women, III 161-3
  compulsion of, III 227
  Don-Juanism, *see* Don Juanism
  & drugs, III 161-2
  fantasies, I 200; II 73, 74
  of girls, III 161-2
'SEELENSUCHER, der' (Groddeck), III 344-8
SELF [*see also* Ego]
  -accusation(s) [reproaches], III 356-7
  -analysis [*see also Healing*], I 129, 256; II 310; III 83, 98-9, 272
  -conviction, patient's, necessity in analysis, II 64
  -cure, pathological [*see also Autotomy*], II 87; III 86
  -defence, *see* Defence [*see also Self-destruction*]
  -destruction [Self-destructive tendency] [*see also Autotomy; Death instinct; Suicide*], II 376, 377; III 102-4
    & being abandoned, III 137-8, 219
    adaptation replacing —, III 221, 225
    & anxiety release, III 249
    in epilepsy, hysteria & melancholia, III 202
    & exhaustion of defensive forces, III 224, 228
    in the newborn, caused by frustration, III 219
    pleasure in, & change of libido direction [*see also Masochism*], III 224-7
    & reconstruction, III 220
    urge for (Freud), III 30
  -dismemberment [Self-mutilation] *see* Autotomy [*see also Self-destruction*]

-gratification, *see* Auto-erotism; Masturbation
-imitatory activity, III 266
-'nursing' by [split-off] parts, III 226, 237-8
-observation [Introspection] [*see also Insight*], III 183-4, 187-90, 193-5, 213-14
 & mathematics, III 183-4, 187-9, 193
 after split of the ego, III 136
 & stage-fright, II *421*
-perception(s) [*see also Insight*], I 217, 258, 272
-preservation, *see* Defence
-reconstruction, *see* Ego reconstruction
-respect [*see also* Respect]
 in general paralysis, III 354, 357-8, 360-1
-sacrifice [*see also Masochism*], as pleasure, III 224-7
-splitting, *see* Split of the ego
SENILE, dementia, *see* Dementia senile [*see also* Age, old]
SENSATIONS, *see* Sense perceptions
SENSE(S) [Sense organ(s))] [*see also* Sense perceptions; & Eye; Hyperaesthesia; Touch; Vision], III 191-92, 195
 functioning of, III 230-1
 role of, III 183, 193
SENSE PERCEPTION(S) [Sensations; Sensory impressions] [*see also Sense*], I 138, 140, 206, 217, 230, 256, 284; III 187-8, 221
 & belief, II 441
 bodily & projected [*see also Projection*], III 260-1
 concentrated & unified —, disadvantages of, III 230
 inhibition of, III 239-40, 244
 pleasure & unpleasure in, III 275
SEQUESTRATION [*see also Autotomy; Fragmentation; Split of the ego*], III 362, 365
SERIES, formation of, I 301
SERIOUSNESS & badness, III 179-80
SEVERN, Elizabeth, III 122, 133
SEX(UAL) [*see also Bisexual; Eros, Erotic; Erotism(s); Erotogenic; Erotomania; Genital; Librido; Sexuality*], I 16, 21, 24, 25, 27, 29, 31-4, 46, 61, 66
 act, *see* Coitus
 aetiology of neurosis, *see* Neuroses
 '— anagogy' in 'active' therapy, II 274
 assault [attack], *see* Assault
 constitution, *see* Biological; Biology; Constitution
 criminality, *see* Jurisprudence, medical; Lust-murder; Seduction
 desires [*see also Oedipus; Sex(ual) impulses; Wish(es)*], I 15, 26, 32; II 20, 95

development, *see* Development
differences [Sexual character], III 167, 243, 366; T 105-6
 in old age, T 106-7
 origin of, III 243-4; T 102-6
 secondary, T 31-2, *96*
 tertiary, T 105
excitement, I 104, 107-10, 188-91; II 171, 300; III 218
 & death, T 95
education, *see* Education, sex
experience, infantile, value of, II 77
fantasies, *see* Fantasies
'— geography' (Freud), II 300
habits, analysis of, II *259*
hunger [*see also Erotomania; Libido; Sexual excitement; Sexual super-performance*], I 25, 39, 45, 46, 48, 57, 61, 64, 66, 73, 78, 87, 103, 156, 168, 184, 187-90, 212, 235, 243, 266, 289, 296, 302, 303, 308, 315; III 271-2, 375
ignorance, *see* Ignorance
impulses [*see also Instinct(s); Libido; Sexual excitement; Sexual hunger*]|
inferiority, I 28-9; III 243; T 105
intercourse, *see* Coitus
jokes, *see* Jokes; Obscene words
life [*see also Coitus; Sexuality*], III 24-5; T 26-7, 29
origin of speech, II 318
super-performance [Hyper-performance], II 264; III 271-2
sureness, I 17
temptation of children, I 26-7
theories, infantile, *see* Infantile theories
trauma, *see* Trauma; Infantile sexual trauma
SEXUALITY [*see also Sex(ual)*], I 17, 86, 233; II 21; III 353; T *1*; W 17-18
 beginnings of, III 68
 female, development of, T 24-6
 identified with oral activity, I 38
 infantile [*see also Child(ren)*], I 108; II 77
 onto & phylogenesis of, *see* Onto & phylogenesis
 & pleasure principle, *see* Pleasure principle
 & regression to womb, T 20, 38-9
 & sleeplessness, T 77
 & speech, *see* Speech
 theory of, II 52, *253*; T *1*
 ubiquity in mental life, I 105
'SEXUALIZATION of everything' [*see also Pansexualism*], I 279
SHAKING, *see* Trembling; Shuddering
SHAME, I 31, 100, 133, 144, 151, 271 (definition) III 376
 after analytic session, II 241
 in childhood, I 31-2, 33; II 327
 & embarrassment, II 202, 315

& group psychology, III 376
& micturition [urethral erotism], I 31-2; III 33
SHOCK ['Erschütterung'] [see also Inhibition; Motor disturbances; Trauma], III 19-20, 137, 253-4, 352
  (definition) III 253
  at end of analytic hour, III 114
  — neuroses, & hope of gain, W 8, 19
  paralysing effect of [see also Inhibition], III 162, 239-40, 244
  passivity induced by, III 239
  psychosis, transitory, as first reaction to —, III 121
  & split of the ego, see Split of the ego
  in trance, III 239-40
  & war-neuroses, II 156; W 6-8
SHOE as symbol, II 358
SHOOTING, dream-figure, I 123
SHORT-SIGHTEDNESS, I 271
SHUDDERING at scratching on glass, II 313
SICKNESS, [see also Mental diseases; Organic diseases], II 93; III 26
SIGHING, displacement to yawning, I 210
SIGNALS, used by child to secure satisfaction, I 223-4
SILBERER, I 207, 217, 261, 266, 277; II 355, 402; III 183, 194
SILENCE,
  'golden', II 250
  technique of, see Psycho-analytic technique, silence
SIMILARITY, principle of, III 192
SIMILES, see Comparisons
SIMMEL, E., II 210; III 124-5; W 16
SIMULATION [see also Mendacity; War neuroses], I 81; III 78
SIN [see also Crime; Guilt; Superego; Totem], enjoyment of, in groups, III 178-9
SINCERITY, see Psycho-analytic rules; Truth; Untruth
SINGER, Kurt, W 9, 10
SINGLE-SYMPTOM NEUROSES, III 25
SISTER, & psychic impotence, I 51
SKILL & calculation, III 183
SKIN,
  burning of the —, & male homosexuality, III 48
  hyperaesthesia of, after masturbation, I 188
  & masochism, II 88
  sensibility of, II 111
SLAVE-MARKET, dream, I 105-6
SLEEP [see also Sleeplessness]
  during analytical session, I 199-200; II 79-80, 249-51
  autoerotism in, T 74
  autoplastic technique in, T 74
  & coitus, T 36, 73-80
  & dream, I 103; III 239; T 78

& epileptic fits, III 198-9, 201
& intrauterine state, T 73
masturbation in, III 216
of newborn, III 198; T 73
& orgasm, T 74, 78
& regression, I 222-3; T 73, 76
no tic during, II 157
& trauma, III 239-40
-walking, exact functioning of the senses during —, III 231
SLEEPLESSNESS [see also Sleep], III 356; T 77
SLIPS, see Mistakes
SMELL [Odour], I 79, 143, 160, 205, 305, 322, 324-8; II 362-5
  as prototype of thought, T 71-2
  & sexuality, T 33, 57, 71
SMILING, see Laughter
SMOKING
  dread of, II 318
  as holding off of death, III 274
'SNAKE-HISS', III 278
SNIFFING, see Smell
SOCIAL
  'aspect' of analytic therapy, II 216
  channels, leading the instincts into —, III 68
  disorders & crime, II 432
  element in wit, II 340
  guilt, III 253
  habits of sleeping, T 76
  helpfulness, III 136, 206, 230
  life
    & paranoia, III 374-5
    & religion, II 444
    & sado-masochism, III 166
  position, consequences of, II 320-1, 413-7
SOCIETY, organization of, II 432
'SOCRATIC art of suggestion', III 260
SOKOLNICKA, E., II 210
SOLIPSISM, see Egoism
SOMA & germplasm, mutual influence, T 65, 68-9
SOMATIC [see also Organic]
  '— compliance', in homosexuals, III 173
  disease, see Organic disease(s)
  phenomena [symptoms], I 193-5; II 126-7; W 11
  sensations of trauma [see also Trauma], II 151,; III 21
SOMNAMBULISM (see also Sleep), a case of, I 76
SON, see Child; Boy; Oedipus complex
SOUL [see also Mind; Psyche]
  '— searcher, the —', review of Groddeck's, III 344-8
  spinal, T 76
SPASM(s), I 200; II 251; III 103, 118, 139-40, 233-4
SPATIAL illusions
  'above', III 222

'beside', III 222-3
rotation, III 221, 222
'up', III 222
SPECTROPHOBIA, II 365
SPECULATION, see Thinking; Thought
SPEECH [see also Talkativeness; Talking; Voice; Words], II 318; III 19-20, 367
& anal erotism, II 251, 403
development of, & projection, I 50
& obscene words, II 226, 251, 403
— signs in place of object-images, I 139
as substitution for gesture, I 229
& thought, I 230
SPENCER, H., on mechanical construction, II 389
SPERBER, I 229; II 318
SPERMATORRHOEA, II 270
SPHINCTER(S) [see also Retention], II 262-3, 265-8
activity, & pleasure-principle, II 265
& amphimixis theory, II 263
anal [-ani] [see also Anal erotism], II 204, 250-1, 259, 284; III 276
education of, see Toilet training
experiments [exercises] in control of, II 226, 261, 263, 266, 268, 274, 277, 282, 289
'— morality', II 266, 267
& obscene words, II 226, 251
paresis of, III 356
tension, II 93, 226, 267, 279
urethral, see Ambition; Urethral erotism
& Yoga, III 276
SPINAL
pain in neurasthenics, III 23
rigidity, instead of erection, III 48
'— soul', T 76
SPIROCHETES [see also Syphilis], & erotogenic zones, III 364
SPITTING [see also Salivation], I 66; II 326
SPLIT(S) OF THE EGO [Split personality; Splitting] [see also Fragmentation], III 78, 135-6, 162-5, 219-25, 228, 230, 237, 241-2, 262, 265, 270
atomization [pulverization], III 223, 234
& being abandoned, feeling of, III 135, 219
'being torn to pieces', feeling of, III 221-2
& the censuring instance, III 241, 242
in the child, after sexual assault, III 163
depth of, III 160
'head being cut off', feeling of, III 135
inhibited, followed by adaptation, III 220
& integration, III 270-1
& narcissism, III 135, 226, 237, 246

in the newborn, III 219
'nursing' part of the self, III 226, 237-8
& plurality of superegos, III 78
psychotic, III 121
& reality sense, III 270
several, increasing in number, III 165
symbols of, III 135, 221, 222, 234
& trance, III 162, 164-5
into unconscious feeling & unfelt knowing, III 237
& unpleasure, III 265
& withdrawal of libido, III 219
'SPOILING', III 58, 116, 136-7
SQUANDERING, see Libido squandering
SQUINT, III 32
STABILITY [see also Security], feeling of, after catharsis, III 223
STABLES, smell of, I 324
STAGE-FRIGHT [see also Anxiety; Fear; Panic]
STAGNANT analysis, 'active' technique in, II 196, 212; III 128-9
STAIRCASE, in dream, III 44
STAMMERING [see also Inhibition, verbal; Motor disturbances; Speech], II 222, 251; T 8
STARING, embarrassment from, I 273; II 49
STÄRCKE, III 102, 364
STEINER, M., I 13, 25, 27-9
STEKEL W., I 13, 25, 39, 40; D 33
STEREOTYPY, & tics, II 144, 153
STERN, W 16
STIGMA(S) [Stigmata] hysterical, II 98, 115, 117; III 218
STIMULUS [Stimuli] [see also Sexual excitement], I 58, 84, 112-13; II 158; III 25-6, 191
external, excluded in sleep & coitus, T 74
of unpleasure, III 220
STOMACH [see also Bowels, Digestion], rumbling, during analysis, I 211
STOOL, see Excrements
STRANGER(S) [see also Public], inhibiting laughter, III 178-9
'STRENGTH' & retention of faeces, II 251
'STRETCHING' & erection, II 269
STRIVING for health, & trauma, III 230-1
STROKING, as encouragement, II 270
STRUGGLE
laughter at senseless —, III 226
of the sexes, III 167
in wooing, T 103
STRÜMPELL, W 8-9, 19
STUBBORNNESS, see Obstinacy
STUDENTS' duels, I 315
STUTTERING, see Stammering
SUBJECT homo-erotism, see Homoerotism; Homosexuality
SUBJECTIVATION, & objectivation, III 265-6

440 INDEX

SUBLIMATION, I 66, 70, 73, 168, 169, 176, 182, 184, 206-9, 245, 296, 305, 314, 315, 323, 328; II 48, 427; D 11, 20
  activation of sublimated activities by 'active therapy', II 206
  of anal erotism, I 324-5
  destruction of, by alcohol, I 162
  & education [see also Education], II 428
  reaction-formation as, II 427
SUBMISSION [Submissiveness]
  infantile, return to, in hypnosis, II 443
  of patient, as repressed criticism, III 158
'SUBSEQUENTNESS' (Freud), I 20, 76, 310
SUBSTITUTION [see also under the respective headings], I 45, 46, 154-5, 185, 193, 307, 310; II 49
SUCKING [see also Oral], I 90; III 219
SUCKLING, see Infant; Newborn
SUFFERING [see also Pain; Unpleasure], II 159; III 354, 357-8, 361
  'economy of —', III 118
  & intelligence, III 243-6
  in mourning, see Depression; Mourning
  & passions, III 166-7
  terrorism of, III 165-6
SUFFOCATION, see Birth; Drowning; Respiration; Trauma
SUGGESTIBILITY [see also Child hypnosis; Suggestion], I 37, 63-4, 305; III 27, 158, 372-3
SUGGESTION(s) [see also Hypnosis; Psychoanalytic method; Suggestibility], I 31, 34, 54, 62, 67, 81, 83-6, 88, 90-3, 154, 181, 305; II 61; D 61
  (definition) II 55, 70, 443, 447; III 254-5
  in analysis [see also Catharsis, neo; Psycho-analytic technique, active], III 133-4, 225, 243, 255, 269-70
  analytic views on, II 27-8, 55, 200
  effect on consciousness ('education in blindness'), II 57
  non-analytic method of, II 27, 28, 235, 447; III 91, 243
  problems & drawbacks of, II 28, 56-7, 60, 61, 444, 447, 448; III 243, 255
  'Socratic art' of, III 260
  & trance, III 259
  & transference, I 58-60; II 186
  & will [see also Will], III 254-5
SUICIDE [Suicidal impulses or tendencies] [see also Self-destruction], III 103, 238, 247, 356-7
  & death coming from outside, III 244
  of foster-mother, I 27
  hesitation between — & duty, II 329
  & melancholia, III 357

'SUM TOTAL', in mathematics & mental life, III 187
SUN
  -bath, II 365
  as father-symbol, I 264; II 246-7, 365
'SUNDAY NEUROSIS', II 174-6
SUPEREGO [see also Ego; Identification; Split]
  (definition) III 73
  biological model of, III 227-31
  ego, id & —, energy-distribution between, III 112-13
  formation, III 72-3, 80, 228
  & habits, II 286
  as imitation (permanent), III 267
  'intelligence', as precondition for, III 228
  '— intropression' in education, III 279
  & mania, III 31
  & mutual devouring, III 230
  omnipotence disappearing in, II 373, 440
  & parental imago, II 266-7, 286
  plurality of, & split personality, III 78
  preconscious, III 100-1
  transformation of, in analysis, III 98, 100-1
  un-assimilated, II 263
SUPERNORMAL capacities [see also Infant prodigies]
  education as unlearning of, II 283
  intellectual super-performances, III 245
SUPERIOR SEX, which? III 243; T 105-6
SUPERIORITY, maintained after defeat (of another kind), III 225-6, 244
SUPERSTRUCTURE, see Conscious superstructure
SUPPRESSION & repression, III 265
SURENESS, sexual & general, I 17
SUSANNA & the elders, III 205
SWALLOWING, see Devouring; Incorporation; Introjection
SWEATING as anxiety symptom, III 24
SWIFT, Jonathan [see also Gulliver], III 57-9, 211
SYMBIOSIS, II 375; T 62
SYMBOL(s) [see also Autosymbolism; Comparison; Dreams of —; Symbolism], I 53, 96, 99, 104, 108, 114, 179, 192, 202, 266, 321-3, 326, 327, 329, 330, 331; II 100, 403, 407
  (definition) I 277-8
  dream —, variety of, I 124
  of ego in external world, I 227-9
  formation of, I 278-81; T 81
  interpretation of, II 352, 355
  limitation of meaning, I 277
  onto & phylogenesis of, I 276, 319; II 356; T 44
  in paraphrenia, II 403

INDEX

various
  animals, small, III 53
  ark, T 49
  bed-linen, II 359
  birth, T 42-3
  bridge, II 352-3
  broken bough, T 48
  bundle, III 228
  burial, II 357
  bursting, III 237
  child, II 320
  cigar, II 357
  coitus, T 42-3
  defaecation, II 101
  earth, T 46-7
  eggs, II 327-8
  empress, III 51
  eyes, I 264, 271, 280; II 84, 317
  face, II 170, 361
  fan, II 361
  finger, III 50
  fish, T 44-5
  foot, I 263
  galoshes, II 358
  great person, growth, III 228
  head, II 170
    cut off, III 135
    Medusa's, II 360
    splitting open, II 123
  hump, III 228
  infection, II 305
  jewels, II 321-2
  kite, II 359-60
  landscape, III 44
  left side, II 111
  leg, I 294
  luggage, II 79
  mice, II 109
  nose, II 101, 283
  oesophagus, II 101
  over-eating, II 101
  paper, rumpled, II 359
  plough, T 48
  robbers, I 108
  sea, T 46-7
  shoe, II 347, 358
  sun, II 246, 365
  toe, II 272
  tooth, I 191-2; II 101
  vermin, II 327, 361
  water, T 48-9
  weapons, I 19
SYMBOLISM [*see also Autosymbolism; Symbol*], I 37, 108, 122-4, 191, 192, 229, *270*, 273-5, 319; II 89, 100-1; III 188; T 47
  & analogical equation, I 278, 280
  functional & poets, I 266
  & genitality, T 87-8
  (mathematical), III 183, 186, 188, 190, 192
  in Oedipus myth, I *253*, 261
  & rediscovery of the loved, II 407

  & repression, I 275, 280
SYMMETRICAL touching, compulsion of, II *242-4*
SYMPATHETIC SYSTEM, & organ neuroses, III 256
SYMPATHY [*see also Affection; Love; Tenderness*], I 21, 43, 62-6, 73, 86
  alleged lack of —, in analyst, III 261
  & trauma-analysis, III *278*
SYMPTOM(s) [*see also* under the respective headings], II 327; III 20, 221
  autosymbolism of, III 221
  — complex, I 14, 88
  exacerbation of, II 213; III 19-20, 27
  'forgetting' of, II *412*
  formation of, I 111, *193*, 197, 198, 201, 211, 212, 235; II 197
  & habits, II 281
  historical representation of, III *221*
  interpretation of [*see Psycho-analytic technique; Interpretation*]
  isolated, II 126-7
  localization of, II 42
  over-determination of, I 197
  passagère, *see* Transitory symptoms
  reappearance in or after trance [*see also Trance*], III 232, 236
  single, III 25
  teleological understanding of, II 26
  therapy of [*see also Psycho-analytic method*], I 11-12; II 26, 61, 197; III 85-6; D 30
SYMPTOMATIC ACTS [*see also Mistakes*], II 38, 195, 242, 401, 411-12
  concealed masturbation as, II 192, 195-6, 315-16
SYNAESTHESIA, II 300-1; T 14
SYPHILIS [Lues] [*see also Spirochetes*], III 364

TABOO(s), II 430
TACT [Tactfulness] [*see also Tactlessness*], of the analyst, III 82, 89, 99-100
  as empathy, III 89-90
  female, III 34
TACTILE SENSATIONS [*see also Touching*], 'disagreeable —', & castration, II 314
TACTLESSNESS [*see also Tact*], III 121
  naughtiness provoked by —, III 132, 219
TAILOR(ing trade), II 418-19
TAILS, & emotion, T 92
TALENT [*see also Genius; Infant prodigies; Intelligence*], II 104; III 186, 189
TALION punishment [*see also Punishment*], I 199, 264, 274
TALKATIVENESS [Verbosity]
  as resistance, II 252
  of the analyst, III 96
TALKING [*see also Speech*], I 210; II 207; D 28
TAMING, of a wild horse, III *336-40*

442   INDEX

TASKS, III 264-5, 271-2
TAUSK, Victor, II 170, 298, 369; III 362
TEASING, fantasies of, II 75
TECHNIQUE, *see* Psycho-analytic technique
TECHNOLOGY [Technological development, discoveries] [*see also Tools*], II 386, 395
TELEKINESIS (definition), III 257
TELEPATHY, III 257
'TELESCOPING', III 263
TEMPERAMENT [*see also Affect(s); Character; Emotion(s); Passionate; Passions*], motor type, II 161
TEMPERATURE, in sleep, T 76
TEMPORAL, *see* Chronological
TENDERNESS [*see also Affection; Object-love*]
 affection, incestuous of adults, masquerading as, III 121
 longing, for, III 104, 121, 123
 need for, III 270
 & passion, III 137-8, *156-67*
 & perversion, III 166
 stage of, III 163-4
TENSION [*see also Discharge; Exaggerated; Relaxation; Retention; Sphincter*], III 251
 in coitus, II 74; T 41, 43, 60, 63, 66, 67
TERATOMA, neurotic personality as, III 123-4
TERMINATION of analysis [treatment], *see* Psycho-analytic treatment, termination
TERROR, *see* Fear; Panic
'TERRORISM of suffering', III 165-6
TERTIARY sexual difference(s) [character] [*see also Sexual difference(s)*]
THALASSAL regression, T 52
THEFT, *see* Kleptomania [*see also Castration*]
'THEORY OF SEXUALITY' (Freud), review of, II *253*
THERAPY, *see* Psycho-analytic method; Psycho-analytic technique; Psychotherapy, non-analytic
 active, *see* Psycho-analytic technique, active
 symptomatic, *see* Symptom(s), therapy of
'THESAURING' of libido, III 253
THING, *see* Lifeless thing; Object
THINKER(s) [*see also Philosophy; Thinking; Thoughts*], II 230-1; III 189
THINKING [*see also Contemplation; Fantasy; Intelligence; Knowledge; Logical relation; Philosophy; Thinker; Thoughts*], (definition) III 190
 animistic, T 70
 & doing, II 187
 as holding off of death, III 274
 & muscle innervation, II *230*

 as objective contemplation, II 372
 & problem solution, III 263
 & reckoning operations, II 378
 smell as prototype of, T 71-2
 speculation distorting reality, III 231
'THIRD SEX' [*see also Homoerotism; Homosexual; Homosexuality*], III 173
THIRST, I 113; III 276
THOUGHT(s) [*see also Intelligence; Knowledge; Logical relations; Philosophy; Speculation; Thinker(s); Thinking*], II 21-2, 51, 232, 403; III 19-20
 abstract, & words, I 139
 development from speech, I 230
 inhibition of, *see* Inhibition of thinking
 — magic, period of, I 230
 obsessional, as substitute for action, II 232
 organic illness, role in the expression of, III 256
 from pleasure principle relatively independent, II 99
THROAT, II 116-17
THUMB, III 219, *325*; T 21
TIC(s) [Tic cases, Tic patients] [*see also Catatonia; Narcissism*], II *142-74*, 282; III *349-50*
 & abreaction, II 153
 aetiology of, II 171, 173, 283
 anal erotic components in, II 171; III 349
 during analysis, II 282
 & catatonia, II 147, 162; III 349
 & character traits, II 152-3; III 81
 & constitutional narcissism, II 145, 151, 161
 contagious in children, II 165
 disappearance during sleep, II 157
 & ego-hysteria, II 173
 & epilepsy, III 201
 & expressive movements, III 26, 278
 & genitalization of parts of body, II 85
 as holding off of death, III 274
 & hyper-sensitiveness, II 145, 152, 417
 & hysteria, II 155, 172-3
 increase & periods of genital stimulation, II 171
 intermediary position between narcissistic & transference neuroses, III *349-50*
 Kovács on, II 271
 & libido, II 145, 147, 160-1, 172
 & masochism, II 160
 & masturbation, II 160, 170, 271
 & obscene words, II 161, 165, 171, 226
 & obsessions, II 169-70, 173-4
 'occupation cramps', II 170
 origin of, III 26
 in paranoiacs & schizophrenics, II 146

pathoneurotic, II 154, 156, 158, 171
'polygonal', II 167, 271
& psychoses, II 161, 162, 163, 165
& sadistic assault, II 160, 226; III 349
& social advancement of family, II 417
& symptomatic acts, II 195
& traumatic neurosis, III 349–50
treatment of, II 48; III 81
TICKLING [Ticklishness] [*see also Itching*], II 113; T 38
TOE, equated with penis, II 272
TOILET-TRAINING [*see also Habits*], II 92; III 66–8
TOLERATION [Tolerance]
of pain, II 280, 287
of unpleasure, III 90, 249, 276–7
TONGUE, paraesthesia of, I 198
TONUS, muscular, *see* Muscle
TOOLS [*see also Technology*] & repressed erotism, II 389
TOOTH [Teeth], -ache, I 196–7; II 82; III 27
& masturbation, I 191–2, 198
'—neurosis', I 192
as primal penis, T 22
-pulling, as castration symbol, I 191–2
as weapons of libido, T 21
TOPIC-dynamic-economic construction of the mental apparatus [*see also Mind; Metapsychology*], III 722 1–2
TOPICAL view, of personality, III 222–3
TOPOGRAPHY (Freud), III 366–
TOPOPHOBIA, II 134
TOTEM sin [*see also Crime*], & the comic, III 178
TOTEMISM, II 429
TOUCHING [*see also Tactile*]
symmetrical, II 242
TOYS, faeces as, I 321–2
TRAINING [*see also Education; Obedience*]
analysis [*see also Psycho-analyst; Lay analysis; 'Wild' analysis*], III 42, 83–4, 98–100; D 39, 60
& active technique, II 220
depth of, III 141–2
as a fundamental rule in analysis, III 88–9
need for, II 187; III 83–4, 124, 153–4, 158
resistance in, II 295
TRANCE (in the course of the analytic process) [*see also Absorption*], III 119, 131, 134, 136, 232–6
(definition), III 233
'acting out' in, III 233–4
awakening from, III 139, 157, 223, 232–3, 236
cathartic affect of, III 223, 232
coma [comatose state] during, III 137, 139, 236
dream analysis in, III 242
fit, hysterical, in, III 233

hallucinatory contents & character of, III 233–4, 259
& hatred, III 157
inhibitions in, III 238, 239, 259
interruptions hindering —, III 259
negative effect of, III 157, 232, 236, 239–40
nightmares in, III 233
& reality, III 223, 232, 259
reappearance of symptoms after, III 232, 236
re-emergence of traumatic scene in, III 223, 224, 234
& silence, III 238
& split of the self [*see also Split*], III 164–5
& suggestion, III 259
TRANSFERENCE [*see also Counter-transference; Patient; Psycho-analyst; Psycho-analytic situation; Psycho-analytic technique*], I *35–93*, 154, 168, 193, 198, 208, 211, 219, 247, 287, 309; II 45–6, 63, 65, *187*, 200, 237, 266, 368–9; III 27, 110, 232–3, 262; D 7–8, 12–13, 20, 58
(definition, Freud's), I 35
& 'active technique', II 208, 219, 237, 272, 289
& analogies, I 42–3
in analysis, I 40; D 22
to analyst, in general [*see also Counter-transference*], II 63–4; III 148; D 40–1
cases of, II 70, 121, 204, 222, 273
at close of treatment, II 233, 369
& conviction, II 229, 438, 442, 445
forced fantasies by aid of, II 72
hatred in, III 157–8
& homosexuality, I 43, 161, 309
in hypnotism, I *58*, 72–4; II 237; T 60, 67
in hypochondria, II 121, 124
& introjection, I *35–42*
& massage, I 55
& medical examination, I 40–1
negative [*see also Patient's criticisms*], I 44; III 83, 91, 93–4, 113, 157–8; D 40
-neuroses, III 31, 349–50, 373
in non-analytic & pre-analytic psychotherapy, I 53–4, 55–7
over-burdening of, III 164
with paranoiacs, III 215
& parental complexes, I 67, 87; III 27
passion for, I 45–7
positive, I 54, 62; II 200, 290–1, 369; III 164, 270, 278
reality as a substitute for, II 369
reciprocal fixations, T 87
as repetition of parent-child relationship, I 67; III 27
— resistance, II 45

submissiveness, as repressed criticism, III 158
& sex of analyst, I 43
in suggestion, I *58*; II *186*
technical handling of, II 290; III 164
universality of, I 36, 65, 155
& weaning from analysis, II *293*; III 164
TRANQUILLITY, III 224-5
TRANSITORY [Passagère]
progressive faculties [see also *Infant prodigies*], III 262
psychoses [see also *Psycho-analytic process*], III 86, 121
states of weakness [see also *Neurasthenia*], I 200-1, 271
symptoms, II 179, 181, *193-212*, 242, 282
TRANSLATION, see Interpretation
TRANSVALUATION, in dreams, I 118-19
TRAUMA(s) [Traumata] [see also *Aetiology; Post-traumatic; Shock; Traumatic*], I 12, 33; II 52, 77, 80, 115, 130, 141, 147, 156, 158, 377; III 221, 227, 230-1, 264-8, 332, 366
(definition), III 276
& affect, II 129, 247
— analysis & sympathy, III *278*
& anxiety, III *249-50*
attempts at mastery of, III 238
& death, see Dead; Death; Dying
& depth of unconsciousness, III 239-41
destruction (partial) after —, III 226
& dream, III *238-42*
fragmentation, as immediate effect of, III 230
genesis of, III 137-8
& hatred, III 166-7, 261
& heterosexuality, III 227
& inability to self-defence, III 253-4
infantile, III 65, 121 [see also *Birth trauma; Infantile; Weaning*]
& intelligence, III 165, *243-6*, 262-3
& intoxication, III 274
of libido-impoverishment, see Impoverishment
maturity, precocious, after — [see also *Infant prodigies*], III 165, 262-3
memory-traces as —, see Memory-traces
of oral frustration (first), III 219
personality before, III 228
physical [see also *Injuries; Wound(s)*], II 129, 151, 156-7; III 354
& primal repression, III 121-2
progressive faculties acquired by [see also *Infant prodigies*], III 243, 246, *262-3*, 362
processes after —, see Post-traumatic
psychosis, transitory, following —, III 121
of punishment, III 121

repetition of, in analysis, III 156-9, 223-4, 234, 238, 261, 268
& self-confidence, lack of, II 134
several (increasing in number), III 165, 362
& split of the ego, III 162, 164-5 [see also *Split*]
& striving for health, III *230-1*
in trance, III 139-40, 223-4, 233-6, 264
TRAUMATIC [see also *Post-traumatic; Shock; Trauma*, and under the respective headings]
aetiology (of neuroses, especially of hysteria) [see also *Aetiology*], II 36-7, 52, 80, 115, 130, 156; III 110, 120, 184; D 48
factors, III 122, 156
neurosis [neuroses], II 83, 156; III 238, 349-50; W 6, 9, 14
primal repression, III 121-2
progression, III 165, 243-6, 262-3, 362
TRAUTOMATOGENIC situation [see also *Psycho-analytic technique*], & analytic situation, III 159-60, 223-4
TRAUMATOLYTIC function, of dream, III 240
TRAUMATOPHILIA, II 139-41, 305
TRAVEL, III 22, 26; W 8
TREATMENT [see also *Psycho-analysis; Psycho-analytic method; Psycho-analytic technique; Psychotherapy, non-analytic*, and under the respective subjects]
anxiety neurosis, II 277
character neuroses, II 211, 214, 262-3, 266
neurasthenia, II 276
neurotic Oedipus complex, II 73, 267
obsessional neurosis, II 48, 210
sexual hunger (insatiable), III 272
tics, II 174
war neuroses, II 210
TREMBLING [Tremor] [see also *Fear; Motor disturbances*], II 125, 126, 137-8; III 24; W 7, 14-15
TROTTER, III 102
TRÖMNER, on sleep, T 79-80
TRUST, see Confidence
TRUTH, acquiring of, by children, passively, III 269
TRUTHFULNESS, of analyst, II 180; III 117
TUBERCULOSIS, I 28, 282-3
TUNES, III *175-6*

Ucs [Unconscious, the] see Instances, the Unconscious; Unconscious; Unconsciousness
UNCONSCIOUS [see also *Instances, psychic, the Unconscious; Unconsciousness*, and under the particular headings]

'dialogues of the —', II 109
emotions & thoughts, expressed by organic illness, III 256
feeling, & unfelt knowing, in the split of the ego, III 237
functioning of 'intelligence', III 228, 230–1
rendering something —, III 221
superego, dissolution of, III 100–1
UNCONSCIOUSNESS [*see also Instances, psychic, the Unconscious; Unconscious*], III 221, 250
depth of, III 199–202, 221, 239–42
UNDER-LINEN, dirty, I 329
UNICELLULAR(s), T 61–2
UNIFICATION [*see also* under the particular heading], III 78, 190–191, 369
after the return of consciousness, III 231
UNIVERSALITY, principle of, III 252
UNORGASTIC, coitus [*see also Coitus; Orgasm*], III 271
UNPLEASANT, ideas [*see also Unpleasure*], II 22–3, 366–78
memories [*see also Memory*], forgetting of, II 20
UNPLEASURE [Unpleasantness] [*see also Pain; Pleasure; Suffering; Unpleasant ideas*], II 314; III 220, 228, 249, 275; T 67
acceptance of, II 366–78; III 80
addiction to, in masochism, III 224, 244
& death instinct, III 220
denial of, as holding off of death, III 274
displaced to others, III 244
elimination of, in erection, T 29
enjoyment of & gratification in, III 244
fertilization, preceded by —, T 67–8
flight from [*see also Pleasure principle*], II 22–3; III 249
& fragmentation, III 220
of the new, III 275
in the newborn, III 199
& play instincts, T 41
& pleasure [*see also Anxiety & pleasure*], III 192, 199, 251; T 34–5, 67–8
& preconsciousness, III 264
principle of, I 38, 56, 64, 65, 255
& split of the ego, III 265 [*see also Split*]
toleration of [*see also Toleration*], III 276–7
'UNREALITY', *see* Reality & 'unreality'
UNSUSPECTING PERSONS, dreams of, II 346
UNTRUTH [*see also Truth*], & psychoanalyst, II 180; III 117

UNWANTED [Unwelcome] child, *see* Child, unwelcome
UPRIGHT posture, I 322
URETHRAL [*see also Anal; Bladder; Micturition; Urethral erotism; Urine*], I 108, 209
character traits, II 172, 266
'— children', II 307
constriction & anxiety, II 268
erotogenic zone & genitality, T 5
fantasies [*see also Fire*], II 75
functioning [*see also Micturition*], II 264–6
habits, II 260, 269
prohibition & anal functioning, II 263
retention, II 261
sphincter, *see* Sphincter
URETHRAL EROTISM [*see also Erotogenic Zones; Urethral*]
& ambition, I 208; III 33
& anal erotism, II 263; T 11
& castration complex, II 122
& emotional outbursts, III 33
& enuresis, nocturnal emission, neurasthenic constitution, masturbation, III 217
& genitality, T 5
& incendiarism [*see also Gulliver fantasies*], II 258
in old people, III 205, 209
& shame, III 33
URINATION, *see* Micturition
URINE [*see also Bladder; Fire; Micturition; Urethral*], I 20, 110, 206, 207, 279, 323
URNING, *see* Homosexual
UTERUS, *see* Womb
UTRAQUISTIC research [utraquism] II 373; III 147–8, 153, 190, 371; D 47
'ÜBERWINDUNG' (Freud), III 35

VAGINA [*see also Erotogenic zones*], I 146–7, 187; II 358; III 34
dentata (Rank on), II 279
displacement of libido from clitoris to, II 89, 228
& female genitality, II 89
frigidity of, & penis envy [*see also Penis envy*], III 34
VANITY & micturition during analysis, I 207
VEGETATIVE tendencies, in the organism, III 229
'VERBAL SALADS', III 19–20
VERBOSITY, *see* Talkativeness
VERIFICATION of analytical explanations, I 193–4
VERMIN, II 327–8, 361
VERTIGO [*see also Giddiness*], III 118, 121–2, 221–2
VIRGINAL anxiety, II 35

VIRGINITY, see Defloration; Virginal anxiety
VISION, I 148; II 116; III 222
VOGT, W 12
VOICE [see also Speech], II *105-9*; II 251
 production, psychogenic anomalies of, II 109
VOLITION, see Will
VOMITING [see also Sickness,], I 66; II 93, 95, 326; III 181; T 86
VORACITY, see Devouring; Hunger
VOWELS & CONSONANTS, senseless, III 265
VOYEUR (Voyeurism), see Scopophilia

WAGNER, I 49
WAKING UP, see Awakening
WALDEN-SCHOOL, the, III 69-71
WAR NEUROSIS [War neuroses], II *124-41*; W 5
 active therapy of, II 210
 atavism in, II 141
 dreams in, see Dream(s)
 ego-injuries in, II 141
 ego-sensitiveness, increased, in, W 18-19
 & hysterical symptoms, II 126-9, 131-2, 138-40; W 19-20
 impotence [reduced potency] in, II 141; W 132
 intermediate position between narcissistic & transference neuroses, III 349-350
 & libido, III 352; W 18
 motor disturbances in, II 125-6, 131-2, 138; W 15
 onto- & phylogenesis of, W 7, 10, 16
 after shock without wounds, II 156
 & sexuality, W 17-18
 symptomatology of, W 14
 the time element in W 10
 & traumata, II 129, 140-1; W 6-7, 15
WAR SHOCK, see War neurosis
WARDING OFF, see Death; Defence; Unpleasure
WASHING-COMPULSION [see also Compulsion; Obsession], II 23, 43, 51, 243
WATER [see also Dream; Rescue], as symbol, T 48-9
WATSON, Dr., III 63
WEAKNESS, see Exhaustion
WEANING [see also Oral erotism], III 65, 219
 from analysis, II *293*
 from libido, D 12
WEAPONS, I 19; T 21
WEEPING, III 179, 181
'WELTUNTERGANG', III 362
WHOOPING-COUGH, displacement of libido after, II 82
'WILD' analysis [analyst], II 188, 209, 219; III 98-9; D 43

WILL [Volition; Will-power], I 232; II 285, 405; III 255
 action without one's own --, III *254-5*
 & formation of organs, T 100
 as holding off of death, III 274
WILLIAMS, Frankwood, III 18
'WISE BABY', II 136, *349*; III 135-6, 165, 271, 274
WISH(ES) [see also Fantasies; Longing; Magic; Sexual desires; Will; Wish-fulfilment], I 235; W 12
WISH-FULFILMENT [see also Wish], I 101-3, 108, 112, 113, 206, 216, 222-4
 conscious reaction against unconscious, I 18
 in day-dreams, I 102
 dreams as, I 101; II 301; III 239, 241
 by non-fulfilment, I 109
 omnipotence of [see also Omnipotence], I 215
 & organic evolution, T 90
 in psychoses, I 223; III 213
 repressed, expressed in obscenity [see also Repression], II 403
 & sleep, T 78
 unconscious, I 17-18, 27, 32, 47, 65, 104, 232; II 95
WIT [see also Comic(al); Jokes; Laughter;] I 42, 71, 115, 124, 140, 255; II 332, 344, 403
 aggressive, II 339
 & comparisons, II 406
 economy of inhibition in, II 334
 libido-distribution in, II 403
 '— & Its Relation to the Unconscious', review of Freud's book, II *332-44*
 a social phenomenon, II 340
WOLLENBERG, W 7
WOMAN [Women] [see also Adult(s); Man; Masculine; Sexual differences], II 25, 206, 262; III 24-5, 34, 47, 182, 205, 243; T 25, 105-7
 aggressiveness in, III 34
 amputated, as love objects, II 361
 analysis of, sign of termination, in case of, III 84
 being a —, III *243-44*
 & brutality of another ego, III 226
 clairvoyant intuition of, III 243
 competitiveness in, III 34
 ejaculatio praecox, effect on, III *291-4*
 esteem of, I 176, 316; III 217
 fat, I 17, 21; III 218
 genitality of, see Genitality
 genitals of, see Genitals
 homosexuality in, III 263
 homosexual, man's attitude to, I 176
 intelligence & intuition in, III 243; T 106

lues in, III 364
menstrual cycle in, T 57, 77
paranoia in, II 25
& penis [*see also Penis envy*], II 314, 317
pleasure-principle, symbolized by, I 262
post-coital depression in, III 209
seduction by, III 161-2, 227
sex development of, T 24-6, 103-4
WOMB, regression to [*see also Intrauterine; Mother; Regression; Thalassal; Woman*], III 36, 220-1, 268-9; T 18, 20, 38-9, 49, 95
WORD(s) [*see also Coprolalia; Etymologizing; Speech; Vowels & consonants*], I 59, 121, 132; II 182
& abstract thoughts, I 139
magic —, period of, I 230
— memories, repressed [*see also Memories*], II 73
obscene [*see also Obscene word(s)*], I *132-53*
& parental complex, I 143
play with, I 140; II 333
proscribed [*see also Words, obscene*], I 132; II 182
reversal of, expressing ridicule, III 170-1
senseless & disconnected, III 19-20, 265
stimulus —, & introjection, I 51
substituted for gesture, I 229
treated as objects, II 442
WORK, III 272
'WORKING THROUGH', II 220, 290; III 82-3, 97; D 3
WORLD, *see* Ego & external world
WORMS, *see* Vermin
WORRY [*see also Anxiety; Depression; Grief; Mourning*], & reality testing, II 411
WOUND(s) [*see also Trauma, physical*], II 156, 352; W 9-10
WRAP, as symbol of neurosis, III 228
WRITERS & psycho-analysis, III 87,

YAWNING, I 209-10
YOGA, III *274-6*

ZELL, Thomas, on eye animals, T 69
ZONE, *see* Erotogenic zone(s)
'ZUHÄLTER' (Dependant man), III 58-9, *217*